AN EXEGETICAL SUMMARY OF
JAMES

AN EXEGETICAL SUMMARY OF JAMES

Second Edition

J. Harold Greenlee

SIL International

Second Edition
© 2008 by SIL International

Library of Congress Catalog Card Number: 2008923521
ISBN: 978-155671-195-4

Printed in the United States of America

All Rights Reserved
No part of this publication may be reproduced, stored in a retrieval system, or transmitted in any form or by any means without the express permission of SIL International. However, brief excerpts, generally understood to be within the limits of fair use, may be quoted without written permission.

Copies of this and other publications
of SIL International may be obtained from

International Academic Bookstore
SIL International
7500 West Camp Wisdom Road
Dallas, TX 75236-5699, USA

Voice: 972-708-7404
Fax: 972-708-7363
academic_books@sil.org
www.ethnologue.com

PREFACE

Exegesis is concerned with the interpretation of a text. Exegesis of the New Testament involves determining the meaning of the Greek text. Translators must be especially careful and thorough in their exegesis of the New Testament in order to accurately communicate its message in the vocabulary, grammar, and literary devices of another language. Questions occurring to translators as they study the Greek text are answered by summarizing how scholars have interpreted the text. This is information that should be considered by translators as they make their own exegetical decisions regarding the message they will communicate in their translations.

The Semi-Literal Translation

As a basis for discussion, a semi-literal translation of the Greek text is given so that the reasons for different interpretations can best be seen. When one Greek word is translated into English by several words, these words are joined by hyphens. There are a few times when clarity requires that a string of words joined by hyphens have a separate word, such as "not" (μή), inserted in their midst. In this case, the separate word is surrounded by spaces between the hyphens. When alternate translations of a Greek word are given, these are separated by slashes.

The Text

Variations in the Greek text are noted under the heading TEXT. The base text for the summary is the text of the fourth revised edition of *The Greek New Testament,* published by the United Bible Societies, which has the same text as the twenty-sixth edition of the *Novum Testamentum Graece* (Nestle-Aland). The versions that follow different variations are listed without evaluating their choices.

The Lexicon

The meaning of a key word in context is the first question to be answered. Words marked with a raised letter in the semi-literal translation are treated separately under the heading LEXICON. First, the lexicon form of the Greek word is given. Within the parentheses following the Greek word is the location number where, in the author's judgment, this word is defined in the *Greek-English Lexicon of the New Testament Based on Semantic Domains* (Louw and Nida 1988). When a semantic domain includes a translation of the particular verse being treated, **LN** in bold type indicates that specific translation. If the specific reference for the verse is listed in *A Greek-English Lexicon of the New Testament and Other Early Christian Literature* (Bauer, Arndt, Gingrich, and Danker 1979), the outline location and page number is given. Then English equivalents of the Greek word are given to show how it is translated by commentators who offer their own translations of the whole text and, after a semicolon, all the versions in the list of abbreviations for translations. When reference is made to "all versions," it refers to only the versions in the list of translations. Sometimes further comments are made about the meaning of the word or the significance of a verb's tense, voice, or mood.

The Questions

Under the heading QUESTION, a question is asked that comes from examining the Greek text under consideration. Typical questions concern the identity of an implied actor or object of an event word, the antecedent of a pronominal reference, the connection indicated by a relational word, the meaning of a genitive construction, the meaning of figurative language, the function of a rhetorical question, the identification of an ambiguity, and the presence of implied information that is needed to understand the passage correctly. Background information is also considered for a proper understanding of a passage. Although not all implied information and background information is made explicit in a translation, it is important to consider it so that the translation will not be stated in such a way that prevents a reader from arriving at the proper interpretation. The question is answered with a summary of what commentators have said. If there are contrasting differences of opinion, the different interpretations are numbered and the commentaries that support each are listed. Differences that are not treated by many of the commentaries often are not numbered, but are introduced with a contrastive 'Or' at the beginning of the sentence. No attempt has been made to select which interpretation is best.

In listing support for various statements of interpretation, the author is often faced with the difficult task of matching the different terminologies used in commentaries with the terminology he has adopted. Sometimes he can only infer the position of a commentary from incidental remarks. This book, then, includes the author's interpretation of the views taken in the various commentaries. General statements are followed by specific statements, which indicate the author's understanding of the pertinent relationships, actors, events, and objects implied by that interpretation.

The Use of This Book

This book does not replace the commentaries that it summarizes. Commentaries contain much more information about the meaning of words and passages. They often contain arguments for the interpretations that are taken and they may have important discussions about the discourse features of the text. In addition, they have information about the historical, geographical, and cultural setting. Translators will want to refer to at least four commentaries as they exegete a passage. However, since no one commentary contains all the answers translators need, this book will be a valuable supplement. It makes more sources of exegetical help available than most translators have access to. Even if they had all the books available, few would have the time to search through all of them for the answers.

When many commentaries are studied, it soon becomes apparent that they frequently disagree in their interpretations. That is the reason why so many answers in this book are divided into two or more interpretations. The reader's initial reaction may be that all of these different interpretations complicate exegesis rather than help it. However, before translating a passage, a translator needs to know exactly where there is a problem of interpretation and what the exegetical options are.

Acknowledgments

This volume has been thoroughly reviewed by Richard C. Blight. He has studied the questions and answers and has made a significant contribution in determining their final forms.

ABBREVIATIONS

COMMENTARIES AND LEXICONS

AB   Reicke, Bo. *The Epistles of James, Peter, and Jude*. The Anchor Bible, edited by W. Albright and D. Freedman. Garden City, NY: Doubleday, 1964.

Alf   Alford, Henry. *Hebrews to Revelation*. Vol 4, Alford's Greek Testament. 1875. Reprinted from the 1875 edition. Grand Rapids: Baker, 1980.

BAGD   Bauer, Walter. *A Greek-English Lexicon of the New Testament and Other Early Christian Literature*. Translated and adapted from the 5th ed., 1958 by William F. Arndt and F. Wilbur Gingrich. 2d English ed. revised and augmented by F. Wilbur Gingrich and Frederick W. Danker. Chicago: University of Chicago Press, 1979.

Bg   Bengel, John Albert. *Gnomon of the New Testament*, Vol. 5. 7th ed. Translated by William Fletcher. Edinburgh: T. & T. Clark, 1877.

BKC   Blue, J. Ronald. *James*. In *The Bible Knowledge Commentary*, edited by John F. Walvoord and Roy B. Zuck. Wheaton, Illinois: Victor Books, 1983.

Blm   Bloomfield, S. T. *The Greek Testament, with English Notes*. London: Brown, Green, and Longmans, 1839.

EBC   Burdick, Donald W. *James*. In vol. 12, *The Expositor's Bible Commentary*, edited by Frank E. Gaebelein. Grand Rapids: Zondervan, 1981.

EGT   Oesterley, W. E. *The General Epistle of James*. In vol. 4, *The Expositor's Greek Testament*, edited by W. Robertson Nicoll. Reprinted from a previous edition, n.d. Grand Rapids: Eerdmans, 1980.

Hb   Hiebert, D. Edmond. *The Epistle of James*. Chicago: Moody, 1979.

Herm   Dibelius, Martin. *James*. 11th ed., 1967. Hermeneia—A Critical and Historical Commentary on the Bible, edited by Helmut Koester. Translated by Michael A. Williams. Philadelphia: Fortress Press, 1976.

HNTC   Laws, Sophie. *A Commentary on the Epistle of James*. Harper's New Testament Commentaries, edited by Henry Chadwick. San Francisco: Harper and Row, 1980.

ICC   Ropes, James Hardy. *A Critical and Exegetical Commentary on the Epistle of St. James*. The International Critical Commentary, edited by Alfred Plummer and Francis Brown. Edinburgh: T. & T. Clark, 1916.

ABBREVIATIONS

Lg	Lange, J. P., and J. J. Van Oosterzee. *The Epistle General of James.* In vol. 12, *Lange's Commentary on the Holy Scriptures.* Translated and edited from the 2d revised German edition, n.d. by J. Isidor Mombert, with editor's additions indicated by the abbreviation Lg(M). Grand Rapids: Zondervan, 1960.
LN	Louw, Johannes P., and Eugene A. Nida. *Greek-English Lexicon of the New Testament Based on Semantic Domains.* 2 vols. New York: United Bible Societies, 1988.
Lns	Lenski, R. C. H. *The Interpretation of the Epistle to the Hebrews and the Epistle of James.* Minneapolis: Augsburg, 1966.
May	Mayor, Joseph B. *The Epistle of St. James.* Reprinted from the 1897 edition. Grand Rapids: Baker, 1978.
Mit	Mitton, C. Leslie. *The Epistle of James.* Grand Rapids: Eerdmans, 1966.
My	Huther, Joh. Ed. *Critical and Exegetical Handbook to the General Epistles of James, Peter, John, and Jude.* Translated from the 3d. German edition by P. J. Gloag, D. B. Croom, and C. H. Irwin. Meyer's Commentary on the New Testament. New York: Funk and Wagnalls, 1887.
NBC	Ward, Ronald A. *James.* In *The New Bible Commentary, Revised.* Edited by D. Guthrie and J. A. Motyer. Grand Rapids: Eerdmans, 1970.
NIC	Adamson, James B. *The Epistle of James.* The New International Commentary on the New Testament, edited by F. F. Bruce. Grand Rapids: Eerdmans, 1976.
NIGTC	Davids, Peter H. *The Epistle of James.* The New International Greek Testament Commentary, edited by I. Howard Marshall and W. Ward Gasque. Grand Rapids: Eerdmans, 1982.
NTC	Kistemaker, Simon J. *Exposition of the Epistle of James and the Epistles of John.* New Testament Commentary. Grand Rapids: Baker, 1986.
TG	Bratcher, Robert G. *A Translator's Guide to the Letters from James, Peter, and Jude.* London, New York, Stuttgart: United Bible Societies, 1984.
TNTC	Moo, Douglas J. *The Letter of James.* The Tyndale New Testament Commentaries, edited by Leon Morris. Grand Rapids: Eerdmans, 1985.
Tsk	Tasker, R. V. G. *The General Epistle of James.* Grand Rapids: Eerdmans, 1956.
WBC	Martin, Ralph P. *James.* Word Biblical Commentary, edited by David A. Hubbard and Glenn W. Barker. Waco: Word, 1988.

GREEK TEXT AND TRANSLATIONS

GNT   Aland, Kurt, Matthew Black, Carlos Martini, Bruce Metzger, and Allen Wikgren. *The Greek New Testament*. 3d ed. (corrected). London, New York: United Bible Societies, 1983.
KJV   *The Holy Bible*. Authorized (or King James) Version. 1611.
NAB   *The New American Bible*. Camden, New Jersey: Thomas Nelson, 1971.
NASB *The New American Standard Bible*. Nashville, Tennessee: Holman, 1977.
NIV   *The Holy Bible: New International Version*. Grand Rapids: Zondervan, 1978.
NJB   *The New Jerusalem Bible*. Garden City, New York: Doubleday, 1985.
NRSV *The Holy Bible: New Revised Standard Version*. New York: Oxford University Press, 1989.
REB   *The Revised English Bible*. Oxford: Oxford University Press and Cambridge University Press, 1989.
TEV   *Today's English Version*, 2d ed. New York: American Bible Society, 1992.
TNT   *The Translator's New Testament*. London: British and Foreign Bible Society, 1973.

GRAMMATICAL TERMS

act.	active
fut.	future
impera.	imperative
indic.	indicative
infin.	infinitive
mid.	middle
opt.	optative
pass.	passive
perf.	perfect
pres.	present
subj.	subjunctive

EXEGETICAL SUMMARY OF JAMES

DISCOURSE UNIT: 1:1–27 [BKC, NTC; NASB]. The topic is the testing of faith [NASB], standing with confidence [BKC], perseverance [NTC].

DISCOURSE UNIT: 1:1–11 [Lg]. The topic is the salutation, and the use of temptation.

DISCOURSE UNIT: 1:1 [AB, BKC, EBC, GNT, Hb, HNTC, ICC, Lns, NBC, NIC, NIGTC, NTC, TG, TNTC, Tsk, WBC; NAB, NIV, NJB, TEV]. The topic is the address and greeting [AB, BKC, HNTC, Lns, My, Tsk, WBC; NJB], the salutation [EBC, Hb, ICC, NBC, NIC, NTC, TNTC], the introduction [NIGTC; TEV].

1:1 **James[a] a-slave[b] of-God and of-(the)-Lord Jesus Christ**
LEXICON—a. Ἰάκωβος (LN 93.158): 'James' [AB, Herm, HNTC, LN, Lns, NIC, TNTC, WBC; all versions]. This name is the Greek form of the Old Testament name 'Jacob' [BKC, Hb, HNTC, May, NIGTC, TG, Tsk, WBC].
  b. δοῦλος (LN 87.76) (BAGD 4. p. 206): 'slave' [BAGD, Herm, LN, Lns], 'bond slave' [NIC], 'bondservant' [LN; NASB], 'servant' [AB, HNTC, WBC; KJV, NAB, NIV, NJB, NRSV, REB, TEV, TNT].
QUESTION—Who is James?
  James is Jesus' half-brother [Bg], the son of Mary and Joseph, who became the leader of the congregation in Jerusalem [AB, Alf, BKC, EBC, Hb, Lns, Mit, My, NIC, NTC, Tsk]. Lns thinks that Jesus was Mary's only child and that Jesus' 'brother' means his cousin (or kinsman [Blm]), so that James was a cousin of Jesus, a son of Mary's sister. A few think that someone other than James used James' name as a literary device [AB, HNTC].
QUESTION—What is meant by being a 'slave' of God and Christ?
  'Slave' is the corollary of calling God 'Lord' [Herm, HNTC, NTC]. It means one who belongs to them [BKC, EBC, ICC, LN, Lns, Mit] and serves them [NTC, TNTC, Tsk]. It is a permanent relationship of submission to the absolute authority of God [Hb, NBC]. It is an expression meaning a worshiper of God and Christ [EGT, HNTC, ICC]. It also is a name suggesting the authority of the office of one who is in the service of the Great King [AB, LN, May, My, NBC, NIGTC, TNTC, Tsk, WBC]. He serves them in the Christian ministry, indicating that he is a Christian leader [TG].

to-the twelve tribes[a] the-(ones) in the dispersion:[b] Greetings.[c]
LEXICON—a. φυλή (LN 10.2; **11.15**) (BAGD 1. p. 868): 'tribe' [AB, BAGD, Herm, HNTC, LN, Lns, NIC, WBC; all versions except TEV]. The phrase 'the twelve tribes' is also translated 'all God's people' [TEV], 'all the people of God' [LN].

b. διασπορά (LN **15.137**) (BAGD 2. p. 188): 'the dispersion' [AB, BAGD, HNTC, NIC, WBC; NAB, NJB, NRSV], 'diaspora' [Herm, LN, Lns], 'the region in which persons have been scattered' [BAGD, LN]. The phrase ἐν τῇ διασπορᾷ 'in the dispersion' is translated 'who are dispersed abroad' [NASB], 'who are dispersed throughout the world' [REB], 'who are scattered throughout the world' [TNT], 'which are scattered abroad' [KJV], 'who are scattered among the nations' [NIV], 'who are scattered over the whole world' [TEV], 'in all the regions where they have been scattered' [LN].

c. pres. act. infin. of χαίρω (LN 33.22) (BAGD 2.b. p. 874): 'greetings' [AB, HNTC, LN; NASB, NIV, NJB, NRSV, REB, TEV], 'greeting' [Herm; KJV, NAB], 'salutation' [NIC], 'be joyful' [Lns]. This was the conventional greeting used in Greek letters [AB, Bg, HNTC, ICC, Lns, May, Mit, NIC, NIGTC, NTC, TG, TNTC, Tsk].

QUESTION—Who are the twelve tribes in the dispersion?

The phrase 'the twelve tribes' is a Jewish expression for the twelve tribes of Israel [Bg] and means the Jewish people as a whole [AB, Alf, BKC, EBC, Hb, ICC, May, My, NBC, NIC, NTC]. The dispersion is a technical term applied to the Jews outside of Palestine who had been scattered among the Gentiles as their ancestors had been scattered during the Captivity [Alf, BKC, Blm, Hb, Lns, My, TNTC, Tsk].

1. The phrase is used figuratively to indicate that all Christians, both Jewish Christians and Gentile Christians, were the new, spiritual Israel [AB, BAGD, HNTC, ICC, LN, NBC, TG; TEV]: to all God's people throughout the world. The Christian church is now the true Israel, whose homeland is in heaven and is considered to be away from home and dispersed in the world [BAGD, HNTC, ICC, TG].

2. The phrase is used in a restricted sense to refer to all the Christian Jews who are scattered in various parts of the world [Alf, BKC, EBC, Hb, Lns, May, My, NIGTC, NTC, TNTC, Tsk, WBC]: to the Jewish Christians who are scattered throughout the world. The Jewish Christians are the true Israel [NIGTC, WBC]. They could have been members of the church led by James in Jerusalem, and had scattered to other places at the time of the persecution (Acts 8:1) [EBC, Lns, TNTC, Tsk]. This designation does not mean that what is written to the Jewish Christians does not apply to the Gentile Christians [My, NTC].

3. The phrase refers primarily to Christian Jews outside Palestine, but includes other Jews who had not actually rejected Jesus as the Messiah [Lg].

4. The phrase is used in a non-restricted sense to include all Jews [NIC]: to the Jews who are scattered throughout the world. James is writing to all Jews, both Christian Jews and non-Christian Jews, whether they lived outside Palestine or in Palestine. He wants the Jews as a whole to turn to Christ [NIC].

5. The phrase refers to Jews outside Palestine [Blm].

JAMES 1:2

DISCOURSE UNIT: 1:2–27 [NIGTC; REB]. The topic is the opening statement [NIGTC], faith under trial [REB].

DISCOURSE UNIT: 1:2–20 [ICC]. The topic is various religious realities.

DISCOURSE UNIT: 1:2–19a. [WBC]. The topic is enduring trial.

DISCOURSE UNIT: 1:2–18 [AB, EBC, Hb, Herm, ICC, Lns, TNTC, Tsk; NIV]. The topic is trials and temptations [EBC, Herm, Lns; NIV], the tests of faith [Hb], patience in the midst of afflictions [AB], the formation of character [ICC], trials and Christian maturity [TNTC, Tsk].

DISCOURSE UNIT: 1:2–12 [BKC, EBC, Hb]. The topic is the testing of faith [EBC], the believer's trials [Hb], rejoicing in trials [BKC].

DISCOURSE UNIT: 1:2–11 [NIC, NIGTC, NTC]. The topic is trials [NTC], testing, wisdom, and wealth [NIGTC], enduring temptations [My], the Christian faith [NIC].

DISCOURSE UNIT: 1:2–8 [GNT, HNTC, TG, WBC; TEV]. The topic is faith and wisdom [TEV], trial and integrity [HNTC], trials, wisdom, and faith [WBC], poverty and wealth [TG].

DISCOURSE UNIT: 1:2–4 [AB, Hb, Lns, NBC, NIC, NIGTC, NTC, TNTC, Tsk; NAB, NJB]. The topic is endurance [NAB], the privilege of trials [NJB], the testing of faith [NTC], dealing with trials [NBC], the proper attitude towards trials [Hb], how to consider trials [Lns], letting trials fulfill their intended purpose [TNTC, Tsk], the testing, training, and fruits of testing [NIC], afflictions leading to steadfastness and perfection [AB], testing producing joy [NIGTC].

1:2 Consider[a] (it) all[b] joy,[c] my brothers, whenever you-experience[d] various[e] trials/temptations,[f]

LEXICON—a. aorist mid. (deponent = active) impera. of ἡγέομαι (LN 31.1) (BAGD 2. p. 343): 'to consider' [BAGD, LN, Lns; NASB, NIV, NJB, NRSV, TEV], 'to regard' [AB, BAGD, Herm, HNTC, LN], 'to deem' [NIC], 'to count' [KJV, NAB, REB], 'to treat as' [WBC], 'you should be (very happy)' [TNT]. The aorist tense indicates that each special case of testing is to be considered an occasion for joy [ICC, May], or that they are to make this their attitude by a definite act [Hb, Lns, Mit].

b. πᾶς (LN 59.23; 78.44) (BAGD 1.a.δ. p. 631): 'all' [BAGD, LN, Lns; KJV, NASB], 'complete' [AB, LN], 'wholly' [HNTC], 'altogether' [WBC], 'nothing but' [NIC; NRSV], 'pure' [NAB, NIV], 'sheer' [Herm], 'great' [NJB], 'very' [TNT], 'supremely' [REB], not explicit [TEV]. 'All joy' is at the beginning of the clause for emphasis [Hb].

c. χαρά (LN 25.123) (BAGD 1. p. 875): 'joy' [AB, BAGD, Herm, LN, Lns; KJV, NAB, NASB, NIV, NJB, NRSV], 'gladness' [LN], 'great happiness' [LN], 'a matter for joy' [HNTC], 'an occasion for joy' [NIC, WBC], '(count yourselves) happy' [REB], '(to be) happy' [TNT], '(consider yourselves) fortunate' [TEV]. This focuses on the occasion for the joy [Hb, HNTC, ICC, May, NBC, NIC, Tsk, WBC].

d. aorist act. subj. of περιπίπτω (LN **90.71**) (BAGD 2. p. 649): 'to experience' [LN], 'to be involved in' [BAGD; NAB], 'to encounter' [BAGD, Herm, NIC; NASB], 'to face' [NIV, NRSV, REB], 'to meet' [WBC], 'to suffer' [TNT], 'to fall into' [AB, HNTC; KJV], 'to fall foul of' [Lns], 'to have (trials) come upon one' [NJB], '(when trials) come your way' [TEV]. This often indicates an unplanned and undesired incident [Hb, ICC, NIGTC]. The aorist tense indicates that these varied afflictions are individual experiences [Hb].

e. ποικίλος (LN 58.45) (BAGD 1. p. 683): 'various' [AB, Herm, HNTC, Lns; NASB], 'of various kinds' [BAGD, LN, WBC], 'in their various forms' [NIC], 'of many kinds' [NIV, NJB], 'of any kind' [NRSV], 'every sort of' [NAB], 'all sorts of' [REB], 'all kinds of' [TEV], 'diversified' [BAGD, LN], 'divers' [KJV], 'whatever' [TNT]. This is emphatic because it is separated from its noun and occurs clause final [Hb, NIC].

f. πειρασμός (LN 27.46; 88.308) (BAGD 2.b. p. 641): 'trial' [AB, Herm, HNTC, Lns; NAB, NASB, NIV, NRSV, REB, TEV, TNT], 'testing' [LN; NJB], 'examination' [LN], 'trying assaults of evil' [NIC], 'temptation' [BAGD, LN (88.308); KJV], 'enticement to sin' [BAGD].

QUESTION—What is meant by πᾶσαν 'all (joy)'?

1. It indicates a high degree of joy in the sense of 'full, utter, sheer joy' [BAGD, Blm, EBC, Herm, ICC, Lg, Lns, May, TNTC, Tsk; KJV, NASB, NRSV, REB, TNT]: consider it to be an occasion for full joy.
2. It qualifies the joy in the sense that joy is not to be mixed with other reactions that would detract from it [BKC, HNTC, Mit, My, NIC, NIGTC, NTC; NAB, NIV]: consider it to be an occasion for nothing but joy, for unmixed joy. It should not be mixed with grief [BKC].
3. Every kind of testing is to be met with every kind of joy [Alf, Bg, Hb]: consider them to be occasions for every kind of joy. The various kinds of testing are matched by various kinds of joy [Hb].

QUESTION—What is meant by πειρασμοῖς 'trials/temptations'?

1. These are external trials of affliction, in contrast with internal temptations to sin [AB, Alf, Bg, BKC, Blm, EBC, Hb, Herm, HNTC, Lns, May, Mit, NIGTC, NTC, TNTC, Tsk, WBC]. They were undesirable events [Hb], such things as sickness [AB, Tsk], poverty [AB, Tsk], hardships of the poor [ICC], and persecution [AB, Blm, EBC, Hb, Herm, HNTC, May, NIGTC, Tsk, WBC] in its social, economic, or physical aspects [NIGTC, Tsk]. Internal 'temptations' with which one is tempted (1:13–15) are not occasions for joy [Hb, ICC, May]. The plural forms indicate the great variety of trials [Hb].
2. These are both external afflictions and internal temptations to sin [Alf, EGT, Lg, My, NIC]. Both are tests of one's faithfulness. The defects inherent in a person make it possible for him to be tempted into committing sin whether it be external or internal stimuli [NIC].

1:3 knowing[a] that the testing/approvedness[b] of-your faith[c] causes[d] endurance.[e]

LEXICON—a. pres. act. participle of γινώσκω (LN 28.1) (BAGD 6.c. p. 161): 'to know' [AB, BAGD, Herm, HNTC, LN; KJV, NASB, NIV, NRSV, TEV, TNT], 'to well know' [NJB], 'to realize' [Lns, NIC; NAB]. This participle is also translated 'in the knowledge that' [WBC; REB].
  b. δοκίμιον (LN **27.45**; 73.3) (BAGD 1. p. 203): 'testing' [AB, BAGD, HNTC, **LN**, WBC; NASB, NIV, NJB, NRSV, REB], 'means of testing' [BAGD, Herm], 'the testing out' [Lns], 'trying' [KJV], 'when (faith) is tested' [NAB], 'approbation' [NIC], 'genuineness' [LN], 'when (faith) succeeds in facing (trials)' [TEV], 'as (faith) is proved' [TNT].
  c. πίστις (LN 31.85) (BAGD 2.d.α.γ. p. 663): 'faith' [AB, BAGD, Herm, HNTC, LN, Lns, WBC; all versions], 'constancy' [NIC].
  d. pres. mid. (deponent = active) indic. of κατεργάζομαι (LN 13.9) (BAGD 2. p. 421): 'to cause' [LN]; 'to result in' [LN], 'to bring about' [BAGD, HNTC, LN], 'to develop' [NIV], 'to produce' [AB, BAGD, Herm, WBC; NASB, NJB, NRSV], 'to work' [KJV], 'to work out' [Lns], 'to accomplish' [NIC], 'to make for' [NAB, REB], 'the result is' [TEV], '(you) learn' [TNT]. The present tense indicates a continuous process of testing [Hb].
  e. ὑπομονή (LN 25.174) (BAGD 1. p. 846): 'endurance' [AB, BAGD, Herm, HNTC, LN, NIC; NAB, NASB, NRSV], 'perseverance' [BAGD; NIV, NJB], 'constancy' [Lns], 'steadfastness' [BAGD], 'fortitude' [BAGD], 'strength to endure' [REB], 'ability to endure' [TEV], 'patient endurance' [WBC], 'patience' [BAGD; KJV]. This noun is also translated as a verb: 'to endure' [TNT].

QUESTION—What relationship is indicated by the use of the participle γινώσκοντες 'knowing'?
  It indicates the grounds for the previous exhortation [Alf, BKC, Blm, EBC, Hb, Herm, Lg, Lns, Mit, NIGTC, NTC, Tsk]: consider trials pure joy since you know that they produce endurance in you.

QUESTION—What is meant by τὸ δοκίμιον 'the testing/approvedness' of one's faith?
  1. It means the process of testing [Alf, Bg, Blm, HNTC, ICC, LN, Lns, NTC, TNTC, Tsk]: you know that the testing of your faith produces endurance. The act of testing is in view [ICC].
  2. It means the means of testing [Hb, Herm, Lg, May, NIGTC, Tsk, WBC]: you know that the means by which their faith is tested (the trials) cause its true nature to be revealed. This implies that there is something genuine to survive the testing [NIGTC].
  3. It means the result of testing [BKC, EGT, My, NIC]: that which is genuine or approved in your faith produces endurance. It is the true faith that develops endurance [BKC]. NIC thinks that the text must be emended so that endurance (in the accusative case), instead of being the result of obtaining approval, be changed to the dative case and the verb be taken as

passive, so that the text would then read 'knowing that approval is accomplished by endurance'.

QUESTION—What is meant by ὑπομονήν 'endurance'?

It is the quality of remaining loyal to God in the face of hostility [Mit, NIGTC]. Rather than an act of endurance, it is the frame of mind that bravely endures hardships and holds up under pressure [Blm, EGT, Hb, Lg, May]. It means a permanent trait of steadfastness from which endurance springs [ICC, TNTC]. This was valuable because only those with such a tested character could know that they would endure to the end [NIGTC]. It is a quality needed by Christians when they face temptation and persecution [Tsk].

1:4 And/But^a (let) endurance have^b (its) full^c work,^d

LEXICON—a. δέ (LN 89.94; 89.87; 89.124): 'and' [AB, HNTC; NASB, NJB, NRSV], 'now' [Lns], 'but' [NIC; KJV, TNT], not explicit [Herm, WBC; NAB, NIV, REB, TEV].

b. pres. act. impera. of ἔχω (LN 90.51) (BAGD I.4. p. 333): 'to have' [BAGD, Lns; KJV, NASB, NRSV], 'to bring about' [BAGD, LN], 'to cause' [BAGD, LN], 'to produce' [LN], 'to yield' [WBC], 'to effect' [Herm], 'to do' [HNTC]. The phrase 'to have its full work' is translated 'to complete its work' [LN (68.23); NASB], 'to finish its work' [NIV], 'to perfect its work' [NIC; REB], 'to come to its perfection' [NAB], 'to carry one all the way without failing' [TEV], '(to endure) to the very end' [TNT]. The present tense indicates that it is their continuing duty to do so [Hb, Lns]. This imperative indicates that endurance is active, not passive [HNTC]. It is emphatic [Lg].

c. τέλειος (LN **68.23**) (BAGD 1.a.α. p. 809): 'full' [AB; NRSV], 'complete' [BAGD, LN, WBC], 'whole' [HNTC], 'perfect' [BAGD, Herm; KJV, NASB], 'having attained the end or purpose' [BAGD].

d. ἔργον (LN 42.11; 42.12) (BAGD 1.b. p. 308): 'work' [BAGD, HNTC, Lns, NIC, WBC; KJV, NASB, NIV, REB], 'deed' [BAGD, LN], 'result' [NASB], 'effect' [AB; NRSV], 'product' [Herm], 'result of what has been done' [LN], 'manifestation' [BAGD].

QUESTION—What relationship is indicated by δέ 'and/but'?

1. It indicates an addition [AB, HNTC, ICC, NIGTC, WBC; NASB, NJB, NRSV]: 'and, now'. This turns to an essential, more remote, consequence of the trials [ICC].

2. It indicates a contrast [Alf, Blm, EGT, Hb, NIC; KJV, TNT]: but. Endurance is important, but it should lead to something even more important [ICC, NIGTC]. This points to a possible danger to be avoided [Alf, EGT, Hb]: do not stop enduring, but let it have its full work.

3. It explains the implications in 1:2–3 [Lns].

JAMES 1:4

QUESTION—What is the 'full work' of endurance?
1. It is the perfect character which is described in the following clause [BKC, Herm, HNTC, Lns, Mit, NIGTC, TNTC, Tsk]: let endurance persist to cause you to become perfect and whole.
2. It is the full and proper fruits that make up completeness of character [Blm, Hb, ICC]. That fruit is a perfect character that is developed as endurance is allowed to work out its intended effect [Hb], carrying out the practical implications of the Christian faith [Lg].
3. It is the development of a perfect endurance [Alf, May, My]: let endurance persist until it becomes a perfect endurance. The trial should be met with steadfastness to the end.

in-order-that/namely-that[a] **you-may-be perfect/mature**[b] **and complete,**[c] **lacking**[d] **in nothing.**

LEXICON—a. ἵνα (LN 89.59; 91.15): 'in order that' [LN, Lns], 'so that' [AB, Herm, HNTC, NIC, WBC; NAB, NASB, NIV, NRSV, TEV, TNT], 'that' [KJV, NASB, REB].
b. τέλειος (LN 88.36; 88.100) (BAGD 2.d. p. 809): 'perfect' [BAGD, Herm, LN (88.36), NIC; KJV, NASB, TEV, TNT], 'perfected' [REB], 'mature' [AB, BAGD LN (88.100); NAB, NIV, NRSV], 'fully developed' [NASB], 'whole' [HNTC], 'complete' [BAGD, Lns, WBC].
c. ὁλόκληρος (LN 59.30) (BAGD p. 564): 'complete' [BAGD, Herm, HNTC; NASB, NIV, NRSV, TEV, TNT], 'complete in every part' [NIC], 'whole' [BAGD, LN], 'entire' [LN, Lns; KJV], 'fully' [NAB], 'perfect' [AB], 'sound throughout' [REB], 'blameless' [WBC].
d. pres. pass. participle of λείπω (LN **57.43**) (BAGD 1.a. p. 470): 'to lack' [AB, BAGD, Herm, HNTC, LN, Lns, NIC; NAB, NASB, NIV, NRSV, REB, TEV], 'to want' [KJV], 'to fail' [TNT], 'to fall short' [BAGD], 'to be deficient' [NASB], 'with no deficiency' [WBC].

QUESTION—What relationship is indicated by ἵνα 'in order that'?
It indicates the purpose of letting endurance have its full work [AB, Alf, BKC, Hb, HNTC, ICC, Lg, Lns, My]: let endurance have its full work in order that you be perfect and complete. It also explains what the full work in the preceding clause is [NIGTC, TNTC, Tsk]. It is the ultimate purpose of the trials [TNTC, Tsk].

QUESTION—What is meant by τέλειοι 'perfect/mature'?
1. It means spiritually mature [BKC, EBC, Hb, May, NIGTC, NTC]. It is a maturing of character that includes uprightness [NIGTC]. The person's character has reached full development [Hb]. This is attainable in this life [Hb, Tsk].
2. It means perfect [ICC, Mit, My, NIC, TNTC, Tsk]. It means complete in the sense of perfect or finished [Blm, ICC, Lg]. It is a goal to be strived for, but cannot be attained until the new age of salvation [Mit, TNTC, Tsk]. It is a right relationship to God which is shown by full obedience

and an unblemished life [NIC]. It means reaching full development [Mit, My].
3. Together with 'complete' it means a complete person [HNTC, Lns]. He is one who has integrity, not like the divided man of 1:6–8 [HNTC]. It also means blameless [HNTC].

QUESTION—What is meant by ὁλόκληροι 'complete'?
It means complete in all its parts [Blm, ICC, NTC], entire [My], without any unfinished part [Mit]. It emphasizes that the perfection includes all facets [NIGTC], all those virtues that characterize a mature believer [Hb]. It is used in combination with the preceding word to emphasize the single idea of perfection [Mit, My, WBC]. It refers to the manifestation of completeness [Lg].

QUESTION—What is meant by ἐν μηδενὶ λειπόμενοι 'in nothing lacking'?
This explains what is meant by ὁλόκληροι 'complete' [EGT, Hb, ICC, NIGTC, NTC]. It is also a negative counterpart to the preceding two positive qualities [Alf, Blm, Hb, HNTC, Lg, Lns, May, My], lacking nothing needed to do every good work [Blm]. He will be all that God wants him to be [BKC].

DISCOURSE UNIT: 1:5–8 [AB, Hb, Lns, Mit, NBC, NIC, NIGTC, NTC, TNTC, Tsk; NAB, NJB]. The topic is prayer for wisdom [AB, NIGTC, NTC; NAB], prayer for guidance [NIC], prayer with confidence [NJB], prayer with faith [Herm, ICC], wisdom, prayer, and faith [TNTC, Tsk], prayer in the midst of trials [Hb, Lns], wisdom [Mit].

1:5 **And/But[a] if anyone of-you lacks[b] wisdom,[c]**
LEXICON—a. δέ (LN 89.94; 89.124): 'and', 'now' [AB, Lns], 'but' [Herm, NIC, WBC; NASB, TEV], not explicit [HNTC; KJV, NAB, NIV, NJB, NRSV, REB, TNT].
  b. pres. pass. indic. of λείπω (LN 57.43) (BAGD 1.b. p. 470): 'to lack' [AB, BAGD, Herm, HNTC, LN, Lns, NIC, WBC; KJV, NASB, NIV, NJB, NRSV, REB, TEV], 'to not have' [LN], 'to be without' [BAGD; NAB], 'to be in need of' [BAGD, LN], 'to fail in' [TNT]. This conditional clause assumes that the need is real [EBC, Hb, WBC].
  c. σοφία (LN 32.32) (BAGD 2. p. 759): 'wisdom' [AB, BAGD, Herm, HNTC, LN, Lns, WBC; all versions], 'knowledge of God's way and will' [NIC].

QUESTION—What relationship is indicated by δέ 'and/but'?
  1. It indicates an addition [AB, Hb, Lns, Tsk]: and. One of the important virtues a Christian may lack is wisdom [Tsk]. Wisdom is necessary to deal with trials [AB, Lns]. If a reader feels that he is not able to regard his trials as just indicated, he should ask God for the needed wisdom [Hb].
  2. It indicates contrast [Bg, Herm, My, NIC, WBC; NASB, TEV]: but. They should be perfect and lack nothing, but they will find that they lack wisdom and they should ask God for it [My]. This clause tells how to deal with temptation [Bg].

QUESTION—In what respect would they need wisdom?
Wisdom would enable them to become and remain perfect and complete [NIGTC, Tsk]. It would enable them to understand the testing [Blm, EBC, May] and to resist and endure it [EBC, Hb, NIGTC] with decisions consistent with God's will [Blm, Hb]. It would enable them to know and practice righteousness [ICC]. It would enable them to know God's will and to apply it in life [Tsk]. It would enable them to have the proper perspective on trials as James described it in 1:2–3 [Hb, Lns, My], so that they could understand God's purpose in placing them in such trials [Lns]. But this wisdom is not confined to the preceding verses and has a wider application to all areas of conduct where wisdom is needed [Hb]. The lack of wisdom is one that only God can supply [HNTC].

let-him-ask[a] from God the-(one) giving[b] to-all generously[c] and not reproaching,[d] and it-will-be-given to-him.

LEXICON—a. pres. act. impera. of αἰτέω (LN 33.163) (BAGD p. 26): 'to ask' [AB, BAGD, Herm, HNTC, LN, Lns, NIC, WBC; all versions except TEV], 'to pray' [TEV]. The present tense indicates that this asking is an activity that is continuing [Hb, Mit], or repeated [EBC, NBC].
  b. pres. act. participle of δίδωμι (LN 57.71): 'to give' [AB, Herm, HNTC, LN, Lns, NIC, WBC; all versions except REB], 'to be a giver' [REB]. The participle is attributive and since it is in the present tense, it indicates that God's nature is to be continually giving [Hb].
  c. ἁπλῶς (LN **57.107**) (BAGD 2. p. 86): 'generously' [AB, BAGD, LN; NAB, NASB, NIV, NJB, NRSV, TEV, TNT], 'liberally' [KJV], 'freely' [HNTC], 'as a simple gift' [NIC], 'without hesitation' [Herm, WBC], 'without reserve' [BAGD], 'without reservation' [Lns]. This adverb is also translated as an adjective: 'generous (giver)' [REB].
  d. pres. act. participle of ὀνειδίζω (LN 33.422) (BAGD 1. p. 570): 'to reproach' [BAGD, LN; REB], 'to chide' [NIC], 'to reprimand' [LN], 'to find fault' [NIV], 'to scold' [NJB], 'to upbraid' [Lns; KJV], 'to grumble' [Herm], 'to grudge' [HNTC]. This participle is also translated as a noun: 'reproach' [NASB]; and as an adverb: 'ungrudgingly' [AB; NAB, NRSV, TNT], 'graciously' [TEV], 'without recrimination' [WBC].

QUESTION—Why is this description of God added here?
It describes the character of God that is pertinent to a request for wisdom and it is a ground for assurance that their requests will be answered [BKC, Blm, Hb, HNTC, ICC, Lns, My, NIGTC].

QUESTION—What is meant by saying that God gives ἁπλῶς 'generously'?
  1. This means that he gives without hesitation or mental reservation [Bg, EGT, Hb, Herm, Lns, May, My, NIC, NIGTC, Tsk, WBC]. He gives it freely, just for the asking [NIC] and unconditionally [May, WBC]. He gives wholeheartedly [Tsk]. He has the single motive of helping the one who asks [TNTC] and has no ulterior motive and no desire to get something in return [EGT, Hb].

2. It means that he gives generously [AB, ICC, LN, Mit; NAB, NASB, NIV, NJB, NRSV, TEV, TNT]. This is not in contrast with the first meaning, since if God gives wholeheartedly and unconditionally, he will also give generously [Hb].
3. It means both of the above [Blm, HNTC, Lg]. There are contrasts mentioned with each: God gives generously, not grudgingly (next clause) and God gives without hesitation, unlike the man who hesitates to ask in the following verse.

QUESTION—What is it that God does not reprimand?

God does not scold them for bothering him [Blm, TG]. He does not bring up conscious or unconscious sins and failures [Bg, NIC, TNTC, Tsk], or say that they are unworthy to approach him [My]. He does not scold about their lack of wisdom [Lns]. After giving a request, God does not complain about giving it to us [ICC, NIC], or remind us endlessly of the value of the gift [TNTC, Tsk]. God doesn't grant the request and then criticize us for asking [Hb]. He doesn't scold because we have improperly used previous gifts or rebuke us for repeated lack of wisdom [Hb]. This does not mean that God does not rebuke us for sin [Hb]. He doesn't give scornfully, nor withhold his gifts from those who are penitent, nor place a limit on his giving [Blm]. He does not complain about the size of the gift that is asked [Herm].

1:6 But^a let-him-ask in^b faith,^c nothing doubting;^d

LEXICON—a. δέ (LN 89.124): 'but' [Herm, HNTC, Lns, NIC; all versions except NAB], 'yet' [NAB], 'however' [WBC], not explicit [AB].
  b. ἐν (LN 89.84): 'in' [AB, Herm, HNTC, Lns, NIC; KJV, NAB, NASB, NRSV, REB, TNT], 'with' [LN, WBC; NJB], not explicit [NIV, TEV].
  c. πίστις (LN 31.85) (BAGD 2.a. p. 663): 'faith' [AB, BAGD, Herm, HNTC, LN, Lns, NIC, WBC; KJV, NAB, NASB, NJB, NRSV, REB, TNT], 'trust' [BAGD, LN]. This noun is also translated as a verb: 'to believe' [NIV, TEV].
  d. pres. mid. participle of διακρίνω (LN **31.37**) (BAGD 2.b. p. 185): 'to doubt' [AB, BAGD, Herm, HNTC, LN, Lns; NAB, NASB, NIV, NJB, NRSV, TEV], 'to waver' [BAGD; KJV], 'to have doubt' [REB, TNT], 'to halt between two opinions' [NIC].

QUESTION—What is the object of this faith and what should not be doubted?

1. It is a certainty that the request will be granted [Alf, Blm, EBC, EGT, Herm, HNTC, Mit, My, TG]: let him ask in the belief that God will do what he asks him to do. It is a belief that God will heed his prayer and either grant it or, in his greater wisdom, deny it [NIC]. It does not refer to his steadfast faith toward God (1:3) [NIC]. He should not doubt that God would do what he asks [EBC, NIC, TG]. It may refer to doubt whether God is willing or able to grant the prayer, or to wavering about whether he really wants something or whether he shrinks from the change it would make in his life [Mit]. Included in this is faith in the character of God [EGT]

2. It is his Christian faith in God [Hb, ICC, Lg, Lns, NBC, NIGTC, TNTC, Tsk]: let him ask with a firm faith in God and Christ. A doubter's whole attitude toward God lacks the steadfastness of 1:3–4 [NIGTC], his allegiance to God wavers [ICC]. Without this faith, he is only a nominal Christian [NBC]. This general teaching about prayer has been attached to praying for wisdom and he may fully expect to receive something from God (1:7) [ICC]. The doubt is not an intellectual doubt, but a conflict of loyalty to God [TNTC, Tsk]. A doubter has competing desires, he wants what he asks for, then changes his mind and desires something else—his desires are divided between God and the world [Hb, Lns].

for[a] the-(one) doubting is-like[b] a-wave[c] of-(the)-sea[d] being-driven-by-wind[e] and being-tossed.[f]

LEXICON—a. γάρ (LN 89.23): 'for' [AB, Herm, HNTC, Lns, NIC, WBC; KJV, NAB, NASB, NRSV, REB, TNT], 'because' [NIV, NJB], not explicit [TEV].
  b. perf. act. indic. of ἔοικα (LN **64.4**) (BAGD p. 280): 'to be like' [AB, BAGD, Herm, HNTC, LN, Lns, NIC, WBC; all versions].
  c. κλύδων (LN 14.25) (BAGD p. 436): 'wave' [AB, HNTC, LN, Lns; KJV, NIV, NRSV, REB, TEV], 'waves' [NJB], 'surf' [BAGD; NAB, NASB], 'billow' [LN], 'surge' [LN], 'rough water' [BAGD]. This noun is also translated as an adjective describing 'sea': 'surging' [Herm; TNT], 'billowing' [WBC].
  d. θάλασσα (LN 1.70) (BAGD 1.a. p. 350): 'sea' [AB, BAGD, Herm, HNTC, LN, Lns, NIC, WBC; all versions except NAB], 'lake' [LN], not explicit [NAB].
  e. pres. pass. participle of ἀνεμίζω (LN **15.164**) (BAGD p. 64): 'to be driven by the wind' [AB, Herm, LN, WBC; KJV, NAB, NASB, NRSV, TEV, TNT], 'to be blown by the wind' [NIC; NIV], 'to be blown about by the wind' [HNTC], 'to be wind-driven' [Lns], 'to be moved by the wind' [BAGD]. The phrase is also translated 'the waves thrown up in the sea by the buffeting of the wind' [NJB], 'tossed hither and thither by the wind' [REB]. The present tense indicates a continuous impact on the waves [Hb].
  f. pres. pass. participle of ῥιπίζω (LN **16.11**) (BAGD p. 736): 'to be tossed' [BAGD, Herm, HNTC; KJV, NAB, NASB, NIV, NRSV], 'to be tossed about' [LN, WBC; TNT], 'to be tossed hither and thither' [AB], 'to be tossed up and down' [Lns], 'to be blown about' [TEV], 'to be beaten under' [NIC]. Some consider this to be synonymous with the preceding verb [Alf, HNTC, My, TG].

QUESTION—What relationship is indicated by γάρ 'for'?
  1. It indicates the reason why it is important to ask in faith and not waver [ICC, Lg, TNTC, Tsk]: let him ask in faith because one who doubts is unstable and will not receive anything. It illustrates what is wrong with such doubting [Hb].

2. It explains what doubting is like, with the following γάρ (1:7) giving the reason [My].

QUESTION—What does the wind do to the waves?

The wind drives the waves first in one direction and then in another [Lns, NIC], raises the sea into waves [Blm], or causes the sea to constantly surge [TNTC, Tsk]. The wind changes directions from one day to another [NIC]. This means no more than normal winds, not a storm [Hb, NIC]. Instead of individual waves, it is probably used in a collective sense of the surge of the sea [Herm, ICC], the surf [HNTC], or a succession of waves, one ridge after another moving with the wind [Hb].

QUESTION—In what way is the doubter like the wind-driven waves?

The point of comparison is instability [AB, Blm, EBC, EGT, Hb, ICC, Lns, My, NTC], unfixed direction [TNTC, Tsk]. The unsettled behavior, going first in one direction and then in another, is like a person inclining towards believing that God will grant his prayer and then inclining towards the opposite alternative and never able to settle on either [NIC]. The water has no inner stability to withstand outside forces and neither does the doubter [AB, Hb]. One commentator makes the comparison with a boat being rocked in turbulent water [WBC].

1:7 For^a (let) that person^b not suppose^c that he-will-receive anything from the Lord,

LEXICON—a. γάρ (LN 89.23) (BAGD 1.b., 3. p. 152): 'for' [BAGD; KJV, NASB, NRSV], 'certainly' [BAGD, Herm], 'yea' [Lns], 'by all means' [BAGD], not explicit [AB, Herm, HNTC, NIC, WBC; NAB, NIV, NJB, REB, TEV, TNT].

b. ἄνθρωπος (LN 9.1; 9.24) (BAGD 4.b. p. 69): 'person' [Herm, LN, Lns, WBC; NJB], 'man' [AB, BAGD, HNTC, LN, NIC; KJV, NAB, NASB, NIV, REB, TNT], 'human being' [BAGD, LN], 'you' [TEV], not explicit [NRSV].

c. pres. mid. impera. of οἴομαι (LN **31.29**) (BAGD p. 562): 'to suppose' [BAGD, **LN**], 'to expect' [BAGD, Herm, HNTC; NAB, NASB, NJB, NRSV, TNT], 'to imagine' [AB, LN, NIC], 'to presume' [LN], 'to believe' [LN], 'to think' [BAGD, LN, Lns, WBC; KJV, NIV, REB, TEV]. The negative with this present imperative verb indicates that the person should stop supposing this [Hb, NTC]. This form can also mean 'do not be doing this in the future'.

QUESTION—What relationship is indicated by γάρ 'for'?

1. It indicates a second reason why a person should ask in faith without doubting [Alf, Blm, Hb, ICC, Lg, My, NBC, NIGTC]: let him ask in faith, with no doubting, because he who doubts is like a wave and because such a person will not receive anything from the Lord. The phrase μὴ γάρ 'for not' is emphatic: 'not by any means' [Lg].

2. It indicates certainty [AB, Lns]: let him ask in faith without doubting, because he who doubts is like a wave, and certainly a person like that will not receive anything from the Lord.

QUESTION—Who is ὁ ἄνθρωπος ἐκεῖνος 'that person' and how is 1:8 connected to him?

'That person' refers to one who doubts (1:6) [AB, Alf, Blm, EBC, Hb, Herm, HNTC, ICC, Lg, Lns, May, Mit, My, NBC, NIC, NIGTC, NTC, TNTC, Tsk, WBC; all versions]: let not that person who doubts suppose that he will receive anything from God. The 'man' in 1:8 is in apposition to 'that person' and describes the character of such a man [AB, Hb, HNTC, ICC, Lns, May, My, NIGTC, TNTC, Tsk]. Some translate 1:8 as a comment describing that person [AB, HNTC, Lns, NIC; KJV, NIV, REB, TNT]: let not that person suppose that he will receive anything; he is a man who is double-minded and unstable in all his ways. Another translation makes 1:8 more of a separate sentence: a double-minded man is unstable in all his ways [KJV]. Some translate with 1:8 inserted after 'that person' [Herm; NAB, NJB, TEV]: let not that person, a man who is double-minded and unstable in all his ways, suppose that he will receive anything. Some comment or translate with the implication that 1:8 is the reason why the doubter will not receive anything [AB, Tsk; NASB]: let not that person suppose that he will receive anything, being a double-minded man who is unstable in all his ways.

QUESTION—What is included in τι 'anything'?

He will not receive anything at all [Lg], let alone such a great gift as wisdom [Lns]. 'Anything' is limited to anything that he asks for [Alf, Hb, Lg(M), My], since God does give general benefits to all people [Hb, Lg(M)], such as rain, food, and clothing [Alf].

QUESTION—Who is the Lord?
1. The Lord is God, the Father [AB, Alf, BKC, Blm, EGT, HNTC, ICC, Lg, May, My, NIGTC, TG, TNTC]. Prayer for wisdom is addressed to God in 1:5 [HNTC].
2. The Lord is Jesus Christ [Lns]. The title *Lord* is given to Jesus Christ in 1:1 [Lns].
3. The Lord refers to the triune Godhead [Hb].

1:8 a-man[a] double-minded,[b] unstable[c] in all his ways.[d]

LEXICON—a. ἀνήρ (LN 9.24; 9.1) (BAGD 4. p. 66): 'man' [AB, BAGD, Herm, HNTC, LN, Lns, NIC; KJV, NASB, NIV], 'person' [LN, WBC; TNT], not explicit [NAB, NJB, NRSV, REB, TEV].

b. δίψυχος (LN 31.38) (BAGD p. 201): 'double-minded' [AB, BAGD, Herm, HNTC, LN, Lns, WBC; KJV, NASB, NIV, NRSV, TNT], 'in two minds' [NJB, REB], 'of two minds' [NIC], 'doubting' [BAGD, LN], 'devious' [NAB], 'unable to make up his mind' [TEV].

c. ἀκατάστατος (LN 37.32) (BAGD p. 30): 'unstable' [AB, BAGD, HNTC, Lns; KJV, NASB, NIV, NRSV, REB, TNT], 'unsteady' [NIC], 'uncontrolled' [LN], 'erratic' [NAB], 'inconsistent' [NJB], 'undecided' [TEV], 'vacillatory' [Herm], 'restless' [BAGD], 'distracted' [WBC].

d. ὁδός (LN 41.16) (BAGD 2.b. p. 554): 'way' [AB, Lns, NIC; KJV, NASB, NRSV], 'conduct' [BAGD, Herm, WBC; TNT], 'activity' [NJB], 'way of life' [BAGD, LN], '(all) that he does' [HNTC; NAB, NIV, REB, TEV].

QUESTION—What is indicated by the change from ἄνθρωπος 'person, man' in 1:7 to ἀνήρ 'man' in this verse?

Some think that the change is merely for the sake of variety with no difference of meaning intended [AB, Hb, ICC]. Others think that ἄνθρωπος 'person' is a generic term in reference to people in general [EGT, May] and ἀνήρ 'man' is more specific and better suited to qualifying words [EGT, May].

QUESTION—What is meant by a δίψυχος 'double-minded' person?

It means a person who holds two conflicting opinions [Bg, TNTC], who is divided between faith and the world [Blm, ICC, Lg]. His mind is distracted by lusts and temptations [NIC]. He does not have total allegiance to God [NIGTC]. The impulse or tendency towards good is in conflict with the tendency towards evil [HNTC, Tsk]. Belief and unbelief battle in his soul [Hb].

QUESTION—What is meant by ἀκατάστατος 'unstable'?

He is unreliable in all of his dealings [EGT, Hb]. He is uncertain in making decision and in what he does [AB]. He cannot act decisively or reliably [HNTC] and is indecisive in business and social life [EBC].

DISCOURSE UNIT: 1:9–11 [AB, GNT, Hb, HNTC, Lns, Mit, NBC, NIC, NIGTC, NTC, TG, TNTC, Tsk, WBC; NAB, NJB, TEV]. The topic is humility [NAB], the lot of the rich [NJB], the folly of boasting about riches [AB], the assessment of wealth [NBC], poverty and riches [ICC, TNTC, Tsk; TEV], the poor and the rich [HNTC], reversing fortunes [WBC], comforting the poor and chastening the rich [NIC], wisdom that is good amid trials [Lns], poverty excelling wealth [NIGTC], the correct estimate of trials [Hb], taking pride [NTC].

1:9 And/But[a] (let) the brother the lowly[b] (one) boast[c] in his elevation,[d]

LEXICON—a. δέ (LN 89.124; 89.94): 'now' [Lns], 'but' [NASB], not explicit [AB, Herm, HNTC, NIC, WBC; KJV, NAB, NIV, NJB, NRSV, REB, TEV, TNT].

b. ταπεινός (LN 87.61) (BAGD 1. p. 804): 'lowly' [BAGD, Herm, LN, Lns, WBC; NRSV], 'of low degree' [KJV], 'of humble circumstances' [NASB], 'in humble circumstances' [HNTC; NAB, NIV, NJB, REB, TNT], 'humble' [AB, LN], 'of humble degree' [NIC], 'low position' [BAGD], 'of no account' [BAGD], 'poor' [BAGD; TEV].

c. pres. mid. impera. of καυχάομαι (LN 33.368) (BAGD 1. p. 425): 'to boast' [BAGD, Herm, HNTC, LN, Lns, WBC; NRSV], 'to take pride' [NAB, NIV, REB], 'to be proud' [TNT], 'to glory' [AB, BAGD; NASB,

NJB], 'to exalt' [NIC], 'to rejoice' [KJV], 'to be glad' [TEV]. Although the verb is often used in a negative sense of arrogant boasting, here it has the positive meaning of rejoicing [ICC, NIC, NIGTC, Tsk], of glorying in God [NIGTC], of the pride possessed by one who values what God values [Tsk]. The present imperative commands the believer to adopt this as a characteristic response [Hb].

    d. ὕψος (LN **87.19**) (BAGD 2.a. p. 850): 'high position' [BAGD, LN, Lns; NASB, NIV], 'eminence' [NAB], 'exaltation' [AB, Herm, HNTC]. This noun is also translated as a verb: 'to be exalted' [WBC; KJV, REB], 'to be lifted up' [NJB, TEV, TNT], 'to be raised up' [NRSV], 'to be made high' [NIC].

QUESTION—What relationship is indicated by δέ 'and/but'?

    1. It indicates a transition [Hb, HNTC, Lns, NIC, TNTC, Tsk, WBC]: and/now. This word appears at 1:5, 9, 19, 22 and each time marks a transition between subsections of the two parts of the chapter [NIGTC]. This begins a new theme which does not seem to have a close tie to the preceding paragraph [EGT, Herm, HNTC, TNTC, Tsk]. Some see a closer connection with the theme of trials, a constant testing for the poor brother [EBC, ICC, WBC]. The writer may think that poverty provides a testing of one's faith in God [WBC].

    2. It indicates a contrast [Alf, Lg; NASB]: but. There is a contrast between double-mindedness (1:8) and the brother who has wisdom to properly regard his status in life [Alf, Hb, Lg].

QUESTION—What is meant by a brother who is ταπεινός 'lowly'?

    1. This refers to his social status as being lowly [May, My, NIC, NTC, TNTC]: the lowly brother. It is a state despised by the rest of the populace [NIC]. It does not refer to the virtue of a humble attitude [ICC, NIC]. Slaves and beggars would be so described [NIC]. It is the social status of the poor people [EGT, Lns, Mit, NTC, TNTC, Tsk, WBC].

    2. This refers especially to his poverty [Alf, Blm, EBC, Hb, HNTC, ICC, NIGTC, TG]: the poor brother. This meaning is in contrast with the wealthy man in the next verse [Hb, HNTC, NIGTC, WBC]. His poverty would put him in a low social status also [Hb, TG].

    3. This refers to Jewish Christians, or Jews, in their oppressed religious condition in contrast with the heathen secular powers [Lg].

QUESTION—What is meant by his ὕψει 'high position'?

    1. This refers to his present spiritual status as a Christian [BKC, EBC, Hb, Lg, Lns, May, Mit, My, NIC, NIGTC, NTC, TNTC, Tsk, WBC]. He is now a member of God's family [Hb, Lns, May, NTC] and has a high position in Christ [EBC] and is valued by God [Mit]. He also has the privilege of suffering for the sake of Christ [EBC]. He is to look beyond the present circumstances to the coming blessings—God has chosen him for an exalted position [Hb, Herm, HNTC, Lg, May, My, NIGTC, NTC, TNTC, Tsk, WBC]. James points to the combination of present status and

future blessings in 2:5 [TNTC, Tsk, WBC]. Another view is that this is the moral gain he achieves through the trials mentioned in 1:2 [ICC].
2. This refers to circumstances that enable the poor man to become wealthy [EGT, TG]. He is to be congratulated when his circumstances change for the better [EGT]. God will reward him either before or after he dies [TG].

1:10 but/and^a the rich^b (man) in his humiliation,^c

LEXICON—a. δέ (LN 89.124; 89.94): 'but' [Herm, HNTC, WBC; KJV, NIV], 'on the other hand' [Lns], 'and' [AB, LN, NIC; NAB, NASB, NJB, NRSV, TEV], not explicit [REB, TNT].
b. πλούσιος (LN 57.26) (BAGD 1. p. 673): 'rich' [BAGD, LN; KJV, NJB, NRSV], 'wealthy' [BAGD, LN], 'well-to-do' [LN]. With the article, the substantive is translated 'the rich man' [Herm, HNTC, WBC; NAB, NASB], 'the rich one' [Lns], 'the one who is rich' [NIV], 'the rich Christian' [TEV], 'the/a rich brother' [AB, NIC; TNT], 'the wealthy member' [REB].
c. ταπείνωσις (LN **88.51**; 87.60) (BAGD 1. p. 805): 'humility' [LN], 'humiliation' [AB, BAGD, Herm, HNTC; NASB], 'humble behavior' [LN], 'lowliness' [NAB], 'low position' [NIV], 'lowly position' [Lns], 'low status' [LN], 'low estate' [LN]. This noun is also translated as a verb: 'to be made low' [NIC; KJV], 'to be brought low' [WBC; NJB, NRSV, REB], 'to be brought down' [TEV, TNT].

QUESTION—Is the rich man a member of the church and what is the ταπεινώσει 'humiliation' of the rich man?
1. He is a member of the church [AB, Bg, BKC, Blm, EBC, EGT, Hb, ICC, Lg, Lns, May, Mit, NBC, NIC, TG, TNTC, Tsk; REB, TEV, TNT]: the rich brother.
   1.1 This concerns his self-abasement [Bg, Blm, Hb, Lg, Lns, May, NIC, Tsk]. It is the adoption of humility before God as urged in 4:10, 13–16 [NIC, TNTC] and identification with Christ [TNTC]. He understands his human frailty [BKC]. The attitudes of both the poor and the rich are the result of spiritual wisdom and the results look in opposite directions [Hb, Lns, TNTC]. His humility is to come from realizing that he will fade away [Bg].
   1.2 This concerns the bringing low of the rich man through the loss of his property or standing [EBC, EGT, ICC, Mit, NBC, TG]. This might be a consequence of becoming a Christian [EBC, ICC, Mit], or any other cause [ICC]. He should boast in such a trial, since trials are of benefit to his moral welfare [ICC].
2. He is not a member of the church [Herm, HNTC, My, NIGTC, NTC, WBC]: the rich man. The exhortation to boast is then ironic [Hb, Herm, HNTC, My, NIGTC, NTC, WBC]: let him boast about what is really his shame. He will be brought low at the day of judgment [HNTC, Tsk], or the rich man has a lot to rejoice about now, but it will all be gone at the last day and the only thing left for him to 'boast' about then will be his

humiliation [Herm, NIGTC]. His humiliation is the fool's paradise in which he lives, thinking his riches are important; but he will shocked to find the true system of values in the coming age [NIGTC, WBC]. His true position in God's estimation, not seen by the rich man but by a discerning Christian, is humiliation [NTC].

because^a as a-flower^b of-grass^c he-will-pass-away.^{d}
LEXICON—a. ὅτι (LN 89.33): 'because' [AB, Herm; KJV, NASB, NIV, NRSV], 'for' [HNTC, NIC, WBC; NAB, NJB, REB, TEV], 'seeing that' [Lns], not explicit [TNT].
  b. ἄνθος (LN **3.56**) (BAGD 1. p. 67): 'flower' [AB, BAGD, Herm, HNTC, LN, NIC, WBC; all versions except NASB], 'blossom' [BAGD], 'bloom' [Lns]. This noun is also translated as an adjective modifying 'grass': 'flowering' [NASB].
  c. χόρτος (LN 3.15) (BAGD p. 884): 'grass' [AB, BAGD, Herm, LN, NIC, WBC; KJV, NASB], 'small plants' [LN], 'wild plant' [TEV], 'herbage' [Lns], 'field' [NAB, NRSV], 'meadow' [HNTC]. This noun is also translated as an adjective modifying 'flower': 'wild' [NIV, NJB, REB, TNT].
  d. fut. mid. indic. of παρέρχομαι (LN 13.93) (BAGD 11.b.α. p. 626): 'to pass away' [AB, BAGD, Herm, HNTC, LN, Lns, NIC; KJV, NASB, NIV, TEV, TNT], 'to cease to exist' [LN], 'to come to an end' [BAGD], 'to disappear' [BAGD, WBC; NAB, NRSV, REB], 'to last (no longer than)' [NJB]. This verb is gnomic and speaks of the rich men in general, the typical rich person [NIC].
QUESTION—What relationship is indicated by ὅτι 'because'?
  1. This indicates the grounds for the preceding exhortation that the rich Christian should boast in his humiliation [Hb, ICC, NIC, TNTC, Tsk]: let the wealthy brother boast in his humiliation, because wealth is transitory and not worth boasting about.
  2. This indicates the grounds for saying the rich will be humiliated [TG]: let the rich man 'boast' of his humiliation, since he will be humiliated when his wealth passes away.
QUESTION—What kind of flowers are being referred to?
  Grass does not have flowers. The expression 'flowers of the grass' is an expression which means 'wild flowers' [EBC, Hb, ICC, Mit, NTC]. Some explain that it means the flowers that are among the grass, not flowers produced by grass [HNTC, Mit, NIC]. Another takes 'grass' to mean weeds or wild plants which grow in the fields and do have flowers [TG]. The flowers could be anemone [HNTC, NIC], cyclamen [NIC], poppies [HNTC], or lilies [NIC].
QUESTION—What is the point of comparison in this simile and what is being compared?
  1. The comparison is with the transitoriness of the bloom of a flower and the possession of wealth [BKC, ICC, NBC, TG], or the world in general

[TNTC]. The riches will pass away and he will cease to be a rich man [ICC, TG]. The rich man as being rich will pass away when he has lost his wealth [NBC]. This does not remind the rich of death, but of the transitoriness of wealth [ICC] and social position [BKC]. This does not mean that he will die, since the poor are sure to die also [ICC].
2. The transitoriness of the bloom of a flower and the life of the rich are compared [EBC, Hb, Lns, May, Mit, NIC, NIGTC, NTC, Tsk]. Both the man and his riches will come to an end [NIC]. Life is brief and uncertain [Hb]. The rich man cannot take his riches with him to the next world [May, Tsk]. This points out how meaningless riches are in the face of death [NIGTC]. Life is transitory for the poor man also, but this is applied to the rich man because while living in luxury he is more prone to forget it [Hb].

QUESTION—How is this clause a reason for a rich man to boast of his humiliation?

It indicates the meaninglessness of wealth in the face of death [NIGTC, WBC]. It indicates that wealth is not the true basis for security [Hb], that he must guard against depending on his wealth [TNTC].

1:11 For[a] the sun rose[b] with the scorching-heat/wind[c] and withered[d] the grass and its flower fell[e] and the beauty[f] of its appearance[g] perished;[h]

LEXICON—a. γάρ (LN 89.23): 'for' [AB, Herm, HNTC, NIC; KJV, NASB, NIV, NRSV], not explicit [WBC; NAB, NJB, REB, TEV, TNT].
  b. aorist act. indic. of ἀνατέλλω (LN 15.104) (BAGD 2. p. 62): 'to rise' [AB, BAGD, Herm, HNTC, LN, WBC; KJV, NASB, NIV, NRSV, TEV, TNT], 'to arise' [NIC], 'to come up' [NAB, NJB], 'to be up' [REB]. The aorist tense here and in the three following verbs is the gnomic aorist, which indicates what is of universal and timeless application [EGT, Hb, ICC, Lns, May, Mit, NIC, NIGTC, NTC, Tsk, WBC], or it may represent the Hebrew perfect to emphasize the suddenness and completeness of the withering [NIC, NTC, Tsk, WBC]. These are best translated in English with the timeless present tense [EGT, Lns, Mit, WBC]. They are historical aorists [Lg].
  c. καύσων (LN 14.67) (BAGD p. 425): 'scorching heat' [BAGD, Herm, LN; NAB, NIV, NRSV, REB, TNT], 'burning heat' [AB, HNTC; KJV], 'blazing heat' [TEV], 'scorching wind' [NIC; NASB], 'scorching hot wind' [WBC]. This noun is also translated as an adjective: 'scorching (sun)' [NJB].
  d. aorist act. indic. of ξηραίνω (LN 79.82) (BAGD 1. p. 548): 'to wither' [AB, Herm, LN; KJV, NASB, NIV, NJB, NRSV, TNT], 'to parch' [NIC; NAB, REB], 'to burn' [TEV], 'to dry up' [HNTC, WBC].
  e. aorist act. indic. of ἐκπίπτω (LN 15.120) (BAGD 1. p. 243): 'to fall' [AB, Herm, HNTC, LN, WBC; KJV, NIV, NJB, TNT], 'to fall off' [BAGD, LN, NIC; NASB, TEV], 'to droop' [NAB], 'to wither' [REB].

f. εὐπρέπεια (LN 79.13) (BAGD p. 324): 'beauty' [AB, BAGD, LN, NIC; NASB], 'loveliness' [LN], 'grace' [KJV]. The phrase 'the beauty of its appearance' is also translated 'its loveliness' [HNTC; NAB], 'its beauty' [AB; NIV, NJB, NRSV, TEV, TNT], 'its attractive beauty' [WBC], 'attractiveness' [**LN**], 'what was lovely to look at' [REB].

g. πρόσωπον (LN 24.24) (BAGD 1.d. p. 721) 'appearance' [AB, BAGD, LN, NIC; NASB], 'fashion' [KJV].

h. aorist mid. indic. of ἀπόλλυμι (LN 20.31) (BAGD 2.a.β. p. 95): 'to perish' [Herm, HNTC, NIC; KJV, NRSV, REB], 'to pass away' [BAGD], 'to fade away' [AB], 'to vanish' [TNT], 'to be destroyed' [LN; NASB, NIV, TEV], 'to be lost' [BAGD; NJB], 'to be gone' [WBC; NAB].

QUESTION—What relationship is indicated by γάρ 'for'?

1. It indicates the grounds for making a comparison of the rich man with a flower in the previous verse [Alf, Blm, Hb].
2. It indicates an elaboration of the figure of the fading flower in the preceding verse [HNTC, Lns, My, NIC, TNTC, Tsk].

QUESTION—What is meant by καύσωνι 'scorching heat/wind'?

1. It refers to the heat of the sun [AB, Alf, BAGD, Herm, HNTC, LN, Lns, Mit, My, NIGTC; all versions except NASB].
2. It refers to the heat of the wind [Blm, EGT, May, NIC, Tsk, WBC; NASB]. It refers to the sirocco, a scorching wind from the southeast which blows every spring [NIC, Tsk, WBC].

thus also the rich-man in[a] his goings/business[b] will-fade-away.[c]

LEXICON—a. ἐν (LN 83.9): 'in' [Lns, NIC; KJV], 'in the midst of' [AB, Herm, WBC; NASB, NRSV, TNT], 'in the middle of' [NJB], 'in mid (career)' [HNTC], 'amid' [NAB]. The phrase ἐν ταῖς πορείας αὐτοῦ 'in his goings' is translated 'while he goes about his business' [NIV, TEV], 'as he goes about his business' [REB], 'while pursuing his business' [LN (57.200)].

b. πορεία (LN **57.200**) (BAGD 1.2. p. 692): 'goings' [Lns], 'business endeavors' [LN], 'business activity' [LN], 'pursuit of business' [LN], 'all his business affairs' [TNT], '(business) journeys' [BAGD], 'undertakings' [BAGD], 'pursuits' [BAGD; NASB], 'enterprises' [AB, WBC], 'ways' [BAGD, NIC; KJV], 'projects' [NAB], 'conduct' [Herm], 'busy life' [NJB, NRSV].

c. fut. pass. indic. of μαραίνομαι (LN **13.94**): 'to fade away' [BAGD, LN, Lns, WBC; KJV, NASB, NIV, REB], 'to wither' [Herm, NIC; NJB], 'to wither away' [HNTC; NAB, NRSV], 'to be destroyed' [TEV], 'to perish' [AB], 'to disappear' [TNT], 'to end up being no one' [LN], 'to finally count for nothing' [LN].

QUESTION—What is meant by 'in his business/goings'?

1. This refers to the varied activities the rich man is engaged in [AB, Bg, Blm, EBC, Hb, Herm, HNTC, ICC, Lns, Mit, My, NIC, NIGTC, NTC, TG, WBC]: in the midst of his activities, the rich man will die. It means

his way of life [NIGTC, WBC], his experiences [ICC], his business affairs [EBC, LN, TG], and his plans [AB]. It implies that the rich man will unexpectedly die while engaged in his busy life [EBC, Hb].
2. This refers to the business trips made by the rich man [May, TNTC, Tsk]: while on a business trip, the rich man will die.

QUESTION—In what sense will the rich man fade away?
1. This refers to the death of the rich man [Bg, Blm, EGT, Lns, Mit, My, NIC, NIGTC, NTC, TNTC, Tsk]. It continues the comparison with the flower which fades away [NIC] and this word is suitable to refer both to the withering of plants and the death of a person [Alf, NIGTC]. Although the poor man will also die, this figure does not apply since he does not bloom like a rich man [Lns]. The fact of mortality has a special lesson for the rich, since it will separate him from his riches [NIC] and from all his deeds [NIGTC]. His wealth is meaningless after death [NIGTC]. Some see the scorching heat to imply God's judgment which will follow [NIGTC].
2. This refers to the loss of the rich man's riches [ICC, TG].

DISCOURSE UNIT: 1:12–27 [NIC, NIGTC]. The topic is the gospel promise [NIC], discussion of testing, proper speech, and generosity [NIGTC].

DISCOURSE UNIT: 1:12–21 [NIC]. The topic is faithful endurance against temptations.

DISCOURSE UNIT: 1:12–19a [WBC]. The topic is the source, mischief, and rationale of testing.

DISCOURSE UNIT: 1:12–18 [AB, GNT, HNTC, NIGTC, TNTC, Tsk; TEV]. The topic is the blessing produced by testing [AB, NIGTC], trials and temptations [GNT, TNTC, Tsk; TEV], gifts of God [HNTC].

DISCOURSE UNIT: 1:12–15 [Mit, NBC, NIGTC, TG, Tsk; NAB, NJB]. The topic is temptation [NAB, NJB], trial [Mit], tests and temptations [TG, Tsk], the results of the evil impulse [NIGTC], recognizing temptation [NBC].

DISCOURSE UNIT: 1:12 [Hb, Lg, Lns, NTC]. The topic is the blessedness of the man who is tested out by trial [Lg, Lns], the outcome of enduring testing [Hb], enduring the trial [NTC].

1:12 Blessed [a] (is) (the) man who endures[b] trial/temptation,[c]

LEXICON—a. μακάριος (LN 25.119) (BAGD 1.b. p. 486): 'blessed' [Herm, HNTC, Lns, WBC; KJV, NASB, NIV, NJB, NRSV], 'happy' [AB, LN, NIC; NAB, REB, TEV, TNT].
   b. pres. act. indic. of ὑπομένω (LN 39.20; 68.17; 25.175) (BAGD 2. p. 846): 'to endure' [AB, Herm, HNTC, LN, WBC; KJV, NRSV], 'to endure with constancy' [NIC], 'to hold one's ground' [LN,], 'to hold out to the end' [NAB], 'to still continue (to trust)' [LN], 'to remain faithful' [TEV], 'to remain constant' [Lns], 'to persevere' [NASB, NIV, NJB], 'to

stand up to' [REB], 'to stand firm' [TNT]. The present tense indicates continued steadfastness under the trial until it is ended [Hb].
- c. πειρασμός (LN 27.46; 88.308) (BAGD 2.b. p. 640): 'trial' [AB, Herm, HNTC, LN, Lns; NAB, NASB, NIV, NJB, REB, TEV], 'temptation' [KJV, NRSV, TNT], 'trying assaults of evil' [NIC], 'time of testing' [WBC]. See this word at 1:2.

QUESTION—What is meant by πειρασμόν 'trial/temptation'?
1. This continues the meaning of the word in 1:2 as 'trials' or 'tests' and is different from the temptations spoken of in 1:13 [AB, BKC, EBC, Hb, Herm, HNTC, ICC, Lns, Mit, NBC, NTC, TG, TNTC, Tsk; NAB, NASB, NIV, NJB, NRSV, REB, TEV], or as 'trials and temptations' and different from the temptations spoken of in 1:13 [NIC]. 'Trial' is meant because temptation must be resisted rather than endured [EBC, Hb, ICC, NBC]. The noun is a collective singular [Hb, Lns], indicating that characteristic feature of human experience [Hb].
2. This changes from the meaning of the word in 1:2 and is the same as the verb form in 1:13 'temptation' [WBC; KJV, NRSV, TNT]. The testings were to be met with endurance (1:2), while here the temptations are to be resisted with resolution [WBC].

because[a] having-become approved[b] he-will-receive the crown[c] of life,[d] which he-promised[e] to-the-(ones) loving him.

TEXT—The subject of the verb ἐπηγγείλατο 'he promised' is specified by some manuscripts as ὁ κύριος 'the Lord' and by other manuscripts as ὁ θεός 'God'. GNT leaves out the subject with an A rating, indicating that the text is certain. 'The Lord' is read by Blm, KJV, NASB, and NJB. 'God' is in NIV, REB, TEV, and TNT, although none of these accept 'God' as part of the Greek text.

LEXICON—a. ὅτι (LN 89.33): 'because' [WBC; NIV, TEV], 'for' [AB, Herm, HNTC, NIC; KJV, NASB, TNT], 'seeing that' [Lns], not explicit [NAB, NJB, NRSV, REB].
- b. δόκιμος (LN 30.115) (BAGD 1. p. 203): 'approved' [NASB]. The phrase 'having become approved' is translated 'to be approved' [AB, Herm, NIC], 'to be proved' [HNTC; NAB], 'to stand the test' [WBC; NIV, NRSV, TNT], 'to pass the test' [REB], 'to be of proven worth' [NJB], 'to be considered good' [LN], 'to be tried' [KJV], 'to succeed in passing a test' [TEV], 'to be tested out' [Lns].
- c. στέφανος (LN 6.192; 57.121) (BAGD 2.a. p. 767): 'crown' [AB, Herm, HNTC, LN, Lns, NIC, WBC; KJV, NAB, NASB, NIV, NJB, NRSV], 'wreath' [LN], 'prize' [LN; NJB], 'reward' [LN; REB, TEV, TNT].
- d. ζωή (LN 23.88) (BAGD 2.b.β. p. 341): 'life' [AB, Herm, HNTC, LN, Lns, NIC, WBC; all versions except TNT], 'the gift of life' [TNT].
- e. aorist mid. indic. of ἐπαγγέλλομαι (LN 33.286) (BAGD 1.b. p. 281): 'to promise' [AB, Herm, HNTC, LN, Lns, NIC, WBC; all versions].

QUESTION—What relationship is indicated by ὅτι 'because'?

It indicates the reason a man who successfully endures trial is blessed [Hb, Lns, My, NIC, NTC]: he is blessed because he will be rewarded with eternal life. Almost all who comment take this as an eschatological reward at the end of the age [Hb, HNTC, Lns, Mit, NIGTC, Tsk, WBC] when salvation is completed [NIGTC]. It concerns living in the joy of the new age that God will bring about [WBC], enjoying God's presence into eternity [Tsk]. It is eternal life in the complete and final sense of the term [Hb]. Another view is that this life is the present spiritual life [BKC].

QUESTION—What relationship is indicated by the aorist participle γενόμενος 'having become'?

It is temporal [Blm]: when he has become approved.

QUESTION—How does a man become approved?

A man becomes approved by God by successfully enduring trials [Alf, EBC, ICC, Lg, Lns, Mit, NBC, NIC, NIGTC]. To endure the trials means that he keeps a genuine faith [NIGTC]. It is to show constancy under the trials [ICC, Lns]. He remains strong in faith and devotion to God [EBC, Mit].

QUESTION—How are the nouns related in the genitive construction τὸν στέφανον τῆς ζωῆς 'the crown of life' and what is the figure involved?

1. 'Life' is in apposition to 'crown', the crown consists of life [Alf, BKC, Hb, HNTC, ICC, Lns, May, My, NBC, NIGTC, TG, TNTC, Tsk]. Some commentators take the crown to be a head-wreath given as a prize to the victor in athletic games [EBC, NIC, TG, TNTC, Tsk]. Some take it to be another type of crown given by a king to his friends as a mark of honor [Alf, ICC, My]. The point of comparison is that both a crown and life are rewards [AB, EBC, EGT, Hb, ICC, Mit, NIC, NIGTC, Tsk, WBC]. Like an athlete is rewarded with a crown, a man who has been approved for enduring trials is rewarded with eternal life [EBC, NIC], or like a man is rewarded with a crown by the king, a man who has been approved for enduring trials is rewarded with eternal life [Hb, ICC]. Unlike an athletic crown which was rewarded only to one of the competitors, all Christians can pass the test and all be rewarded with life [NIC].

2. It means the crown granted to a worthy life [Lg].

QUESTION—Who promised this crown of life?

1. God promised the crown [AB, Alf, BKC, EBC, Herm, HNTC, ICC, Lg, Mit, NBC, NIC, NIGTC, TG, TNTC, WBC; NIV, NRSV, REB, TEV, TNT]. The absence of the subject for the verb follows the Jewish reluctance to name God [NIGTC]. The 'crown of life' is a generalized statement of OT promises [NIGTC], such as Exod. 20:5–6; Deut. 7:9 [NIGTC]; or, since this specific phrase is not found in the OT, this is an unrecorded statement by Jesus [NIC].

2. The Lord Jesus promised the crown [Blm, Hb, Lns]. It may be that this refers to some unrecorded promise of Jesus [Hb], or it is a general summary of all that Jesus had in view [Hb, Lns].

JAMES 1:13

DISCOURSE UNIT: 1:13-18 [BKC, EBC, Lg, Lns]. The topic is the source of temptation [EBC], how temptation works in a person [Lns], resisting deadly temptation [BKC], warning against attributing temptation to God [Lg].

DISCOURSE UNIT: 1:13-16 [Hb]. The topic is the nature of temptation.

DISCOURSE UNIT: 1:13-15 [NTC]. The topic is temptation to desire.

1:13 (Let) no-one being-tempted[a] say, "By/From[b] God I-am-tempted";

LEXICON—a. pres. pass. participle of πειράζω (LN 88.308) (BAGD 2.d. p. 640): 'to be tempted' [AB, BAGD, Herm, LN, Lns; all versions except NJB], 'to be led into temptation' [LN], 'to be put to the test' [NJB], 'to be under trial' [HNTC], 'to be under trying assault of evil' [NIC]. This is also translated as 'in time of trial' [WBC]. The present tense indicates that the temptation is going on at the time of the writing [Hb].

b. ἀπό (LN 90.7) (BAGD V.6. p. 88): 'by' [AB, Herm, HNTC, LN; NAB, NASB, NRSV, REB], 'from' [Lns, NIC; TEV], 'of' [KJV], 'by command of, caused by' [BAGD]. God is also made the subject of the verb: 'God is tempting' [WBC; NIV, NJB, TNT].

QUESTION—What is meant by πειραζόμενος 'being tempted'?

The noun form πειρασμός and the verb form πειράζω can refer to outward trials that test a person who is then approved if he comes through them successfully, or they can refer to temptations that exert pressure to commit sin [EBC, Hb, ICC, Lns, May, Mit, TG, Tsk]. From the meaning of 'trial' in 1:2-12, the meaning now is changed to 'temptation' [AB, BAGD, Bg, BKC, Blm, EBC, Hb, Herm, HNTC, ICC, LN, Lns, May, Mit, TNTC, Tsk; all versions except NJB]. Some show a transition connecting the same events being experienced with the two meanings [Hb, HNTC, Lns, May, My, Tsk]: blessed is the person who endures trials (1:12), but if he feels tempted by such trials, he must not say that God is tempting him. The trial may be ordered by God, but the inner solicitation to sin which is aroused by the outer trial is from the person himself [May, Mit]. Others treat this verse as being concerned with experiences other than trials [Herm]: blessed is the person who is tested with trials and endures, but when something else tempts him, he must not say that God is tempting him. Those who take 1:2 to include temptation to do evil, continue the same meaning here [Alf, NIC]. EGT takes it to mean temptation to lust.

QUESTION—What relationship is indicated by the participle πειραζόμενος 'being tempted'?

1. It is temporal [AB, Alf; KJV, NASB, NIV, NJB, NRSV, REB]: when he is being tempted.
2. It is conditional [TEV]: if he is tempted.
3. It is indefinite attributive [Bg; NAB, TNT]: who is being tempted.

QUESTION—What is meant by saying that one is tempted ἀπό 'from' God?

Some commentators think that ἀπό 'from' is used instead of ὑπό 'by' (1:14) in order to indicate that God is the ultimate cause of the temptation even though the temptation is ὑπό 'by' intermediate agents [BAGD, BKC, Lns, May, My]. Others apparently think that this distinction is not intended and merely translate it to say that God tempts people [Blm, NTC, TG, WBC; NIV, NJB, TNT].

for[a] God is not-tempted[b] of-evils,[c] and he himself tempts no-one.

LEXICON—a. γάρ (LN 89.23): 'for' [AB, Herm, HNTC, Lns, NIC, WBC; KJV, NASB, NIV, NRSV, REB, TEV], not explicit [NAB, NJB, TNT].

b. ἀπείραστος (LN **88.309**) (BAGD p. 83): 'not tempted' [HNTC], 'without temptation' [BAGD], 'unable to be tempted' [Herm, LN], 'beyond the grasp' [NAB], 'invincible to assault' [NIC]. The phrase ἀπείραστος ἐστιν 'is not tempted/temptable' is translated 'cannot be tempted' [BAGD, Herm, **LN**, Lns, WBC; all versions except NAB].

c. κακός (LN 88.106) (BAGD 1.c. p. 397): 'evil' [LN, NIC; NAB], 'evil deeds' [BAGD]. In the genitive case it is here translated 'by evil' [AB, Herm, HNTC, WBC; NASB, NIV, NJB, NRSV, REB, TEV, TNT], 'with evil' [KJV], 'as regards things base' [Lns].

QUESTION—What relationship is indicated by γάρ 'for'?

It indicates the grounds for the exhortation that no one should say that he is tempted by God [Hb, Herm, HNTC, My, NIGTC, TNTC, Tsk].

QUESTION—What is meant by ἀπείραστος 'not tempted' and how does this clause fit into the argument?

1. It means that God is incapable of responding to temptations to do evil [BKC, Blm, EGT, Hb, Herm, HNTC, ICC, May, Mit, My, NIC, NTC, TG, Tsk]. Trying to tempt God cannot be successful [Bg]; God fully resists any temptation or invitation to sin [EBC, Lg]. Evil is repugnant to God [Hb]. To tempt others, God would have to enjoy evil, but he is incapable of this [EBC, NIC]. God's character makes it impossible for him to tempt people, and in his activity he does not, in fact, tempt them [Hb]. Just as nothing evil can tempt God, so God on his part never tempts anyone [Lns, NTC]. God cannot be tempted with the wish to tempt people [EGT]. Our belief in the holy character of God makes it impossible to suppose that temptations to sin can come from him [May, Mit].
2. It means that God is separated from evil [Alf, Lg(M), WBC]. God is unversed in evil things and has no experience of them [Alf, Lg(M)]. The argument is that God has nothing to do with the evil conditions that tested them in 1:2, and therefore it cannot be said that God is using evil to entice them to commit the sin of denying him [WBC].
3. It means that God should not be tested by evil people [NIGTC]. In trials, people tend to challenge God [NIGTC].

1:14 But[a] each-one is-tempted by[b] his-own desires,[c] being-drawn-away[d] and being-enticed;[e]

LEXICON—a. δέ (LN 89.124): 'but' [AB, Lns, NIC; KJV, NASB, NIV, NRSV, TEV], 'rather' [WBC; NAB], 'instead' [Herm], not explicit [HNTC; NJB, REB, TNT].
  b. ὑπό (LN **89.26**) (BAGD 1.a.β. p. 843) 'by' [AB, BAGD, Herm, HNTC, Lns, NIC, WBC; NASB, NIV, NJB, NRSV, REB, TEV, TNT], 'because of' [LN], 'of' [KJV, NAB]. This denotes the agent or cause [BAGD].
  c. ἐπιθυμία (LN 25.20) (BAGD 3. p. 293): 'desire' [AB, BAGD, Herm, HNTC, LN; NRSV, REB], 'evil desire' [LN, WBC; NIV, TEV, TNT], 'wrong desire' [NJB], 'lust' [LN, Lns, NIC; KJV, NASB], 'passion' [NAB]. Although in some contexts the word can refer to good desires, here it refers to evil desires [BAGD, EBC, Lns, My, NTC, TG]. It is not only sexual lust, but other strong desires such as greed for gain, desire for power and prominence, perverted desires to inflict cruelty on others [Mit]. The singular form indicates an innate tendency towards sin [Tsk].
  d. pres. pass. participle of ἐξέλκω (LN **31.74**) (BAGD p. 274): 'to be drawn away' [AB, LN; KJV, TEV], 'to be drawn out' [HNTC, Lns], 'to be led away' [LN], 'to be lured' [Herm; NRSV], 'to be lured away' [LN], 'to be dragged away' [BAGD; NIV, REB], 'to be dragged off' [WBC], 'to be taken in tow' [BAGD], 'to be carried away' [NASB], 'the tug of' [NAB], 'to be attracted' [NJB], 'to feel the pull of its distraction' [NIC]. The passive voice is also translated actively: '(his evil desire) drags away' [TNT]. The present tense here and in the following participle indicates a repeated experience characteristic of all people [Hb], or they indicate a process [Lg].
  e. pres. pass. participle of δελεάζω (LN **88.303**) (BAGD p. 174): 'to be enticed' [AB, BAGD, Herm, **LN**, WBC; KJV, NASB, NIV, NRSV], 'to be seduced' [NJB], 'to be lead astray' [LN], 'to be lured' [REB], 'to be lured away' [HNTC], 'to be lured into sin' [LN], 'to be lured with bait' [Lns], 'to be trapped' [TEV], 'to feel the enticement' [NIC], 'the lure of' [NAB]. It is the word used for catching fish [Blm]. The passive voice is also translated actively: '(his evil desires) entice' [TNT].

QUESTION—What relationship is indicated by the use of the two participles ἐξελκόμενος καὶ δελεαζόμενος 'being drawn away and being enticed'?
  1. They indicate the manner in which his desires tempt him [EGT, Lns, May, WBC]: he is tempted by his evil desires drawing him away and enticing him.
  2. They indicate an explanation of being tempted [Alf, Lg]: he is tempted in the sense that he is drawn away and enticed by his own desires.

QUESTION—What metaphor is involved in the two participles?

'Desire' is the agent of the two participles [Hb, Herm, HNTC, ICC, May], and it is personified [EBC, Hb, Herm, May, WBC].
  1. The two participles are in sequence, the second leading to the first. The imagery is concerned with fishing [Blm, TNTC, Tsk]. Like a baited hook

entices and then draws out a fish, so a person's evil desire entices and overcomes him [TNTC, Tsk]. Or there are two images, fishing and then hunting [NIGTC]: like a fish is drawn out by a hook and like an animal is trapped by bait, so a person lured to sin is overcome by his evil impulses.
2. The two participles are different aspects of the same event [Hb, Herm, ICC, TG]. They are virtually synonymous in meaning without any progression from one event to another [TG]. The imagery is from hunting or fishing [Hb, ICC, Lns, TG]: like a hunter or fisherman lures his prey and entices it to his trap or hook, so one's evil desire endeavors to make the person sin. This figure was also ascribed to the activities of a harlot [EGT, Hb].
3. The two participles are in sequence, the first leading to the second [Bg, BKC, Blm, EBC, EGT, HNTC, Lg, May, Mit]. The initial stage of temptation is when a person is drawn out from his normal restraints [Bg, Mit]. Then it is finished by his being enticed to commit sin [Bg, HNTC, May, Mit]. It is like a fish being drawn out from its hiding place and then being enticed by a lure [BKC, EBC, EGT]. It is like when an animal is lured from its lair and enticed by a tempting bait [Mit].

1:15 then the desire having-conceived[a] gives-birth-to[b] sin,[c]

LEXICON—a. aorist act. infin. of συλλαμβάνω (LN 23.49) (BAGD 1.b. p. 776): 'to conceive' [AB, BAGD, Herm, HNTC, LN, Lns, NIC, WBC; all versions], 'to become pregnant' [BAGD, LN].

b. pres. act. indic. of τίκτω (LN 23.52) (BAGD 2. p. 817): 'to give birth to' [AB, BAGD, Herm, LN, Lns, NIC; all versions except KJV, TNT], 'to bear' [BAGD, HNTC, LN], 'to bring forth' [KJV], 'to produce' [WBC; TNT].

c. ἁμαρτία (LN 88.289): 'sin' [AB, Herm, HNTC, LN, Lns, NIC, WBC; all versions]. Here sin is a knowing disobedience to God's will [Mit]. Without the article this refers to some general act of sin of one kind or another, the exact kind being immaterial [Alf, Hb, My], but it is some definite act of sin [Bg, Lns]. In the following clause, the article with sin refers the sin to whatever particular sin is here produced [Alf, Hb].

QUESTION—What is the metaphor intended here?

The metaphor concerns the process of human reproduction. Like a woman conceives and gives birth to a child, so lust produces sin [Alf, BKC, Blm, EBC, Hb, Lns, May, Mit, NBC, NIC, NIGTC, NTC, TG, TNTC, Tsk, WBC]. In this sense lust is personified [EGT, NIGTC, TNTC, WBC]. The human will is seduced by lust (in the preceding verse) to produce sin as their offspring [Alf, Hb, May, NBC, NIC, Tsk, WBC]. However, others do not see such a full correspondence and deny that this implies a union between lust and the will [ICC]. Another explanation is that the devil is the implied father [BKC, NIC]. The two steps, 'conceives' and 'gives birth', are meant to be a single process of producing sin [NIC]. Or they may be viewed as distinct steps: allowing an evil desire to remain in the heart is spoken of desire conceiving, and then as surely as conception leads to birth, so does the unrepentant desire lead to sin [Mit].

QUESTION—What relationship is indicated by the participle συλλαβοῦσα 'having conceived'?

1. It is temporal [AB; KJV, NAB, NASB, NIV, NRSV]: when it has conceived, it gives birth.
2. It is parallel to the following verb [NJB, REB, TEV, TNT]: it conceives and gives birth.

and the sin having-become-full-grown[a] causes/gives-birth-to[b] death.[c]

LEXICON—a. aorist pass. participle of ἀποτελέω (LN **68.22**) (BAGD 1. p. 101): 'to become complete' [Herm, LN, Lns], 'to run its course' [BAGD], 'to reach maturity' [NAB], 'to become mature' [HNTC], 'to reach full growth' [NJB], 'to be fully grown' [NIC, WBC; NIV, NRSV, REB, TEV, TNT], 'to ripen' [AB], 'to be finished' [KJV], 'to be accomplished' [NASB],

b. pres. act. indic. of ἀποκυέω (LN **13.12**) (BAGD p. 94): 'to cause' [**LN**], 'to produce' [AB; TNT], 'to give rise to' [LN], 'to give birth to' [BAGD, HNTC, LN, WBC; NIV, NJB, NRSV, TEV], 'to bear' [BAGD], 'to beget' [NAB], 'to bring forth' [Herm, Lns, NIC; KJV, NASB], 'to breed' [REB]. Some commentators think that there is no significant difference between this word and τίκτω 'to give birth' in the preceding clause [Hb, HNTC, Lns, WBC].

c. θάνατος (LN 23.99) (BAGD 2.a. p. 351): 'death' [AB, BAGD, Herm, HNTC, LN, Lns, NIC, WBC; all versions]. This is a figurative use of death, meaning spiritual death [BAGD, Hb, Lns, Mit, TG]. But it also includes physical death and the ultimate eternal death [Hb, Mit, NBC, NTC, TG].

QUESTION—What relationship is indicated by the participle ἀποτελεσθεῖσα 'having become full-grown'?

It is temporal [AB, Alf; KJV, NAB, NASB, NIV, NJB, NRSV, REB, TEV, TNT]: when it has become full-grown.

QUESTION—What is the metaphor intended here?

1. This concerns human growth and reproduction. Like a child grows up and then, in turn, has a child, so sin develops until it is complete and produces death [Alf, BKC, Blm, EBC, NIC, TG, TNTC, Tsk]. Three generations are involved in the two clauses, lust gives birth to sin which, in turn, gives birth to death [Blm, EBC, Hb, TG, Tsk]. The 'maturing' of sin refers to the complete development of sin [NIGTC]. When sin becomes a fixed state and habit, it brings forth death [May, My, NIC]. Or this means the sinful act brings about a series of results which bring the person to bondage to sin [Alf]. Sin is complete at the point where its result is death [ICC]. This should not be understood to mean that only when sin has matured will it result in death since the penalty of sin of any kind is

spiritual death [EBC]. The purpose of the metaphor is simply to trace the results of temptation when a person yields to it [EBC].
2. This concerns reproduction only [Bg, Lns]. Sin is not to be thought of as growing up. Sin does not conceive, it is pregnant with death from the start [Bg]. It is brought to completion when it is not repented of and then it brings about death [Lns].

DISCOURSE UNIT: 1:16–27 [NAB]. The topic is the response to God's gift.

DISCOURSE UNIT: 1:16–18 [Mit, NBC, NIGTC, NTC, TG, Tsk; NJB]. The topic is receiving the word and putting it into practice [NJB], receiving perfect gifts [NTC], God's gifts [TG], recognizing that all good gifts come from God [NBC, Tsk].

1:16 Do not be-deceived,[a] my beloved[b] brothers.
LEXICON—a. pres. mid. impera. of πλανάω (LN 31.8) (BAGD 2.c.γ. p. 665): 'to be deceived' [BAGD, Herm, LN, Lns; NASB, NIV, NRSV, TEV], 'to be misled' [BAGD, LN], 'to be led astray' [WBC; TNT], 'to go astray' [AB], 'to make a mistake' [**BAGD**, Herm, NIC; NAB, NJB, REB], 'to err' [KJV]. This present imperative with the negative μή cautions against falling into deception [Blm], against misunderstanding the preceding and following comments [HNTC, May]. Here μή with the present imperative warns against making a habit of doing something; only the context can indicate whether it is something already in progress, thus meaning 'stop doing this' [EBC, Hb, Lns], or something not yet being done, thus meaning 'don't be doing this'. Here the context leaves both possibilities open.
  b. ἀγαπητός (LN 25.45) (BAGD 2. p. 6): 'beloved' [AB, BAGD, Herm, HNTC, LN, Lns, NIC; KJV, NASB, NRSV], 'dear' [LN, WBC; NAB, NIV, NJB, REB, TEV, TNT].
QUESTION—What would someone be deceived about?
The warning refers to being deceived into thinking that God is the author of temptation [Bg, EBC, EGT, Herm, Lg, May, Mit, NBC, NTC, TG, TNTC, Tsk]. Since it also marks a transition to the following text, it could also mean that they are not to be deceived about the true gifts of God [Blm, HNTC].

DISCOURSE UNIT: 1:17–18 [Hb]. The topic is God's actions in people's affairs.

1:17 Every good[a] giving/gift[b] and every perfect[c] gift[d] is from-above,[e] coming-down[f] from the Father of-the lights,[g]
LEXICON—a. ἀγαθός (LN 65.20; 88.1) (BAGD 1.a.β. p. 2): 'good' [AB, BAGD, Herm, HNTC, LN, Lns, NIC, WBC; KJV, NASB, NIV, NJB, REB, TEV, TNT], 'beneficial' [BAGD], 'worthwhile' [NAB], 'generous' [NRSV]. This word describes the gift as being useful and beneficial [Hb].
  b. δόσις (LN 57.73) (BAGD 1. p. 204): 'giving' [Lns, WBC], 'generous action' [REB], 'act of giving' [NRSV]. This noun is also translated as a

JAMES 1:17

verb; 'to be given' [NJB]. Then there is distinction between this noun and the following noun 'gift' [Hb, Lns, May]. Instead of the act of giving in the active sense of the word, the focus on the thing given in the passive sense of the word is also taken: 'gift' [AB, BAGD, Herm, HNTC, LN, NIC; KJV, NAB, NIV, TEV, TNT], 'thing bestowed' [NASB]. Then there is no significant difference in meaning from the following noun δώρημα 'gift' [Alf, Herm, HNTC, ICC, Mit, My, NBC, NIGTC, TG, TNTC, Tsk, WBC]. The variation is for rhetorical effect [NBC, TNTC, Tsk, WBC] because of the poetical or proverbial nature of the text [NIGTC].

c. τέλειος (LN 88.36; 79.129) (BAGD 1.a.α. p. 809): 'perfect' [AB, BAGD, Herm, HNTC, LN, NIC, WBC; KJV, NASB, NIV, NJB, NRSV, REB, TEV, TNT], 'genuine' [NAB], 'complete' [Lns]. This word describes the gift as being complete [Blm, Hb] and fully meeting the needs of the recipient [Hb] and having no element of evil [EBC, ICC] or defect [Blm].

d. δώρημα (LN **57.84**) (BAGD p. 210): 'gift' [BAGD, Herm, LN, NIC; KJV, NASB, NIV, NRSV, REB, TNT], 'present' [HNTC; TEV], 'benefit' [NAB], 'bequest' [AB], 'bounty' [WBC], 'thing given' [Lns]. This noun is also translated as a verb: 'to be given' [NJB].

e. ἄνωθεν (LN 84.13) (BAGD 1. p. 77): 'from above' [AB, BAGD, Herm, HNTC, LN, Lns, NIC, WBC; KJV, NAB, NASB, NIV, NJB, NRSV, REB, TNT], 'from heaven' [TEV].

f. pres. act. participle of καταβαίνω (LN **15.107**) (BAGD 1.b. p. 408): 'to come down' [AB, BAGD, Herm, HNTC, LN, NIC, WBC; KJV, NASB, NIV, NJB, NRSV, REB, TEV], 'to descend' [Lns; NAB], 'to come (from above)' [TNT]. The present tense pictures the gifts as continually coming down [Hb, Lg].

g. φῶς (LN 14.36) (BAGD 1.b.α. p. 872): 'light' [BAGD, Herm, HNTC, LN; KJV, NASB, NJB, NRSV], 'heavenly lights' [Lns; NIV, TEV, TNT], 'luminaries' [AB], 'heavenly luminaries' [NAB], 'lights of heaven' [NIC, WBC; REB]

QUESTION—What are the gifts?

They are gifts that affect a person's soul [Hb]. There is the gift of new birth (1:18) [Mit, Tsk], wisdom (1:5 and 3:15) [HNTC, WBC], salvation [Mit], the kingdom of God [Mit], the sending of his Son [NTC], the coming of the Holy Spirit [Mit, NTC], and all good things from him, in contrast with the rejected idea that he sends temptation [NIGTC]. This includes both spiritual and material gifts [NTC].

QUESTION—What relationship is indicated by the use of the participle καταβαῖνον 'coming down'?

1. The participial phrase adds an explanation that 'from above' means that the good gifts come down from God [AB, Bg, Hb, HNTC, ICC, Lns, May, My, NIC, NIGTC, TNTC, Tsk, WBC; NAB, NASB, NIV, NRSV, TEV, TNT]: every good and perfect gift is from above, that is, it comes down from the Father of lights. It also explains why the gifts are good and perfect [ICC].

2. The participle is to be taken with 'is' as a periphrastic construction [Alf, Herm; REB]: every good and perfect gift is coming down from above, it is from the Father of lights.
  3. It states an additional fact [KJV, NJB]: it is from above and it comes down from the Father of lights.

QUESTION—How are the nouns related in the genitive construction τοῦ πατρὸς τῶν φώτων 'the Father of lights'?

  It means that the Father who created the lights [Lg], i.e., the heavenly bodies: the sun, moon, and stars [Alf, Blm, EBC, Hb, HNTC, ICC, My, NBC, NIGTC, NTC, TG, TNTC, Tsk; REB, TEV, TNT] also controls them [EBC, Hb, WBC]. Describing God as 'Father' alludes to his creative work [Alf, EBC, Herm, HNTC, ICC, Mit, My, TG, Tsk]. The purpose of this description is to remind the readers of God's power manifested in his good creation (Gen. 1) [TNTC, Tsk].

with whom there-is[a] no change[b] or shadow[c] of-turning.[d]

TEXT—Instead of ἢ τροπῆς ἀποσκίασμα 'or of-turning a-shadow', some manuscripts have ἢ (or ἡ) τροπῆς ἀποσκιάσματος 'the (variation which consists of) turning of a shadow'. GNT selects the first reading with 'or' with a B rating, indicating that the text is almost certain. Only EBC and ICC have the second reading.

LEXICON—a. pres. act. indic. of ἔνι (LN **13.70**) (BAGD p. 266): '(there) is' [AB, BAGD, HNTC, LN, Lns, WBC; KJV, NASB, NJB, NRSV, REB]. The Father is also made the subject of the verb: 'who does not change like shifting shadows' [NIV], 'who cannot change and who is never shadowed over' [NAB], 'who does not change or cause darkness by turning' [TEV], 'he never varies, nor turns away from us and leaves us in the shadows' [TNT], 'who himself is without change and knows neither turning nor eclipse' [Herm], 'whose nature suffers neither the variations of orbit nor any shadow' [NIC].

  b. παραλλαγή (LN **58.44**) (BAGD p. 620): 'change' [BAGD, Herm, LN; NAB], 'variation' [BAGD, HNTC, Lns, NIC; NASB, NRSV, REB], 'variableness' [KJV], 'wavering' [WBC], 'alteration' [NJB], 'change of position' [AB]. This noun is also translated as a verb: 'to change' [NIV, TEV], 'to vary' [TNT].

  c. ἀποσκίασμα (LN **14.61**) (BAGD p. 98): 'shadow' [BAGD, HNTC, LN, Lns, NIC, WBC; KJV, NASB, NIV, NJB, NRSV, REB, TNT], 'darkness' [TEV], 'eclipse' [Herm], 'concealment' [AB]. The phrase is also translated 'who is never shadowed over' [NAB]

  d. τροπή (LN **16.15**) (BAGD 2. p. 827): 'turning' [BAGD, Herm, **LN**; KJV, TEV], 'variation' [BAGD, LN], 'change' [BAGD, HNTC, Lns; NJB, NRSV], 'variation of orbit' [NIC], 'eclipse' [WBC]. This noun is also translated as an adjective: 'shifting (shadows)' [LN (14.61); NASB, NIV], '(play of) passing (shadows)' [REB], 'periodic (concealment)' [AB]. It is also translated as a verb: 'to turn away' [TNT].

QUESTION—What is meant by 'there is no change with God'?
Most commentators think that this carries over the reference to the heavenly bodies [Alf, Blm, HNTC, ICC, Lns, Mit, NBC, Tsk, WBC]. Heavenly bodies are seen to change by their own movements [HNTC]. It emphasizes the unchangeable nature of God (in his understanding or will [Bg]) in contrast with the changeableness of creation [Blm, TNTC, Tsk]. The changes refer to regular movements of the heavenly bodies [TNTC, Tsk], such as the movement of stars in their orbits [NBC, WBC]. Or it refers to the variations to the intensity of light given by the sun and moon [Alf, Hb, ICC, Lns, Mit] and the differences of length of the day through the year [ICC]. Since God gives good and perfect gifts and his good character does not change, then it is clear that he cannot be trying to tempt people to sin [Herm, NIGTC].

QUESTION—How are the nouns related in the genitive construction τροπῆς ἀποσκίασμα 'shadow of turning'?
It means a shadow caused by turning [Alf, Hb, HNTC, LN, Lns, TNTC, WBC; NJB, NRSV, TEV, TNT]. It is not clear whether the shadow is caused by the changing positions of the heavenly bodies as they appear from earth [Alf, My, NIGTC, NTC, TG, TNTC, Tsk], by the phases of the moon [Alf, TNTC], by occurrences of eclipses of the sun or moon [Alf, Herm, NIC, NIGTC, NTC, TNTC, Tsk, WBC], by clouds blocking light from above, by the changing position of the sun during the day [BKC, EBC, Mit, NBC, NTC], or by nighttime which alternates with daytime [Alf, NIGTC, NTC, Tsk]. The purpose of this clause is to highlight the changeableness of nature and contrast it with the changelessness of God [TNTC, Tsk]. God is unchangeably good in contrast to the shadows which change as the sun moves across the sky [WBC]. God does not change and is not changed [NIGTC], not even by a 'shadow' or slightest change [Bg]. God does not turn away from people and leave them in darkness [TG].

1:18 Having-purposed[a] he-gave-birth-to[b] us by-a-word[c] of-truth,[d]

LEXICON—a. aorist passive participle of βούλομαι (LN 30.56) (BAGD 2.b. p. 146): 'to purpose' [LN], 'to will' [Lns, WBC; NAB], 'to choose' [NIV], 'to plan' [LN], 'to want to do' [TNT]. This participle is also translated as a prepositional phrase: 'of/ according to his will' [BAGD, HNTC, NIC; KJV], 'in accordance with his will' [Herm], 'in the exercise of his will' [NASB], 'by his own will' [TEV], 'with good will' [AB], 'by/of his own choice' [NJB, REB], 'in fulfillment of his own purpose' [NRSV]. It was his spontaneous decision [TNTC]. Some commentators mention that the position of this word at the beginning of the sentence makes it emphatic [Herm, ICC, NIC], while others think that this is the normal unemphatic position for it [NIGTC].

b. aorist act. indic. of ἀποκυέω (LN **13.87**) (BAGD p. 94): 'to give birth' [HNTC, WBC; NJB, NRSV], 'to bring to birth' [NAB], 'to bring someone to birth' [NIV, REB], 'to beget' [AB, NIC; KJV], 'to bring forth' [Herm, Lns; NASB], 'to bring into being' [BAGD, LN; TEV,

TNT], 'to cause to exist' [LN]. This is a figurative use of 'to give birth to' [BAGD, LN], and is the same verb used in 1:15. The aorist tense looks back to the time of conversion [Hb, Lg, WBC].

c. λόγος (LN 33.98; 33.260) (BAGD 1.b.β. p. 478): 'word' [AB, BAGD, Herm, HNTC, LN, Lns, NIC, WBC; all versions except NJB, TNT], 'message' [LN; NJB], 'what is preached' [LN], 'gospel' [BAGD, LN]. This noun is also translated as a participle: '(by) declaring' [TNT]. The dative form indicates the means by which he brought us forth [Hb, Lns, May, Mit, NBC, TG, Tsk, WBC] and this is indicated by the prepositions 'by' [AB; NASB, NJB, NRSV, REB], 'by means of' [Lns], 'through' [NIV, TEV], 'with' [KJV, NAB].

d. ἀλήθεια (LN 72.2) (BAGD 2.b. p. 36): 'truth' [AB, BAGD, Herm, HNTC, LN, Lns, NIC, WBC; all versions].

QUESTION—What relationship is indicated by the use of the participle βουληθείς 'having purposed'?

1. This indicates the reason God gave birth to us [Alf, Bg, Hb, Lns, May, TG; REB]: God gave birth to us because he purposed to do so.
2. This functions as an orienter to the following statement [WBC; NAB, NIV, TNT]: God purposed to give birth to us.
3. It confirms the statement that every good gift comes from God [Blm]: it is certain that all good gifts come from God, because it was by his will that we were born.
4. It expresses the basis of his giving birth to us [NASB, NJB, NRSV, TEV]: in the exercise of his will he gave us birth.

QUESTION—What is meant by the metaphor 'God gave birth to us'?

The image is of a mother giving birth to her child [Hb, HNTC, May, Mit, NBC, NIC, NIGTC, WBC]: like a mother gives birth to a child, so God brought to life his spiritual children. The point of comparison is giving life to a person. It means that God gave spiritual life to believers [AB, Alf, EBC, EGT, Hb, Herm, ICC, Lns, May, Mit, My, NIC, NTC, TG, TNTC, Tsk, WBC]. It is similar to the use of the metaphor of 'new birth' for the entrance into spiritual life [Hb, Mit, My, NBC, NIC, NIGTC, NTC, Tsk]. The verb is the same as the one used in 1:15 and makes a contrast with that metaphor of giving birth: sin produces death, but God produces spiritual life [Hb, HNTC, ICC, Lns, Mit, NIGTC, NTC, TG, Tsk]. Although the normal meaning of the verb refers to a mother giving birth to a child, it can be loosely applied to the father's responsibility in the birth of the child [Mit]. However, some commentators see no problem with comparing God to a mother instead of to a father [May, NBC, NIC, TG, WBC].

QUESTION—What word is referred to, and how are the nouns related, in the genitive construction λόγῳ ἀληθείας 'a word of truth'?

1. The word is the message of the gospel [AB, Alf, Bg, EBC, Hb, Herm, ICC, Lg, Lns, Mit, My, NBC, NIC, NIGTC, NTC, TG, TNTC, Tsk].
   1.1 'Truth' is an attribute of 'word' and it means a word which is true [Alf, My, NTC]: God produced spiritual life in us by means of the true word.

It is a word which consists of truth [Alf], it is a word which was spoken in truth [NAB].

1.2 'Truth' is an attribute of an implied Christian doctrine and it means a message which proclaims the truth [Hb, May, Mit, NBC]: God produced spiritual life in us by means of the message about the true gospel. It is the preaching or proclamation of the gospel [Mit].

2. The word is God's spoken word which expresses his purpose and is true [EGT, WBC]; God produced spiritual life in us by a true word of command. The background for this is God speaking at creation where his word expressed and executed his will [WBC].

that we should be a-kind-of[a] firstfruits[b] of-his creatures.[c]

LEXICON—a. τις (LN 92.13) (BAGD 2.b.α. p. 820): 'a kind of' [BAGD, Herm, HNTC, Lns, NIC, WBC; KJV, NAB, NIV, NRSV, REB, TNT], 'a sort of' [NJB], 'a' [AB], 'something important' [LN], 'as it were' [NASB], not explicit [TEV]. This word indicates a figurative use of the word 'firstfruits' [Alf, ICC, Mit, My, NIC]. It is used to moderate a figure that is too definite [AB, BAGD, Hb, Herm, Lns] and not quite adequate for the comparison [TG].

b. ἀπαρχή (LN 53.23) (BAGD 1.b.α p. 81): 'firstfruits' [AB, BAGD, Herm, HNTC, Lns, NIC, WBC; all versions except TEV], 'first offering' [LN], 'first portion' [LN]. This noun is also translated 'to have first place' [TEV]. The singular form in Greek is a collective singular and refers to a group [Lns, WBC].

c. κτίσμα (LN 42.38) (BAGD p. 456): 'creature' [AB, BAGD, Herm, HNTC, LN; KJV, NAB, NASB, NRSV, TEV, TNT], 'creation' [NIC; NJB, REB], 'what has been created' [BAGD, LN], 'what he created' [WBC], 'all he created' [NIV], 'created thing' [Lns].

QUESTION—What relationship is indicated by εἰς τὸ εἶναι ἡμᾶς 'in order that we might be'?

This indicates the purpose God had for giving birth to us [EBC, Hb, Herm, May, Mit, NIGTC, Tsk, WBC]: God gave birth to us in order that we be a kind of firstfruits of his creatures. This purpose was realized when we received spiritual life [Hb]. Some consider this to indicate result [Lns].

QUESTION—What is the meaning of the metaphor 'firstfruits' and who are the 'creatures'?

The 'firstfruits' were the first products of the grain or fruit [NBC, TG], and also of a person or animal [Alf, EGT, ICC, Lns, Mit, NIC, NIGTC, NTC].

1. 'Firstfruits' focuses on what is first in order [EGT, Hb, Herm, NIGTC, Tsk]: as the firstfruits of a crop is the first portion of the whole that is still to come, so we are the first to be redeemed of the total number of God's creatures to be redeemed.

    1.1 'Creatures' refers to people who will believe later in time [EGT].

    1.2 'Creatures' refers to all that God created, both animate and inanimate [Hb, Herm, NIGTC, Tsk]. The whole creation is due to be redeemed

(Rom. 8:19–22) [Hb, Herm, Tsk]. Christians are the first installment of God's plan to redeem the universe [Tsk]. This may also include the picture of the Christians being a special possession of God [NIGTC].

2. 'Firstfruits' focuses on that first part of the crop that belongs to God and is offered back to him [AB, Alf, EBC, May, Mit, My, NBC, NIC, NTC, TG, WBC]: as the firstfruits of a crop is dedicated to God so we are the ones dedicated to God among all the rest of God's creatures. 'Creatures' refers to everything God has created, both animate and inanimate [Alf, May, NTC]. The first portion was regarded as belonging to God [Hb, Lns, Mit, NTC] and was offered back to him [EBC, Hb, ICC, May, My]. The word was used not only for first in order, but also first in honor [Bg, NIC] or quality [Mit, TG]. This suggests that the group is especially dedicated to God and it is of fine quality [Mit, NBC, TG]. The 'firstfruits' are Christians in general [Bg, TNTC]. The early Christians were the first converts of all others who will follow [EBC, EGT, Mit, NTC]. Christians live among the rest of God's creatures, but are first in rank and must present themselves as an offering to God [AB]. Of all created things, Christians are in a special relationship to God [Lns].

DISCOURSE UNIT: 1:19–3:18 [Hb]. The topic is the fruit produced by faith.

DISCOURSE UNIT: 1:19–2:26 [ICC, TNTC, Tsk]. The topic is religious realities in instruction and in public worship [ICC], genuine Christianity demonstrated by its deeds [TNTC, Tsk].

DISCOURSE UNIT: 1:19–27 [AB, BKC, EBC, GNT, Hb, Herm, HNTC, Lg, Lns, May, NBC, NTC; NIV, NJB, TEV]. The topic is hearing and doing [Herm, NBC; NIV, TEV], doing what God's word requires [EBC], hearing and doing what God's word requires [GNT, Lns], the importance of doing God's word [AB], how one's faith is revealed by how one responds to God's word [Hb], one's religion as expressed in speaking and actions [HNTC], true religion [NJB], an exhortation to rest in God's truth [BKC], a warning against fanaticism [Lg], agreements [NTC].

DISCOURSE UNIT: 1:19–25 [ICC]. The topic is the importance of obeying as well as hearing.

DISCOURSE UNIT: 1:19–21 [BKC, Mit, NIGTC, NTC, TG, Tsk]. The topic is the absence of anger in pure speaking [NIGTC], the acceptance of the word of God [BKC, NTC], a discussion of human anger [TG], comments about those who hear God's word [Tsk].

DISCOURSE UNIT: 1:19–20 [Hb, TNTC, Tsk]. The topic is responses to God's word [Hb], remarks about speech and anger [TNTC, Tsk].

1:19 **Know/You know**[a] **(this), my beloved brothers,**

TEXT—Instead of ἴστε 'know/you know', some manuscripts have ὥστε 'therefore'. GNT reads ἴστε with a B rating, indicating that the text is almost certain. 'Know/you know' is read by AB, Alf, BKC, EBC, Hb, Herm, HNTC, ICC, Lg, Lns, May, Mit, My, NBC, NIGTC, NTC, Tsk, WBC, and all versions except KJV. 'Therefore' is read by Bg, Blm, NIC, and KJV.

LEXICON—a. perf. (with pres. meaning) act. indic. or impera. of οἶδα (LN 32.4) (BAGD p. 555; 1.i. p. 556): 'to know' [BAGD, Herm, Lns; NASB, TNT], 'to have knowledge' [AB], 'to be certain' [REB], 'to understand' [HNTC, LN; NRSV], 'to comprehend' [LN], 'to take note of' [NIV], 'to note' [WBC], 'to remember' [NJB, TEV], 'to keep in mind' [NAB]. This verb is imperative [BKC, EBC, Herm, HNTC, ICC, Lns, Mit, My, NIGTC, TNTC, WBC; NAB, NIV, NJB, NRSV, REB, TEV]; it is indicative [AB, Alf, Hb, May; NASB, TNT].

QUESTION—What is this phrase connected with?
1. The verb ἴστε 'know/you know' refers to what precedes.
   1.1 It is imperative [Lns, WBC; NAB, REB]: understand/keep in mind what I have just said. Some make a paragraph break following this clause [WBC; NAB], others before this clause [Lns; REB].
   1.2 It is indicative [Alf, Hb, Lg(M), May, Tsk; NASB, TNT]: you know what I have just said. They are not to be content with just knowing this, but are to let that knowledge have practical consequences in their lives [Alf, Hb, Tsk].
2. The verb refers to what follows and is imperative [BKC, EBC, Herm, HNTC, ICC, Mit, NIGTC, TNTC; NIV, NJB, NRSV, TEV]: take note of these commands: let every person be quick to hear, etc. Most do not translate the δέ. Some think that James was quoting a proverb or common saying and δέ 'now' is included because it was part of the original saying [My, NIGTC].
3. The verb ἴστε 'you know' refers to the general knowledge of the gospel and is indicative [AB]: you have knowledge, but it must not be misused, rather let every person be quick to hear, etc.
4. When ὥστε 'therefore' is taken instead of the verb ἴστε 'know/you know', this phrase is part of the following clause [Bg, Blm, NIC; KJV]: therefore let every person be quick to hear, etc. The experience of the new birth should show itself in one's conduct [NIC].

DISCOURSE UNIT: 1:19b–3:18 [WBC]. The topic is instructions on applying God's word.

DISCOURSE UNIT: 1:19b–27 [WBC]. The topic is obedience which springs from faith.

1:19b but/now (let) every person be quick^a for^b the hearing, slow^c for^b the speaking, slow^c for^b wrath;^d

TEXT—Some manuscripts omit δέ 'but' following the verb ἔστω 'let be', and some who omit δέ add καί 'and' before the verb. GNT reads ἔστω δέ 'but let be' with a B rating, indicating that the text is almost certain. δέ is read by Alf, Herm, ICC, Lns, May, My, NIGTC, Tsk; NASB, REB, TNT; ἔστω is read by AB, Blm, HNTC, NIC, WBC, KJV, NAB, NIV, NJB, NRSV, TEV, although some of these probably omit δέ 'but' for stylistic rather than textual reasons; and καὶ ἔστω is read by Lg.

LEXICON—a. ταχύς (LN **67.110**) (BAGD 1. p. 807): 'quick' [BAGD, Herm, HNTC, LN, WBC; all versions except KJV], 'swift' [AB, Lns, NIC; KJV].

b. εἰς with accusative object (LN 90.23): 'to' [AB, Herm, HNTC, NIC, WBC; all versions], 'for' [Lns], 'concerning' [LN].

c. βραδύς (LN **67.123**) (BAGD p. 147): 'slow' [AB, BAGD, Herm, HNTC, LN, Lns, NIC, WBC; all versions]. It means to be humble and patient [NIC].

d. ὀργή (LN 88.173) (BAGD 1. p. 579): 'anger' [AB, Herm, HNTC, LN; NAB, NASB, NRSV], 'human anger' [NJB], 'wrath' [Lns, NIC; KJV]. The phrase εἰς ὀργήν 'for wrath' is translated 'to be angry' [BAGD; REB], 'to become angry' [NIV, TEV], 'to get angry' [WBC], 'to lose one's temper' [TNT]. This refers to anger in general [Herm, ICC, NIGTC], the opposite of self-restraint [NIC], a quarrelsome and censorious temper [My], attitudes of resentment, hatred, or revenge [Tsk], the anger of those who preach angry sermons of condemnation [AB], the anger that arises from controversial conversation [Alf, Lg], from opposition to others' views [Blm], or from argumentative attitudes [EBC, Mit]. It refers to a continuing hostile attitude [Hb, Mit].

QUESTION—What are they to be quick to hear?

1. They should eagerly hear the word of God to guide their lives [AB, Alf, Blm, EBC, Hb, Herm, ICC, Lg, May, NIC, TG, Tsk]: be eager to hear God's word. They are to hear God's word read and listen to instruction in the faith [Hb, Herm], to read the word and listen to God speaking to their conscience [Tsk]. However, the principle applies to hearing good thoughts in general [May].

2. They should have a general attitude of readiness to hear [Lns, Mit, My, NBC, NIGTC, TNTC], although hearing the word of truth is included [My, NBC]. They should be willing to listen to the opinions of others in any discussion [Mit, NBC]. The aorist tense of the infinitive refers to the whole concept of hearing [Lns].

QUESTION—What are they to be slow to speak?

1. They are not to engage in hasty and ill-considered talking [Lg, Mit, NBC, NIC, NIGTC, NTC, TNTC] or reactions to what they hear [Hb]. They are to avoid speaking too much [Alf, EBC, Herm, Lns, My], since this can lead to anger [Alf, Lns], and continual talking interferes with hearing [EBC, Lns]. They are to speak wisely [NTC]. They are not to speak improperly concerning God [Bg].

2. They are to be slow to speak in anger [My].

3. They are to avoid speaking or teaching dictatorially or controversially [Blm, May].

4. They are not to be eager to be the speaker or preacher [AB, Tsk] before they truly understand the message themselves [Tsk], since some engage in angry condemnation in their preaching [AB].

QUESTION—What relationship is indicated by the three prepositional phrases introduced by εἰς 'to'?

They define the areas in which they are to be quick and slow [ICC]: be quick with reference to hearing; be slow with reference to speaking and to becoming angry. The use of εἰς with the articular infinitive is stronger than the simple infinitive [Lns].

1:20 **for wrath of-man (does) not bring-about[a] righteousness[b] of-God.**

LEXICON—a. pres. act. indic. of ἐργάζομαι (LN 13.9) (BAGD 2.a., 2.c. p. 307): 'to bring about' [BAGD, LN; NIV], 'to cause' [LN], 'to achieve' [AB; NASB, TEV], 'to produce' [Herm, HNTC; NRSV], 'to promote' [WBC; REB, TNT], 'to fulfill' [NAB], 'to work' [Lns; KJV], 'to do' [BAGD], 'to be served' [NJB], 'to express in action' [NIC]. The present tense indicates a continuing fact [Hb]; it is inchoate, meaning to begin to accomplish [NIC].

b. δικαιοσύνη (LN 88.13) (BAGD 2.b. p. 196): 'righteousness' [AB, BAGD, HNTC, LN, Lns, NIC; KJV, NASB, NRSV], 'divine righteousness' [Herm, WBC], 'righteous life' [NIV], 'righteous purpose' [TEV], 'righteous purposes' [TNT], 'saving justice' [NJB], 'justice' [NAB, REB]. The phrase δικαιοσύνη θεοῦ 'righteousness of God' is translated 'what is right in God's sight' [BAGD], 'the righteousness that will stand before God' [BAGD]. This noun has no article, so it means conduct whose quality corresponds to what God requires [Hb].

QUESTION—What is this phrase connected with?

It is connected with the preceding phrase giving the reason for being 'slow to wrath' [Alf, BKC, EBC, EGT, Hb, Lg, Mit, My, NBC]: be slow to become angry, because a man's anger does not accomplish the righteousness of God.

QUESTION—How are the two nouns related in the genitive construction ὀργὴ ἀνδρός 'wrath of a man'?

It means the wrath expressed by a man [Bg].

QUESTION— What is meant by ἀνδρός 'man'?

1. The word ἀνδρός 'man' is here a synonym for ἀνθρώπου 'man/human being' [NTC], and the sense is human wrath, not merely a man's wrath instead of a woman's wrath [Hb, NIGTC, NTC, TG]: human wrath. Although this word basically refers to man as distinct from woman, here it has no article and thus is qualitative, emphasizing the kind of wrath it is [Hb]. Since it is in contrast with the righteousness of God, it is not limited to the male gender [Hb].
2. It refers to man's wrath as distinct from woman's [Bg, Lg, May]. Those who would speak in wrath would be men [May].

QUESTION—How are the two nouns related in the genitive construction δικαιοσύνην θεοῦ 'righteousness of God'?
1. The phrase means the righteous life that God approves [BAGD, BKC, EBC, Hb, HNTC, ICC, Lns, May, Mit, My, NBC, NIC, NIGTC, NTC, TG, TNTC; NIV]. This righteousness is defined by God [Hb] and he is its source [Lns, May]. It is God's standard [NIGTC]. It is full obedience to the principles of the Sermon on the Mount [May]. It is a warning against the idea that anger can be a tool of righteousness [ICC].
2. It means God's saving justice [NJB] or saving rule [WBC].

DISCOURSE UNIT: 1:21–27 [TNTC, Tsk]. The topic is being doers of the word.

DISCOURSE UNIT: 1:21 [Hb]. The topic is receiving God's word.

1:21 Therefore,ª having-gotten-rid-of^b all moral-filth^c and abundance^d of-evil,^e

LEXICON—a. διό (LN 89.47): 'therefore' [AB, Herm, HNTC, LN, WBC; NASB, NIV, NRSV], 'wherefore' [KJV, Lns, NIC], 'so' [NJB, TEV, TNT], 'so then' [LN], 'then' [REB], 'for this reason' [LN], not explicit [NAB].
b. aorist mid. participle of ἀποτίθημι (LN 68.37; 85.44) (BAGD 1.b. p. 101): 'to get rid of' [WBC; NIV, TEV, TNT], 'to rid oneself of' [NRSV], 'to put away' [AB, Herm, LN, Lns], 'to put aside' [NASB], 'to lay aside' [BAGD, HNTC], 'to lay apart' [KJV], 'to rid oneself of' [BAGD], 'to strip off' [NIC], 'to strip away' [NAB], 'to do away with' [NJB], 'to remove' [LN], 'to discard' [REB], 'to stop' [LN], 'to cease' [LN]. It has a meaning similar to repentance [Mit, NIGTC]. The aorist tense implies putting off as a single act [Alf, Hb, Mit], a definite break with the past, preceding the reception of the implanted word [Alf, Hb].
c. ῥυπαρία (LN **88.256**) (BAGD p. 738): 'moral filth' [WBC; NIV], 'moral filthiness' [**LN**], 'moral impurity' [LN], 'moral uncleanness' [BAGD], 'filthiness' [AB, LN, NIC; KJV, NASB], 'filth' [BAGD, Herm], 'what is filthy' [NAB], 'filthy habit' [TEV], 'impurities' [NJB], 'sordidness' [NRSV], 'that is sordid' [TNT], 'vulgarity' [HNTC], 'shabbiness' [Lns]. The phrase πᾶσαν ῥυπαρίαν 'all moral filth' is translated 'everything sordid' [REB]. This word is used figuratively here [Alf], referring to lustful impurity [EGT]; it means filth in a strictly religious sense, not general moral filth [Lg]. The absence of the article refers to the quality of evil [Hb].
d. περισσεία (LN **59.53**) (BAGD p. 650): 'abundance' [BAGD, **LN**], 'accumulation' [AB], 'rank growth' [NRSV], 'great mass' [HNTC], 'prodigality' [NIC], 'a lot of' [Lns], 'remnants' [NJB], 'every trace' [WBC], 'superfluity' [KJV], 'all that remains' [NASB], 'what is so prevalent' [NIV]. The phrase περισσείαν κακίας 'abundance of evil' is translated 'vicious excess' [NAB], 'wicked excess' [REB], 'wicked

conduct' [TEV], 'profuse wickedness' [Herm], 'what is unspeakably evil' [TNT]. It refers to a profuse growth of evil [Alf, Mit, My], meaning that there is very much evil [Hb, Herm, Lns]. It refers to any evil that still remains in their life [Mit, Tsk]. The sense is 'manifold', not 'excess', since any κακία 'evil' is too much [EGT]. It refers to the overflowing of evil speech by false teachers to their followers [Lg].
   e. κακία (LN 88.105) (BAGD 1.a. p. 397): 'evil' [AB, LN, WBC; NIV, NJB], 'wickedness' [BAGD, LN; NASB, NRSV], 'vice' [NIC], 'badness' [LN], 'baseness' [Lns], 'malice' [HNTC], 'naughtiness' [KJV]. This wickedness consists of an evil disposition which makes the soul unable to receive the implanted word [Alf], evil attitudes toward others [May, Mit, My] and malice [NIGTC]. The absence of the article focuses on the quality of evil [Hb].

QUESTION—Who is addressed here?
  1. Those addressed are Christians [AB, HNTC, Lns, Mit, My, NBC, NIC, NIGTC, NTC, TNTC, Tsk]. They are being exhorted to let the gospel have its full effect in their lives [EBC, Lns]. They are probably recent converts [AB].
  2. They are not yet Christians and are being urged to meet the necessary conditions [EGT].

QUESTION—What relationship is indicated by διό 'wherefore'?
  1. It introduces the conclusion to be drawn from 1:20 [AB, Alf, BKC, Hb, Herm, HNTC, ICC, Mit, My, NBC, NIC, NIGTC, NTC, Tsk, WBC; all versions except NAB]: a man's anger does not accomplish God's righteousness; therefore put off all evil.
  2. It gives the conclusion from 1:18 [TNTC]: God gave us birth; therefore receive the engrafted word.
  3. It resumes and completes the exhortations in 1:19 [Blm]: be slow to speak and slow to wrath; so then receive the implanted word. Verse 20 gives an illustration concerning being slow to wrath [Blm].

QUESTION—What relationship is expressed by the participle ἀποθέμενοι 'having gotten rid of'?
  1. It is semantically parallel to the following imperative verb δέξασθε 'receive' [AB, BKC, Hb, HNTC, May, NBC, NIC, NIGTC, NTC, TNTC, Tsk, WBC; all versions except NASB]: get rid of all filthiness and receive the implanted word.
  2. It expresses the means for receiving the implanted word [Alf, Lns]: by putting away evil receive the implanted word.
  3. It is semantically the principal verb and the following δέξασθε 'receive' is temporal [Herm]: put away wickedness, and be humble when you receive the implanted word.

QUESTION—What is the genitive noun κακίας 'evil' connected with?
  1. It is connected with περισσείαν 'abundance' [BKC, Hb, Herm, ICC, Lg, Lns, NIGTC, NTC, Tsk; NAB, NASB, NIV, REB, TEV]: abundance of evil. The preceding πᾶσαν 'all' also modifies it: 'all abundance of evil'

[Herm, ICC; NAB, NASB, REB, TEV]. 'Abundance of evil' further identifies the preceding 'filthiness' [May]. This genitive identifies what the 'abundance' is—an abundance which consists of evil [Hb, ICC].

2. It is connected with ῥυπαρίαν καὶ περισσείαν 'filthiness and abundance' [Alf, My]: all evil's filthiness and abundance. The reference is not to all kinds of moral pollution but only that which belongs to κακία 'evil' [Alf].

in^a gentleness^b receive^c the implanted^d word the-(one) being-able^e to-save^f your souls.^g

LEXICON—a. ἐν with dative object (LN 89.84): 'in' [NASB], 'with' [AB, LN, Lns, NIC; KJV, NRSV]. The phrase ἐν πραΰτητι 'in gentleness' is translated 'humbly' [HNTC, WBC; NAB, NIV, NJB, TNT], 'meekly' [REB], 'be meek' [Herm], 'submit to God' [TEV].

b. πραΰτης (LN 88.59) (BAGD p. 699): 'gentleness' [LN], 'mildness' [LN], 'meekness' [LN, Lns, NIC; KJV, NRSV], 'humility' [AB, BAGD; NASB]. This is not weakness, but a considerate and gentle spirit [Hb, My], willingness to learn and to submit to God [Mit], the characteristic of a strong man who is willingly submissive [EBC], strength in restraint [NBC]. It refers to attitudes toward one another [Alf].

c. aorist mid. (deponent = act.) impera. of δέχομαι (LN 34.53; 57.125) (BAGD 3.b. p. 177): 'to receive' [AB, Herm, LN, WBC; KJV, NASB], 'to accept' [BAGD, HNTC, LN, Lns, NIC; NIV, REB, TEV, TNT], 'to welcome' [LN; NAB, NJB, NRSV]. It implies a welcome reception, not merely a passive acceptance [Hb], grasping it with one's heart [My]; it refers to giving attention to God's word [ICC] and acting upon it [NIGTC, Tsk]. This aorist imperative indicates a single decisive act [HNTC, Mit]; it implies urgency [Hb]; it refers both to receiving the word at conversion and also further receiving [Lg, NBC, NIC].

d. ἔμφυτος (LN **85.31**) (BAGD p. 258): 'implanted' [AB, BAGD, Herm, HNTC, LN, Lns, NIC; NASB, NRSV], 'engrafted' [KJV]. This word is translated as a phrase 'that is implanted' [WBC], 'which is implanted within you' [LN], 'planted in you' [NIV], 'planted in your hearts' [REB], 'that he plants in your hearts' [TEV], 'which God has planted in your hearts' [TNT], 'which has been planted in you' [NJB], 'that has taken root in you' [NAB]. The sense is 'implanted' rather than 'grafted' [BKC, Blm], the word planted into the believer's nature [ICC] by regeneration and by habit [Bg]. It has already been implanted in their hearts [Alf, EBC, NIC] and awaits being accepted to develop and grow [Alf]; it takes root in transforming power [Tsk]. It refers to subsequent gifts of grace which take root in our nature [Mit]. The 'implanted word' is the gospel [Alf, Bg, Blm, HNTC, Lg, TG, TNTC, WBC], the same as λόγῳ ἀληθείας 'word of truth' in 1:18 [Alf, Mit, My, WBC]. It refers to Christ as the Word implanted in their hearts [Lg(M)]. Its characteristic is to root itself in one's heart [EGT, Hb, May].

e. pres. mid. (deponent = act.) participle of δύναμαι (LN 74.5): 'to be able' [AB, Herm, HNTC, LN, Lns, NIC; KJV, NASB, TEV], 'to have the power' [NRSV], '(it) can' [LN; NIV, NJB, TNT]. The phrase τὸν δυνάμενον 'the one being able' is translated 'with its power' [NAB, REB]. The phrase τὸν δυνάμενον σῶσαι τὰς ψυχὰς ὑμῶν 'the one being able to save your souls' is translated 'by which you may be saved' [WBC]. It describes the power or ability of the word [My].

f. aorist act. infin. of σῴζω (LN 21.27) (BAGD 2.a.γ. p. 798): 'to save' [AB, BAGD, Herm, HNTC, LN, Lns, NIC; all versions]. The aorist tense implies a completed work [Alf, Hb]. The reference is to final salvation [Mit, My, NIC, NIGTC, TNTC, Tsk]; it includes both present and final salvation [NBC]; it means complete wholeness [NTC].

g. ψυχή (LN 23.88) (BAGD 1.c. p. 893): 'soul' [AB, BAGD, Herm, HNTC, Lns, NIC; KJV, NASB, NJB, NRSV], 'life' [LN]. The phrase τὰς ψυχὰς ὑμῶν 'the souls of you' is translated 'you' [NAB, NIV, REB, TEV, TNT]. The soul implies one's self [NTC, TNTC], the whole person [HNTC, Lns, NIGTC, TG], which may be saved or lost [Alf, Hb], the real self which survives death [Mit].

QUESTION—What is the phrase ἐν πραΰτητι 'with gentleness' connected with?

1. It is connected with what follows [AB, Alf, BKC, Blm, EBC, Hb, HNTC, Lg, Lns, Mit, My, NBC, NIC, NIGTC, NTC, Tsk, WBC; all versions]: humbly receive the word. It is emphatic by word order [Hb, My].
2. It is connected with what precedes [Herm; GNT]: put away wickedness and be humble. The reference is to a good-tempered attitude in general, in contrast with anger (1:20); the preposition ἐν 'in' refers to an accompanying circumstance [Herm].

QUESTION—What relationship is indicated by the attributive participle τὸν δυνάμενον 'the one being able'?

1. It describes 'the implanted word' [AB, EBC, Hb, Herm, HNTC, Lns, NBC, NIC, NTC; KJV, NASB, NIV, NJB, NRSV, TEV]: the implanted word which is able to save. It also implies the reason for receiving the word, 'because it is able to save' [AB, Lns, NIC]. The present tense indicates a continuing ability [Hb].
2. It describes an accompanying quality of the word [NAB, REB]: the implanted word with its power to save.
3. It states the reason for accepting the word [TNT]: accept the implanted word, for it can save.

DISCOURSE UNIT: 1:22–27 [Hb, NIC]. The topic is obeying the word [Hb], the gospel promise for those who obey the word and guard their speech [NIC].

DISCOURSE UNIT: 1:22–25 [BKC, Mit, NIGTC, NTC, TG, Tsk]. The topic is obedience requiring generosity [NIGTC], listening and obeying [NTC, TG], obeying the word [BKC, Tsk].

1:22 But/Now[a] become[b] doers[c] of-(the)-word and not only[d] hearers[e] deceiving[f] yourselves.

LEXICON—a. δέ (LN 89.94; 89.124): 'but' [HNTC, NIC; KJV, NASB, NJB, NRSV], 'only' [REB], 'now' [Lns], 'furthermore' [AB], not explicit [AB; NAB, NIV, TEV, TNT].

  b. pres. mid. (deponent = act.) impera. of γίνομαι (LN 13.3; 13.48): 'to become' [AB, LN, WBC], 'to be' [Herm, HNTC, LN, Lns, NIC; KJV, NRSV], 'to prove oneself' [NASB], 'to show oneself' [WBC]. The phrase γίνεσθε ποιηταί 'become doers' is translated 'do' [NIV], 'you must do' [NJB], 'act on' [NAB], 'be sure you act on' [REB], 'put into practice' [TEV]. This entire verse is translated 'Do not deceive yourselves by just listening to the word without practicing it' [TNT]. The present tense implies that they should continue to obey the word [BKC, Hb, NIC, NIGTC]. This word does not mean that they were not now doers of the word [Alf, Hb, Lns, My, NIGTC], but that they should show more and more that they are doers of the word [May], to make sure that they are doers [Tsk]; it is used as the imperative sense of the verb 'to be' [Hb, Herm, ICC, My, WBC].

  c. ποιητής (LN 42.20) (BAGD 2. p. 683): 'doer' [AB, BAGD, Herm, HNTC, LN, Lns, NIC; KJV, NASB, NRSV], 'one who does' [BAGD, LN], 'one who puts into practice' [WBC]. This noun implies that doing the word should characterize their lives [Alf, Hb, My].

  d. μόνον (LN 58.50) (BAGD 2. c. α. p. 528): 'only' [AB, BAGD, Lns; KJV], 'merely' [Herm, NIC; NASB, NRSV], 'just' [HNTC], 'simply' [WBC], 'alone' [LN]. The phrase καὶ μὴ μόνον ἀκροαταί 'and not only hearers' is translated 'and do not merely listen' [REB], 'and not just listen to it' [NJB], 'by just listening' [TEV]. The phrase καὶ μὴ μόνον ἀκροαταὶ παραλογιζόμενοι ἑαυτούς 'and not only hearers deceiving yourselves' is translated 'if all you do is listen to it, you are deceiving yourselves' [NAB]. This word shows that the author is not disparaging hearing, but is insisting on something in addition [Hb, HNTC, Tsk].

  e. ἀκροατής (LN 24.56) (BAGD p. 33): 'hearer' [AB, BAGD, Herm, LN, Lns, NIC; KJV, NASB, NRSV], 'listener' [HNTC], 'one who listens' [WBC]. The phrase μὴ γίνεσθε μόνον ἀκροαταί 'do not become only hearers' is translated 'do not merely listen' [NIV]. This word refers to hearing the word read [Hb, ICC, Mit, NIC, NIGTC], listening to oral teaching [Hb, Mit, NIC, NIGTC] and private instruction [NIGTC] and worship [Mit].

  f. pres. mid. (deponent = act.) participle of παραλογίζομαι (LN 88.153) (BAGD 1. p. 620): 'to deceive' [AB, BAGD, Herm, HNTC, LN, WBC; all versions except NASB], 'to delude' [NIC; NASB], 'to cheat (oneself) by false reasoning' [Lns]. The meaning is being deceived by false reasoning [BKC, EBC, Hb, Lg, Lns, Mit], by drawing false conclusions [Alf, My]. It is being deceived concerning their salvation [NIGTC]. The present tense implies a continual process of deception [Hb].

QUESTION—What relationship is indicated by δέ 'but'?
1. It is contrastive [BKC, HNTC, ICC, NIC; KJV, NASB, NJB, NRSV]: but. They must be swift to listen, but just listening is not enough [BKC, HNTC, ICC].
2. It is continuative [Hb, Lns]. It explains what is meant by acceptance of the word [Lns]. Obedience is to follow reception of the word [Hb].

QUESTION—What relationship is indicated by the participle παραλογιζόμενοι 'deceiving'?
1. It expresses the result of being hearers only [Hb, NTC, TG, WBC; NIV, REB]: don't be hearers only; the result would be to deceive yourselves. It expresses a warning [Blm]. Merely hearing amounts to self-deception [Herm].
2. It describes 'hearers only' [AB; NASB, NRSV]: hearers who deceive themselves.

QUESTION—What is the participle παραλογιζόμενοι 'deceiving' connected with?
1. It is related to 'you', the subject of γίνεσθε 'become' [Hb, Herm, HNTC, ICC, Lns, May, My, NIC, NTC; all versions except NASB, NRSV]: don't you become hearers only, deceiving yourselves.
2. It is related to ἀκροαταί 'hearers' [AB, Lg, Mit, NIGTC, WBC; NASB, NRSV]: hearers only, deceiving themselves.

QUESTION—In what way does the author think the readers might deceive themselves?

They might think that they could be saved by merely hearing God's word [AB, Alf, BKC, Blm, EBC, Hb, ICC]: don't deceive yourselves by thinking that merely hearing the word will save you.

1:23 Because[a] if anyone is a-hearer[b] of-(the)-word and not a-doer,[c]

LEXICON—a. ὅτι (LN 89.33): 'because' [Herm, LN, Lns], 'for' [AB, HNTC, LN, NIC; KJV, NASB, NRSV], 'since' [LN], not explicit [WBC; NAB, NIV, NJB, REB, TEV, TNT].
  b. ἀκροατής: 'hearer'. See this word at 1:22.
  c. ποιητής (LN 42.20) (BAGD 2. p. 683): 'doer' [AB, BAGD, Herm, HNTC, LN, Lns, NIC; KJV, NASB, NRSV]. This noun is translated as a phrase 'to do' [WBC; NIV], 'to act (on it)' [REB], 'to take no action' [NJB], 'to put (it) into practice' [NAB, TEV], 'to practice (it)' [TNT]. See this word at 1:22.

QUESTION—What relationship is indicated by ὅτι 'because'?

It introduces the grounds for what the author has just said [Alf, Bg, Hb, Lg, My, NBC, WBC]. It explains the meaninglessness of a mere confession of faith [AB] and states why we should be doers and not merely hearers of the word [EBC, May]. It gives an illustration of the non-practicing hearer [Blm, Herm, ICC].

QUESTION—What relationship is indicated by εἰ 'if'?
   It introduces a possible fact, but with no specific person in mind [Alf, Lns]: if anyone is presently a hearer only.
QUESTION—How are the two nouns related in the genitive construction ἀκροατής λόγου 'a hearer of the word'?
   It means that the person hears the word [Lg; NAB, NIV, NJB, REB, TEV, TNT]: if anyone hears the word.

this-one is-like[a] a-man looking-at[b] the face[c] of-the existence[d] of-him in[e] a-mirror.[f]

LEXICON—a. perf. (with pres. meaning) act. indic. of ἔοικα (LN **64.4**) (BAGD p. 280): 'to be like' [AB, BAGD, Herm, HNTC, **LN**, Lns, NIC; all versions], 'to be similar to' [LN, WBC].

   b. pres. act. participle of κατανοέω (LN 30.4) (BAGD 2. p. 415): 'to look at' [BAGD, Herm, WBC; all versions except KJV, TEV], 'to look and see' [TEV], 'to take a good look at' [HNTC], 'to observe' [NIC], 'to perceive' [AB], 'to behold' [KJV], 'to take cognizance of' [Lns], 'to consider closely' [LN]. The present participle implies 'beholding' as a continuing characteristic of the person [Hb]. Some take it to be an ordinary look [Herm, ICC], even a hasty one [Hb, NBC, NIC, TG, Tsk] that reveals something that needs to be changed [Hb]. Others take it to mean a careful observation [Blm, HNTC, Lns], and it implies that the persons are those who have heard and clearly understood God's will for them [EBC].

   c. πρόσωπον (LN 8.18) (BAGD 1.a. p. 720): 'face' [BAGD, HNTC, LN, NIC, WBC; KJV, NAB, NASB, REB], 'countenance' [Lns], 'appearance' [Herm]. The phrase τὸ πρόσωπον τῆς γενέσεως αὐτοῦ 'the face of his existence' is translated 'his face' [NIV], 'his own features' [NJB], 'the shape of his natural features' [AB], 'himself' [TNT], 'himself as he is' [TEV], 'themselves' [NRSV].

   d. γένεσις (LN **13.71**; 23.46) (BAGD 2. p. 154): 'existence' [BAGD, **LN**], 'being' [Lns], 'birth' [LN], 'mortal, physical birth' [NIC], 'created being' [NIC]. This noun is translated as an adjective: 'natural' [BAGD, Herm; KJV, NASB]. The phrase τῆς γενέσεως αὐτοῦ 'of his existence' is translated 'he was born with' [HNTC; NAB], 'nature gave him' [REB], 'that nature gave him' [WBC]. The sense is 'existence' [Herm, Mit] or 'birth' [My, NBC, NIC]. This phrase emphasizes the physical features [Alf, Hb, Lns], his physical face [NIC, Tsk], which constantly changes [Lg, Tsk]; it is in contrast with the character which he finds described in the law [ICC]; it refers to the swiftly passing earthly life in contrast with what relates to eternity [EGT, May, Tsk]; it refers to what the man is in contrast with what God intends him to be [Mit]. This word is emphatic [ICC].

   e. ἐν with dative object (LN 83.13): 'in' [AB, Herm, HNTC, LN, Lns, NIC, WBC; all versions except NAB], 'into' [NAB].

f. ἔσοπτρον (LN **6.221**) (BAGD p. 313): 'mirror' [AB, BAGD, Herm, HNTC, LN, Lns, NIC, WBC; all versions except KJV], 'glass' [KJV]. The mirror is a figurative reference to God's word [AB, BKC, Blm, NBC]. It implies imperfect knowledge [May].

QUESTION—What is meant by ἀνδρί 'man'?
1. Here it is used generically [Hb, Herm, NIGTC; NJB, NRSV, REB]: a person.
2. It refers to a man [Lg, NIC; TEV, TNT]: a man. A woman would probably not forget her appearance [BKC, Lg].

QUESTION—What relationship is indicated by the participle κατανοοῦντι 'beholding'?

It describes the man [BKC, NIGTC; all versions except KJV, REB]: a man who beholds.

QUESTION—How are the two nouns related in the genitive construction πρόσωπον τῆς γενέσεως 'face of the existence'?

The genitive τῆς γενέσεως 'of the existence' describes πρόσωπον 'face' [Alf, Blm, Hb, Lg; KJV, NAB, NASB, REB]: the face he has had since birth [My, NBC, NIC, TG, TNTC; NAB].

QUESTION—What is αὐτοῦ 'of him' connected with?
1. It is connected with γενέσεως 'existence' [Alf, BKC, Hb, Lg, My; REB]: the face of his existence.
2. It is connected with πρόσωπον 'face' [KJV, NASB, NIV, NJB, NRSV]: 'his face'.

1:24 **For he-looked-at**[a] **himself and has-gone-away**[b] **and immediately forgot**[c] **what-sort-of-person**[d] **he-was.**

LEXICON—a. aorist act. indic. of κατανοέω (LN 30.4) (BAGD 2. p. 415): 'to look at' [BAGD, Herm, WBC; NAB, NASB, NIV, NRSV, TNT], 'to take a good look at' [TEV], 'to observe' [NIC], 'to take cognizance of' [Lns], 'to consider closely' [LN], 'to consider carefully' [HNTC], 'to behold' [KJV], 'to glance at' [REB], 'to catch a glimpse of' [AB]. The phrase κατενόησεν ἑαυτόν 'he looked at himself' is translated 'he has seen what he looks like' [NJB]. The verb implies a careful inspection [EBC, HNTC]; it is a hasty inspection [May, Mit, NBC]; it is an ordinary look [Herm, ICC]. The aorist tense is gnomic [EGT, Hb, Herm, ICC, May, NIC, NIGTC], expressing a proverbial, timeless, or general action [Hb, Herm, My, NIC]. It describes an actual event [Lns].

b. perf. act. indic. of ἀπέρχομαι (LN 15.37) (BAGD 1.a. p. 84): 'to go away' [AB, BAGD, Herm, HNTC, LN, Lns; NASB, NIV, NRSV, TEV, TNT], 'to go off' [WBC; NAB, NJB], 'to go one's way' [KJV, REB], 'to go' [NIC], 'to depart' [BAGD, LN], 'to leave' [LN]. The perfect tense implies a continuing state of absence [Alf, Hb, ICC, Lg(M)]; it implies suddenness [May, NIC] and completeness [May], vividness [Lns].

c. aorist mid. (deponent = act.) of ἐπιλανθάνομαι (LN 29.14) (BAGD 1. p. 295): 'to forget' [AB, BAGD, Herm, HNTC, LN, Lns, NIC, WBC; all versions], 'not to recall' [LN]. The aorist tense focuses on the act of forgetting [Alf, Mit] in a specific instance [Lns]; it is gnomic [EGT, Hb, Herm, ICC, NIC], expressing a proverbial, timeless, or general action [Hb, Herm, NIC]. This action is the most important point of the verse [Lg, My], showing the result of the look in the mirror [My].

    d. ὁποῖος (LN **58.30**) (BAGD p. 575): 'what sort of person' [BAGD, **LN**], 'what kind of person' [NASB], 'what kind of' [LN], 'what kind' [Lns], 'what manner of man' [KJV]. The phrase ὁποῖος ἦν 'what sort of person he was' is translated 'what he looked like' [AB, Herm; NAB, REB], 'what he looks like' [WBC; NIV, NJB, TEV, TNT], 'what he was like' [HNTC, NIC], 'what they were like' [NRSV]. The reference is to his appearance in the mirror [Alf, Mit, My, NIC, TG].

QUESTION—Why is this clause mentioned?

    It extends (and explains [NIGTC] or justifies [May]) the illustration of 1:23 [My], showing further what the hearer-only does [Hb], emphasizing the comparison [Herm]: he is like that, for the following is what he does. The emphasis is upon the departure and forgetting [My], showing the uselessness of the viewing [NIGTC].

1:25 But the-one having-looked[a] into[b] (the) perfect[c] law[d] the-(one) of-the freedom[e] and having-remained,[f]

LEXICON—a. aorist act. participle of παρακύπτω (LN 24.13; 27.39) (BAGD 2. p. 619): 'to look' [Herm; KJV, NRSV, REB, TNT], 'to look (in)' [BAGD], 'to look intently' [NASB, NIV], 'to look closely' [Lns; TEV], 'to look steadily' [NJB], 'to gaze' [AB], 'to stoop and look' [LN], 'to bend over to look' [NIC], 'to peer' [NAB], 'to peer intently' [WBC], 'to catch a glimpse of' [HNTC]. The literal sense is to stoop down so as to look intently [BKC, Blm, EBC, EGT, Mit, NBC, NIC], but here means merely to look attentively [Blm, Mit, NTC, TG, WBC]. It implies a more than superficial look [Bg]. The aorist tense refers to the completed act of looking, but none of the commentaries mention this point.

    b. εἰς with accusative object (LN 84.22): 'into' [AB, Herm, LN, Lns, NIC, WBC; all versions except NASB, NJB], 'at' [NASB, NJB], not explicit [HNTC]. This preposition indicates both the direction and intensity of the looking [My].

    c. τέλειος (LN 88.36) (BAGD 1.a.α. p. 809): 'perfect' [AB, BAGD, Herm, HNTC, LN, NIC, WBC; all versions except NAB], 'complete' [Lns], 'ideal' [NAB]. It implies completeness [EBC, Hb, HNTC, TG] and a lasting state [ICC], in contrast with the previous incomplete and preparatory law [EBC].

    d. νόμος (LN 33.333) (BAGD 5. p. 543): 'law' [AB, BAGD, Herm, HNTC, LN, Lns, NIC, WBC; all versions]. This 'law' is the gospel [AB]. It refers to all of God's revelation [EBC, Lns], including both the OT and the NT [ICC], and implies that Christianity is the fulfillment of the OT law [ICC]. It refers to God's requirements for right conduct [NIC], to the will of God

JAMES 1:25

as expressed by Christ [NIGTC]. This noun has no article and is qualitative, implying that God's word has the authority of law [Hb].

e. ἐλευθερία (LN 37.133) (BAGD p. 250): 'freedom' [BAGD, Herm, HNTC, LN; NAB, NIV, NJB], 'liberty' [AB, BAGD, Lns, NIC; KJV, NASB, NRSV]. The phrase τὸν τῆς ἐλευθερίας 'the one of the freedom' is translated 'that makes free' [WBC], 'that makes us free' [REB], 'which sets us free' [TNT], 'that sets people free' [TEV]. The definite article with this noun indicates that it is the well-known freedom from bondage [Hb, Lns] which comes through faith in Christ [Hb]. The freedom is the opposite of slavery [EBC]; it is freedom to obey God freely and spontaneously [Alf, EBC, May], not because of compulsion [EBC]. It refers to freedom from bondage to ceremonies, to the law of sin, and to the minute observance of the Mosaic law [Blm]. It is the ethic of the OT as interpreted by Jesus [NIGTC].

f. aorist act. participle of παραμένω (LN 68.11) (BAGD 2. p. 620): 'to remain' [AB, LN, Lns], 'to abide' [NAB, NASB], 'to stay' [HNTC, NIC], 'to continue' [BAGD, WBC; KJV, NIV], 'to keep to' [NJB], 'to persevere' [Herm; NRSV], 'to go on doing' [TNT], 'to keep on paying attention' [TEV], 'not to turn away' [REB]. The meaning is, not to let it pass from one's thoughts [Alf], to continue to look intently [EBC]. The aorist tense indicates the completed fact of remaining [Lns].

QUESTION—Why is this clause mentioned?

It introduces a contrast with the preceding description [Bg, Hb, Lg, Mit, NTC], a contrast with the 'hearer' and 'doer' of 1:23 [NIGTC], and describes the right conduct [My]: in contrast with the preceding, this is the proper conduct. The preceding description was a simile; what follows is reality [Alf, Hb, Herm].

QUESTION—What relationship is indicated by the participles ὁ παρακύψας ... καὶ παραμείνας 'the one having looked ... and having remained'?

They are substantival, describing the person [Hb]: the person who has looked ... and has remained. Both participles are governed by the one article, since they refer to the same person [My]. Both participles have the prefixed preposition παρα-, which implies proximity [Hb].

QUESTION—Why is the gospel called a 'law' here?

The writer is not implying that the gospel involves external observances; rather, he is presenting the gospel as true 'law' to overcome Jewish zeal for the law of God [AB]. The reference is to the 'implanted word' of 1:21 [Hb, Herm, ICC, Lns, WBC] or 'the word' of 1:22 [Hb]. It is the Gospel [My, TG, TNTC] as the standard of behavior for Christians [NBC]. Christ is the giver of the new law [NIGTC]. It is the law of love and the law written on the heart (2:1–13) [WBC]. It is the commanding aspect of the Word [TNTC].

QUESTION—What is meant by the phrase νόμον τέλειον 'perfect law'?

It means that the gospel is the perfect rule for conduct, and is perfect in itself [Blm], and leads people to freedom and thus is perfect [AB, Blm, NTC]. It is the best law, and thus perfect [TG]. It is God's final and complete revelation [NTC, TG], God's new covenant [Tsk]. It is whole and complete and must be kept in full [HNTC]. It is 'perfect' in the sense that no more perfect law is possible; its perfection is further described by the following phrase [ICC]. It refers to the Gospel as the completion and transformation of the OT law, which makes people free [Lg, May]. It is 'complete', including both the OT law and the Gospel [Lns]. It refers to all of Jesus' teaching about conduct which God approves [Mit]. It is more perfect than Gentile laws, and perfect because it comes from Jesus [NBC].

QUESTION—How are the two nouns related in the genitive phrase τὸν τῆς ἐλευθερίας 'the (law) of the freedom'?

It is the law which is characterized by freedom [ICC]; it is a restatement of τέλειος 'perfect' [AB, Alf, Hb]: the perfect law—that is, the law characterized by freedom. It is the law that makes a person free [Bg, ICC, Tsk, WBC; REB, TEV, TNT]. It refers to the freedom that is involved in willing obedience to God's word when its perfection is realized [Hb, May, Mit, Tsk], the freedom from self-interest and ability to love our neighbors [WBC], the freedom of conscience for differing opinions [Lg]. It sets free those who follow it [NBC, TG].

not having-become a-hearer[a] of-forgetfulness[b] but a-doer[c] of-(the)-work,[d]

LEXICON—a. ἀκροατής (LN 24.56) (BAGD p. 33): 'hearer' [AB, BAGD, Herm, LN, Lns, NIC; KJV, NASB, NRSV], 'listener' [HNTC; NAB]. The phrase οὐκ ἀκροατὴς ἐπιλησμονῆς γενόμενος 'not having become a hearer of forgetfulness' is translated 'not listening and forgetting' [NJB], 'not forgetting what he has heard' [WBC; NIV], 'never forgetting what he hears' [TNT], 'remembers what he hears' [REB], 'who does not simply listen and then forget it' [TEV].

b. ἐπιλησμονή (LN **29.14**) (BAGD p. 250): 'forgetfulness' [BAGD]. This noun is also translated as an adjective: 'forgetful' [AB, BAGD, Herm, HNTC, Lns; KJV, NAB, NASB], and as a phrase: 'who forgets' [NIC; NRSV], 'who then forgets' [LN].

c. ποιητής (LN 42.20) (BAGD 2. p. 683): 'doer' [AB, BAGD, Herm, HNTC, LN, Lns, NIC; KJV, NASB, NRSV]. This noun is also translated as a participle: 'doing' [NIV]. The phrase ποιητὴς ἔργου 'doer of the work' is translated 'putting it into practice' [WBC; NJB, TNT], 'puts it into practice' [TEV], 'one who carries out the law in practice' [NAB], 'he acts on it' [REB].

d. ἔργον (LN 42.11; 42.42) (BAGD 1.a. p. 307): 'work' [HNTC, LN, Lns; KJV], 'act' [LN], 'action' [BAGD], 'deed' [BAGD, LN], not explicit [NIV]. This word is also translated as an adjective: 'effectual' [NASB], 'effective' [AB], 'obedient' [Herm], and as a phrase: 'who act(s)' [BAGD, NIC; NRSV]. It refers to the work required by the law of freedom [Blm].

JAMES 1:25

QUESTION—Why is this participial phrase mentioned?

It describes what the person is not and what he is, in contrast with the preceding phrase which refers to what he does [Hb].

QUESTION—What relationship is indicated by the participial form γενόμενος?

It expresses the result of 'having looked' and 'having remained' [My]: the result is that he has not become a forgetful hearer but a doer of work. This participle indicates that it is by faithful attention that one becomes a true doer of God's word [Lg].

QUESTION—How are the two nouns related in the genitive phrase ἀκροατὴς ἐπιλησμονῆς 'hearer of forgetfulness'?

'Επιλησμονῆς 'of forgetfulness' is a genitive of quality [Alf, May, NIGTC], equivalent to an adjective [Blm, Herm] but stronger than an adjective [Lg]: a forgetful hearer. He is not characterized by forgetfulness [Hb, My].

QUESTION—How are the two nouns related in the genitive phrase ποιητὴς ἔργου 'doer of work'?

Ἔργου is an objective genitive [Herm, Lns, May, My, NIGTC]: he performs work. The noun ἔργου has no article and is abstract, referring to his characteristic activity rather than to specific works [Hb].

this-one shall-be blessed[a] in[b] the doing[c] of-him.

LEXICON—a. μακάριος (LN 25.119) (BAGD 1.b. p. 486): 'blessed' [AB, BAGD, Herm, HNTC, Lns, NIC, WBC; KJV, NASB, NIV, NJB, NRSV], 'blessed by God' [TEV], 'blest' [NAB], 'happy' [LN; TNT]. The phrase μακάριος ἔσται 'he shall be blessed' is translated 'he will find happiness' [REB]. This word indicates being in a state of blessedness [AB] rather than that God has blessed him, but TEV implies the action of God's blessing him.

b. ἐν with dative object (LN 13.8; 67.33; 67.136; 89.5): 'in' [AB, Herm, HNTC, Lns, NIC, WBC; all versions except REB, TNT], not explicit [TNT]. The phrase ἐν τῇ ποιήσει αὐτοῦ 'in his doing' is translated 'by so acting' [REB]. This preposition refers to the element in which the blessedness is to be found [Alf, My].

c. ποίησις (LN **42.7**) (BAGD 1. p. 683): 'doing' [AB, BAGD, Herm, LN, Lns, NIC; NRSV], 'deed' [KJV]. The phrase τῇ ποιήσει αὐτοῦ 'his doing' is translated 'what he does' [HNTC, **LN**, WBC; NASB, NIV, TEV], 'whatever he does' [NAB, TNT], 'every undertaking' [NJB]. This noun implies that there will be blessedness in the act of doing [Alf, Blm, Lg], in what he does [EBC, ICC].

QUESTION—What relationship is indicated by οὗτος 'this (person)'?

It is emphatic, contrasting the person now described with the person who only hears [May, NIGTC]: *this* is the person who will be blessed.

QUESTION—What is signified by the future tense verb ἔσται 'he shall be'?

1. It implies blessedness immediately following the 'doing' [My, NTC; all versions except TEV]: he will be blessed when he does this.

2. It refers to blessedness at the final judgment [NIGTC]: he will be blessed at the last judgment.
3. It includes both of the above [NBC]: he will be blessed when he does this and at the final judgment.

DISCOURSE UNIT: 1:26–27 [BKC, ICC, Mit, NIGTC, NTC, TG, Tsk]. The topic is the summary and transition [NIGTC], serving religiously [NTC], true religion [TG], religious observance [Tsk], receiving and responding to the word [BKC].

1:26 If anyone thinks[a] (himself) to-be religious,[b] not bridling[c] his tongue[d] but deceiving[e] his heart,[f]

TEXT—Some manuscripts add ἐν ὑμῖν 'among you' after θρησκὸς εἶναι 'to be religious'. LN does not mention this variant; only KJV adds this phrase.

LEXICON—a. pres. act. indic. of δοκέω (LN 31.29) (BAGD 1.a. p. 201): 'to think' [AB, BAGD, Herm, HNTC, LN, Lns, NIC; NASB, NRSV, REB, TEV], 'to believe' [BAGD, LN], 'to consider' [BAGD; NIV, TNT], 'to regard' [WBC], 'to suppose' [BAGD, LN], 'to presume' [LN], 'to assume' [LN], 'to imagine' [BAGD; NAB], 'to claim' [NJB], 'to seem' [KJV]. This word refers to one's opinion of himself [Hb], based merely on appearance [Lg].

b. θρησκός (LN 53.6) (BAGD p. 363): 'religious' [AB, BAGD, Herm, HNTC, LN, Lns, WBC; all versions except NAB], 'pious' [LN], 'devout' [LN; NAB], 'a model of piety' [NIC]. This word refers to the outward manifestations of religious service [Alf, BKC, EBC, EGT, Hb, Herm, Lg, Lns, May, Mit, My, NBC, NIC, NIGTC, Tsk] and describes a person who engages in religious practices [ICC, TNTC], a worshiper of God [Bg].

c. pres. act. participle of χαλιναγωγέω (LN **88.85**) (BAGD p. 874): 'to bridle' [AB, BAGD, Herm, HNTC, Lns, NIC; KJV, NASB, NRSV, REB], 'to hold in check' [BAGD, WBC], 'to keep a tight rein on' [NIV, NJB], 'to control' [LN; NAB, TEV, TNT].

d. γλῶσσα (LN 33.74) (BAGD 1.a. p. 162): 'tongue' [AB, BAGD, Herm, HNTC, LN, Lns, NIC, WBC; all versions], 'speech' [LN].

e. pres. act. participle of ἀπατάω (LN 31.12) (BAGD 1. p. 82): 'to deceive' [AB, BAGD, Herm, HNTC, LN, Lns; KJV, NASB, NIV, NRSV], 'to delude' [NIC], 'to mislead' [LN]. The phrase ἀλλὰ ἀπατῶν καρδίαν αὐτοῦ 'but deceiving his heart' is translated 'he deceives himself' [TEV], 'he is deceiving himself' [REB, TNT], 'he is self-deceived' [WBC; NAB], 'this is mere self-deception' [NJB]. The deception arises from the person's incorrect view of his conduct [Hb].

f. καρδία (LN 26.3) (BAGD 1.b.β p. 403): 'heart' [AB, BAGD, HNTC, LN, Lns, NIC; KJV, NASB, NRSV], 'inner self' [LN], 'mind' [BAGD, LN]. The phrase καρδίαν αὐτοῦ 'his heart' is translated 'himself' [Herm; NIV]. This word refers to the person's thoughts [NIGTC], to the center of the person's personality and points out the moral quality of his error [Hb].

QUESTION—What is this verse connected with?

It expands on the command to be slow to speak in 1:19 [Alf, Lns, WBC], although the absence of a connecting word gives it partial independent status [Hb]. It is connected with 1:25 by its similar emphasis [Mit], with 1:24 by the theme of self-deception [WBC]. This and the following verse give a summary of this chapter and prepare for the following chapter [NIGTC]. This verse points out the futility of piety which does not result in moral purity [Herm, Mit] or concern for those in need [Mit].

QUESTION—What is meant by 'not bridling his tongue'?

It means using words that are slanderous [Blm, EGT, NTC, Tsk], boastful, defiling [Blm, EGT, Mit, NTC], hurtful [Mit]; not controlling one's talk [TG]. It refers to speaking empty religious platitudes and orthodox confessions not supported by deeds [WBC]. It refers to zealous speaking which the person considers to be evidence of being religious [My]. It refers to persons pretending to be teachers who are causing dissension by their words [NIGTC].

QUESTION—What relationship is indicated by the use of the participle χαλιναγωγῶν 'bridling'?

1. It expresses concession [Herm, NTC; NASB, NIV]: he thinks he is religious although he does not bridle his tongue.
2. It describes the person referred to [Hb, Lg, NBC, NIC; NAB]: the person who thinks he is religious but who does not bridle his tongue. The present tense indicates that the condition is a continuing one [Hb].
3. It states in what way the person described is 'religious' [My]: he thinks he is religious in not bridling his tongue.

QUESTION—What relationship is indicated by the use of the participle ἀπατῶν 'deceiving'?

1. It expresses a second concession and also expresses the consequence of not bridling his tongue [Herm]: although he does not bridle his tongue but rather as a result is deceiving himself.
2. It expresses the consequence of not bridling his tongue [Lg, My; NAB, NIV]: he does not bridle his tongue and therefore is deceiving himself.
3. It further describes the true state of the person [Hb, NBC, NIC]: the person who does not bridle his tongue but who is deceiving himself. The present tense indicates that the condition is a continuing one [Hb].

of-this-person worthless[a] **(is) the religion.**[b]

LEXICON—a. μάταιος (LN **65.37**) (BAGD p. 495): 'worthless' [BAGD, Herm, HNTC; NASB, NIV, NJB, NRSV, TEV, TNT], 'futile' [**LN**, WBC; REB], 'useless' [LN], 'pointless' [NAB], 'empty' [BAGD, LN], 'vain' [AB, Lns, NIC; KJV]. The meaning is that it fails to enable him to reach the proper goal of his religion [Hb, ICC, Lns, Mit, Tsk], which is to please God [Tsk], to honor and obey God [Mit]; it is without contents [My], of no value [TG].

b. θρησκεία (LN **53.1**) (BAGD p. 363): 'religion' [AB, BAGD, Herm, HNTC, **LN**, Lns, WBC; all versions except NAB], 'piety' [LN, NIC], 'worship' [NAB]. This word refers primarily to the externals of religious worship [ICC, Mit, NBC, NIC, NIGTC, Tsk].

QUESTION—How is this clause connected to the preceding one?

It expresses the consequence of the first part of the verse [My, NIGTC; NASB, NRSV]: if anyone does that, his religion is futile.

QUESTION—What is implied by the word order of this clause?

Both the forefronted genitive τούτου 'of this person' and the predicate adjective μάταιος 'worthless' preceding the subject indicate emphasis—primary emphasis on 'of this person' and secondary emphasis on 'worthless' (but none of the commentaries mention this).

1:27 **Religion[a] pure[b] and undefiled[c] in-the-sight-of[d] the God and Father is this:**

LEXICON—a. θρησκεία: 'religion'. See this word at 1:26.

    b. καθαρός (LN 53.29) (BAGD 3.b. p. 388): 'pure' [AB, BAGD, Herm, HNTC, LN, Lns, NIC, WBC; all versions except TNT], 'genuine' [TNT]. This is the positive aspect of religion [Alf, ICC, NIGTC, NTC].

    c. ἀμίαντος (LN **53.36**) (BAGD 1. p. 46): 'undefiled' [AB, BAGD, Herm, LN, Lns, NIC; KJV, NASB, NRSV], 'untainted' [**LN**, WBC], 'unstained' [HNTC], 'without stain' [NAB], 'unspoilt' [NJB], 'pure' [BAGD; TNT], 'faultless' [NIV, REB], 'genuine' [TEV]. This is the negative synonym of the preceding adjective 'pure' [Alf, ICC, NIGTC, NTC]. It presents purity as the absence of what would defile [My].

    d. παρά with dative object (LN 90.20) (BAGD II.2.b. p. 610): 'in the sight of' [BAGD, LN; NASB, REB], 'in the eyes of' [NJB], 'before' [AB, Herm, HNTC, Lns; KJV, NAB, NRSV], 'in the opinion of' [LN], 'in the judgment of' [BAGD, LN], not explicit [NIC, WBC; NIV, TEV, TNT]. It means acceptable by God [Hb, ICC], in the judgment of God [My], in the sight of God [Lg, Mit, NIGTC, WBC].

QUESTION—What is implied by the phrase τῷ θεῷ καὶ πατρί 'the God and Father'?

    1. The one article unites the two nouns [Alf, Hb, HNTC, Mit, NIGTC] and implies the possessive [Alf, Hb]: him who is both our God and our Father. The addition of 'Father' implies love [My] or the concept of family [NTC].

    2. The sense is 'God, even the Father' [Blm].

to-visit[a] orphans[b] and widows[c] in[d] the affliction[e] of-them,

LEXICON—a. ἐπισκέπτομαι (LN 34.50) (BAGD 2. p. 298): 'to visit' [HNTC, LN, Lns, NIC; KJV, NASB], 'to go to see' [LN], 'to look after' [BAGD, Herm, LN; NAB, NIV, REB, TNT], 'to care for' [AB; NRSV], 'to take care of' [LN, WBC; TEV], 'to come to the help of' [NJB]. It implies visiting for the purpose of caring for needs [Hb, HNTC, Lg, Lns, Mit, My, NIC, TG, Tsk, WBC] with personal involvement [Mit]. It manifests

caring love [My, NTC]. The present tense implies a continuing attitude [Hb].
b. ὀρφανός (LN 10.40) (BAGD 1. p. 583): 'orphan' [AB, BAGD, Herm, HNTC, LN, Lns, WBC; all versions except KJV], 'fatherless' [NIC; KJV].
c. χήρα (LN 10.61) (BAGD 1. p. 881): 'widow' [AB, BAGD, Herm, HNTC, LN, Lns, NIC, WBC; all versions].
d. ἐν with dative object (LN 13.8; 67.136): 'in' [AB, Herm, HNTC, LN, Lns, NIC, WBC; all versions], 'during' [LN].
e. θλῖψις (LN 22.2) (BAGD 1. p. 362): 'affliction' [HNTC, Lns, NIC; KJV], 'suffering' [LN; TEV], 'trouble' [REB, TNT], 'distress' [AB, Herm, WBC; NAB, NASB, NIV, NRSV], 'hardships' [NJB], 'difficult circumstances' [BAGD]. Their troubles consisted of their bereavement [HNTC, ICC], their poverty [HNTC, NIC], their lack of legal status [Hb, HNTC, Mit, NTC] which left them in danger of exploitation by unscrupulous persons [Hb, Mit, WBC], and widows' old age or illness [NIC].

QUESTION—What relationship is indicated by the phrase ἐν τῇ θλίψει αὐτῶν 'in their affliction'?

It indicates the reason for visiting them [Alf]: because they are being afflicted. Widows and orphans were the two groups most in need of aid [Hb, HNTC, ICC, Lns, Mit, WBC] and of special concern to God [HNTC, Lg, TG, Tsk]. These are named as representing all who were in need [Mit, NIGTC].

to-keep[a] himself unspotted[b] from/by[c] the world.[d]
LEXICON—a. τηρέω (LN 13.32) (BAGD 2.b. p. 815): 'to keep' [AB, BAGD, Herm, HNTC, LN, NIC, WBC; all versions], 'to guard' [Lns]. The sense is 'to maintain' [WBC].
b. ἄσπιλος (LN 88.33) (BAGD 2. p. 117): 'unspotted' [AB, BAGD, Lns, NIC; KJV, NAB], 'morally spotless' [LN], 'unstained' [Herm; NASB, NRSV], 'untarnished' [REB], 'uncontaminated' [NJB], 'undefiled' [HNTC], 'pure' [LN, WBC], 'from being polluted' [NIV], 'from being corrupted' [TEV], 'free' [TNT].
c. ἀπό with genitive object (LN 89.25; 89.122; 90.7; 90.15) (BAGD under ἄσπιλος 2. p. 117, under κόσμος 7. p. 446): 'from' [Herm, LN, Lns, NIC, WBC; KJV, TNT], 'by' [AB, BAGD, HNTC, LN; all versions except KJV, TNT], 'because of' [LN], 'separated from' [LN].
d. κόσμος (LN 41.38) (BAGD 7. p. 446): 'world' [AB, BAGD, Herm, HNTC, LN, Lns, NIC; all versions except TNT], 'world system' [LN], 'world's evil' [TNT], 'contaminations of the world's influence' [WBC]. It refers to the entire world system, separated from God and lying in sin [Alf, EBC, Hb, Herm, ICC, Lg(M), My, Tsk], mankind with its false values and self-centeredness [HNTC, Lg, Lns, Mit, My, NIGTC].

QUESTION—How is this infinitive phrase 'to keep . . .' related to the preceding infinitive phrase 'to visit . . .'?

Both phrases are part of the description of 'pure and undefiled religion' [Alf, Lns, Mit, My, Tsk, WBC]: pure religion consists both of visiting orphans and widows and of keeping oneself morally undefiled. The first phrase refers to one's conduct, the second to one's character [BKC], indicating the need for both social concern and personal purity and holiness [Hb, Tsk]. These phrases do not define true religion but rather describe its chief aspects [Blm, EBC, Lns, My, NIC, Tsk], a principle [NTC], the evidence of true religion [WBC] in social and personal standards [Hb] which are better than mere religious forms [ICC]. They do not imply obtaining acceptance by God through good deeds and behavior, but rather conduct resulting from salvation by faith [Hb, Lg]. Both phrases are in apposition to αὕτη 'this' [May].

QUESTION—What is implied by the forefronting of ἄσπιλον ἑαυτόν 'unspotted himself' before the infinitive τηρεῖν 'to keep'?

The forefronting of ἄσπιλον 'unspotted' emphasizes the necessity of personal purity [Lg] as the chief thought [My]; the forefronting of ἑαυτόν 'himself' emphasizes the responsibility for personal cooperation with God's keeping power [Hb].

QUESTION—What is ἑαυτόν 'himself' connected with?

It refers back to τις 'anyone' in 1:26 as the subject of the infinitive ἐπισκέπτεσθαι 'to visit' [Alf]: for someone to visit . . . and to keep himself unspotted.

QUESTION—What is implied by the forefronting of ἄσπιλον ἑαυτόν 'unspotted himself' before the infinitive τηρεῖν 'to keep'?

The forefronting of ἄσπιλον 'unspotted' emphasizes the necessity of personal purity [Lg] as the chief thought [My]; the forefronting of ἑαυτόν 'himself' emphasizes the responsibility for personal cooperation with God's keeping power [Hb].

QUESTION—What is ἑαυτόν 'himself' connected with?

It refers back to τις 'anyone' in 1:26 as the subject of the infinitive ἐπισκέπτεσθαι 'to visit' [Alf]: for someone to visit . . . and to keep himself unspotted.

DISCOURSE UNIT: 2:1–26 [BKC, Lg, NIC, NIGTC, NTC; REB]. The topic is serving compassionately [BKC], faith [NTC], the Christian life [NIC], love for one's neighbor [REB], the excellence of being poor and of being generous [NIGTC], a warning against partiality [Lg], a discussion of the third form of temptation [Lg].

DISCOURSE UNIT: 2:1–13 [AB, BKC, EBC, GNT, Hb, Herm, Lg, Lns, NBC, NIC, NIGTC, NTC, TG, TNTC, Tsk, WBC; NAB, NASB, NIV, NJB, TEV]. The topic is a condemnation of favoritism [EBC, GNT, NIGTC, TG; NAB, NASB, NIV, TEV], one's reaction to favoritism as a test of his faith [Hh], a discussion of favoritism [Herm, Lns, NBC], showing respect for poor persons [NJB], the inappropriateness of seeking the favor of rich people [AB], acceptance of others [BKC], social compassion amid social divisions [NIC], faith and the law [NTC], impartiality related to the law of love [TNTC, Tsk], problems in the assembly [WBC].

DISCOURSE UNIT: 2:1–9 [HNTC]. The topic is the sin of partiality.

DISCOURSE UNIT: 2:1–7 [ICC, Lns, Mit, Tsk]. The topic is partiality [Tsk], the sin of favoring the rich [ICC, Lns] and neglecting the poor [ICC].

DISCOURSE UNIT: 2:1–4 [BKC, Hb, NIGTC, NTC]. The topic is a rebuke against showing partiality [Hb], an illustration of partiality in the assembly [NIGTC], avoiding favoritism [NTC], showing courtesy to everyone [BKC].

2:1 My brothers,[a] (do) not with[b] partialities[c] have[d] the faith[e] of-our Lord Jesus Christ of-the glory.[f]

LEXICON—a. ἀδελφός (LN 11.23): 'brother' [AB, HNTC, Lns, WBC; all versions except NRSV, REB], '(Christian) brother' [LN], 'brother and sister' [Herm; NRSV], 'fellow believer' [LN], 'friend' [REB], not explicit [NIC]. The reference is to fellow believers in Jesus [BKC].

b. ἐν with dative object (LN 89.84): 'with' [LN, NIC, WBC; KJV, NASB, NRSV], 'together with' [HNTC], 'connected with' [Lns], not explicit [AB; NAB, NIV, NJB, TNT]. The phrase ἐν προσωπολημψίαις 'with partiality' is translated 'and at the same time show partiality' [Herm]. The phrase μὴ ἐν προσωπολημψίαις ἔχετε 'do not have with partiality' is translated 'you must always be impartial' [REB], 'you must never treat people in different ways according to their outward appearance' [TEV]. This preposition indicates acts with which the partiality was shown [ICC] or the many ways in which partiality shows itself [May].

c. προσωπολημψία (LN 88.238) (BAGD p. 720): 'partiality' [BAGD, Herm, LN], 'favoritism' [WBC; NAB, NIV, TNT], 'act of favoritism' [NRSV], 'personal favoritism' [NASB], 'class distinction' [NJB], 'discrimination between people' [HNTC], 'respect of persons' [KJV], 'respect to persons' [Lns], 'currying favor with people' [AB], 'worship of men's social status' [NIC]. This phrase is emphatic by forefronting [Alf, Hb] and refers to a circumstance accompanying their holding the Christian faith [Herm]. The plural form points out the various incidents and types of partiality [Alf, ICC, Lg, May, My, NBC]; it is a Semitic usage [EGT, NTC].

d. pres. act. impera. of ἔχω (LN 90.65): 'to have' [LN; KJV], 'to hold' [Herm, HNTC; NASB], 'to allow' [NAB], 'to let be connected with' [Lns], 'to let enter into' [NJB], 'to use' [AB], 'to try to combine' [NIC, WBC]. The phrase ἔχετε τὴν πίστιν 'have the faith' is translated 'you believe' [NRSV, REB], 'as believers' [NIV, TEV], 'you are men who believe' [TNT].

e. πίστις (LN 31.102; 31.104) (BAGD 2.b.β. p. 663): 'faith' [AB, BAGD, Herm, HNTC, LN, Lns, NIC, WBC; KJV, NAB, NASB, NJB], 'beliefs'

[LN]. This is the Christian faith as found in the gospel [Hb], active faith in Christ [ICC].

f. δόξα (LN 12.49; 79.18) (BAGD 1.a. p. 203): 'glory' [BAGD, HNTC, LN, Lns, NIC; KJV, REB, TEV], 'glorious power' [LN], 'splendor' [LN], 'majesty' [BAGD], 'wonderful being' [LN]. This noun is also translated as an adjective: 'glorious' [AB, Herm, WBC; NAB, NASB, NIV, NRSV, TNT], and as a participle: 'glorified' [NJB]. It is the majesty and splendor which surrounds God and belongs also to the Messiah [ICC].

QUESTION—What is implied by the use of ἀδελφοί μου 'my brothers'?

It indicates a change to a new point [BKC, Hb, ICC, Lg, Lns]. This section continues the exhortation of the necessity of acting in accordance with the gospel [Blm, EBC, HNTC, NIC]. This phrase brings a brotherly spirit into the admonishing [Lns, May, NTC]. It indicates the equality of believers [Bg], and shows that the people in general, not merely their leaders, were referred to [My].

QUESTION—What is the meaning of μὴ ἔχετε 'do not have'?

1. It is imperative [Alf, BKC, Blm, EBC, EGT, Hb, Herm, ICC, Lg, May, Mit, My, NBC, NIC, NIGTC, NTC, WBC; all versions except NRSV]: don't show partiality. To interpret it as a QUESTION would imply expecting a negative answer, "You don't, do you?" contrary to the following context, which implies that they did show partiality [Hb]. The meaning is, "Don't *try* to combine faith and partiality" [WBC], since it is really impossible to do so [NIC].

2. It is interrogative [NRSV]: do you really have the faith?

QUESTION—What is meant by not having faith with partiality?

It means that they are not to let partiality pervert their faith [Lns, May, Mit, My, NIC, Tsk, WBC; TEV]: don't let partiality intrude into your faith. They must not combine their faith with favoritism for the rich [My, NIC, Tsk, WBC] and depreciation of the poor [My, NIC, WBC], evaluating a person by what he possesses (by appearances [TG; TEV]) rather than by what he is [NBC]. They should not let their faith be a pretext for partiality [AB] nor hold their faith in such a way as to show partiality [Blm]. Partiality should not be made an integral part of their faith [Lg].

QUESTION—How is the noun πίστιν 'faith' related to the genitive noun phrase τοῦ κυρίου ἡμῶν Ἰησοῦ Χριστοῦ 'of our Lord Jesus Christ'?

1. The genitive construction refers to their faith in Christ [BKC, Hb, ICC, Lns, May, Mit, NBC, NIC, NTC, TG, WBC; all versions except KJV]. Both James and his readers are included in ἡμῶν 'our' [Hb, Lns, NTC].

2. The genitive construction refers to the Christian faith which Christ brought to the world [Alf, EGT]. The meaning is thus stronger than personal faith in Christ [Alf].

QUESTION—What is the noun phrase τῆς δόξης 'of glory' related to?

1. It describes κυρίου 'Lord', i.e., our Lord Jesus Christ, the Lord of glory [Alf, Blm, Lg(M), Mit, TNTC; KJV, NJB, TEV, TNT]. It means 'our glorious Lord' [Blm, Mit, TNTC; TNT] or 'our glorified Lord' [NJB].

2. It describes the entire reference to Jesus [BKC, Herm, ICC, My, NTC, WBC; NAB, NASB, NIV, NRSV]: our glorious Lord Jesus Christ.
3. It gives another title to Jesus [Bg, EGT, Hb, HNTC, May, NBC, NIC, Tsk]: our Lord Jesus Christ, who is the glory. He is compared to the Shekinah glory of the OT [EGT, Hb, NIC]. James thinks of Jesus as the glory of God in the midst of his people [Hb]. Jesus reflected the glory of God on the earth [Tsk].
4. It is related to ἡμῶν 'our', reflecting the Shekinah glory of the OT [NIC]: the Lord Jesus Christ, who is our glory. This view amends the text by transferring 'our' to the end of the sentence [NIC].
5. It makes a comment about Christ [REB]: our Lord Jesus Christ who reigns in glory.
6. It describes πίστιν 'faith' [AB]: their glorious faith in our Lord Jesus Christ..

2:2 For[a] if there-enters[b] into your synagogue[c] a-man gold-ringed[d] in[e] shining[f] clothing,[g]

LEXICON—a. γάρ (LN 89.23): 'for' [Herm, LN, Lns, NIC; KJV, NASB, NRSV], 'because' [LN], 'thus' [AB], 'to illustrate' [WBC], 'now' [NJB], not explicit [HNTC; NAB, NIV, REB, TEV, TNT].

b. εἰς with accusative object (LN 84.22): 'into' [Herm, HNTC, LN, Lns, NIC; NAB, NASB, NIV, NJB, NRSV, TNT], 'unto' [KJV], 'to' [TEV], not explicit [AB, WBC; REB].

c. συναγωγή (LN **11.44**; **7.20**) (BAGD 2.b. and 5. p. 783): 'synagogue' [AB, Lns; NJB], 'assembly place' [BAGD, **LN**], 'assembly' [Herm, **LN**, NIC; KJV, NAB, NASB, NRSV], 'meeting' [BAGD, HNTC, WBC; NIV, REB, TEV, TNT], 'congregation' [LN]. The singular is generic, referring to all such places [Blm, EGT, May]. This word indicates the Jewish character of the situation [BKC, NTC] and of the writer and his readers [NTC].

d. χρυσοδακτύλιος (LN **6.191**) (BAGD p. 888): 'gold-ringed' [HNTC], 'wearing a gold ring' [LN, WBC; NIV, TEV], 'with a gold ring' [AB, NIC; KJV, NASB, NJB], 'with gold rings' [Herm; NRSV, REB], 'with a gold ring on his finger' [Lns], 'with gold rings on his fingers' [NAB], 'with a gold ring on one's finger' [BAGD], '(one) wears a gold ring' [TNT]. The word implies ostentatiously wearing many rings on the fingers [Hb, WBC]. The reference is figurative, meaning Judaizers who prided themselves on their Jewish heritage [Lg].

e. ἐν with dative object (LN 13.8): 'in' [AB, LN, Lns; KJV, NASB, NRSV], 'with' [LN], 'dressed in' [WBC], 'wearing' [HNTC; TEV], not explicit [Herm, NIC; NIV]. The phrase ἐν ἐσθῆτι λαμπρᾷ 'in shining clothing' is translated 'fashionably dressed' [NAB], 'well-dressed' [NJB, REB], '(is) finely dressed' [TNT].

f. λαμπρός (LN 14.50; 79.20) (BAGD 3. p. 465): 'shining' [BAGD, LN, Lns], 'bright' [BAGD, LN], 'splendid' [AB, HNTC, LN, WBC], 'fine'

[Herm, NIC; NASB, NIV, NRSV, TEV], 'goodly' [KJV]. The reference is to fine (and white [EGT, Hb, Lns]) garments worn by wealthy persons [EBC, EGT, Lns].

g. ἐσθής (LN 6.162) (BAGD p. 312): 'clothing' [BAGD, Herm, LN], 'clothes' [HNTC, Lns, NIC, WBC; NASB, NIV, NRSV, TEV], 'apparel' [LN; KJV], 'garment' [AB].

QUESTION—What relationship is indicated by γάρ 'for'?
1. It indicates the grounds for the preceding exhortation by giving an illustration [Hb, ICC, Lg].
2. It explains what he means by giving an illustration of partialities [Alf, HNTC, My, NIGTC, TNTC, Tsk, WBC].

QUESTION—What relationship is indicated by ἐάν 'if'?
It indicates a condition which probably did occur at times [Alf, Hb, Lg, TNTC, WBC], which often occurred [My], or which could occur [HNTC, Lns, NBC]: if this should happen. It is a hypothetical condition [Alf, BKC, EBC, Hb, HNTC, NTC, TNTC]. The protasis (the 'if' clause) of this condition includes 2:2-3 [Herm, My], and the apodosis (conclusion) is 2:4 [Herm, Lg, My, NIGTC].

QUESTION—What is meant by συναγωγή 'synagogue'?
1. It refers to a meeting place of Christian worship [Alf, EGT, Hb, Lns, May, Mit, My].
2. It refers to the assembled persons [Bg, ICC, NIGTC, NTC, TG, TNTC; NIV, REB, TEV, TNT].
3. It refers to a church court assembly [NIGTC, WBC].

QUESTION—Who is the rich man?
He is a stranger [HNTC, ICC, Lns, NBC, NIC, NIGTC, TG, Tsk, WBC].
1. He is a non-Christian [ICC, My, NBC, Tsk], a Jew [Lns].
2. He is a wealthy Christian who is visiting [WBC] or a new convert [NIGTC, WBC].

and there-enters also a-poor[a] (man) in[b] dirty[c] clothing,[d]

LEXICON—a. πτωχός (LN **57.53**) (BAGD 1.a. p. 728): 'poor' [AB, BAGD, Herm, HNTC, LN, Lns, NIC; all versions], 'destitute' [LN]. This adjective is translated as a noun: 'beggar' [WBC]. While most refer this to a poor man, some add that he is a beggar [EBC, HNTC, WBC].

b. ἐν with dative object: 'in' [Herm, HNTC, NIC, WBC; NIV, NJB, REB, TEV, TNT].

c. ῥυπαρός (LN 57.53; 79.52) (BAGD 1. p. 738): 'dirty' [BAGD, LN, NIC; NASB, NRSV], 'filthy' [AB, Herm, HNTC, LN, WBC; TNT], 'grimy' [REB], 'shabby' [Lns; NAB, NIV, NJB], 'ragged' [LN; TEV], 'vile' [KJV].

d. ἐσθής (see in the preceding clause): 'clothing' [AB], 'clothes' [NJB, REB, TNT].

QUESTION—Who is the poor man?
He is a stranger [HNTC, ICC, Lns, NBC, NIC, NTC, TG, Tsk, WBC].

1. He is not represented as a Christian [ICC, My, NBC, Tsk]; he is a Jew [Lns].
2. He is a visiting Christian [WBC].

2:3 **and you-pay-special-attention**[a] **to**[b] **the-(one) wearing**[c] **the shining clothing**
LEXICON—a. aorist act. subj. of ἐπιβλέπω (LN **24.12**; **87.17**) (BAGD p. 290): 'to pay special attention to' [**LN**; NASB, REB], 'to pay attention to' [AB, Herm, WBC], 'to show special attention to' [NIV], 'to pay special respect to' [**LN**], 'to show more respect to' [TEV], 'to pay observance to' [NIC], 'to have respect to' [KJV], 'to look at' [BAGD, HNTC], 'to look upon' [Lns], 'to consider' [BAGD], 'to take notice of' [NAB, NJB, NRSV, TNT], 'to notice especially' [**LN**], 'to care about' [BAGD]. The meaning is to look with favor on someone [Blm, EBC, Hb]. It is emphatic [Lg].
   b. ἐπί with accusative object (LN 90.57): 'to' [AB, Herm, LN, NIC, WBC; KJV, NASB, NIV, REB, TEV], 'at' [HNTC], 'upon' [Lns], not explicit [NAB, NJB, NRSV, TNT]. This preposition always follows the verb ἐπιβλέπω 'to pay special attention to' [WBC].
   c. pres. act. participle of φορέω (LN 49.11) (BAGD 1. p. 865): 'to wear' [AB, BAGD, Herm, HNTC, LN, Lns, NIC; KJV, NASB, NIV, NRSV]. This participle is translated as a preposition: 'with' [WBC]. The phrase τὸν φοροῦντα τὴν ἐσθῆτα τὴν λαμπράν 'the one wearing the shining clothing' is translated 'the well-dressed man' [NAB, NJB, REB, TEV, TNT].

and you-say, "You sit here well/please,"[a]
LEXICON—a. καλῶς (LN **33.177**; **87.25**) (BAGD 1. p. 401): 'well' [BAGD], 'please' [Herm, **LN**, Lns; NAB, NRSV, REB, TNT], 'if you will' [WBC]. This adverb is translated as a phrase: 'in a good place' [BAGD, HNTC; KJV, NASB], 'in this good seat' [NIC], 'in the best place' [AB]; as an adjective: 'best' [**LN**], 'important' [**LN**]. This entire phrase is translated 'and say to him, "Have this best seat here" ' [LN; TEV], 'and say, "Here's a good seat for you" ' [NIV], 'and say, "Come this way to the best seats" ' [NJB].
QUESTION—What is meant by καλῶς 'well/please'?
   1. It describes the place where they are to sit [AB, Alf, Hb, HNTC, My, NIC, NTC; NIV, NJB, TEV]. It is a good place [AB, Alf, Hb, HNTC, NIC], or, more specifically, a good seat [NTC; NIV], a comfortable one [EGT, My, NIC], perhaps an elevated seat [NIC, NTC], and it is the best seat there [NJB, TEV].
   2. It is an idiom meaning 'please' [Herm, ICC, Lns, Mit, WBC; NAB, NRSV, REB, TNT].
QUESTION—What is implied by the plurals εἴπητε 'you say' here and in the next clause?
   The double use of the verb adds emphasis [WBC]. The second person plurals mean that this is the attitude of the group (but not all of them [WBC]) even

though it is expressed to the two visitors by one person [Hb, NBC, TG] or by several persons [WBC].

QUESTION—What is implied by the two singular pronouns σύ 'you'?

They are emphatic [Hb]: *You* sit here . . . *you* stand there. The different treatment of the two persons is then indicated by the contrasted 'sit' and 'stand', 'here' and 'there', and 'well' and 'under my footstool' [Lg, My].

and to-the poor[a] (man) you say, "You stand there or sit under[b] my footstool,"[c]

TEXT—Instead of στῆθι 'stand there or sit', some manuscripts read 'stand or sit there'; others add ὧδε 'here' after κάθου 'stand there or sit here'. GNT reads 'stand there or sit' with a B rating, indicating that the text is almost certain. 'Stand there or sit' is read by AB, Alf, EBC, Hb, Lns, NIGTC, WBC, NASB, NIV, NJB, NRSV, TNT. 'Stand or sit there' is read by ICC, NAB. 'Stand there or sit here' is read by Blm, NIC, KJV, REB, TEV.

LEXICON—a. πτωχός: 'poor'. See this word at 2:2.

b. ὑπό with accusative object (LN 83.51) (BAGD 2.a.α. p. 843): 'under' [BAGD, HNTC, LN, NIC; KJV], 'at' [AB, BAGD, WBC; NRSV, TNT], 'by' [Lns; NAB, NASB, NIV, NJB, REB, TEV]. The phrase ὑπὸ τὸ ὑποπόδιόν μου 'under my footstool' is translated 'near me on the floor' [Herm]. The meaning of this phrase is 'on the floor' [EGT, Hb, Herm, May, My], 'beside my footstool' [Alf, May, TNTC].

c. ὑποπόδιον (LN 6.117) (BAGD p. 846): 'footstool' [BAGD, HNTC, LN, Lns, NIC; KJV, NASB, REB], 'foot-rest' [NAB, NJB], 'feet' [AB, WBC; NIV, NRSV, TEV, TNT].

QUESTION—What is implied by the conjunction ἤ 'or'?

1. It introduces the alternative choice offered to the poor man [AB, Alf, EBC, Hb, HNTC, Lg, Mit, My, NBC, NIGTC, NTC, Tsk, WBC; KJV, NASB, NRSV, TEV]: "Stand there or sit here."
2. It introduces a different direction which the speaker might give to the poor man [Herm, Lns, NIC; NAB, NIV, NJB, NRSV, TNT]: he might say, "Stand there," or he might say, "Sit here."

2:4 not have-you-made-distinctions[a] among/in[b] yourselves and become judges[c] of-evil[d] reasonings?[e]

LEXICON—a. aorist pass. (deponent = act.) indicative of διακρίνω (LN 30.113) (BAGD 2.b. p. 185): 'to make a distinction' [AB, Herm, HNTC, LN; NASB, NJB, NRSV], 'to create a distinction' [TEV], 'to make class-distinctions' [TNT], 'to discriminate' [NAB, NIV, REB], 'to be partial' [KJV], 'to doubt' [BAGD], 'to get into doubt' [Lns], 'to waver' [BAGD], 'to be at odds with oneself' [BAGD], 'to become divided' [WBC]. The phrase οὐ διεκρίθητε ἐν ἑαυτοῖς 'have you not made distinctions among/in yourselves' is translated 'have you not lost your bond of unity' [NIC].

b. ἐν with dative object (LN 83.9; 83.13): 'among' [AB, Herm, LN, WBC; all versions except KJV, NAB], 'in' [HNTC, LN, Lns; KJV, NAB].

JAMES 2:4

c. κριτής (LN 56.28) (BAGD 1.b. p. 453): 'judge' [AB, BAGD, Herm, HNTC, LN, Lns, NIC, WBC; KJV, NAB, NASB, NIV, NRSV], not explicit [NJB]. The phrase ἐγένεσθε κριταί 'have you become judges' is translated 'you are judging' [REB], 'you are making judgments' [TEV]. The phrase ἐγένεσθε κριταὶ διαλογισμῶν πονηρῶν 'have you become judges of evil reasonings' is translated 'your standards of judgment are all wrong' [TNT].

d. πονηρός (LN 88.110) (BAGD 1.b.β. p. 691): 'evil' [BAGD, LN; KJV, NASB, NIV, NRSV, TEV], 'wrong' [AB, REB, TNT], 'wicked' [BAGD, Herm, LN, Lns], 'pernicious' [NIC], 'corrupt' [HNTC; NAB, NJB], 'immoral' [LN]. The phrase διαλογισμῶν πονηρῶν 'of evil reasonings' is translated 'criminally minded' [WBC]. It means ethically evil [Hb].

e. διαλογισμός (LN 30.10; 30.16) (BAGD 1. p. 186): 'reasoning' [BAGD, LN], 'thought' [BAGD; KJV, NIV, NRSV], 'consideration' [Lns], 'opinion' [BAGD], 'decision' [HNTC; NAB], 'motive' [Herm; NASB, TEV], 'standard' [AB; NJB, REB, TNT], 'distinction' [NIC].

QUESTION—How is this clause connected with the preceding one?

It is the apodosis (conclusion) of the two preceding verses.

1. It is stated as a QUESTION [Alf, EBC, Hb, Herm, Lg, My, NIGTC, NTC, TG, TNTC, WBC], and the introductory οὐ 'not' expects an affirmative answer [BKC, EBC, Hb, Herm, My, NIGTC, NTC, TG, TNTC, WBC]: if you do that, haven't you discriminated and become judges of evil reasonings?
2. It is stated as a fact, and the first verb is differently interpreted [Bg]: you have not discriminated correctly, and you have become judges of evil reasonings.

QUESTION—What is the meaning of διεκρίθητε 'to make a distinction'?

1. It means that they are making distinctions, favoring one class above another [Blm, EBC, Herm, HNTC, NIGTC, NTC; all versions]: you are acting with partiality.
2. It means that they are acting inconsistently with their professed faith [NBC, NIC, Tsk]: your actions are inconsistent with your faith.
3. It means that they are introducing doubts on this issue into their faith [Alf, ICC, Lns, My], by introducing a contradiction to their faith [My].
4. It means that sinful motives cause their minds to be divided [TNTC].
5. It means that their actions cause divisions among them [AB, EGT, Hb, Lg, May, TG].
5.1 The division is their recognition of differences in social rank [AB, EGT, Hb, May, TG].
5.2 They are divided in their individual minds by the dissension [Lg].
5.3 They are divided in their opinion of how to treat rich and poor persons [WBC].
6. The meaning includes 1, 2, and 4 above [WBC].

7. The meaning is to discriminate properly, which would have resulted in equal treatment of the two visitors [Bg]: you have not discriminated properly.

QUESTION—What is the meaning of ἐν ἑαυτοῖς 'among/in yourselves'?
1. It refers to the group [AB, EGT, Herm, My, NIGTC, NTC, TG, WBC; all versions except KJV, NAB]: among yourselves.
2. It means within the minds of the individuals [Alf, HNTC, Lg, Lns, May, NBC, TNTC; KJV, NAB]: within your own minds.

QUESTION—How are the two nouns related in the genitive construction κριταὶ διαλογισμῶν πονηρῶν 'judges of evil reasonings'?
1. 'Evil reasonings' is a qualitative genitive, describing the judges [AB, Alf, BKC, Blm, EBC, EGT, Hb, Herm, ICC, Lg, Lns, May, My, NBC, NIGTC, NTC, TG, TNTC, Tsk, WBC; all versions except KJV, NAB]: judges motivated by evil thoughts.
2. 'Evil reasonings' is an objective genitive [HNTC, NIC; NAB]: judges who render evil decisions.
3. It means that they tacitly approve the evil reasonings which characterize the rich man [Bg]: you are approvers of the rich man's evil thoughts.

DISCOURSE UNIT: 2:5–11 [Hb]. The topic is the result of discrimination.

DISCOURSE UNIT: 2:5–9 [BKC]. The topic is compassion for everyone.

DISCOURSE UNIT: 2:5–7 [NIGTC, NTC]. The topic is a rational argument against discrimination [NIGTC], an exhortation to be rich in faith [NTC].

2:5 Listen,[a] my beloved[b] brothers;

LEXICON—a. aorist act. impera. of ἀκούω (LN 31.56; 32.1): 'to listen' [AB, Herm, HNTC, LN, Lns, NIC; all versions except KJV], 'to hearken' [KJV], 'to hear' [WBC], 'to understand' [LN], 'to comprehend' [LN].
    b. ἀγαπητός (LN 25.45) (BAGD 2. p. 6): 'beloved' [AB, BAGD, Herm, HNTC, LN, Lns, NIC; KJV, NASB, NRSV], 'dear' [BAGD, LN, WBC; NAB, NIV, NJB, REB, TEV, TNT].

QUESTION—What is the function of this phrase?
It calls the readers' attention to what the author is about to say [Alf, BKC, EBC, Herm, Lns, Mit, NIGTC, NTC], giving it emphasis [ICC, Lg, NBC, NTC] with loving concern [Lns, May, NBC, NIGTC, NTC, WBC]. It indicates the author's fervor [EGT, Lg].

(has) not God chosen[a] the poor (persons) in/to-the world[b] rich in[c] faith[d]

TEXT—Instead of the dative τῷ κόσμῳ 'in/to the world', some manuscripts read τοῦ κόσμου 'of the world', and others read τοῦ κόσμου τούτου 'of this world'. LN does not deal with this variant. Only HNTC reads 'of the world'; Blm, Tsk, KJV, NASB, and TEV read 'of this world'.

LEXICON—a. aorist mid. (deponent = act.) indic. of ἐκλέγομαι (LN **30.86**; 30.92) (BAGD 3.c. p. 242): 'to choose' [AB, BAGD, Herm, HNTC, **LN**, Lns, WBC, all versions], 'to select' [LN, NIC]. The aorist tense refers to

God's past action of choosing [Hb]. The author does not mean that poverty was the reason for the choosing [Bg, EBC, Hb, HNTC, ICC], nor that all of the poor will be saved [Bg, Hb, TNTC], nor that no rich persons will be included [TNTC].

b. κόσμος (LN 1.39; 9.23) (BAGD 5.a. p. 446): 'world' [AB, BAGD, Herm, HNTC, LN, Lns, NIC, WBC; all versions], 'earth' [LN]. The reference is to non-Christian people [EBC].

c. ἐν with dative object (LN 89.5): 'in' [AB, Herm, HNTC, LN, NIC, WBC; all versions], 'in connection with' [Lns], 'with regard to' [LN].

d. πίστις (LN 31.85; 31.102) (BAGD 2.d.α. p. 663): 'faith' [AB, BAGD, Herm, HNTC, LN, Lns, NIC, WBC; all versions]. The meaning here is trust [EGT].

QUESTION—What is implied by οὐχ 'not'?

It indicates that the author expects an affirmative answer to this question [Hb, NIGTC, NTC, TG, WBC]: hasn't God chosen the poor…?

QUESTION—What is meant by the phrase πτωχοὺς τῷ κόσμῳ 'poor in/to the world'?

1. It means poor in the view of, or by the standards of, the non-Christian world [EBC, EGT, Hb, Herm, ICC, Lg, May, Mit, My, NIGTC, TG, WBC; NAB, NIV, NJB, REB, TNT]. They are not really poor [EBC].
2. It means poor in material things of the world [Alf, BKC, Blm, HNTC, Lns, NBC, TNTC], with reference to the world [Lg(M)]. It is because of this that the world judges them to be poor [NBC].

QUESTION—How are the phrases πλουσίους ἐν πίστει καὶ κληρονόμους τῆς βασιλείας 'rich in faith and heirs of the kingdom' related to τοὺς πτωχοὺς τῷ κόσμῳ 'the poor in/to the world'?

1. These phrases tell what God intends for the poor [AB, Alf, Hb, Herm, HNTC, ICC, Mit, NBC, WBC]: God has chosen the poor to become rich in faith and heirs of the kingdom.
2. It describes the poor [Bg, Blm, EBC, Lns, My, NIC]: God has chosen the poor, who are rich in faith and are heirs of the kingdom.

QUESTION—What is meant by the phrase ἐν πίστει 'in faith'?

1. It refers to the area in which they are rich [Alf, BKC, Blm, Hb, Herm, HNTC, ICC, Lns, May, My, NBC, NIC, NIGTC, TG]: rich in the area of faith, of spiritual things. They are rich because of their faith [HNTC, Lg, TG], rich by God's standards [TG]; they become rich through their faith [NBC, NTC]. The riches consist of salvation with all of its blessings [Hb]. They are rich in that they have a place in God's kingdom [Lns, My, WBC]. It does not imply that all poor people are rich in faith [EBC] or will be saved [NIC, NTC], nor that no rich people will be saved [NIC, NTC], but that the poor are not less favored than the rich [Hb].
2. Their riches consist of their faith [Mit].

and heirs[a] of-the kingdom[b] which he-has-promised[c] to-the-(ones) loving him?

LEXICON—a. κληρονόμος (LN **57.133**) (BAGD 2.b. p. 435): 'heir' [AB, BAGD, Herm, HNTC, LN, Lns, NIC; KJV, NAB, NASB, NJB, NRSV], 'receiver' [LN], 'sharer' [WBC]. This noun is also translated as a verb: 'to inherit' [NIV], 'to possess' [REB, TEV], 'to take possession of' [TNT], 'to receive' [**LN**].

b. βασιλεία (LN 1.82; 37.64) (BAGD 3.g. p. 135): 'kingdom' [AB, BAGD, Herm, HNTC, LN, Lns, NIC, WBC; all versions], 'reign' [BAGD, LN]. This word refers to God's ruling, not to a place [Mit].

c. aorist mid. (deponent = act.) of ἐπαγγέλλομαι (LN 33.286) (BAGD 1.b. p. 281): 'to promise' [AB, BAGD, Herm, HNTC, LN, Lns, NIC, WBC; all versions]. The aorist tense refers to God's action in making the promise [Hb], but not to any specific occasion [ICC].

QUESTION—What does τῆς βασιλείας 'the kingdom' refer to?
1. The reference is to the future eternal kingdom [Bg, EBC, Hb, Herm, HNTC, ICC, Mit, My, NIC, NIGTC, TG, TNTC, Tsk].
2. It refers to the Messianic kingdom on earth [EGT, Lg, May].

2:6 But you have-dishonored[a] the poor (person).

LEXICON—a. aorist act. indic. of ἀτιμάζω (LN 87.74; 88.127) (BAGD p. 120): 'to dishonor' [AB, BAGD, Herm, Lns; NASB, NJB, NRSV, TEV], 'to cause to be dishonored' [LN (87.74)], 'to cause to suffer dishonor' [LN], 'to humiliate' [REB, TNT], 'to disgrace' [WBC], 'to treat shamefully' [BAGD, LN (88.127); NAB], 'to despise' [KJV], 'to insult' [BAGD, HNTC; NIV], 'to have contempt for' [NIC], 'to mistreat' [LN]. The meaning is to treat disdainfully and actively [NIC], to dishonor [Tsk], to withhold someone's rights [EGT]. This verb is contrasted with ἐξελέξατο 'chose' [My]. The aorist tense refers to the general attitude toward the poor [Herm, Lg, My, NIGTC], which is illustrated by the specific example mentioned in 2:2–3 [Lg, My, NBC, NIGTC].

QUESTION—What relationship is indicated by ὑμεῖς δέ 'but you'?
Δέ 'but' indicates the contrast [Lg, My, NIGTC, NTC, TNTC], and ὑμεῖς 'you' is emphatic [Hb, WBC], pointing out the difference between God's treatment of the poor and theirs [Hb, Lg, My, NIGTC, NTC, TNTC]: God has chosen the poor, but *you* have dishonored them.

QUESTION—How did they dishonor the poor?
They have dishonored the poor by their discourtesy [Hb, Mit, NBC], by their partiality to the rich [ICC, NIGTC]; their favor to the rich is implied [NBC]. They showed that they held them in contempt by ordering them to sit on the floor [Hb]. The singular noun πτωχόν 'poor' is generic, referring to poor people in general [ICC, TG].

(Do) not the rich (people) oppress[a] you

LEXICON—a. pres. act. indic. of καταδυναστεύω (LN 22.22) (BAGD p. 410): 'to oppress' [AB, BAGD, Herm, HNTC, LN, NIC; KJV, NASB, NRSV,

TEV, TNT], 'to cause severe hardship' [LN], 'to tyrannize' [Lns], 'to exploit' [BAGD, WBC; NAB, NIV], 'to dominate' [BAGD], 'to lord it over' [NJB]. This entire phrase is translated 'are not the rich your oppressors' [REB]. The meaning is to use power or position to mistreat [Alf, Hb, HNTC, My], to deprive of one's rights tyrannically [EBC]. The reference is to social and economic mistreatment, not religious persecution [Hb, Herm, HNTC, ICC, TNTC, WBC]. It is legal action concerning wages, debts, and rent [ICC]. The present tense implies actual repeated offenses [Hb, WBC]. The reference is to rich non-Christians in general [Herm, My, NBC, NTC], or to rich Jews but not all of them [Lns].

QUESTION—What is implied by this and the following clause?

It is an argument against showing favoritism to rich people [Alf, Blm, Hb], since they are unworthy [Bg, Blm]. It does not mean that all rich people mistreat Christians, but that some do so [AB, Bg, Hb, Lg]. It refers to non-Christian rich people [Alf, NIGTC]. The introductory οὐχ 'not' means that an affirmative answer is expected [Hb, NIGTC, NTC, TG].

and (do not) they-themselves drag[a] you into[b] courts?[c]

LEXICON—a. pres. act. indic. of ἕλκω (LN 15.178) (BAGD 1.a. p. 251): 'to drag' [AB, BAGD, Herm, HNTC, LN, NIC; all versions except KJV, NAB], 'to hale' [BAGD, Lns, WBC; NAB], 'to draw' [KJV]. This word implies acting violently [Alf, Bg, EBC, My, WBC], or forcibly [Hb, Herm], through court procedures [Mit, My, NIGTC, TG]. It refers both to rich Gentiles and to rich Jews [Herm].

b. εἰς with accusative object (LN 84.22): 'into' [Herm, HNTC, LN; NAB, NASB, NIV, NJB, NRSV, REB], 'to' [Lns, NIC; TNT], 'before' [AB, WBC; KJV]. The phrase εἰς κριτήρια 'into courts' is translated 'before the judges' [TEV].

c. κριτήριον (LN **56.1**) (BAGD 1. p. 453): 'court' [AB, BAGD, Herm, HNTC, **LN**, Lns, NIC; all versions except KJV, TEV], 'law court' [BAGD], 'court of justice' [LN], 'tribunal' [BAGD, WBC], 'judgment seat' [KJV]. The reference is to Jewish courts [Hb, Lns, NIC], or courts in general, both Jewish and Gentile [My, NIGTC].

QUESTION—How is this clause related to its context?

1. It is a continuation of the first question [AB, Alf, Hb, HNTC, Lns; KJV, NASB, TEV]: Don't the rich oppress you and drag you into court?
2. It is a second question [BKC, EBC, Herm, NIC, NTC, WBC; NIV, NJB, NRSV, REB, TNT]: Don't the rich oppress you? And don't they drag you into court?
3. It is a statement of fact [NAB]: Don't the rich oppress you? And they drag you into court.

QUESTION—What is implied by this clause?

It implies that their oppressors act with the outward forms of justice, but in fact they act unjustly [Bg].

QUESTION—What is implied by the pronoun αὐτοί 'they themselves'?
   1. It emphasizes the identity of their oppressors [Alf, Hb, ICC, Lns, My, NBC, NIC, NIGTC; NAB, NIV, NJB, NRSV, REB, TNT]: are not *they* the ones who do this? The very ones whom they improperly favor [Hb], the same ones who oppress them [NIGTC], are the ones who drag them into court [Hb]. This word is forefronted for emphasis [My], contrasting them with the poor [NIC].
   2. It implies that the rich personally drag them into court [EBC, May; NASB].

2:7 (Do) not they-themselves blaspheme^a the good^b name^c the-(one) having-been-named^d upon^e you?

LEXICON—a. pres. act. indic. of βλασφημέω (LN 33.400) (BAGD 2.b.δ. p. 142): 'to blaspheme' [BAGD, Herm, LN, Lns; KJV, NAB, NASB, NRSV], 'to slander' [HNTC; NIV], 'to defame' [LN], 'to revile' [AB, LN], 'to speak evil of' [TEV], 'to insult' [NJB], 'to pour contempt on' [REB, TNT], 'to sin impiously against' [NIC], 'to bring into disgrace' [WBC]. The reference is to blasphemous speech [Alf, EBC, Lg, May, My, NIC, NIGTC, TNTC] or indirect comments [NIGTC] by non-Christians [Alf, Bg, My], and especially by wealthy Jews who rejected Jesus [Hb, ICC, Lns, May].
   b. καλός (LN 88.4) (BAGD 2.c.β. p. 400): 'good' [AB, BAGD, HNTC, LN; TEV], 'fine' [LN, WBC], 'fair' [NASB, TNT], 'worthy' [KJV], 'noble' [Lns, NIC; NAB, NIV], 'honorable' [Herm; NJB], 'honored' [REB], 'excellent' [NRSV], 'praiseworthy' [LN]. This word refers to high esteem and honor [EBC, Hb] and it contrasts with the shameful blasphemy [Lg, My].
   c. ὄνομα (LN 33.126) (BAGD I.4.b. p. 571): 'name' [AB, BAGD, Herm, HNTC, LN, Lns, NIC, WBC; all versions]. The name is 'Christ' [Alf, EBC, ICC, Lg, May, Mit, My, TNTC, Tsk]; it is 'Jesus' [BKC, EGT, Hb, Herm, HNTC, Lns, NBC, NIGTC, NTC]; it is the name 'Christian' [NIC]; it is God's name [Bg].
   d. aorist pass. participle of ἐπικαλέω (LN 33.131) (BAGD 1.b.β. p. 294): 'to be named' [BAGD, Herm, LN], 'to be invoked' [AB; NRSV], 'to be called' [HNTC, LN, Lns; KJV], 'to be pronounced' [NJB]. The phrase τὸ ἐπικληθὲν ἐφ' ὑμᾶς 'the one having been named upon you' is translated 'by which you have been called' [WBC; NASB], 'by which you are called' [NIC], 'by the which ye are called' [KJV], 'by which God has claimed you' [REB], 'which has made you God's own' [NAB], 'of him to whom you belong' [NIV]. The phrase τὸ καλὸν ὄνομα τὸ ἐπικληθὲν ἐφ' ὑμᾶς 'the good name the one having been named upon you' is translated 'him who called you by his own fair name' [TNT], 'that good name which has been given to you' [TEV]. The aorist tense refers to the event in which the name was invoked upon them [HNTC, WBC], namely, at their baptism [HNTC, NIGTC, TG].

JAMES 2:7

e. ἐπί with accusative object (LN 83.9; 83.46; 90.57) (BAGD III.1.a.ζ. p. 288): 'upon' [AB, HNTC, LN, Lns], 'on' [LN], 'over' [BAGD, Herm, LN; NJB, NRSV], 'to' [TEV], 'among' [LN].

QUESTION—What is the function of this clause?
It continues the argument against showing favoritism to the rich [BKC, EBC, Hb, Herm, HNTC, Lg, Mit, My, NBC, NIGTC, TNTC, Tsk, WBC].

QUESTION—What is meant by τὸ ἐπικληθὲν ἐφ' ὑμᾶς 'the one having been named upon you'?
1. It refers to the fact that they belong to Jesus [BKC, Hb, Herm, ICC, NIGTC, TNTC], to Christ [EBC, Lg(M)]. The name of Jesus was named over them at their baptism [Alf, Herm, HNTC, Lns, May, NBC, NIGTC]. It does not necessarily refer to baptism [ICC].
2. It means that they belong to God and are under his protection [EGT].
3. It refers to their being called the people of God [Bg]: you have been called God's people.

DISCOURSE UNIT: 2:8–13 [Lns, Mit, Tsk]. The topic is the results of breaking one law [Lns], the royal law [Tsk].

DISCOURSE UNIT: 2:8–12 [NIGTC]. The topic is the biblical argument for the excellence of being poor and being generous.

DISCOURSE UNIT: 2:8–11 [ICC, NTC]. The topic is an exhortation to keep the royal law [NTC].

2:8 Indeed/But-on-the-one-hand[a] if you-fulfill[b] (the) royal[c] law[d] according-to[e] the scripture, "You-shall-love[f] your neighbor[g] as[h] yourself," you-do well;

LEXICON—a. μέντοι (LN 89.130; **89.136**) (BAGD 1. p. 503): 'indeed on the one hand' [**LN**], 'indeed' [HNTC, NIC], 'really' [BAGD, Herm; NIV, NRSV, TNT], 'truly' [WBC], 'actually' [BAGD], 'well' [NJB], 'but' [LN (89.130)], 'however' [Lns; NAB, NASB, REB], 'nevertheless' [LN], 'on the contrary' [AB], not explicit [KJV, TEV]. This word is emphatic in its sense [HNTC].
b. pres. act. indic. of τελέω (LN 36.20) (BAGD 2. p. 811): 'to fulfill' [AB, BAGD, Herm, HNTC, NIC, WBC; KJV, NAB, NASB, NRSV, TNT], 'to obey' [LN; TEV], 'to keep' [BAGD, LN; NIV, NJB], 'to carry out' [BAGD, Lns], 'to perform' [BAGD], 'to observe' [REB]. It is emphatic by its position [Alf].
c. βασιλικός (LN 37.69) (BAGD p. 136): 'royal' [AB, BAGD, Herm, HNTC, LN, Lns; KJV, NASB, NIV, NRSV, TNT], 'sovereign' [NIC; REB], 'supreme' [WBC; NJB], 'of the kingdom' [NAB, TEV]. This word is nonrestrictive; it is not intended to distinguish this law from some other inferior law [ICC]. It is made prominent by its position [Hb].
d. νόμος (LN 33.333) (BAGD 5. p. 543): 'law' [AB, BAGD, Herm, HNTC, LN, Lns, NIC, WBC; all versions], 'ordinance' [LN], 'rule' [LN]. It is the

law of God [ICC]. The absence of the article emphasizes its royal quality [Hb, Lns, NIGTC].
e. κατά with accusative object (LN 89.8) (BAGD II.5.a.α. p. 407): 'according to' [AB, BAGD, HNTC, Lns, NIC, WBC; KJV, NASB, NRSV], 'in accordance with' [BAGD, Herm, LN]. The phrase κατὰ τὴν γραφήν 'according to the scripture' is translated 'found in (the) scripture' [NIV, TEV], 'laid down in scripture' [REB, TNT], 'of scripture' [NJB], 'scripture has it' [NAB].
f. πλησίον (LN 11.89) (BAGD 1.b. p. 672): 'neighbor' [AB, BAGD, Herm, HNTC, LN, Lns, NIC, WBC; all versions]. Jesus made this term inclusive of everyone whom we can help [Hb].
g. fut. act. indic. of ἀγαπάω (LN 25.43) (BAGD 1.a.α. p. 4): 'to love' [all commentaries and translations]. The future indicative has imperative meaning [BKC, EBC, Hb, Herm, HNTC, ICC, Lg, Lns, May, Mit, My, NBC, NIC, NIGTC, NTC, TG, TNTC, Tsk, WBC; NIV, REB, TEV, TNT]: you must love your neighbor as yourself.
h. ὡς (LN 64.12): 'as' [AB, Herm, HNTC, LN, Lns, NIC, WBC; all versions], 'like' [LN]. It indicates both the manner and the extent of the love, [Hb]: you must love in the way and to the extent that you love yourself.

QUESTION—What relationship is indicated by μέντοι 'indeed/but'?
  1. It indicates a continuation of the argument [BAGD, Hb, HNTC, LN, My, NIC; NIV, NJB, NRSV, TNT]. It implies affirmation [NTC]. It grants this fact to the readers and at the same time has in view the contrast contained in the next clause [My].
  2. It indicates a contrast with what precedes [AB, Alf, EGT, Hb, ICC, Lg(M), Lns, NIGTC, TNTC; NAB, NASB, REB]. They do evil in dishonoring the poor, but if they fulfill the royal law, they will do well [TNTC]. It contrasts their actual behavior with the behavior described in this clause [NIGTC]. Although many do dishonor the poor, James pauses to show that he knows there were some who do well [Hb].

QUESTION—What is implied by εἰ 'if' and the indicative mood in this conditional clause?
  1. It implies that his readers claim that they are obeying the royal law [HNTC, Mit, My]. Such a claim would be the result of dishonesty or deceiving themselves [Mit].
  2. It anticipates obedience by his readers [BKC].
  3. It means that he knew that not all of his readers were guilty of favoritism [Hb].
  4. The construction in itself is noncommittal, merely referring to actual circumstances [NTC]: if you are doing this. (The same construction follows in 2:9, with the opposite implication.)

QUESTION—What law is meant by the phrase νόμον βασιλικόν 'royal law'?
1. It refers to the command to love one's neighbor [AB, Bg, BKC, EBC, EGT, HNTC, Lns, May, My, NBC, NTC]. To fulfill this commandment is to fulfill the whole law [ICC].
2. It refers to the law as a whole [Blm, EGT, Hb, Herm, ICC, Lg, Mit, NIC, NIGTC], the whole of God's will for believers [TNTC, WBC], of which the command to love is only a part [Herm, ICC], and which has royal authority [Herm, Mit]. However, the whole law is fulfilled by fulfilling the command to love [Herm, ICC, Mit, WBC]. The reference is to the entirety of God's will for his people [TNTC].

QUESTION—Why is it called βασιλικόν 'royal'?
1. It is 'royal' because of its nature—it is the highest law [Alf, Bg, Blm, EBC, Hb, Lg(M), Lns, My], summing up the Decalogue [Bg], summing up all of the OT [Lns, My], summing up all other laws concerning human relationships [EBC].
2. It is 'royal' because of its source—it is given by the Supreme King [Bg], Christ [AB, NIC] or God [EGT, WBC]. It has Christ's authority [Lg, NIGTC] and is the law of God's kingdom [HNTC, NIGTC].

QUESTION—What is the meaning of the phrase κατὰ τὴν γραφήν 'according to the scripture'?
It gives the standard by which the 'royal law' is to be fulfilled [Hb]: fulfill the royal law in the way this scripture indicates. It implies that love for one's neighbor is at the heart of God's law [AB, TNTC].

QUESTION—What is implied by the singulars 'you', 'your', and 'yourself' in the scripture quoted?
It points out that the duty is for each individual [Hb]: each of you must do this.

QUESTION—What is meant by the apodosis (the conclusion) of the 'if' clause καλῶς ποιεῖτε 'you do well'?
1. It indicates that fulfilling the royal law is highly commendable [Hb, HNTC, Mit, My, NIGTC, NTC, TG]: if you are doing this, it is a very fine thing.
2. It means that he recognizes that they know they must love their neighbors, and he agrees that in doing so they are doing well [HNTC].
3. It means that if their deference to the rich man (a Jew [Lns]) was simply to fulfill the command to love their neighbor, he approves their action [Lns, May].

2:9 if on-the-other-hand[a] you-show-partiality,[b] you-commit[c] sin,
LEXICON—a. δέ (LN **89.136**): 'on the other hand', 'but on the other hand' [LN], 'but' [AB, Herm, HNTC, Lns, NIC, WBC; all versions].
b. pres. act. indic. of προσωπολημπτέω (LN **88.238**) (BAGD p. 720): 'to show partiality' [BAGD, Herm; NASB, NRSV, REB], 'to show favoritism' [LN, WBC; NAB, NIV, TNT], 'to show discrimination' [HNTC], 'to be partial' [LN], 'to have respect of persons' [Lns], 'to have

respect to persons' [KJV], 'to make class distinctions' [NJB], 'to be swayed by men's social status' [NIC], 'to treat one person better than another' [**LN**], 'to treat people according to their outward appearance' [TEV], 'to try to curry favor with people' [AB].
  c. pres. mid. (deponent = act.) of ἐργάζομαι (LN 90.47) (BAGD 2.a. p. 307): 'to commit' [AB, BAGD, Herm, HNTC, Lns, NIC, WBC; all versions except NIV, TEV], 'to do' [LN], 'to be guilty of' [TEV]. The phrase ἁμαρτίαν ἐργάζεσθε 'you commit sin' is translated 'you sin' [NIV]. This verb implies intentional action [Hb, Mit]; it is stronger than the common word meaning merely 'to do' [Lg].
QUESTION—Why is this clause mentioned?
  It describes the conduct which breaks the law commanding love for one's neighbor, in contrast (indicated by δέ 'but' [Hb, NIC, NIGTC, WBC]) to the good behavior described in 2:8 [EBC, NIGTC, TNTC, WBC].
QUESTION—What is implied by εἰ 'if' and the indicative mood in this conditional clause?
  It indicates that he is dealing with a factual and not hypothetical situation [Hb, NTC] (but without stating that they are showing partiality). The action is deliberate, not accidental [Hb].
QUESTION—What is implied by ἁμαρτίαν 'sin'?
  It is emphatic by forefronting [Alf, Hb]. It refers to willful sin [EGT, Mit]. The absence of the definite article makes it qualitative [Lns]: it is sin that you are committing.

being-convicted[a] by[b] the law[c] as[d] transgressors.[e]
LEXICON—a. pres. pass. participle of ἐλέγχω (LN 33.417) (BAGD 2. p. 249): 'to be convicted' [AB, BAGD, Herm, Lns, NIC, WBC; NAB, NASB, NIV, NRSV], 'to stand convicted' [HNTC; REB], 'to be rebuked' [LN], 'to be reproached' [LN], 'to be convinced' [KJV], 'to be under condemnation' [NJB]. The phrase ἐλεγχόμενοι ὑπὸ τοῦ νόμου 'being convicted by the law' is translated 'the Law condemns you' [TEV, TNT]. This verb indicates that they are proven wrong by the law [Hb].
  b. ὑπό with genitive object (LN 90.1): 'by' [AB, Herm, HNTC, LN, Lns, NIC, WBC; NAB, NASB, NIV, NRSV, REB], 'of' [KJV]. The phrase ὑπὸ τοῦ νόμου ὡς παραβάται 'by the law as transgressors' is translated 'for breaking the Law' [NJB]. This preposition implies agency, suggesting that the law is personalized as a witness against them [Hb, May, Mit, NBC].
  c. νόμος (LN 33.55) (BAGD 5. p. 543): 'law' [AB, BAGD, Herm, HNTC, LN, Lns, NIC, WBC; KJV, NAB, NASB, NIV, NRSV, REB], 'the Law' [LN; TEV, TNT]. The reference is to the law mentioned in 2:8 [TNTC]—the royal law [EBC, HNTC, Lns], the law commanding love for one's neighbor [Blm, EBC, HNTC, Lns, Mit, NTC, TNTC], the whole law [Herm, My]. It refers to the law forbidding partiality in Deut. 16:19 [Lg], in Lev. 19:15 [Blm, Hb, ICC, May, Mit, NBC].

d. ὡς (LN 64.12) (BAGD III.1.c. p. 898): 'as' [AB, BAGD, Herm, HNTC, LN, Lns, NIC, WBC; all versions except NJB].
e. παραβάτης (LN 36.29) (BAGD p. 612): 'transgressor' [AB, BAGD, Herm, HNTC, LN, Lns, NIC, WBC; KJV, NAB, NASB, NRSV], 'offender' [REB], 'lawbreaker' [NIV, TEV, TNT]. This word implies passing into a prohibited area, indicating violation of a known law [Hb, Mit, NTC]. Such a person is one who breaks or disobeys the law [LN]. Here it means being transgressors of the whole law [Herm, My], of the royal law of love [HNTC].

QUESTION—What relationship is indicated by the present participle ἐλεγχόμενοι 'being convicted'?
1. It adds an additional aspect of their condemnation [Herm, HNTC, NIC, WBC; all versions]: you are committing sin and are convicted by the law.
2. It expresses the reason why they are committing sin in showing partiality [Alf, Lns]: you are committing sin because you are convicted by the law.
3. This participial phrase restates their guilt [My, NIGTC, NTC]: you are committing sin; indeed, you are convicted by the law.
4. It expresses the result of their sin [Bg]: you are committing sin, and as a result you are convicted by the law.

DISCOURSE UNIT: 2:10–13 [BKC, HNTC]. The topic is the whole law [HNTC], being consistent [BKC].

2:10 For[a] whoever keeps[b] all the law but stumbles[c] in[d] one (thing) has-become[e] guilty[f] of-all.

LEXICON—a. γάρ (LN 89.23): 'for' [AB, Herm, HNTC, LN, Lns, NIC; KJV, NASB, NIV, NRSV, REB], 'because' [LN], 'it follows that' [WBC], not explicit [NAB, NJB, TEV, TNT].
b. aorist act. subj. of τηρέω (LN 36.19) (BAGD 5. p. 815): 'to keep' [AB, BAGD, Herm, HNTC, LN, WBC; all versions except TEV, TNT], 'to obey' [LN], 'to observe' [BAGD, NIC], 'to fulfill' [BAGD], 'to guard' [Lns], not explicit [TEV, TNT]. The sense is to guard the law against being violated [EGT].
c. aorist act. subj. of πταίω (LN **88.291**) (BAGD 1. p. 727): 'to stumble' [LN, Lns, WBC; NASB, NIV], 'to trip up' [HNTC; NJB], 'to fail' [AB, Herm; NRSV], 'to sin' [BAGD, **LN**], 'to fall into sin' [NAB], 'to err' [LN], 'to offend' [KJV], 'to contravene' [NIC]. The phrase πταίσῃ ἐν ἑνί 'stumbles in one' is translated 'breaks one commandment' [TEV], 'breaks just one commandment' [REB], 'breaks only one point of the Law' [TNT].
d. ἐν with dative object (LN 89.5): 'in' [Herm, HNTC, LN, Lns; KJV, NASB, NRSV], 'on' [NAB, NJB], 'at' [AB; NIV], 'in the case of' [LN], 'with regard to' [LN], 'about' [LN], 'over' [WBC], not explicit [NIC].
e. perf. act. indic. of γίνομαι (LN 13.48): 'to become' [AB, LN, Lns, NIC, WBC; NAB, NASB, NRSV], 'to be' [KJV, NIV, NJB, REB, TEV, TNT]. The phrase γέγονεν ἔνοχος 'has become guilty' is translated 'has sinned

against' [Herm], 'has become answerable in respect (of)' [HNTC]. The perfect tense implies a (guilty) state resulting from his action [Hb, Lns].
  f. ἔνοχος (LN 88.312) (BAGD 2.b.γ. p. 268): 'guilty' [AB, BAGD, LN, Lns, NIC, WBC; all versions except NRSV], 'accountable' [NRSV].

QUESTION—What relationship is indicated by γάρ 'for'?
  It introduces the explanation for the claim that the person who does not love his neighbor is a law-breaker [EBC, NIGTC, TNTC], a confirmation that their favoritism was evil and a violation of God's law [Hb, My].

QUESTION—What is the meaning of this verse?
  1. It means that the law is a unit [Alf, Blm, Hb, Lns, NBC, NIGTC, NTC, TNTC], and breaking one point breaks the law as a whole [AB, Alf, Blm, EBC, Hb, ICC, Lns, Mit, NBC, NTC, TNTC, WBC]. The singular noun νόμον 'law' refers to the law as a whole [Alf, My]. Moreover, the law commanding love for one's neighbor is basic to the law as a whole [Blm]. Any transgression reveals the person's attitude toward the law and the lawgiver [NIGTC].
  2. It means that breaking one point of the law reveals a nature which will break the law in other points [Hb, Herm, NIGTC]. It is not that the person has broken all parts of the law or that all violations of the law are equally serious, but that the sinner has been brought under the condemning power of the whole law [Hb].

QUESTION—What is implied by the two aorist subjunctive verbs, τηρήσῃ 'keeps' and πταίσῃ 'stumbles'?
  They mean that James is dealing with the situation as a contingency or real possibility rather than referring to a specific instance or instances [Hb, Lns, NTC]: whoever at any time does this. It is a hypothetical situation [Lg]; it has the same meaning as a conditional clause [NTC; REB, TNT].

QUESTION—What is meant by the phrase ἐν ἑνί 'in one thing'?
  It refers to any one point of the law [EBC, EGT, Hb, Herm, HNTC, ICC, Lg, Lns, TNTC, Tsk, WBC], any specific law [My]: whoever breaks any point of the law. Since the law as a whole details the manner of loving one's neighbor, to break any single law breaks the law of love [Blm, Lns, NBC, TG]. Since the command to love is the supreme commandment, to break that law is to violate the heart of God's law [WBC].

2:11 For[a] the-(one) having-said, "(Do) not commit-adultery,"[b] said also, "(Do) not commit-murder";[c]

LEXICON—a. γάρ (LN 89.23): 'for' [Herm, HNTC, LN, Lns, NIC, WBC; all versions except NJB], 'because' [LN], 'thus' [AB], not explicit [NJB].
  b. aorist act. subj. of μοιχεύω (LN 88.276) (BAGD 1. p. 526c): 'to commit adultery' [AB, BAGD, Herm, HNTC, LN, Lns, NIC, WBC; all versions]. The aorist tense implies a prohibition of even a single act [Hb, Lns].
  c. aorist act. subj. of φονεύω (LN 20.82) (BAGD p. 864): 'to commit murder' [BAGD, LN; NASB, REB, TEV], 'to murder' [BAGD, Herm, HNTC, LN, WBC; NIV, NRSV, TNT], 'to kill' [AB, BAGD, Lns, NIC;

KJV, NAB, NJB]. The reference is not to actual murder but to anger and harsh words [AB]. The aorist tense implies a prohibition of even a single act [Hb, Lns].

QUESTION—What relationship is indicated by γάρ 'for'?

It indicates the continuation of the grounds for what he has just said [Alf, Blm, EBC, Herm, TNTC, WBC], namely, that the law is a unity [Hb, TNTC], and serves to explain and illustrate it [Blm, EBC, Hb].

QUESTION—What is implied by the aorist participial phrase ὁ εἰπών 'the one having said'?

This manner of reference to the scriptures focuses attention on God as the author [Bg, HNTC, Lg, May, My, NBC, NIGTC, NTC, TG, TNTC] and thus points up the unity of the law [Bg, May, My, NIGTC, TNTC, WBC]. The καί 'also' shows that God gave both commandments [WBC]. This expression is a Jewish way of avoiding using God's name [NIC, NTC, WBC].

QUESTION—Why does the author use the commandments against adultery and murder as his examples?

They are the central ethical commandments, used to support the argument that all violations of the law are transgressions [NIGTC]. These two were commonly used as examples of the requirements of God's law [TNTC]. They are extreme examples that show how absurd their inconsistent behavior is [BKC, Mit]. Also, breaking either of these commandments violates the law of love [Mit]. He uses them because they are the first two in the Decalogue which relate to relations to one's neighbors [Alf, My, NTC, Tsk]. Symbolically, they refer to spiritual fornication by involvement with heathenism, and murder by hating fellowmen [Lg].

and[a] if not you-commit-adultery but[b] you-commit-murder, you-have-become[c] a transgressor[d] of-(the)-law.[e]

LEXICON—a. δέ (LN 89.94): 'and' [LN], 'now' [Lns; KJV, NASB, NJB, NRSV], 'even' [TEV], 'therefore' [NAB], 'so' [HNTC], not explicit [AB, Herm, NIC, WBC; NIV, REB, TNT]. This word introduces the proof of the argument [Hb].

b. δέ (LN 89.124): 'but' [AB, Herm, HNTC, LN, Lns, NIC, WBC; NAB, NASB, NIV, NRSV, TNT], 'and' [LN], 'yet' [KJV], not explicit [NJB, REB, TEV]. This word indicates a contrast with the preceding commandment [Hb].

c. perf. act. indic. of γίνομαι: 'to become'. See this word at 2:10.

d. παραβάτης: 'transgressor'. See this word at 2:9.

e. νόμος (LN 33.55) (BAGD 3. p. 542): 'law' [AB, BAGD, Herm, HNTC, LN, Lns, NIC, WBC; KJV, NAB, NASB, NRSV, REB], 'the Law' [BAGD, LN; NJB, TNT], 'ordinance' [LN]. The reference is to the law as a whole [Hb].

QUESTION—What is implied by the construction εἰ 'if' with the indicative verbs οὐ μοιχεύεις 'you do not commit adultery' and φονεύεις 'you commit murder'?

It is a conditional clause dealing with reality [Hb], implying a real possibility [NIGTC]; it is a hypothetical case [Tsk].

QUESTION—What is implied by the phrase γέγονας παραβάτης νόμου 'you have become a transgressor of the law'?

It is the apodosis (the result) of the preceding 'if' clause [My] and means that they have violated the morality which underlies the whole law [Blm]. The perfect tense of the verb implies a state of being a transgressor [Hb]. From the generalized ὅστις 'whoever' of 2:10, the author now moves to the definite singular 'you', indicating the individual guilt [Hb, Lns]. Since the law is a unity, violation of one part violates the law as a whole [Bg, EBC, My, NTC, WBC].

DISCOURSE UNIT: 2:12–13 [Hb, NTC]. The topic is an appeal for living consistently [Hb], showing mercy [NTC].

2:12 So[a] speak and so[a] act[b] as[c] being-about[d] to-be-judged[e] through[f] a/(the) law[g] of freedom.[h]

LEXICON—a. οὕτως (LN 61.9; 61.10) (BAGD 2. p. 598): 'so' [Herm, LN, Lns, NIC; KJV, NASB, NRSV], 'thus' [BAGD, LN], 'in this way' [BAGD, LN], 'as follows' [BAGD, LN], 'in every respect' [HNTC], 'always' [NAB, REB], not explicit [AB, WBC; NIV, NJB, TEV, TNT]. The repetition of this word before the two verbs adds emphasis [EBC, Hb, May, My, NTC, TNTC, WBC] or solemnity [NIGTC], and gives equal prominence to both verbs [EBC, Hb, May, TNTC].

b. pres. act. impera. of ποιέω (LN 42.7) (BAGD I.2.a.α. p. 682): 'to act' [AB, BAGD, Herm, HNTC, LN, Lns, NIC, WBC; all versions except KJV, NJB], 'to behave' [NJB], 'to do' [BAGD, LN; KJV], 'to perform' [LN].

c. ὡς (LN 64.12) (BAGD I.2.a. p. 897): 'as' [AB, BAGD, Herm, HNTC, LN, Lns, NIC, WBC; all versions except NJB], 'like' [LN; NJB].

d. pres. act. participle of μέλλω (LN 67.62): 'to be about (to)' [LN, Lns], 'to be going (to)' [AB, HNTC; NIV, NJB], 'to be destined for' [NAB]. This participle is translated 'they that shall' [KJV], 'people who will' [TEV], 'those who will' [NIC], 'those who are (to)' [Herm, WBC; NASB, NRSV], 'men who are (to)' [REB, TNT]. This participle implies the certainty of the future judgment [Hb, NIGTC, WBC] and a deliberate choice [NIC].

e. pres. pass. infin. of κρίνω (LN 56.20) (BAGD 4.b.α. p. 452): 'to be judged' [AB, BAGD, Herm, HNTC, LN, Lns, NIC, WBC; all versions except NAB], 'to be evaluated' [LN], 'to be destined for judgment' [NAB]. The judgment is that of believers at Christ's judgment seat [EBC, Hb, Mit] to assess their character [Hb, Mit, TNTC]. The passive voice implies that the judgment will be made through the law of freedom [WBC]

f. διά with genitive object (LN 90.8): 'through' [LN], 'by means of' [LN, Lns], 'by' [AB, Herm, WBC; all versions except NAB, REB], 'under' [NAB, REB], 'in accordance with' [NIC], 'in terms of' [HNTC]. It indicates the framework (the condition [ICC]) within which they should speak and act [HNTC, ICC], the instrument of the judgment [TNTC, WBC].

g. νόμος (LN 33.333) (BAGD 5. p. 543): 'law' [AB, BAGD, Herm, LN, Lns, NIC, WBC; all versions].

h. ἐλευθερία (LN 37.133) (BAGD p. 250): 'freedom' [BAGD, Herm, HNTC, LN; NAB, NIV, NJB], 'liberty' [AB, BAGD, Lns, NIC; KJV, NASB, NRSV]. This noun is translated as a phrase: 'which makes free' [REB], 'that sets free' [WBC; TEV], 'which sets free' [TNT].

QUESTION—How is this verse related to its context?

It is the conclusion and summary of the preceding argument [Alf, Blm, EBC, Herm, ICC, Lg, My, NIC, NIGTC], of 2:8–9 [TNTC]. It is a general exhortation [Blm, Mit, My] and warning [Mit].

QUESTION—What are the two instances of οὕτως 'so' connected with?

1. They refer to the ὡς 'as' clause which follows [Alf, BAGD, EBC, Hb, Lns, May, NIGTC, NTC; KJV, NAB, NASB, NRSV, REB]: speak and act as being about to be judged.
2. They refer to what precedes [Lg, My]: speak and act according to the rule stated in 1:10–11. The following ὡς 'as' clause is an added confirmation [My] or reason [Lg].

QUESTION—What do the present tense imperative verbs, λαλεῖτε 'speak' and ποιεῖτε 'act', indicate?

They exhort habitual conduct [Alf, BKC, EBC, Hb, Lns, TNTC, WBC]: habitually speak and act thus. These verbs express a duty, not merely an option [Hb]. These two verbs include all of a person's conduct [NIGTC].

QUESTION—What relationship is indicated by ὡς 'as'?

1. It introduces the manner of doing so [Hb; KJV, NAB, NASB, NJB, NRSV]: in the manner of being about to be judged.
2. It introduces the reason for speaking and acting properly [EBC, Lg, My]: because you are going to be judged.

QUESTION—What relationship is indicated by the use of the participial phrase, μέλλοντες κρίνεσθαι 'being about to be judged'?

1. It indicates manner [Alf]: in the manner of being about to be judged.
2. It identifies the persons referred to [AB, BKC, Hb, Herm, HNTC, NIC, NTC, Tsk, WBC; all versions]: as people who are going to be judged. (Grammatically, this is unacceptable; to be an attributive participle, a definite article would be required with the participle since it modifies 'you' which is definite. Probably many have translated in this way merely because it is simpler, without intending to imply that it is attributive.)

QUESTION—What is the meaning of νόμου ἐλευθερίας 'law of freedom'?

It is the law commanding love [AB, EBC, WBC], the perfection of the Jewish law [AB] as interpreted by Jesus, focusing on the law of love [NIGTC], the gospel [TG], God's will as expressed in the gospel [TNTC], the perfect expansion of God's will, based on the principle of love [Alf], new life in Christ which frees from the law's restrictions [Lg]. The absence of the article from both nouns emphasizes the quality or character of the law [Hb, Lns, May]. It refers to 'the word of truth' of 1:18 [Hb], to 'the law of freedom' in 1:25 [Herm, Lns, May, Mit, My].

QUESTION—How are the two nouns related in the genitive construction νόμου ἐλευθεραίς 'law of freedom'?

It means that the law brings freedom [BKC, EBC, Hb, NTC, TG, Tsk, WBC; NIV, REB, TEV, TNT]: the law that sets people free.

DISCOURSE UNIT: 2:13 [NIGTC]. The topic is an exhortation to obedience.

2:13 For^a the judgment (is) without-mercy^b to the-(one) not having-done^c mercy;

LEXICON—a. γάρ (LN 89.23): 'for' [AB, Herm, HNTC, LN, Lns, NIC; KJV, NASB, NRSV, TEV], 'because' [LN; NIV], not explicit [WBC; NAB, NJB, REB, TNT].

b. ἀνέλεος (LN 88.82) (BAGD p. 64): 'without mercy' [AB, Herm, Lns; KJV, NIV, NJB, NRSV], 'unmerciful' [LN], 'merciless' [BAGD, HNTC, LN, WBC; NAB, NASB, TNT], 'without pity' [NIC]. The phrase ἡ κρίσις ἀνέλεος 'the judgment (is) without mercy' is translated 'in that judgment there will be no mercy' [REB], 'God will not show mercy when he judges' [TEV]. The reference is to God's mercy [Herm; TEV], while ἔλεος 'mercy' in the following clause refers to human mercy [Herm, ICC].

c. aorist act. participle of ποιέω (LN 42.7; 90.45) (BAGD I.1.c.β. p. 682): 'to do' [BAGD, LN], 'to show' [AB, BAGD, Herm, HNTC, NIC, WBC; KJV, NAB, NASB, NRSV, REB, TNT], 'to practice' [BAGD, LN], 'to act' [LN; NJB], 'to carry out' [LN], 'to exercise' [Lns]. The phrase τῷ μὴ ποιήσαντι ἔλεος 'to the one not having done mercy' is translated 'to anyone who has not been merciful' [NIV], 'the person who has not been merciful' [TEV]. The aorist tense looks at the actions of the person's whole life from the point of view of the future judgment [Alf, Hb]; his lack of mercy removes him from God's mercy [Hb].

QUESTION—What relationship is indicated by γάρ 'for'?

1. It indicates the grounds for the exhortation of 2:12 [Alf, EBC, Hb, ICC, My, NIC, TNTC]: speak and act thus, for the following reason(s). It also refers to 1:27 [My].

2. It indicates the grounds for an understood thought, namely, "this is a fearful threat" [NBC]: you will be judged (2:12); this is a fearful threat since judgment is without mercy.

3. It summarizes the preceding thought with a proverb and leads into the discussion of charity [NIGTC].
4. It is only loosely connected with 2:12 [HNTC] or is an isolated saying not connected with it [Herm]. It is a comment about the topic of judgment [HNTC].

QUESTION—What is the meaning of ἡ κρίσις 'the judgment'?

It refers to the coming judgment [Alf, Bg, EBC, Hb, Lns], the judgment referred to in 2:12 [Hb], as the definite article indicates [Alf, Hb].

mercy boasts-against^a judgment.

LEXICON—a. pres. mid. (deponent = act.) indic. of κατακαυχάομαι (LN **74.11**) (BAGD 2. p. 411): 'to boast against' [Herm, Lns], 'to boast in the face of' [HNTC], 'to laugh at' [NJB], 'to triumph over' [AB, BAGD, **LN**, NIC, WBC; NAB, NASB, NIV, NRSV, REB, TEV], 'to be more powerful than' [LN], 'to rejoice against' [KJV]. This clause is translated 'but the man who has shown himself merciful has nothing to fear from the judge' [TNT]. This verb is emphatic by its position [Hb].

QUESTION—What is the meaning of this clause?

The asyndeton (the absence of a connecting particle) adds emphasis [Lg]; it indicates that this clause states a general principle [Hb, May, NBC].
1. The meaning is that those who show mercy need not fear the judgment [AB, Alf, Blm, EBC, Hb, Herm, HNTC, ICC, May, My, NIC, NIGTC, TG, TNTC, Tsk; TNT]. Their mercy cancels out the judgment [Alf]. It is the converse of the preceding clause [ICC]. The judge is God [NIC, NIGTC, TG]. This does not mean that showing mercy earns salvation and God's mercy; rather, that being merciful shows that the person has been transformed by God's grace and therefore needs not fear the judgment [Hb].
2. It means that God's mercy triumphs over judgment [Mit, NBC, WBC].

DISCOURSE UNIT: 2:14–26 [AB, BKC, EBC, GNT, Hb, Herm, HNTC, ICC, Lg, Lns, NBC, NIC, NIGTC, NTC, TG, TNTC, Tsk, WBC; NAB, NASB, NIV, NJB, TEV]. The topic is a discussion of faith and deeds [GNT, Herm, HNTC, NTC, TG, Tsk, WBC; NAB, NASB, NIV, NJB, TEV], the relationship between faith and action [EBC], testing faith by its deeds [Hb], faith expressed in deeds [NIC], the faith that saves [TNTC], an exhortation to help other people [BKC], the worthlessness of faith not exercised [AB], having faith is not an excuse for not doing good deeds [ICC], unproductive faith [Lns], faith at work [NBC], the necessity of being generous [NIGTC].

DISCOURSE UNIT: 2:14–20 [Hb]. The topic is a description of useless faith.

DISCOURSE UNIT: 2:14–17 [Lns, Mit, NIGTC, NTC]. The topic is faith without deeds [NTC], faith without deeds is dead [Lns], an illustration of an ineffective Christian [NIGTC].

2:14 What (is) the advantage,[a] my brothers,[b] if someone says[c] to-have faith[d] but (does) not have deeds?[e]

LEXICON—a. ὄφελος (LN 65.40) (BAGD p. 599): 'advantage' [LN], 'benefit' [BAGD, LN], 'profit' [Lns], 'good' [AB, BAGD, HNTC, NIC, WBC; NAB, NIV, NRSV, REB, TEV, TNT], 'use' [Herm; NASB], 'help' [NJB]. This noun is also translated as a verb: 'to profit' [KJV]. The definite article makes this noun emphatic [Lg].

  b. ἀδελφός (LN 11.23): 'brother' [AB, HNTC, Lns, NIC, WBC; all versions except NRSV, REB, TEV], 'friend' [REB, TEV], 'fellow believer' [LN]. The plural ἀδελφοί is translated 'brothers and sisters' [Herm; NRSV]. This term indicates the author's tender concern for his readers [Hb].

  c. pres. act. subj. of λέγω (LN 33.69) (BAGD I.1.b.β. p. 468): 'to say' [AB, BAGD, HNTC, LN, NIC; KJV, NASB, NRSV, REB, TEV], 'to profess' [NAB], 'to claim' [Herm, WBC; NIV, NJB, TNT], 'to declare' [Lns]. James accepts the supposed person's claim but without necessarily agreeing that he does have true faith [Hb]. Such a person has no real faith; he only claims to have it [AB, BKC, HNTC, Lns]. This verb does not imply a false claim; it is used simply because faith without deeds can only be known by a statement [My].

  d. πίστις (LN 31.85; 31.102) (BAGD 2.d.δ. p. 664): 'faith' [AB, BAGD, Herm, HNTC, LN, Lns, NIC, WBC; all versions]. It is emphatic by forefronting, indicating that faith is the center of the discussion [Hb]. It refers to mere assent to Christian truth [Blm, EBC, Hb, ICC, Lg, NTC, Tsk] unaccompanied by appropriate deeds [Lg(M), Mit, NIGTC, TNTC, WBC], the type of faith described in the following verses, 2:15–16 [WBC]. It is the Christian faith [Herm, ICC, My] but without receiving Christ for new life [My]. It is only the Jewish belief in the unity of God, not faith as Paul uses it in Romans [EGT].

  e. ἔργον (LN 42.11) (BAGD 1.a. p. 307): 'deed' [BAGD, LN, WBC; NIV], 'work' [AB, Herm, HNTC, Lns, NIC; KJV, NASB, NRSV], 'act' [LN; NJB], 'action' [BAGD; REB, TEV]. The phrase ἔργα δὲ μὴ ἔχῃ 'but does not have deeds' is translated 'without practicing it' (i.e., faith) [NAB], 'but has nothing to show for it' [TNT]. The reference is to deeds which are evidence of faith [Alf, EBC, Hb, Herm, Lns, Mit, My, TG, TNTC] and the plural implies that numerous deeds should be involved [Hb].

QUESTION—How is this verse related to its context?

It introduces a further test of true faith [Hb, May]. It deals with the relationship between faith and deeds [Herm, HNTC, My]. It introduces the conclusion of the appeal for pure religion [TNTC].

  1. It is closely connected with the preceding [My, NIGTC, WBC]; it is the persons described in 2:1–13 who are condemned here [WBC].

  2. It is independent of the preceding passage and states the point of the following section [Herm].

JAMES 2:14   89

QUESTION—How are the two parts of this verse related?
   It consists of two related (rhetorical [Hb, Herm, NBC, TG, TNTC, Tsk, WBC]) questions [AB, Alf, EBC, Hb, Herm, Lns, My, NBC, NIC, NIGTC, NTC, TG, TNTC, Tsk, WBC; all versions]: What is the profit…? Is his faith able to save him? The use of these questions involves the readers in thinking about the matter [Hb].
QUESTION—What is the implied answer to the first question?
   The implied response is that there is no benefit [Lns, My, NIGTC, NTC, TG, TNTC, Tsk, WBC] for final salvation [NIGTC], which the second question confirms [My].
QUESTION—What is implied by the present tense of the infinitive ἔχειν 'to have' and the subjunctive ἔχῃ 'has'?
   The present tenses imply a continuing claim to have faith but a continual lack of appropriate deeds [Hb, WBC]. The two verbs are of equal importance [Lns].

Not is-able the faith[a] to-save[b] him?
LEXICON—a. πίστις: 'faith'. See this word in the preceding clause. The definite article indicates the faith referred to in the preceding clause [Alf, EBC, Hb, Lg, Lns, My, NIC, NTC, TNTC, WBC; NASB, NIV, NJB, REB, TEV, TNT]; it refers to the hypothetical person's faith [AB, HNTC, Mit]; it refers to Christian faith but which has no deeds [Herm, Lg].
   b. aorist act. infin. of σῴζω (LN 21.27) (BAGD 2.a.γ. p. 798): 'to save' [AB, BAGD, Herm, HNTC, LN, Lns, NIC, WBC; all versions except NJB], 'to bring salvation' [NJB]. Some think that the aorist tense implies obtaining salvation [NIC], or refers to present salvation already possessed [Lg]. Others think it refers to the event of final salvation [Hb, Herm, Mit, My, NIGTC, TNTC, WBC], especially since δύναται 'is able' implies a future event [Herm].
QUESTION—What is implied by μή 'not' which introduces this QUESTION?
   It expects a negative response [BKC, EBC, Hb, Herm, HNTC, ICC, Lns, May, NBC, NIC, NIGTC, NTC, TG, TNTC, Tsk, WBC; NAB]: it can't save him, can it? The pronoun αὐτόν 'him' shows that James does not deny that faith can save, but that it cannot save the person described here [Alf, My].

2:15 If[a] a-brother or sister be[b] naked[c] and lacking[d] the daily[e] food,[f]
TEXT—Some manuscripts add δέ 'but' after ἐάν 'if'. GNT does not deal with this variant; only Alf, Bg, Blm, Lg, and My add this word.
LEXICON—a. ἐάν (LN 89.67): 'if' [AB, Herm, HNTC, LN, Lns, NIC, WBC; KJV, NAB, NASB, NJB, NRSV, TNT], 'suppose' [NIV, REB, TEV].
   b. pres. act. subj. of ὑπάρχω (LN 13.5) (BAGD 2. p. 838): 'to be' [AB, BAGD, HNTC, LN, Lns, NIC, WBC; all versions except NAB, TEV]. The phrase γυμνοὶ ὑπάρχωσιν 'be naked' is translated 'has nothing to wear' [Herm; NAB], 'needs clothes' [**LN**], 'who need clothes' [TEV]. The verb implies a condition from the past still existing [Hb, NIC, Tsk, WBC], and that the needy persons are accessible to the one who claims to

have faith [Alf]. The plural, although the two subjects are singular and alternatives, is required for the sake of the following plural participle [Lns].

c. γυμνός (LN 49.22) (BAGD 3. p. 168): 'naked' [AB, LN, Lns; KJV, NRSV], 'without clothes' [NIC; NIV], 'without clothing' [NASB], 'in need of clothes' [NJB], 'poorly clad' [TNT], 'poorly dressed' [BAGD], 'ill-clad' [WBC], 'in rags' [REB], 'scantily dressed' [HNTC], 'to need clothes' [LN (57.43)]. The reference is to being actually or nearly naked [Alf, LN, My]; it is probably an overstatement to emphasize the extreme need [EBC]; it indicates lack of appropriate clothing [EGT, TNTC], being ill-clothed [Hb, ICC, Mit, NIGTC, NTC, TG, Tsk, WBC].

d. pres. mid. participle of λείπω (LN **57.43**) (BAGD 1.b. p. 470): 'to lack' [AB, BAGD, HNTC, LN, Lns, WBC; NRSV], 'to be in lack of' [Herm], 'to be in need of' [BAGD, LN; NASB], 'to be in want of' [NIC], 'to have not' [LN], 'to have not enough' [NJB, TNT], 'to be with not enough' [REB], 'to be without' [BAGD; NIV], 'to be destitute of' [KJV]. The phrase λειπόμενοι τῆς ἐφημέρου τροφῆς 'lacking the daily food' is translated 'has nothing to eat each day' [**LN**], 'has no food for the day' [NAB], 'has not enough food for one day' [TNT], 'don't have enough to eat' [TEV]. This participle is related to ὑπάρχωσιν [May].

e. ἐφήμερος (LN **67.183**) (BAGD p. 330): 'daily' [AB, BAGD, Herm, LN, Lns, NIC, WBC; KJV, NASB, NIV, NRSV], 'for the day' [BAGD, HNTC; NAB, REB], 'each day' [**LN**], 'on each day' [LN], 'to live on' [NJB]. The reference is to food for each day's need [Alf, EGT, ICC, My, NIC, NTC, WBC], food for even a single day [Hb], not knowing from day to day where his next meal will come from [Mit], indicating the urgent need [EGT, Hb, ICC].

f. τροφή (LN 5.1) (BAGD 1. p. 827): 'food' [AB, BAGD, Herm, HNTC, LN, Lns, NIC; all versions except TEV], 'sustenance' [WBC], 'nourishment' [BAGD].

QUESTION—How is this verse related to its context?

1. Verses 15–17 deal with the unprofitableness of faith without deeds [Bg, Blm, Hb, ICC, May, My, NIGTC, TNTC, Tsk], showing that the absence of deeds shows the absence of love or concern [Lg]. Verses 15–16 give a comparison [Bg, Blm, Herm], an illustration [EGT, Hb, HNTC, Lns, May, Mit, My, NIC, Tsk, WBC], a parable [ICC, NIGTC], which is hypothetical [Tsk] (as indicated by ἐάν 'if' [NBC, NIGTC, TG]) but very possible [BKC, Hb, Herm]; it is a real situation [WBC], with which the readers would agree [Mit]; it is almost ludicrous [EBC]. Verse 2:15 is parallel to 2:14, giving a second illustration of what one professes in contrast to the reality [Hb, May].

2. It refers symbolically to the attitude of Jewish Christians to Gentile Christians, their nakedness consisting of their lack of proper Jewish background, and their lack of daily food their lack of knowledge of God's word by Judaistic standards [Lg].

QUESTION—What is implied by the reference here to ἀδελφὸς ἢ ἀδελφή 'brother or sister'?
  The meaning is that they are fellow Christians [NIGTC, NTC, TNTC, Tsk, WBC; NRSV], making stronger the obligation to help [Alf, Hb, Mit, My]. The addition of ἀδελφή 'sister' points to distinctively Christian influence [EGT], insisting on equal treatment for both sexes [Hb]. Although the subject is 'brother *or* sister' (showing that no specific instance is in mind [Herm, NBC]), the plural verb ὑπάρχωσιν 'they be' implies that both are being considered together [Hb], as is indicated also by the plurals γυμνοί 'naked' and λειπόμενοι 'lacking' which refer to both nouns together [NTC].
QUESTION—What is implied by mentioning the two lacks, of clothing and of food?
  1. It indicates extreme destitution, leaving the person both cold and hungry [Hb].
  2. The reference is not to destitution but to a degree of poverty which might not call for immediate relief and which could be dismissed with hopeful wishes [HNTC].

2:16 **and someone of[a] you says to-them, "Go[b] in[c] peace,[d] keep-warm[e] and keep-well-fed,"[f]**
LEXICON—a. ἐκ with genitive object (LN 63.20): 'of' [AB, Herm, HNTC, LN, Lns, NIC, WBC; all versions except NAB, TEV], 'among' [LN], not explicit [TEV]. The phrase τις ἐξ ὑμῶν 'someone of you' is translated 'you' [NAB]. The reference is to someone from among the believers themselves [Alf].
  b. pres. act. impera. of ὑπάγω (LN 15.35; 15.52) (BAGD 1. p. 836): 'to go' [AB, HNTC, LN, Lns, NIC, WBC; NASB, NRSV], 'to go away' [BAGD, LN], 'to leave' [LN], 'to depart' [LN; KJV]. The phrase ὑπάγετε ἐν εἰρήνῃ 'go in peace' is translated 'go, I wish you well' [NIV], 'I wish you well' [NJB], 'may things go well for you' [Herm], 'keep well' [BAGD (2. p. 227)], 'good-bye' [REB], 'good-bye to you' [TNT], 'good-bye and good luck' [NAB], 'God bless you' [TEV].
  c. ἐν with dative object (LN 13.8): 'in' [AB, HNTC, LN, Lns, NIC, WBC; KJV, NASB, NRSV]. The sense is to depart in a state of peace [NIC] as an attendant circumstance [WBC].
  d. εἰρήνη (LN 22.42; 25.248) (BAGD 2. p. 227): 'peace' [AB, BAGD, HNTC, LN, Lns, NIC, WBC; KJV, NASB, NRSV], 'tranquility' [LN], 'freedom from worry' [LN].
  e. pres. mid. or pass. impera. of θερμαίνω (LN 79.73) (BAGD p. 359): 'to keep warm' [BAGD, NIC; NAB, NIV, NRSV, REB, TEV, TNT], 'to keep oneself warm' [NJB], 'to warm oneself' [BAGD, LN], 'to get warm' [WBC], 'to dress warmly' [BAGD], 'to clothe oneself warmly' [Herm]; as a passive 'to be warmed' [AB, HNTC, Lns; KJV, NASB]. The person is to be warmed by being properly clothed [My, NIGTC].

f. pres. mid. or pass. impera. of χορτάζω (LN 23.16) (BAGD 2.a p. 884): 'to keep well fed' [NAB, NIV], 'to have a good meal' [REB], 'to have a good dinner' [TNT], 'to eat well' [NIC; TEV], 'to eat one's fill' [BAGD, Herm, LN; NRSV], 'to eat plenty' [NJB], 'to be satisfied with food' [LN], 'to be satisfied' [BAGD], 'to be filled' [BAGD, HNTC, Lns, WBC; KJV, NASB]; as a passive 'to be fed' [AB, BAGD]. The meaning is to have their hunger satisfied [NIGTC, NTC].

QUESTION—What relationship is indicated by δέ 'and'?

It indicates the slight contrast between the need and the way in which it is supposedly met [Alf]. This verse is a continuation of the conditional proposition begun in the preceding verse [WBC]; it gives the hypothetical response to the hypothetical situation of the preceding verse [NIGTC, TNTC].

QUESTION—What is implied by the aorist tense of εἴπῃ 'says'?

It implies that he does nothing more after saying this [Lns].

QUESTION—What is implied by the words spoken to the needy persons?

1. They express a wish for their welfare [BKC, Blm, EBC, EGT, Hb, Herm, HNTC, Mit, My, NIGTC, TG, TNTC]. This is a common Hebrew farewell [EBC, Hb, HNTC, ICC, Mit, NIGTC, TG, TNTC].
    1.1 They are a comment based on faith without deeds [BKC, Blm, EBC, Hb, Herm, Mit, TNTC]: may your needs be met without my help.
    1.2 They indicate a mistaken idea or hope that God would meet their needs [EGT, HNTC] and that the Christian community need not help them [EGT]: may God meet your needs.
    1.3 They imply that the needs have been met [Alf]: go in peace with your needs met.
2. They express a rejection [Bg, Lg, May, NIC].
    2.1 They imply "Don't expect any help from me" [Bg, NIC].
    2.2 They express a rejection of help, but clothed in words which seemingly express good will [Lg, May].

QUESTION—What is implied by the two imperative verbs θερμαίνεσθε καὶ χορτάζεσθε 'keep warm and keep well fed'?

The present tense of both verbs implies a continuing state [Alf, NIC]: be continually warm and well-fed. The imperatives express an exhortation, not a command [My, WBC].

1. Both verbs are middle voice, with a reflexive sense, implying that they should get food and clothing for themselves [Bg, EBC, Herm, Lg, My, NIGTC, NTC, TG, Tsk, WBC]: clothe and feed yourselves. The thought is preposterous [EBC].
2. Both verbs are passive [Hb, HNTC, ICC, Lns, May, Mit, NIC], implying that the needed help should be given by someone else [Hb, Lns], by God [HNTC].

but you-give not to-them the needed^a (things) of-the body,

LEXICON—a. ἐπιτήδειος (LN 57.48) (BAGD p. 302): 'needed' [LN], 'needful' [KJV], 'necessary' [BAGD, LN; NASB], 'essential' [LN]. The phrase τὰ ἐπιτήδεια τοῦ σώματος 'the needed things of the body' is translated 'what the body needs' [AB], 'what their body needs' [NIC], 'the things their bodies need' [LN], 'their bodily needs' [WBC; NAB, NRSV, REB], 'the bodily necessities' [Herm, HNTC], 'the necessities for the body' [Lns], 'the necessities of life' [TEV], 'these bare necessities of life' [NJB], 'his physical needs' [NIV], not explicit [TNT].

QUESTION—What is implied by δέ 'but'?

It indicates the contrast from what they say to what they fail to do [WBC].

QUESTION—What is implied by μὴ δῶτε 'you do not give'?

Although only one person (τις ἐξ ὑμῶν 'someone of you') is represented as having wished the poor persons well, the failure to meet the needs is referred to all of the believers [Alf, Hb, My, NIGTC, Tsk]: all of you have failed to meet the needs. It indicates a failure to help even though they were well able to do so [Hb].

what (is) the advantage?^a

LEXICON—a. ὄφελος: 'advantage'. See this word at 2:14.

QUESTION—What is implied by this QUESTION?

This is the apodosis (conclusion) of the condition begun with ἐάν 'if' in 2:15 [WBC]. The QUESTION is rhetorical [Hb]. It implies that good words and good will are of no benefit if not accompanied by good deeds [Blm, EBC, EGT, Hb, Lg, Lns, My, NBC, NIC, WBC]. This is not irony, but rather is a correction of a mistaken idea [EGT].

2:17 Thus^a also the faith,^b if it-has^c not deeds,^d is dead^e by^f itself.

LEXICON—a. οὕτως (LN 61.9): 'thus' [AB, LN], 'so' [Herm, LN, Lns, NIC, WBC; NAB, NRSV, REB, TEV], 'even so' [KJV, NASB], 'in this way' [LN], 'in the same way' [NIV, NJB], 'in just the same way' [HNTC], 'like that' [TNT].

b. πίστις: 'faith'. See this word at 2:14. This word virtually refers to the person [Alf]. The definite article refers this faith to the faith mentioned in 2:14 [Hb, Lns, WBC].

c. pres. act. subj. of ἔχω (LN 90.51) (BAGD I.4. p. 333): 'to have' [BAGD, Herm, HNTC, Lns, WBC; KJV, NASB, NRSV], 'to include' [TEV], 'to include in itself' [BAGD], 'to be accompanied by' [AB; NIV], 'to produce' [LN], 'to bring about' [BAGD], 'to lead to' [REB], 'to cause' [BAGD, LN]. The phrase ἐὰν μὴ ἔχῃ ἔργα...καθ᾽ ἑαυτήν 'if it has not deeds...by itself' is translated 'without deeds...by itself' [NIC], 'if good deeds do not go with it' [NJB], 'that does nothing in practice' [NAB], 'if there is nothing to show for it' [TNT].

d. ἔργον: 'deed'. See this word at 2:14. The reference is to deeds which are the natural fruit of faith [My].

e. νεκρός (LN 65.39) (BAGD 1.b.β. p. 535): 'dead' [AB, BAGD, HNTC, Lns, NIC, WBC; all versions except NAB, REB], 'lifeless' [NAB, REB], 'useless' [BAGD, LN], 'barren' [Herm], 'futile' [LN], 'vain' [LN].

f. κατά with accusative object (LN 89.4) (BAGD II.1.c. p. 406): 'by' [BAGD, NIC; NASB, NIV, NRSV, REB], 'in' [AB, HNTC], 'in relation to' [LN], 'in regard to' [LN], 'according to' [Lns]. The phrase καθ' ἑαυτήν 'by itself' is translated 'alone' [Herm], 'being alone' [KJV], 'if it is alone' [TEV], 'on its own' [WBC].

QUESTION—What relationship is indicated by οὕτως 'thus'?

It introduces the application of the preceding illustration to inactive faith [Hb, Herm, ICC, My, NBC, NIGTC, TNTC, WBC].

QUESTION—What is implied by the clause ἐὰν μὴ ἔχῃ ἔργα 'if it does not have deeds'?

It means a faith that is not accompanied by appropriate deeds [Alf, Bg, Hb, ICC, Lg, May, Mit, TG] which true faith normally produces [Bg, Hb, Lg, May]. The conditional clause leaves open the conclusion concerning the nature of the faith, but the problem may be real [WBC]; in the situation being dealt with, the faith is without appropriate deeds [Hb]. This clause is an expansion of καθ' ἑαυτήν 'by itself' [Mit].

QUESTION—What is the meaning of νεκρά 'dead'?

It means that the professed faith is worthless [BKC, Blm, EBC, EGT, ICC, Mit, My, NIGTC, NTC, TG, TNTC, WBC], without power to save [My], although it is a kind of faith [EBC, ICC, Lns, My, NTC], an assent to the Christian faith [Lns]. The professed faith does not exist [Bg, NIC, Tsk]; it is not faith at all [Tsk].

QUESTION—What is the meaning of καθ' ἑαυτήν 'by itself'?

1. It means when it remains alone without appropriate deeds [BKC, Hb, Mit, NBC, NIC, NIGTC, NTC, Tsk, WBC; NIV, NJB, NRSV, REB, TEV]: faith alone without deeds. This phrase is emphatic by its final word order in the clause [WBC].

2. It means that it is dead in itself [Alf, Blm, EGT, HNTC, ICC, Lg(M), May], with no root to make it alive [Alf]. This phrase adds emphasis to νεκρά 'dead' [ICC].

3. It means with reference to itself [Bg, Lg, My]: faith in respect to itself.

DISCOURSE UNIT: 2:18–26 [Mit].

DISCOURSE UNIT: 2:18–20 [BKC, Lns, NIGTC]. The topic is the evidence of genuine faith [BKC], a rational argument [NIGTC].

DISCOURSE UNIT: 2:18–19 [NTC]. The topic is faith, deeds, and one's creed.

2:18 But someone will-say, "You have faith, and-I have deeds."
QUESTION—What relationship is indicated by ἀλλά 'but'?
1. It indicates that an objection (a partial objection [BKC]) will be raised to what precedes [EGT, Herm, My, NBC, NIGTC, WBC]: however, someone will say the following.
2. It carries on the argument [AB, Alf, Bg, Lg, May], as an adversative after implied negatives, with the sense of 'yes' [NIC]: yes, to continue my reasoning, someone will say the following.

QUESTION—Who is τις 'someone' who makes this comment?
1. It is representative of anyone who agrees with the author in objecting to the idea of faith which is not accompanied by deeds [Alf, Bg, Lg, NBC, NIC].
2. It is merely a hypothetical person who is introduced so that the author may present his own view by contrast [EBC, Herm, HNTC, ICC, Mit, TNTC]: suppose someone should say. Both κἀγώ 'and I' and σύ 'you' in the quotation are hypothetical, equivalent to the objector's saying, "One person has faith and another person has deeds," implying that faith and deeds are independent of one another [EBC, HNTC, ICC, Mit, TNTC].
3. It represents a hypothetical someone who stresses deeds at the expense of faith, although agreeing that faith not accompanied by deeds is dead [BKC].
4. It represents someone who objects to James's insistence on deeds to give evidence of faith [Hb, Lns, My, Tsk, WBC].
   4.1 The objector is telling Gentile Christians that a confession of faith is sufficient for them, leaving to others the practice of charitable deeds [AB].
   4.2 The objector means that a one-sided insistence on deeds is as improper as a one-sided insistence on faith [My].

QUESTION—What is the extent of the quotation in this verse?
1. It includes only the words "You have faith and I have deeds" [EBC, Hb, Herm, HNTC, ICC, Lns, Mit, My, NIGTC, NTC, TG, TNTC, Tsk; NAB, NIV, NRSV, REB, TEV, TNT].
2. It extends to the end of this verse [Alf; KJV, NASB].
3. It extends through 2:19 [AB, Bg, BKC, May, NBC, NIC, WBC].

QUESTION—What is implied by this clause?
1. For those who close the quotation in the middle of the verse:
   1.1 It is an assertion that faith and deeds are independent of one another [EBC, Hb, ICC, Lns, Mit, My, NIGTC, NTC, TG, TNTC, Tsk; REB, TEV, TNT]: you have faith, and I have deeds. The speaker means that both are acceptable [EBC, Hb, ICC, Lns, Mit, My, TG, TNTC, WBC; REB, TEV, TNT]. The σύ 'you' and κἀγώ 'and I' are equivalent to 'one person' and 'and another person' [ICC, NTC, TG, TNTC, Tsk; REB, TEV, TNT]. 'You' is a member/members of the church, and 'I' is James [Lns] (but this would require an *indirect* quotation here, "Someone will say *that* you have faith and I have deeds").

1.2 The reference is to faith without deeds [Herm]: you have faith without deeds.
2. For those who extend the quotation to the end of this verse, it implies that the person addressed cannot show his faith apart from deeds [Alf]: you can't demonstrate your faith if you do not have appropriate deeds.
3. For those who include 2:19 in the quotation [AB, Bg, BKC, NIC, WBC]:
   3.1 It implies that the person addressed cannot show that he has faith if he does not have deeds to support it [Bg, BKC, NBC, NIC].
   3.2 The objector is attempting to make faith and deeds separate from one another [AB, WBC].
   3.2.1 He implies that each of the two can be demonstrated by the other [WBC].
   3.2.2 He implies that faith without deeds is sufficient [AB].

Show[a] me your faith apart-from[b] the deeds, and-I will-show to-you the faith from[c] my deeds.

LEXICON—a. aorist act. impera. of δείκνυμι (LN 28.47) (BAGD 2. p. 172): 'to show' [AB, Herm, HNTC, LN, Lns, WBC; all versions], 'to make known' [LN], 'to demonstrate' [LN], 'to explain' [BAGD], 'to prove' [BAGD], 'to let one see' [NIC]. The meaning is to demonstrate visibly [Hb].

b. χωρίς with genitive object (LN 89.120) (BAGD 2.b.β. p. 890): 'apart from' [Herm, LN, WBC; NRSV, TNT], 'without' [AB, HNTC, LN, Lns, NIC; KJV, NAB, NASB, NIV, NJB, TEV], 'without making use of' [BAGD], 'independent of' [LN]. The phrase χωρὶς τῶν ἔργων 'apart from the deeds' is translated 'with no actions' [REB].

c. ἐκ with genitive object (LN 89.3; 89.77) (BAGD 3.g.β. p. 235): 'from' [HNTC, LN, Lns], 'by' [Herm, WBC; all versions except NAB], 'by means of' [LN], 'through' [AB, NIC], 'that underlies' [NAB].

QUESTION—What is implied by this clause?
1. For those who close the quotation in the middle of the verse, the latter part of the verse declares that faith cannot be demonstrated apart from deeds [EBC, Hb, Herm, HNTC, ICC, Lns, Mit, My, NIGTC, NTC, TG, TNTC, Tsk]. Faith does not necessarily imply deeds, but deeds do imply faith [Herm, ICC, Lns, My, NIGTC, NTC, TG]. By their word order, σοι 'to you' and ἐκ τῶν ἔργων μου 'by my deeds' are emphatic [Hb].
   1.1 James is speaking of his own deeds which demonstrate his faith [EBC, Hb, Herm, HNTC, NTC, Tsk]. He declares that he himself does have faith, and that his deeds demonstrate that he does [Hb, Herm].
   1.2 James is speaking in general terms, not of his own deeds; the κἀγώ 'and I' and σοι 'to you' are 'one person' and 'another person' as in the first part of the quotation [ICC].
2. For those who extend the quotation to the end of this verse, it continues the argument against faith without deeds [Alf]. The speaker does have

faith as well as deeds [Alf, NIC], and his deeds are evidence of his faith [NIC].
3. For those who include 2:19 in the quotation [AB, Bg, BKC, NIC, WBC]:
3.1 This latter part of 2:18 continues the argument against faith without deeds [Bg, BKC, NBC, NIC].
3.2 This latter part of 2:18 continues the argument that faith is sufficient without accompanying deeds [AB, WBC].

2:19 You believe that God is one;^a you-do^b well.

TEXT—Instead of εἷς ἐστιν ὁ θεός 'one is God', some manuscripts read εἷς θεός ἐστιν or εἷς ὁ θεός ἐστιν 'one God is', or ὁ θεὸς εἷς ἐστιν 'God one is'. The first reading means 'God is one' (or 'One is God' [Lns]); the second reading means 'there is one God'; the third and fourth reading can probably be translated either way. GNT has the first reading with a B rating, indicating that the text is almost certain. 'God is one' is read by AB, Alf, EGT, Hb, Herm, HNTC, Lg, Lns, May, NIGTC, WBC, NAB, NASB, NRSV; 'there is one God' is read by Bg, NIC, KJV, NIV, REB, TEV, TNT; NJB reads 'you believe in the one God'.

LEXICON—a. εἷς (LN 60.10; 63.4) (BAGD 2.b. p. 231): 'one' [AB, Herm, HNTC, LN, Lns, NIC, WBC; all versions], 'only one' [BAGD], 'single' [BAGD].
  b. pres. act. indic. of ποιέω (LN 90.45) (BAGD I.2.a.α. p. 682): 'to do' [AB, BAGD, Herm, HNTC, LN, Lns; KJV, NASB, NRSV]. The phrase καλῶς ποιεῖς 'you do well' is translated 'you are quite right' [NAB], 'good!' [NIC; NIV, TEV, TNT], 'excellent!' [WBC; REB], 'that is creditable enough' [NJB].

QUESTION—Who is speaking in this verse and what is the argument?
1. For those who limit the quotation in 2:18 to the first part of that verse, James is stating that acceptance of the Jewish "Shema," the belief in one God, is not enough [EBC, Hb, Herm, Lns, Mit, My, NIGTC, NTC, TG, TNTC]. The people addressed are self-satisfied in their orthodox intellectual belief [Mit].
2. For those who extend the quotation in 2:18 to the end of 2:18, James is now speaking directly, and no longer through the objector, to the person who has faith without deeds [Alf]: now I personally say to you.
3. For those who extend the quotation in 2:18 through 2:19:
3.1 James is ironically quoting the objector [AB]: you are saying that even the demons have that kind of faith! James implies that that would make the Christian faith identical with natural religion [AB].
3.2 The objector is continuing his argument.
3.2.1 He argues that mere belief in one God is good, but it is deeds that really count [BKC], since faith cannot prove that it exists apart from deeds [May]; he thus puts too much emphasis on deeds [BKC]. Such a faith is consistent with demons' faith [May].

3.2.2 He is continuing to make faith and deeds independent of one another; he points out that Jews, Christians, and even demons acknowledge one God [WBC].

QUESTION—Why is the existence or unity of God used as an illustration here?

It is used because this aspect of belief distinguishes biblical religion from heathenism [Blm, My, TNTC]. The author knows that he can compare this type of belief to the belief which the demons have, and that his readers will agree [NIGTC]. The Jews and Jewish Christians so pridefully held to the declaration of the Jewish Shema that it kept them from accepting the full Christian faith and resulted in terror of God [Lg].

QUESTION—Is this a statement or a QUESTION?

1. It is a statement [AB, Alf, Bg, BKC, EGT, Hb, Herm, ICC, Lg, Lns, May, My, NIC, NIGTC, NTC, TNTC, Tsk; KJV, NASB, NIV, NJB, NRSV, REB]: You believe.
2. It is a question [HNTC, NBC, WBC; NAB, TEV, TNT]: Do you believe?

QUESTION—What does the speaker state or ask concerning what the person addressed believes?

1. For those who read ὅτι εἷς ἐστιν ὁ θεός 'that God is one':
    1.1 The reference is to the unity of God [AB, EGT, Hb, Herm, HNTC, May, My, TNTC, WBC; NAB, NASB, NRSV]: God is one. The basis of this belief is the Jewish Shema [May, WBC].
    1.2 The reference is to their belief that there is only one God [EBC, Mit].
    1.3 The reference is to the identity of God [Lns]: One is God. This is the sense of all the textual readings [Lns].
2. For those who follow the other textual readings:
    2.1 The meaning is that there are no other gods [Blm, NTC; KJV, NIV, REB, TEV, TNT].
    2.2 The meaning is that God exists [NIC]: there is (only) one God.
    2.3 The meaning is primarily that there is only one God, but it includes God's existence and unity as well [ICC].
3. The meaning is that the person believes in the one true God [NJB]: you believe in the one God.

QUESTION—What is meant by καλῶς ποιεῖς 'you do well'?

1. It is favorable [AB, Alf, BKC, EBC, EGT, Hb, HNTC, ICC, Tsk; KJV, NAB, NASB, NJB, NRSV].
    1.1 It is James's comment, with reservation [Alf, EBC, EGT, Hb, HNTC, ICC, Tsk; NAB, NASB, NRSV], but with a touch of irony [ICC].
    1.2 It is the objector's comment [BKC]: that is good, so far as it goes.
    1.3 It is the objector's comment without reservation [AB]: that is good; even demons believe that.
2. It is ironic [Herm, Lns; NIV, REB, TEV, TNT]: Good! Even the demons believe that!
3. It is favorable since the belief is true, but what follows introduces the irony [Lg, May, Mit, My, NBC, NIGTC, TG, TNTC], which rises to sarcasm in the final words of the verse [My].

The demons[a] also believe and tremble.[b]

LEXICON—a. δαιμόνιον (LN 12.37) (BAGD 2. p. 169): 'demon' [BAGD, Herm, HNTC, LN, Lns, WBC; all versions except KJV], 'evil spirit' [AB, BAGD, LN], 'devil' [NIC; KJV]. The reference is to the evil spirits often mentioned in the Gospels [Hb, ICC, Lns, May].

b. pres. act. indic. of φρίσσω (LN **25.260**) (BAGD p. 866): 'to tremble' [AB; KJV, REB], 'to tremble with fear' [**LN**; NJB, TEV], 'to shudder' [BAGD, Herm, HNTC, Lns, NIC, WBC; NAB, NASB, NIV, NRSV, TNT], 'to shudder with fear' [LN], 'to be extremely afraid' [LN]. The present tense indicates their characteristic reaction [Hb].

QUESTION—What is implied by the phrase καὶ φρίσσουσιν 'and they tremble'?

It means that they are terrified [EBC, Hb, Herm, HNTC, ICC, Lg, Lns, Mit, My, NBC, NIGTC, TG, Tsk, WBC; NJB], since their belief merely makes them certain of their own terrible destiny [Alf, Bg, Hb, Lg, Mit, My, NIGTC, Tsk]. The demons' belief is not merely intellectual; it produces a response [HNTC, Mit]. This negative effect of belief adds force to the author's argument [Bg]. A faith which causes the person to tremble in fear is clearly not a true Christian faith [Herm, ICC].

QUESTION—What is meant by this statement?

The meaning is that mere intellectual faith is worth nothing [AB, Alf, Blm, EBC, EGT, Hb, Herm, HNTC, ICC, Lns, Mit, My, NIC, NTC, Tsk], is not enough without deeds [BKC, NBC, NIGTC, TNTC, WBC]. James is protesting the practice of some leaders who try to gain converts by telling them that mere faith is sufficient for their salvation [AB].

DISCOURSE UNIT: 2:20–24 [NTC]. The topic is Abraham's faith.

2:20 But do-you-wish[a] to-know,[b] O foolish[c] man, that the faith apart-from[d] the deeds is idle?[e]

TEXT—Instead of ἀργή 'idle', some manuscripts have νεκρά 'dead'. GNT reads ἀργή with a B decision, indicating that the text is almost certain. Only Bg, Blm, KJV read νεκρά.

LEXICON—a. pres. act. indic. of θέλω (LN 25.1) (BAGD 1. p. 355): 'to wish' [BAGD, HNTC, LN], 'to want' [BAGD, Herm, LN; NAB, NIV, NRSV, TEV, TNT], 'to desire' [BAGD, LN], 'to like' [NJB], 'to will' [Lns; KJV], 'to be willing' [NASB]. The phrase θέλεις γνῶναι 'do you wish to know' is translated 'do you have to be told' [REB], 'will you accept the truth' [NIC], 'don't you understand' [WBC], 'please consider' [AB].

b. aorist act. infin. of γινώσκω (LN 28.1) (BAGD 3.c p. 161): 'to know' [LN; KJV, NJB], 'to understand' [BAGD, HNTC, WBC; TNT], 'to comprehend' [BAGD], 'to realize' [Lns], 'to recognize' [NASB]. This active infinitive is also translated in the passive voice: 'to be shown' [Herm; NRSV, TEV], 'to be told' [REB]; and as a noun: 'proof' [NAB], 'evidence' [NIV].

c. κενός (LN 32.60) (BAGD 2.a.β. p. 427; 2.b. p. 428): 'foolish' [AB, BAGD, LN; NASB, NIV], 'senseless' [BAGD; NRSV], 'silly' [TNT], 'empty-headed' [WBC], 'stupid' [HNTC, LN], 'vain' [NIC; KJV], 'empty' [BAGD, Lns]. The phrase ὦ ἄνθρωπε κενέ 'O foolish man' is translated 'fool' [NJB], 'you fool' [**LN**; REB, TEV], 'you ignoramus' [NAB], 'you braggart' [Herm]. The sense is that the person is undependable [May], morally wrong [EBC, NIGTC, TNTC, WBC], intellectually wrong [NIGTC, TNTC, WBC], spiritually wrong [EBC]; he lacks knowledge and serious intention [Alf], good moral sense [Hb], real faith [Hb, Lg] and spiritual strength [Lg], spiritual understanding [EBC, Tsk]; his words are empty and vain [Bg]; the truth is so obvious that the person should hardly require proof [Blm]. It implies that James is impatient with the objector [Hb].

d. χωρίς with genitive object: 'apart from'. See this word at 2:18.

e. ἀργός (LN 42.46; **65.36**) (BAGD 3. p. 104): 'idle' [LN; NAB], 'useless' [AB, BAGD, Herm, HNTC, **LN**; NASB, NIV, NJB, TEV, TNT], 'unproductive' [BAGD], 'ineffectual' [WBC], 'barren' [Lns; NRSV], 'sterile' [NIC], 'futile' [REB]. There is an intentional play on words here—faith that does not have 'works' (ἔργων) does 'not work' (ἀργή = ἀ- ἔργον) [Herm, ICC, Lns, NTC, TNTC, WBC]. The meaning is that it does not work [TNTC], is without result [Alf]. This word reflects the author's strong objection to this empty faith [ICC].

QUESTION—What is the function of this verse?

The argument of these verses is not contradictory to Paul's theology; Paul argues that faith alone secures salvation, while James argues that faith which does not result in appropriate deeds is futile [BKC, HNTC].

1. It begins the illustration of Abraham's faith supported by deeds [Alf, Bg, EBC, My, TNTC]: I will now give you an illustration.
2. It is transitional, connected both with what precedes and what follows [Blm, EGT, Hb, Herm, May, Mit, NIGTC]. The author is continuing his objection to 'faith without deeds' [Herm].
3. It is the conclusion to the preceding [AB]: so do you see that faith without deeds is useless?

QUESTION—What relationship is indicated by δέ 'but'?

It introduces the further illustration [Alf, Hb, NIGTC, WBC], connecting it with what precedes [Lns].

QUESTION—Who is speaking in this verse?

The author is now speaking directly [EBC, EGT, May, Mit, My, NBC, NIGTC, NTC, TNTC, WBC].

JAMES 2:20   101

QUESTION—What is implied by the use of the phrase 'do you wish to know'?
It is a rhetorical QUESTION [TG]: I will now show you. This phrase is the equivalent of the future tense, 'will you know?' but implying the activity of the will [NTC].
1. It implies that the knowledge is clear [NIC, WBC] and can be rejected only by perverse intention [Alf, Hb]. This form of expression is common in this type of Greek argument, the diatribe [NIC, WBC].
2. It implies that the speaker is confident that he has won the argument [My].
3. It is the equivalent of a conditional clause [May, TNTC]: If you wish to have proof.
4. It continues the reproof [EBC, EGT, NTC]: Do you want evidence?
5. It is a courteous form [Bg]: Are you willing to know?

QUESTION—Who is the ἄνθρωπε κενέ 'foolish man'?
1. It is the objector [AB, Alf, BKC, EBC, Hb, Herm, HNTC, ICC, Mit, NTC, TNTC, WBC]. However, the objector is primarily a hypothetical figure which the author uses as a basis for presenting his own ideas [Herm, TNTC]. The objector is perhaps trying to impress with his cleverness rather than seeking truth [Mit].
2. It is the church member whom the objector is trying to influence [Lns].

QUESTION—What is implied by the term ἄνθρωπε κενέ 'foolish man'?
The seemingly harsh phrase [EBC] is typical of this type of Greek argument called the diatribe [Herm, HNTC, ICC, NBC, NIGTC, WBC]. The strong expression [BKC] (intensified by the ὦ 'O' [Lg, Lns, My, WBC], which strengthens the reproof [Alf, My, WBC]), results from his indignation [My], and impatience [NTC], since the truth is so obvious [Blm].

QUESTION—What is implied by the definite article with 'faith' ἡ πίστις 'the faith'?
It refers back to the kind of faith being discussed in the preceding verses [Hb].

QUESTION—What is implied by the definite article with 'deeds' τῶν ἔργων 'the deeds'?
The reference is to the deeds which naturally result from a proper faith [Hb].

DISCOURSE UNIT: 2:21–26 [BKC, NIGTC]. The topic is examples of true faith [BKC], a biblical argument with Abraham and Rahab as examples [NIGTC].

DISCOURSE UNIT: 2:21–25 [Hb]. The topic is saving faith manifested through works.

DISCOURSE UNIT: 2:21–24 [Lns]. The topic is the inclusion of works with Abraham's faith.

2:21 (Was) not Abraham our father[a] justified[b] by[c] deeds, having-offered[d] Isaac his son upon[e] the altar?[f]

LEXICON—a. πατήρ (LN 10.20) (BAGD 2.e. p. 635): 'father' [AB, BAGD, Herm, HNTC, Lns, NIC, WBC; KJV, NAB, NASB, NJB, REB, TNT], 'forefather' [LN], 'ancestor' [LN; NIV, NRSV, TEV].

b. aorist pass. indic. of δικαιόω (LN 88.16) (BAGD 3.a. p. 197): 'to be justified' [AB, Herm, HNTC, NIC; KJV, NAB, NASB, NJB, NRSV, REB], 'to be put right with God' [TEV], 'to be made right with God' [TNT], 'to be acquitted' [BAGD], 'to be declared righteous' [Lns], 'to be considered righteous' [NIV], 'to be pronounced and treated as righteous' [BAGD], 'to be shown to be right' [LN], 'to be proved to be right' [LN], 'to be proved righteous' [WBC]. This word refers to being *declared* righteous [NIGTC] (as the suffix -οω normally indicates), not to *being* righteous [EBC, ICC, Lg, May, My]; it means here to be shown to be justified [Tsk]. The passive voice implies God as the one who justified him [Hb, Lns, My, NIGTC].

c. ἐκ with genitive object (LN 89.25; 89.77): 'by' [AB, Herm, HNTC, NIC, WBC; all versions except NIV, TEV], 'by means of' [LN (89.77)], 'through' [TEV], 'because of' [LN (89.25)], 'as a result of' [Lns]. The phrase ἐξ ἔργων 'by deeds' is translated 'for what he did' [NIV]. This preposition indicates the source of the justification [EBC, Lns].

d. aorist act. participle of ἀναφέρω (LN **53.17**) (BAGD 2. p. 63): 'to offer' [AB, Herm, LN, NIC, WBC; all versions except NASB], 'to offer up' [BAGD, HNTC, **LN**; NASB], 'to bring up' [Lns]. The meaning is to *bring* as a sacrifice, not to *make* a sacrifice [My].

e. ἐπί with accusative object (LN 83.46): 'upon' [Herm, LN, Lns; KJV, REB], 'on' [AB, HNTC, LN, NIC, WBC; all versions except KJV, REB].

f. θυσιαστήριον (LN 6.114) (BAGD 1.c. p. 366): 'altar' [AB, BAGD, Herm, HNTC, LN, NIC, WBC; all versions], 'altar of sacrifice' [Lns].

QUESTION—What is indicated by οὐκ 'not'?

It indicates that the QUESTION expects an affirmative answer [Hb, Lns, My, NBC, NIGTC, WBC]: Abraham was justified by deeds. It implies that James assumes that his readers will agree [Lns, My] and his opponents as well [My]. The QUESTION is rhetorical [TG].

QUESTION—What is meant by the phrase 'Ἀβραὰμ ὁ πατὴρ ἡμῶν 'Abraham our father'?

This phrase is forefronted for emphasis upon Abraham as the example [Hb].

1. It implies that James and his readers were Jews, since Abraham was their forefather [Alf, EBC, Lns, May, My].
2. It does not necessarily mean that James's readers were all Jews, since Paul calls Abraham the father of gentile Christians (Rom. 4:11, 16–17) [Hb, Herm, HNTC, ICC, Mit, NIC, TG, Tsk] and all Christians claimed Abraham as their father [Mit, NIC].

JAMES 2:21

QUESTION—What is meant by ἐξ ἔργων ἐδικαιώθη 'he was justified by deeds'?
1. It is not a contradiction of Paul's theology, but simply means that faith should be accompanied by Christian deeds [AB, Bg, BKC, Blm, EBC, Hb, ICC, Lg, Lns].
2. James's position that justification requires deeds as well as faith is not in agreement with Paul's position [HNTC].

QUESTION—What is meant by ἐδικαιώθη 'he was justified'?
1. It means that he was considered or declared to be righteous [Alf, Bg, BKC, EBC, Hb, Herm, ICC, Lg, Lns, May, My, NIGTC, NTC, TG, TNTC, WBC; NIV] by a deed which resulted from his faith [Bg, EBC, Hb, Herm, ICC, Lns], a deed which was the evidence of his faith [BKC]. He was justified by God [Bg, EBC, Herm, Lg, Lns, My, NIGTC, NTC, TG, TNTC, WBC].
2. It means that he was shown to be righteous by his deed [Blm, Mit, NIC, Tsk] which arose from his faith [Mit].
3. It means that God recognized that Abraham was righteous as a result of his deed [Herm, HNTC, NBC].
4. It means that he was put right with God [HNTC; TEV, TNT].

QUESTION—What relationship is indicated by ἐκ 'by'?
1. It indicates means [AB, Alf, WBC]: by means of his deed. His deed was the means by which his righteousness was demonstrated [WBC].
2. It indicates the source [EBC, Hb, Lns, TG]: his deed was the source of the justification.
3. It indicates the reason for his justification [My]: he was justified because of his deed.

QUESTION—What is the significance of the plural form ἔργων 'deeds'.
1. The plural ἔργων 'deeds' refers to deeds as a category (meaning 'by his conduct' [Herm]), of which this act was a crowning example [Alf, Hb, Herm, Lg, Lns, My].
2. The plural refers to the ten different testings Abraham endured according to Jewish scholars. The crowning test was that of giving up Isaac [NIGTC].

QUESTION—What relationship is indicated by the participial form ἀνενέγκας 'having offered'?
1. It expresses the grounds of his justification [AB, Blm, EBC, ICC, Tsk; NJB, REB]: he was justified because he offered his son.
2. It expresses the means of his justification [TNT]: he was justified by offering his son.

QUESTION—What does the aorist tense of the participial form ἀνενέγκας 'having offered' indicate?
  The aorist tense refers to the event of God's pronouncement upon Abraham's act of obedience [Hb, Lns] and considers his act as completed even though it was not carried out [Hb].

1. It indicates that his obedience was prior to God's pronouncement [Hb]: he was justified after offering his son.
2. It indicates that his obedience was simultaneous to God's pronouncement [Alf]: he was justified when he offered his son.

2:22 **You see**[a] **that the faith was-working-together**[b] **with-his deeds and by**[c] **the deeds the faith was-perfected,**[d]

LEXICON—a. pres. act. indic. of βλέπω (LN 24.7; 32.11) (BAGD 7.b. p. 144): 'to see' [AB, Herm, HNTC, LN, Lns, NIC, WBC; all versions], 'to understand' [LN], 'to perceive' [LN], 'to recognize' [LN], 'to discover' [BAGD], 'to find' [BAGD]. The verb is singular [Hb, Herm, Lns, NBC, NIGTC, TNTC, WBC], referring to the person mentioned in the preceding verses [NBC, NIGTC, TNTC, WBC].

b. imperf. act. indic. of συνεργέω (LN 42.15) (BAGD p. 787): 'to work together' [NIV, TEV, TNT], 'to work together with' [AB, LN; NJB], 'to work with' [BAGD; KJV, NASB], 'to be at work with' [WBC], 'to be at work in' [REB], 'to be active together with' [LN], 'to be active along with' [NRSV], 'to share in' [NIC], 'to assist' [Herm; NAB], 'to aid' [BAGD], 'to help' [Lns], 'to cooperate with' [HNTC]. This verb indicates the close connection between Abraham's faith and his deeds; but with the deeds supporting his faith, not as an equal factor with faith [Hb, Lns]. The imperfect tense implies that this cooperation was characteristic of Abraham's life [Hb, NIC, NTC, TNTC, Tsk, WBC].

c. ἐκ with genitive object: 'by'. See this word at 2:21.

d. aorist pass. indic. of τελειόω (LN 68.22) (BAGD 2.e.β. p. 810): 'to be perfected' [BAGD; NASB, REB], 'to be made perfect' [AB; KJV, TEV], 'to become perfect' [NJB], 'to be completed' [LN; TNT], 'to be made complete' [HNTC; NIV], 'to be brought to completion' [WBC; NRSV], 'to be implemented' [NAB], 'to be consummated' [NIC], 'to be brought to one's goal' [Lns]. The phrase ἐκ τῶν ἔργων ἡ πίστις ἐτελειώθη 'by the deeds the faith was perfected' is translated 'deeds perfected his faith' [Herm]. The aorist tense indicates a completed act [Alf]. This verb implies that Abraham's faith existed before his deed, and the deed brought faith to its proper goal [Hb, ICC, Lg, Lns, Mit, My, NBC, NIGTC], to maturity [NIC, TNTC, WBC]. His deed showed that his faith was genuine [Bg, EBC, Tsk]. The passive voice implies that the perfecter was God [Hb, Lns].

QUESTION—What is the form of this verse?
1. It is a statement [AB, Alf, EGT, Hb, Herm, HNTC, Lg, Lns, May, Mit, My, NIGTC, TG, TNTC; NAB, NASB, NIV, NJB, NRSV]: you see. It is the logical deduction from the preceding [EGT, Hb, My, NIGTC; NAB]; the necessity of faith was granted both by James and his objectors, and this verse shows the importance of deeds [My, TNTC]. It explains θέλεις γνῶναι 'do you wish to know' in 2:20 [May, TG]. It implies that the conclusion is obvious [Alf, Hb].

2. It is an exhortation [WBC]: you ought to see. This is an attempt to persuade James's opponent that faith and deeds are not to be considered as separate [WBC].
3. It is a question [Blm, Tsk; KJV, REB, TEV, TNT]: do you see? It expects an affirmative answer [REB, TNT].

QUESTION—How much is included under βλέπεις ὅτι 'you see that'?
1. For those who interpret this verse as a statement:
1.1 It includes through 2:23 [EGT, ICC, Lns]: You see that his faith and deeds worked together . . . and he was called a friend of God.
1.2 It includes only 2:22 [Herm, HNTC, WBC; NAB, NIV, NJB, NRSV]: you see that his faith and deeds worked together to perfect his faith.
1.3 It includes only part of 2:22 [AB]: You see that his faith and deeds worked together; so his faith was made perfect by his works.
2. For those who interpret this verse as a question:
2.1 It includes only 2:22 [Blm; KJV, REB, TEV]: Do you see that his faith and deeds worked together to perfect his faith?
2.2 It includes only part of 2:22 [TNT]: Do you see that his faith and deeds worked together? His faith was completed by what he did.

QUESTION—Where is the emphasis in the two clauses following ὅτι 'that'?
'Faith' is emphasized in the first clause and 'deeds' in the second [Bg].

QUESTION—What meaning is implied by the article ἡ 'the' with πίστις 'faith'?
1. It implies possession and refers to Abraham's faith [Hb; NIV, NJB, TEV, TNT]: his faith.
2. It is abstract in both instances [Alf]: faith.

QUESTION—What is the meaning of the plural nouns ἔργοις and ἔργων 'deeds'?
They are the plural of the category, actually referring to only one work, as in the preceding verse [Alf, Hb].

QUESTION—What relationship is indicated by ἐκ 'by'?
1. It sets forth the deed as the grounds or source [Alf, Lns]: the grounds for the perfection of his faith was his deed. The deed demonstrated the faith [Hb].
2. It states how Abraham's faith became really faith [Herm]: through his deed his faith was perfected.

2:23 and was-fulfilled[a] the Scripture the-(one) saying, "And Abraham believed[b] God, and it-was-credited[c] to-him as[d] righteousness";[e]

LEXICON—a. aorist pass. indic. of πληρόω (LN 13.106) (BAGD 4.a. p. 671): 'to be fulfilled' [AB, BAGD, Herm, HNTC, LN, Lns, NIC, WBC; all versions except REB, TEV], 'to be fulfillment' [REB], 'to come true' [TEV], 'to be caused to happen' [LN]. The passive voice implies that it was fulfilled by God [Lns].
b. aorist act. indic. of πιστεύω (LN 31.85) (BAGD 1.b. p. 661): 'to believe' [AB, BAGD, Herm, HNTC, Lns, WBC; all versions except NJB, REB],

'to believe in' [LN], 'to put one's faith in' [NIC; NJB, REB], 'to have faith in' [LN], 'to trust in' [LN].
  c. aorist pass. indic. of λογίζομαι (LN 57.227) (BAGD 1.a. p. 476): 'to be credited' [BAGD; NAB, NIV], 'to be reckoned' [AB, HNTC, Lns, WBC; NASB, NRSV], 'to be reckoned to one's credit' [NIC], 'to be counted' [REB], 'to be imputed' [KJV], 'to be considered' [NJB], 'to be put into one's account' [LN], 'to be recorded in one's account' [Herm]. The phrase ἐλογίσθη αὐτῷ εἰς δικαιοσύνην 'it was accounted to him as righteousness' is translated 'God accepted him as righteous' [TEV, TNT]. The passive voice implies that God did this [WBC].
  d. εἰς with accusative object (LN 13.62): 'as' [AB, Herm; NAB, NASB, NIV, NJB, NRSV, REB], 'for' [HNTC, LN, Lns, NIC, WBC; KJV].
  e. δικαιοσύνη (LN 88.13) (BAGD 3. p. 197): 'righteousness' [AB, BAGD, Herm, LN, Lns, NIC, WBC; KJV, NASB, NIV, NRSV, REB], 'justification' [HNTC], 'justice' [NAB], 'making (him) upright' [NJB].
QUESTION—What relationship is indicated by the initial καί 'and'?
  1. It introduces the additional result of Abraham's act [Hb, ICC]: his faith was perfected by his deed and, in addition, the Scripture passage was fulfilled.
  2. It introduces the confirmation of the preceding argument [WBC].
QUESTION—What is meant by the Scripture being 'fulfilled'?
  1. It was in Abraham's offering up Isaac that this Scripture passage received its full realization [Alf, Blm, EBC, ICC, NBC, NIC, NIGTC], its second fulfillment [Bg], its verification [Lg], its proof [May]. God's previous justification of Abraham was vindicated by Abraham's obedience here [EBC, Hb, TNTC]. He was declared to be righteous because he obeyed God [NIC]. This verse is the principal point of the argument [Herm].
  2. In Abraham's obedient life in general, and in his offering up Isaac as a specific example, this Scripture passage received its full realization [NTC, Tsk].
  3. Abraham's faith expressed years earlier was vindicated when God now maintained his prophecy by rescuing Isaac [Lns].
QUESTION—What is implied by the phrase ἐπίστευσεν τῷ θεῷ 'he believed God'?
  1. It means that he put his faith in God [NJB, REB].
  2. The dative case τῷ θεῷ 'God' implies that Abraham believed what God said, not that he believed *in* God [ICC, Lns, TNTC]. He believed that God would fulfill the promise to grant him an heir [ICC].

and he-was-called[a] friend[b] of-God.
LEXICON—a. aorist pass. indic. of καλέω (LN **33.131**) (BAGD 1.a.β. p. 399): 'to be called' [AB, BAGD, Herm, HNTC, LN, Lns, NIC, WBC; KJV, NASB, NIV, NRSV, REB, TEV], 'to be addressed as' [BAGD], 'to be designated as' [BAGD], 'to receive the title' [NAB], 'to receive the name' [NJB]. This clause is translated 'and God called him his friend' [TNT].

b. φίλος (LN 34.11) (BAGD 2.a.β. p. 861): 'friend' [AB, BAGD, Herm, HNTC, LN, Lns, NIC, WBC; all versions].

QUESTION—What relationship is indicated by καί 'and'?

It indicates that Abraham's obedient act had this further result [Hb, Lns, TNTC; NAB] or reward [Herm, ICC]. It was a second manifestation of the fulfillment of the Scripture [Lg]: the Scripture was also fulfilled in his being called a friend of God. It states the proof of Abraham's justification [May]: as a proof that he was justified, he was called a friend of God.

QUESTION—Where is Abraham called the friend of God?
1. He is thus indirectly designated in Isa. 41:8 and 2 Chron. 20:7 [Alf, Bg, Hb, HNTC, ICC, Lns, May, Mit, My, NIC, NIGTC, TG, TNTC, Tsk, WBC].
2. He was thus regarded by God when he offered up Isaac [My].

2:24 You-see[a] that by[b] deeds a-man is-justified[c] and not by[b] faith[d] only.

LEXICON—a. pres. act. indic. of ὁράω (LN **32.11**) (BAGD 1.c.α. p. 578): 'to see' [AB, Herm, HNTC, NIC; all versions except NAB], 'to understand' [BAGD, LN], 'to perceive' [Lns; NAB], 'to be aware' [WBC]. The verb is plural, addressed to all the readers [EGT, Hb, Herm, NBC, NIC, NIGTC, NTC, TG, TNTC, Tsk, WBC].

b. ἐκ with genitive object: 'by'. See this word at 2:22.

c. pres. pass. indic. of δικαιόω: 'to be justified'. See this word at 2:21.

d. πίστις: 'faith'. See this word at 2:17.

QUESTION—What is the form of this verse?
1. It is a statement [AB, Alf, Bg, Herm, HNTC, ICC, Lg, Lns, My, TNTC, Tsk; all versions except NAB]: you see.
2. It is an exhortation [NTC, WBC; NAB]: you should see.
3. It is a rhetorical question [NIC]: do you see?

QUESTION—What is meant by this verse?

It is a general conclusion [EBC, EGT, HNTC, NIGTC] based on Abraham's example [Alf, Blm, Mit, My, NTC, TNTC, Tsk]. It answers the QUESTION in 2:14 [Hb, ICC]. It means that a person is justified by faith, but not by faith alone [EBC, NIC], at the final judgment [My, NIGTC, TNTC]. His justification must be demonstrated by appropriate deeds [AB, Alf, Bg, Hb]; deeds help to show that a person is justified [Blm, EBC]. James argues against a superficial faith which produces no deeds [AB, EBC, HNTC, Lns, NIGTC, WBC]. Paul's argument was that deeds could not earn justification [AB, EBC, Lns, NIGTC, TNTC, WBC]. James probably wrote earlier than Paul's epistles [Hb]; he had not read Romans [NIGTC].

DISCOURSE UNIT: 2:25–26 [Lns, NTC]. The topic is faith and righteousness [NTC], Rahab's faith included deeds [Lns].

2:25 And likewise[a] (was) not also[b] Rahab the prostitute[c] justified[d] by deeds,

LEXICON—a. ὁμοίως (LN 64.1) (BAGD p. 568): 'likewise' [BAGD, LN, Lns; KJV, NRSV], 'similarly' [BAGD, NIC], 'in the same way' [BAGD, Herm, HNTC; NASB, NIV], 'it was the same' [TEV], 'the same is true' [REB], 'the same was true' [AB], 'to give another instance' [WBC], 'there is another example of the same kind' [NJB], not explicit [NAB, TNT]. This word (together with δὲ καί 'and also' [NIGTC, WBC]) indicates the similarity of this and the preceding example [Alf, Hb, Lg, Lns, My, NIGTC, WBC].
  b. καί (LN 89.93): 'also' [Herm, LN, Lns, NIC; KJV, NASB, NRSV, REB], 'in addition' [LN], 'too' [TNT], 'even' [NIV], not explicit [AB, HNTC, WBC; NAB, NJB, TEV].
  c. πόρνη (LN 88.275) (BAGD 1. p. 693): 'prostitute' [LN, NIC, WBC; NIV, NJB, NRSV, REB, TEV, TNT], 'harlot' [AB, BAGD, Herm, HNTC, Lns; KJV, NAB, NASB]. This word has its literal meaning here [Alf, EGT, Hb, ICC, Mit, NIC]. The definite article with this noun indicates that she is the well-known Rahab [Lg].
  d. aorist pass. indic. of δικαιόω: 'to be justified'. See this word at 2:21.

having-received[a] the messengers[b] and by-another way having-sent-(them)-out?[c]

LEXICON—a. aorist mid. (deponent = act.) participle of ὑποδέχομαι (LN 34.53) (BAGD p. 844): 'to receive' [AB, BAGD, Herm, LN, Lns, NIC; KJV, NASB], 'to welcome' [BAGD, HNTC, LN, WBC; NJB, NRSV, REB, TEV, TNT], 'to give lodging' [NIV], 'to harbor' [NAB]. The word implies welcome and entertainment as guests [Hb, Lg].
  b. ἄγγελος (LN 33.195) (BAGD 1.a. p. 7): 'messenger' [AB, BAGD, Herm, HNTC, LN, Lns, NIC, WBC; all versions except NIV, TEV], 'spy' [NIV, TEV]. The use of 'messengers' rather than 'spies' suggests that they were God's messengers to Rahab [Hb]. They were 'messengers' only in that they were to report back to Joshua [HNTC].
  c. aorist act. participle of ἐκβάλλω (LN 15.68) (BAGD 2. p. 237): 'to send out' [Herm, HNTC, LN, NIC, WBC; KJV, NAB, NASB, NRSV], 'to send off' [NIV], 'to send away' [AB, BAGD; REB, TNT], 'to hurry (someone) out' [Lns], 'to help to escape' [TEV]. The phrase καὶ ἑτέρᾳ ὁδῷ ἐκβαλοῦσα 'by another way having sent (them) out' is translated 'and showed them a different way to leave' [NJB]. Haste is implied [Alf, Hb, Lg, My], effort [Lg], difficulty [NIC], and fear [Alf, Hb] for the messengers' safety [Hb].

QUESTION—Why is this verse mentioned?

It is another instance of the necessity of good deeds [AB, Herm, Lns, Mit, NIGTC, NTC, Tsk, WBC]. Having mentioned a devout Jewish man, James now mentions a previously non-devout gentile woman [Bg, EBC, Lg, Lns, NTC, TNTC, Tsk], to make his argument inclusive [Bg, Hb, Mit, NTC, Tsk] and more compelling [NIC]. Rahab was justified in the same way as Abraham, by deeds proceeding from faith [Blm, EBC, Hb, Herm, HNTC, Mit, NIC, TNTC]. Her faith is not mentioned but is assumed [Herm, HNTC, NIC, NIGTC, NTC, TNTC, Tsk, WBC]. Rahab's identity is emphasized by forefronting [Hb, Lns].

QUESTION—What is implied by this QUESTION?
The use of a question challenges the readers to give attention to the example [Hb]. The question is rhetorical [NIGTC, NTC, TG, WBC], and οὐκ 'not' shows that the question expects an affirmative answer [Hb, NIGTC, NTC, TG, WBC].

QUESTION—What is meant by καί 'also/even'?
1. It means Rahab in addition to Abraham [AB, Hb, Herm; KJV, NASB, NRSV, REB, TEV, TNT]: Rahab also.
2. It means even such a person as Rahab [BKC, EBC, HNTC, ICC, NTC, Tsk; NIV]: even Rahab. She is sharply contrasted with Abraham [HNTC, ICC].

QUESTION—What relationship is indicated by the use of the participial forms ὑποδεξαμένη 'having received' and ἐκβαλοῦσα 'having sent out'?
1. They state the reason for her justification [Blm, NIC, NTC, Tsk; NJB, TEV, TNT]: God justified her because she received them and showed them a different way.
2. They identify her deeds [ICC, Lns, My, TNTC; REB]: her deeds consisted of welcoming them and sending them away by a different route.

DISCOURSE UNIT: 2:26 [Hb]. The topic is the union of faith and deeds.

2:26 For^a just-as^b the body apart-from^c spirit^d is dead,

LEXICON—a. γάρ (LN 89.23): 'for' [Herm, HNTC, LN, Lns, NIC; KJV, NASB, NRSV], 'because' [LN], 'so then' [TEV], not explicit [AB, WBC; NIV, NJB, REB, TNT]. The phrase ὥσπερ γάρ 'for just as' is translated 'be assured, then' [NAB].

b. ὥσπερ (LN 64.13) (BAGD 1. p. 899): 'just as' [AB, BAGD, Herm, HNTC, LN; NASB, NRSV], 'as' [BAGD, LN, Lns, NIC, WBC; KJV, NIV, NJB, REB, TEV], not explicit [TNT].

c. χωρίς with genitive object (LN **89.120**) (BAGD 2.b.γ. p. 890): 'apart from' [BAGD, LN, WBC], 'without' [AB, Herm, HNTC, **LN**, Lns, NIC; all versions except REB], 'without possessing' [BAGD]. The phrase χωρὶς πνεύματος 'apart from spirit' is translated 'when there is no breath left in it' [REB].

d. πνεῦμα (LN 23.186; 26.9) (BAGD 2. p. 674): 'spirit' [AB, BAGD, LN (26.9), NIC; KJV, NASB, NIV, NJB, NRSV, TEV], 'life-spirit' [BAGD], 'soul' [BAGD, Herm], 'breath' [BAGD, HNTC, LN (23.186), Lns, WBC; NAB, REB, TNT].

QUESTION—What relationship is indicated by γάρ 'for'?
1. It is the general conclusion to the argument [Alf, Bg, BKC, Blm, EBC, Hb, ICC, My, NIGTC, NTC, TG, TNTC, WBC], stated as a comparison

[Alf, Blm, Hb, My, NIGTC], as an illustration [EBC, NTC]. The comparison is indicated by ὥσπερ ... οὕτως καί 'just as ... thus also' [Hb]; in both parts of the comparison, if the second member is missing, the result is death [Hb, Lns].
2. It indicates that the truth of the preceding verse is derived from the axiom expressed in the present verse [Alf, Hb, My, WBC]: it is true that Rahab was justified by her deeds, because faith without deeds is dead.

QUESTION—What is implied by the presence of the definite article with the first member of each pair in the comparison, and the absence of the definite article with the second member?

The definite article makes 'body' [Lg] and 'faith' generic, including all instances in general; while the absence of the article makes 'spirit' and 'deeds' qualitative, emphasizing their nature [Hb]. The article with 'deeds' indicates the deeds appropriate to faith [My].

QUESTION—What is the meaning of πνεῦμα 'spirit' here?
1. It means the inner being, the human spirit or soul [AB, Bg, EBC, Hb, Herm, ICC, Lg, Mit, My, NIC, NTC, TG; KJV, NASB, NIV, NJB, NRSV, TEV].
2. It means breath [EGT, Lns, WBC; NAB, REB, TNT].

thus^a also^b the faith apart-from^c deeds is dead.

LEXICON—a. οὕτως (LN 61.9): 'thus' [LN], 'so' [AB, Herm, HNTC, LN, Lns, NIC, WBC; all versions except NAB, TEV], 'in this way' [LN], not explicit [NAB, TEV].
  b. καί (LN 89.93): 'also' [AB, Herm, LN, Lns, WBC; KJV, NASB, TEV], 'too' [TNT], not explicit [HNTC, NIC; NAB, NIV, NJB, NRSV, REB].
  c. χωρίς with genitive object (LN 89.120) (BAGD 1.b.β. p. 890): 'apart from' [LN, WBC], 'without' [AB, Herm, HNTC, LN, Lns, NIC; all versions except REB], 'without making use of' [BAGD], 'without practicing (something)' [BAGD], 'divorced from' [REB], 'that does not express itself in' [BAGD].

QUESTION—Why is this clause mentioned?
It is the principal point of the argument [Hb, Herm].
  c. χωρίς with genitive object (LN 89.120) (BAGD 1.b.β. p. 890): 'apart from' [LN, WBC], 'without' [AB, Herm, HNTC, LN, Lns, NIC; all versions except REB], 'without making use of' [BAGD], 'without practicing (something)' [BAGD], 'divorced from' [REB], 'that does not express itself in' [BAGD].

QUESTION—Why is this clause mentioned?
It is the principal point of the argument [Hb, Herm].

DISCOURSE UNIT: 3:1–4:12 [NIGTC, TNTC]. The topic is an insistence on pure speech [NIGTC], quarrels among the believers [TNTC].

DISCOURSE UNIT: 3:1–18 [BKC, Hb, ICC, Lg, NIC, NTC; TEV]. The topic is the need to speak with care [BKC], faith tested by the presence of self-control

[Hb], the vocation of a teacher [ICC], propagandism as the fourth form of temptation [Lg], the need for restraint [NTC], the tongue [TEV].

DISCOURSE UNIT: 3:1–12 [AB, BKC, EBC, GNT, Herm, HNTC, ICC, Lns, NIGTC, NTC, TG, TNTC, WBC; NAB, NASB, NIV, NJB, REB]. The topic is a discussion concerning the use of the tongue [GNT, Herm, NTC], the power of the tongue [HNTC], the tongue is a fire [NASB], the danger of a poisoned tongue [AB], the need to control one's tongue [BKC, EBC, TG; NAB, NIV], the effects of the tongue not controlled [TNTC; NJB], pure speech without anger [NIGTC], the Christian manner of speaking [REB], the responsibility of teachers and the danger of the tongue [ICC, Lns, WBC].

DISCOURSE UNIT: 3:1–5 [BKC, Mit]. The topic is the power of the tongue [BKC].

DISCOURSE UNIT: 3:1–5a [Tsk]. The topic is the teacher's responsibility.

DISCOURSE UNIT: 3:1–2 [Hb, NTC]. The topic is the importance of a tongue properly controlled [Hb], the discipline of speech [NTC].

DISCOURSE UNIT: 3:1–2a [NIGTC]. The topic is a warning against exalting oneself.

DISCOURSE UNIT: 3:1 [NIC]. The topic is a discussion of who should be a teacher.

3:1 (Do) not many (of you) become teachers,^a my brothers,^b

LEXICON—a. διδάσκαλος (LN 33.243) (BAGD p. 191): 'teacher' [AB, BAGD, Herm, HNTC, LN, Lns, WBC; all versions except KJV], 'instructor' [LN], 'master' [KJV], 'rabbi' [NIC]. The reference is to an official position in the church [HNTC, ICC, Mit, NIGTC, NTC, TG, TNTC, WBC], to unofficial teachers who spoke in the assemblies [BKC, EGT, Hb, Lns, My], or to private instructors [Blm].

b. ἀδελφός (LN 11.23): 'brother' [AB, HNTC, Lns, NIC, WBC; all versions except NRSV, REB], '(Christian) brother' [LN], 'brother and sister' [Herm; NRSV], 'fellow believer' [LN], 'friend' [REB].

QUESTION—How is this verse related to its context?
1. This verse introduces a new point [Herm], as the phrase ἀδελφοί μου 'my brothers' indicates [BKC, Hb, ICC, NIGTC].
2. It takes up the warning of 1:19, 26 about controlling the tongue [EBC, EGT, Hb, HNTC], insisting that true faith results in proper control of the tongue [Hb].
3. It continues the preceding discussion, cautioning that the belief that works are not necessary would encourage more people to want to become teachers [Alf, Lg].

112   JAMES 3:1

QUESTION—What is the meaning of this exhortation?
  1. It implies that there should be a limited number of qualified teachers [Hb, Lns, My, NIGTC, WBC] so that only some should become teachers [Hb, Lns, My, NIGTC].
  2. It is an exhortation against unauthorized teachers [May] such as Judaistic proselyting teachers [Lg]. This is an ironical rebuke, telling them not to end up being a great number of teachers [Lg].
QUESTION—What is μή 'not' connected with?
  1. It is connected with πολλοὶ διδάσκαλοι 'many teachers' [Hb, Lns, My, NIGTC]: not many of you should become teachers.
  2. It is connected with the verb γίνεσθε 'become' [NTC, WBC]: many of you should not become teachers. The negative and the verb are separated for emphasis on the verb [NTC], on the negative [WBC].

knowing[a] that we-shall-receive[b] greater judgment.[c]
LEXICON—a. perf. (with pres. meaning) act. participle of οἶδα (LN 28.1): 'to know' [AB, Herm, HNTC, LN, Lns, NIC; KJV, NASB, NIV, NRSV, TEV, TNT], 'to realize' [NAB], 'to be aware' [WBC], 'to be certain' [REB], 'to bear in mind' [NJB]. It indicates that this warning was already known to them [Hb, NIGTC, WBC].
  b. fut. mid. (deponent = act.) indic. of λαμβάνω (LN 57.125) (BAGD 2. p. 465): 'to receive' [AB, BAGD, Herm, HNTC, LN, Lns, WBC; KJV, NJB], 'to incur' [NASB], 'to be called to' [NAB], 'to face' [REB], 'to be adjudged' [NIC]. The phrase μεῖζον κρίμα λημψόμεθα 'we shall receive greater judgment' is translated 'we will be judged more strictly' [NIV, TNT], 'we will be judged with greater strictness' [NRSV, TEV]. By the first person plural 'we' (which he rarely uses elsewhere in the epistle [EGT]), James includes himself as a teacher [EGT, Hb, ICC, Lg(M), Lns, May, Mit, NBC, NIGTC, NTC, Tsk, WBC].
  c. κρίμα (LN 30.110; 56.24; 56.30) (BAGD 4.b. p. 450): 'judgment' [HNTC, LN, Lns, WBC; NASB, NJB, REB], 'account' [NAB], 'condemnation' [AB, BAGD, LN; KJV], 'sentence of condemnation' [BAGD], 'penalty' [Herm], 'punishment' [BAGD, NIC]. The phrase κρίμα λημψόμεθα 'we will receive judgment' is translated 'we will be judged' [NIV, NRSV, TEV, TNT], 'we will be condemned' [BAGD]. This word is neutral in its connotation [EBC, Lg]. In the NT it usually implies condemnation [AB, Hb, Herm, HNTC, NIC; KJV], but since this includes James, it is neutral here [HNTC, Lg]. The judgment is from God [TG, WBC] at the final judgment day [ICC].
QUESTION—What relationship is indicated by the use of the participle εἰδότες 'knowing'?
  It indicates the grounds for the preceding exhortation [AB, Alf, Hb, HNTC, ICC, Lns, My, WBC; NIV, NRSV, REB]: because you know. It is a warning that being a teacher is a serious responsibility, and involves greater condemnation if he fails in his responsibility [AB, Blm], since he claims to

have knowledge [BKC]. James warns against substituting talking for deeds [Blm], speaking to exalt themselves [BKC], teaching without being qualified [Blm, EBC, Hb, HNTC], seeking the prestige [Hb, NIGTC] given to rabbis [BKC], seeking to be teachers for wrong motives [TNTC].

QUESTION—What is meant by κρίμα 'judgment'?
It means careful scrutiny [EBC, Lns, NIGTC, TG; NAB, NIV, NRSV, TEV, TNT]. In the case of failure, there will be greater condemnation [Alf, My, NIC, TNTC, Tsk, WBC], penalty [Herm], or punishment [Herm, NIC], since there will be more occasions for failure [Bg]. Increased influence means increased responsibility [Hb]. At the final judgment, teachers will be judged more severely [Hb, NTC].

DISCOURSE UNIT: 3:2–18 [NIC]. The topic is some items of Christian advice.

DISCOURSE UNIT: 3:2–12 [NIC]. The topic is the tongue's potential for evil.

3:2 For[a] much[b] we-all stumble.[c]

LEXICON—a. γάρ (LN 89.23): 'for' [AB, Herm, HNTC, LN, Lns, NIC; KJV, NASB, NJB, NRSV], 'because' [LN], not specific [WBC; NAB, NIV, REB, TEV, TNT].

b. πολύς (LN 59.1; 59.11) (BAGD I.2.b.β. p. 688): 'much' [LN], 'greatly' [BAGD], 'often' [BAGD; TEV], 'many' [LN], 'again and again' [REB], 'in many things' [Lns; KJV], 'in many respects' [AB; NAB], 'in many ways' [HNTC, WBC; NASB, NIV, NJB]. The phrase πολλὰ πταίομεν 'we stumble much' is translated 'we make many mistakes' [NRSV, TNT], 'we commit many sins' [Herm], 'we are guilty of many sins' [NIC]. This word is used adverbially [My], meaning 'many times' [Alf, Lg; REB] or 'in many ways' [AB, BAGD, HNTC, WBC; NAB, NASB, NIV, NJB, TEV]; it is adjectival, meaning 'many things' [BAGD Hb, Herm, Lns, NIC, TNTC; KJV, NRSV, TNT].

c. pres. act. indic. of πταίω (LN 88.291) (BAGD 1. p. 727): 'to stumble' [LN, Lns; NASB, NIV], 'to trip up' [NJB], 'to err' [HNTC, LN], 'to go wrong' [REB], 'to go astray' [WBC], 'to make mistakes' [BAGD; NRSV, TEV, TNT], 'to offend' [KJV], 'to give offense' [AB], 'to fall short' [NAB], 'to sin' [LN], 'to commit sins' [Herm]. The reference is to our entire conduct [Alf], to any slip of the tongue [Bg], to any moral failure [Hb, Lg, My, WBC]; it means to sin [EBC, Mit]. James includes himself [BKC, NIGTC, NTC, TNTC, WBC]. The present tense indicates repeated actions [Hb, Lns] that do not include fatal falling [Lns]. See this word at 2:10.

QUESTION—What relationship is indicated by γάρ 'for'?
1. It indicates the grounds for the preceding warning [EBC, Hb, ICC, My, NBC, NIC]: the teacher's responsibility is great because it is difficult to control the tongue.

2. It introduces the transition from the teacher to the use of speech in general [HNTC, Mit].
3. It introduces the reason for an implied thought [Blm]: we ought to fear this judgment, for we all stumble.

QUESTION—What is meant by ἅπαντες 'all'?

It is an emphatic form of πάντες 'all' [Alf, Bg, Hb, My] and is emphatic by its position [Hb], referring to all people [NIGTC, TG, WBC], not merely teachers [Hb, My]: we all without exception. The author includes himself [Bg, Hb, HNTC, Lg].

DISCOURSE UNIT: 3:2b–5a [NIGTC]. The topic is a warning concerning the tongue's power.

3:2b **If someone in^a word^b does not stumble,**

LEXICON—a. ἐν with dative object (LN 89.5; 89.76; 90.10): 'in' [AB, Herm, HNTC, LN, Lns, WBC; all versions except REB], 'with regard to' [LN], 'by' [LN], 'by means of' [LN], 'with' [LN]. This clause is translated 'a man who never says anything wrong' [REB], 'only if such a man there be as never sins in what he says' [NIC]. This word indicates the sphere in which the stumbling occurs [My].

  b. λόγος (LN 33.99) (BAGD 1.a.β. p. 477): 'word' [Lns; KJV], 'speech' [AB, HNTC, LN; NAB, NJB], 'speaking' [BAGD, Herm, LN; NRSV], 'what he says' [BAGD, NIC, WBC; NASB, NIV, TEV, TNT]. The reference is to those who teach [Alf, Herm]; it refers to speech in general [Hb, Mit, My, NBC, NIGTC, WBC]; it refers to speaking in worship in harmful ways [WBC], or speaking in ways that lead others astray from the truth [WBC].

QUESTION—What relationship is indicated by εἰ 'if'?

It expresses a real condition of fact [Hb]. It is assumed to be true for the sake of argument [NIGTC]. The present tense of the verb implies that his conduct is characterized by not stumbling [Hb]. It is a condition of fact which states the self-evident truth that no one can avoid this [Hb, NTC].

this (person) (is) a perfect/mature^a man, able^b to-bridle^c also^d all the body.^e

LEXICON—a. τέλειος (LN **88.36**; 88.100) (BAGD 2.d p. 809): 'perfect' [BAGD, Herm, HNTC, **LN**, NIC, WBC; all versions except NAB, NJB], 'mature' [AB, LN (88.100)], 'fully developed' [BAGD], 'complete' [Lns], 'in the fullest sense' [NAB]. The phrase τέλειος ἀνήρ '(is) a perfect man' is translated 'has reached perfection' [NJB].

  b. δυνατός (LN 74.2) (BAGD 1.a.β. p. 208): 'able' [AB, BAGD, Herm, HNTC, LN, Lns, NIC, WBC; KJV, NASB, NIV, NJB, NRSV, TEV], 'capable' [REB], 'in a position' [BAGD], '(he) can' [NAB, TNT].

  c. aorist act. infin. of χαλιναγωγέω (LN 88.85) (BAGD p. 874): 'to bridle' [AB, BAGD, Herm, HNTC, Lns; KJV, NASB], 'to keep in check with a bridle' [NRSV], 'as with a bridle to control' [NIC], 'to keep on a tight rein' [NJB], 'to keep in check' [NIV], 'to hold in check' [BAGD], 'to

hold in restraint' [WBC], 'to keep under control' [TNT], 'to control' [LN; NAB, REB, TEV]. It implies restraint from wrong directions and guidance in right directions [Hb].
  d. καί (LN 89.93): 'also' [Herm, HNTC, LN, Lns, NIC; KJV, TEV], 'as well' [AB, WBC; NASB], 'even' [LN], not specific [NAB, NIV, NJB, NRSV, REB, TNT].
  e. σῶμα (LN 8.1; 9.8): 'body' [AB, Herm, HNTC, LN, Lns, NIC, WBC; all versions except TEV, TNT], 'self' [LN; TNT], 'physical being' [LN], 'whole being' [TEV]. The reference is to the person himself [Bg, ICC, TG], to the other members of the physical body [Alf, Hb, Lg, My, TG], to the church [AB, WBC] and especially to the leaders [WBC].

QUESTION—What is signified by the presence of the demonstrative οὗτος 'this person'?

It is emphatic [My], limiting the description to the person who does not stumble [Hb], implying that such persons are rare [Lg]. It refers to teachers whose words need to be controlled [WBC].

QUESTION—What is meant by τέλειος 'perfect/mature'?
  1. It means an unattainable perfection of character [Alf, EBC, ICC, NIC]. Apart from Jesus, there never has been an ideally perfect person [NIC]. This refers to moral perfection [ICC]. Sin is universal, but if anyone could be found who does not sin in what he says, then he would not sin in other ways either [EBC].
  2. It means an attainable maturity of character [AB, BKC, Blm, Hb, HNTC, Lg, NTC, WBC]. This describes spiritual maturity, not sinlessness [BKC, Hb, Lg, NTC].

QUESTION—What is implied by the use of ἀνήρ 'man' (male gender)?
  1. It indicates that the author is referring in particular to the activities of men [Lg].
  2. It means persons in general [Lns; NJB, NRSV, TEV].

QUESTION—What relationship is indicated by the clause introduced by δυνατός 'able'?
  1. It states the second result of his not stumbling in what he says [AB, Blm, HNTC, Lg, Lns, Mit, TNTC, Tsk; REB, TEV, TNT]: if he controls his tongue, he is perfect and is also able to control his whole body.
  2. It states the grounds for saying that he is τέλειος 'perfect' [NAB]: he is perfect, because he is able to control his whole body.
  3. It gives a further description of the perfect man [Bg, Hb, Herm] in apposition with ἀνήρ 'man' [My]: he is a perfect man; he is able to control his whole body.

DISCOURSE UNIT: 3:3–8 [NTC]. The topic is examples of the use of the tongue.

DISCOURSE UNIT: 3:3–6 [Hb]. The topic is the need to control the tongue.

3:3 Now[a] if/since[b] we put the bits[c] of-the horses into[d] the mouths in-order-to[e] (make) them obey[f] us,

TEXT—Instead of εἰ δέ 'now if', some manuscripts read various spellings of ἴδε 'behold', and one important manuscript reads ἴδε γάρ 'for behold'. GNT reads εἰ δέ 'now if' with a C rating, indicating difficulty in deciding which variant to place in the text. Εἰ δέ 'now if' is read by EGT, Hb, Herm, Lg, Lns, My, NIGTC, NTC, TNTC, WBC, NAB, NASB, NIV, NJB, NRSV, and REB; ἴδε 'behold' is read by Bg, Blm, HNTC, ICC, NIC, Tsk, and KJV; ἴδε γάρ 'for behold' is read by AB and May.

LEXICON—a. δέ (LN 89.94): 'now' [Lns; NASB], 'and' [LN], not explicit [Herm, WBC; all versions except KJV, NASB]; different text: 'behold' [KJV], 'look' [HNTC], 'see' [NIC], 'for' [AB].

b. εἰ (LN 89.30; 89.65): 'if' [AB, Herm, LN (89.65), Lns; NASB, NRSV], 'when' [WBC; NAB, NIV, REB], 'once' [NJB], 'since' [LN (89.30)], not explicit [TEV, TNT]. It introduces an action which is, in fact, commonly done [Alf, Hb], as the present tense of the verb indicates [Hb, Lns].

c. χαλινός (LN **6.7**) (BAGD p. 874): 'bit' [AB, BAGD, Herm, HNTC, **LN**, Lns, NIC; all versions], 'bridle' [BAGD, LN, WBC]. The definite article with this word indicates that bits are well-known items [Alf]; it is generic, referring to bits/bridles in general [Hb]. The word refers only to the metal bit [Lg(M), Mit, TG], since it is put into the mouth [Mit]; it refers to the whole bridle [Hb, ICC], because the entire bridle is necessary for guiding the horse [Hb, ICC].

d. εἰς with accusative object (LN 84.22): 'into' [Herm, LN, Lns; all versions except KJV, NJB], 'in' [AB, HNTC, NIC, WBC; KJV, NJB].

e. εἰς with accusative object (LN 89.57): 'for the purpose of' [LN], 'so that' [AB, HNTC, Lns; NASB], 'that' [Herm; KJV], 'to' [NIC, WBC; all versions except KJV, NASB]. This preposition introduces the purpose of the bits [Alf, Lns], which is to control the whole horse, not just its mouth [Hb], adding emphasis to the point being made [My].

f. pres. pass. infin. of πείθω (LN **15.186**; 33.301) (BAGD 3.b. p. 639): 'to make to obey' [**LN**, NIC, WBC; NAB, NIV, NRSV, REB, TEV], 'to obey' [AB, BAGD, Herm, HNTC, LN, Lns; KJV, NASB], 'to control and make to obey' [TNT], 'to make to do what (one) wants' [NJB], 'to be persuaded' [LN]. The present tense implies repeated action [Lns].

QUESTION—What relationship is indicated by δέ 'now'?

It introduces a transition to the illustration in this verse [Alf, Hb, Lns]. It is used to distinguish the illustration from the principle stated in 3:2 [My]. The figure is introduced by the mention of χαλιναγωγῆσαι 'to bridle' in 3:2 [Alf, Hb, HNTC, Lg, Lns, My, NIGTC, TNTC, WBC], which also accounts for the emphatic forefronting of τῶν ἵππων 'of the horses' in this verse [Alf]. The use of 'we' in both verbs indicates that the practice of controlling horses by a bit was common knowledge to James and to his readers [Hb].

QUESTION—What is the point of this illustration?
It is the first of three (two [Blm, Hb, Lg, My, NBC]) illustrations to point out that the tongue is powerful [BKC, EBC, HNTC, Lg, Mit, NIC, TNTC, WBC], that it is important to control the tongue [Blm, Hb], that control of the tongue makes possible control of the whole body [My], that control of the tongue implies the ability to control all the body [Blm, NIC, Tsk], that if a man can control a horse with a small bit in its mouth, he should be able to control his own tongue [Lns, NTC], or to point out what the perfect man can do [NBC]. It is an illustration of how a church leader may control the whole group of believers [WBC] by controlling the preaching [AB], and therefore church leaders must control their tongues [WBC].
1. The smallness of the tongue is in view [BKC, Blm, EBC, Herm, Mit, NBC, NIC, NTC, TG, TNTC].
2. The smallness of the tongue (of the bit [Lg]) is not significant here [ICC, Lg, My].

QUESTION—What is the genitive τῶν ἵππων 'of the horses' connected with?
It is forefronted for emphasis [Alf, Bg, EGT, Hb, ICC, Lg(M), May, My, NTC], to note the parallel between controlling the mouth of a horse and of a person [EGT, Hb, May]. The article [Hb] and the plural [Hb, Lns] refer to horses in general [Hb, Lns].
1. It is connected with τὰ στόματα 'the mouths' [Alf, My], since the emphasis is upon the mouth [My]: the mouths of the horses.
2. It is connected more with χαλινούς 'bits' [EGT, ICC, Lg, May]: the bits of the horses. However, the sense is the same for both interpretations [Lg(M)].

also/and[a] all the body of-them we-lead-about.[b]
LEXICON—a. καί (LN 89.92; 89.93): 'also' [Herm, LN], 'in addition' [LN], 'as well' [NASB], 'and' [LN; KJV, TEV, TNT], not explicit [NAB, NIV, NJB, NRSV, REB].
b. pres. act. indic. of μετάγω (LN **15.186**) (BAGD 1. p. 510): 'to guide' [BAGD, Herm, HNTC, **LN**; NAB, NRSV], 'to steer' [LN], 'to direct' [LN; NASB, REB], 'to control' [AB], 'to have under control' [NJB], 'to turn' [NIC, WBC; NIV], 'to turn about' [Lns; KJV], 'to make to go' [TEV, TNT]. The present tense indicates customary action [Hb, Lns].

QUESTION—What is the area of meaning of καί 'also/and'?
1. For those who read εἰ 'if' at the beginning of this verse, the meaning is 'also' [Hb, Herm, Lns, WBC; NASB] and this clause gives the conclusion [Alf, Hb, Herm, Lg, My]: if we put bits into horses' mouths, we control their whole bodies also.
2. For those who do not translate εἰ 'if' at the beginning of this verse, it is a coordinate connector of the two clauses [HNTC, NIC; KJV, TEV, TNT]: we put bits into horses' mouths and we control them.

3:4 Look, the ships also, being so-large[a] and/even by[b] strong[c] winds being-driven,[d]

LEXICON—a. τηλικοῦτος (LN **79.128**) (BAGD 1. p. 814): 'so large' [AB, BAGD, **LN**; NIV, NRSV], 'so great' [BAGD, Herm, LN, Lns; KJV, NASB], 'so huge' [WBC]. The phrase τηλικαῦτα ὄντα 'being so large' is translated 'no matter how big' [NJB], 'big as they are' [HNTC; TNT], 'so great as they are' [NIC], 'big as it is' [TEV], 'however large they are' [NAB], 'large though it may be' [REB].
  b. ὑπό with genitive object (LN 90.1) (BAGD 1.a.β. p. 843): 'by' [AB, BAGD, Herm, HNTC, LN, Lns, NIC, WBC; NAB, NASB, NIV, REB, NRSV, TNT], 'of' [KJV]. The phrase ὑπὸ ἀνέμων σκληρῶν ἐλαυνόμενα 'by strong winds being driven' is translated 'even if a gale is driving them' [NJB], 'that it takes strong winds to drive them' [NRSV].
  c. σκληρός (LN **20.3**; **76.15**) (BAGD 1.b. p. 756): 'strong' [BAGD, Herm, HNTC, LN (20.3); NASB, NIV, NRSV, TEV, TNT], 'stiff' [Lns], 'powerful' [LN (76.15), WBC], 'rough' [BAGD], 'violent' [LN (20.3)], 'fierce' [AB, NIC; KJV, NAB]. The phrase ἀνέμων σκληρῶν 'strong winds' is translated 'gales' [REB]. The implication is that these winds cannot be swayed from their course [Hb, Lns]. This word contrasts with the smallness of the rudder [ICC].
  d. pres. pass. participle of ἐλαύνω (LN **15.161**) (BAGD p. 248): 'to be driven' [AB, BAGD, Herm, HNTC, **LN**, Lns, NIC; KJV, NAB, NASB, NIV, REB, TEV], 'to be driven along' [LN, WBC], 'to be carried along' [LN; TNT].

QUESTION—How is this verse related to its context?

It is a further illustration of what the 'perfect man' can do [NBC]. The καί adds emphasis [Lg] and means 'not only horses but even (καί) ships' [Bg, Lg], or 'ships also as well as horses' [Hb, ICC].

QUESTION—What is the function of ἰδού 'look'?
  1. It is an exclamatory particle [Alf, Hb, Lg, Lns, May, My; NASB] (τὰ πλοῖα 'the boats' is nominative [May]) adding vividness to the illustration [Hb, Lg, Lns, My] by calling attention to what is to follow [Hb]: look!
  2. It is treated as a verb [AB, Herm, HNTC, Mit; KJV, NRSV]: look at the ships.

QUESTION—What is the point of the illustration?
  1. The point is how a large object can be controlled by a small object [AB, BKC, Hb, HNTC, Lg, Lns, Mit, NBC, NTC, TNTC, WBC].
  2. The point is how control of the tongue influences the direction of the whole life [EBC, TNTC, Tsk]; if we can control the tongue, we can more easily (we should be able to [NIC, NTC]) control the whole body [ICC, NIC, WBC], or if the teachers' tongues are controlled, the spiritual health of the congregation will be good [WBC]. The ships represent the church, the rudder represents the preaching, the winds represent conflicting human interests, and the pilot is the leader of the congregation [AB].

JAMES 3:4

QUESTION—What relationship is indicated by the use of the participles ὄντα 'being' and ἐλαυνόμενα 'being driven'?

They are concessive [AB, Alf, Hb, Herm, Lg, Lns, My, NTC, WBC; KJV, NAB, NASB, NIV, NJB, REB]: although they are so great and driven by strong winds, they are guided by a very small rudder. They point out the difficulty of steering the ships, in order to emphasize the power of the small rudder [My]. The factors to be dealt with are the size of the ships [Bg, EBC, Hb], the force of the winds [Bg, EBC], and the smallness of the rudder [EBC].

QUESTION—What relationship is indicated by καί 'and/even'?

1. The καί is translated 'and' and connects two coordinate participial phrases [AB, Alf, Hb, Herm, Lns, My, NTC, WBC; KJV, NAB, NASB, NIV, REB]: although they are so great and are driven by strong winds, they are guided by a very small rudder.
2. The καί is translated 'even' [NJB, TNT] and adds emphasis to the illustration [Tsk]: although they are so great, even when they are driven by strong winds they are guided by a very small rudder.
3. The second participial phrase emphasizes their large size [NRSV]: although they are so great that it takes strong winds to drive them, they are guided by a very small rudder.

they-are-steered[a] by[b] a-very-small[c] rudder[d] wherever[e] the impulse[f] of-the-(one) steering[g] desires.[h]

LEXICON—a. pres. pass. indic. of μετάγω (LN **15.186**) (BAGD 1. p. 510): 'to be steered' [BAGD, **LN**, WBC; NIV, REB, TEV], 'to be guided' [AB, BAGD, Herm, HNTC, LN; NRSV], 'to be directed' [LN; NAB, NASB, NJB], 'to be turned' [Lns; TNT], 'to be turned about' [KJV], 'to be turned this way and that' [NIC]. The repetition of this word from the preceding verse emphasizes the parallel between the two illustrations [ICC].

b. ὑπό with genitive object: 'by'. See this word in the preceding clause.

c. ἐλάχιστος (LN **79.125**) (BAGD 2.a p. 248): 'very small' [BAGD, Herm, LN, Lns, NIC, WBC; all versions except NJB], 'tiny' [AB, HNTC; NJB].

d. πηδάλιον (LN **6.50**) (BAGD p. 656): 'rudder' [AB, BAGD, Herm, HNTC, LN, Lns, NIC, WBC; all versions except KJV], 'helm' [KJV], 'steering paddle' [BAGD].

e. ὅπου (LN 83.5) (BAGD 1.b.α. p. 576): 'wherever' [AB, Herm, LN; NASB, NIV, NJB, NRSV, TEV], 'whither' [Lns], 'whithersoever' [KJV], 'where' [BAGD, HNTC, LN], 'in any direction' [TNT], 'in whatever direction' [NIC], 'on whatever course' [NAB, REB], 'which course' [WBC].

f. ὁρμή (LN **26.12**) (BAGD p. 581): 'impulse' [AB, BAGD, HNTC, LN; NAB], 'whim' [NJB], 'will' [Herm, **LN**; NRSV], 'desire' [LN, NIC], 'inclination' [NASB], 'choice' [WBC], 'push' [Lns], not explicit [KJV, NIV, REB, TEV, TNT]. The phrase ὅπου ἡ ὁρμὴ τοῦ εὐθύνοντος βούλεται 'wherever the impulse of the one steering desires' is translated

'wherever the impulse of the steersman leads him' [BAGD], 'wherever the pilot wants it to go' [**LN**]. The reference is to the thought or intention [Alf, Blm, Herm, ICC, Lg(M), LN, Mit, My, NIC, NTC, TG, Tsk; NASB, NIV, NJB, NRSV]; it refers to the physical action of moving the rudder [Bg, Hb, Lns, May], to both thought and action [Lg].
- g. pres. act. participle of εὐθύνω (LN **54.21**) (BAGD 2. p. 321): 'to pilot' [**LN**], 'to steer' [LN], 'to guide straight' [BAGD]. The phrase τοῦ εὐθύνοντος 'of the one steering' is translated 'of the steersman' [HNTC, Lns], 'the steersman's' [NIC; NAB], 'of the helmsman' [NJB], 'the helmsman' [REB, TNT], 'the pilot' [NIV, TEV], 'the pilot's' [AB, WBC], 'of the pilot' [BAGD, Herm; NASB, NRSV], 'the governor' [KJV]. The present tense implies a characteristic function [Hb]. The reference is to the man who actually handles the rudder [Mit, My, TG].
- h. pres. pass. (deponent = act.) of βούλομαι (LN 25.3) (BAGD 2.a.ζ. p. 146): 'to desire' [LN; NASB], 'to want' [LN; NIV, TEV], 'to will' [LN], 'to wish' [BAGD; TNT], 'to intend' [Lns], 'to select' [NAB], 'to choose' [NIC; REB], 'to decide' [WBC; NJB], 'to direct' [AB, Herm, HNTC; NRSV], 'to list' [KJV].

QUESTION—What is meant by ὁρμή 'impulse'?
1. It means the thought or intention of the helmsman [Alf, Blm, Herm, ICC, Lg(M), LN, Mit, My, NIC, NTC, TG, Tsk; NASB, NIV, NJB, NRSV, REB, TEV, TNT].
2. It means the physical pressure exerted by the helmsman [Bg, Hb, Lns, May]. It is the slight pressure of his hand on the tiller [May].

QUESTION—How are the noun and the substantival participle related in the genitive construction ἡ ὁρμὴ τοῦ εὐθύνοντος βούλεται 'the impulse of the one steering'?
1. The genitive participle expresses the source of the impulse [Lns]: the impulse given by the pilot.
2. The noun and participle are combined into one concept [KJV, NIV, TEV, TNT]: the helmsman.

3:5 Thus also the tongue is a small member[a] and boasts[b] great (things).

LEXICON—a. μέλος (LN 8.9) (BAGD 1. p. 501): 'member' [BAGD, Herm, LN, Lns; KJV, NAB, NRSV], 'member of the body' [NIC], 'organ' [AB], 'limb' [HNTC], 'body part' [LN], 'part of the body' [WBC; NASB, NIV, NJB, TNT], not explicit [REB, TEV].
- b. pres. act. indic. of αὐχέω (LN **33.368**) (BAGD p. 124): 'to boast' [BAGD, Herm, HNTC, LN, Lns; KJV, NASB, NRSV, TEV], 'to vaunt' [NIC], 'to make boasts' [AB; NIV], 'to make pretensions' [NAB], 'to make claims for itself' [WBC], 'to be a great braggart' [TNT]. This verb is also translated as a noun: '(its) boasts' [NJB], '(its) pretensions' [REB]. This verb refers to the power which the tongue actually has (for good or evil [Blm, NTC, TNTC]), not to empty claims [Blm, EGT, Hb, HNTC, ICC, Lg, May, Mit, NBC, NTC, TNTC; TEV]. The phrase μεγάλα αὐχεῖ

(the verb μεγαλαυχεῖ [Alf, Bg, Tsk]) 'boasts great things' is usually derogatory, and is so here [AB, Alf, Bg, EBC, NIGTC, Tsk, WBC; NAB, NIV, REB, TNT]. It is an arrogant proclamation [Hb, ICC].

QUESTION—How is this clause related to its context?

It applies the comparison in the two (especially the last [Blm, My]) preceding illustrations to the tongue [Alf, Blm, EBC, HNTC, Lns, My, NIGTC, TNTC], as οὕτως 'thus' implies [Hb, NIGTC]: in a similar way the small tongue does great things. Μεγάλα 'great things' is forefronted before the verb for emphasis [Hb]. It also prepares the way for the judgment pronounced on the tongue in what follows [Herm, My]. The point is the small tongue and its great effect [Lns, Mit, NBC, NIGTC, NTC]. The reference is to the teacher whose teaching is producing harm [WBC]. The meaning is that speech, which is considered relatively insignificant, controls actions, which we consider much more significant [May]; it means that the tongue has great influence [Mit].

DISCOURSE UNIT: 3:5b–12 [NIGTC, Tsk]. The topic is a warning against the deceitfulness of the tongue [NIGTC], the havoc which the tongue can cause [Tsk].

3:5b Look, how-much[a] fire kindles[b] how-much[c] forest;[d]

TEXT—Instead of ἡλίκον 'how much' (implying 'little'), some manuscripts have ὀλίγον 'little'. LN does not mention this variant. Bg, Blm, and probably KJV read ὀλίγον; most others who translate 'small' or something similar probably nevertheless read ἡλίκον.

LEXICON—a. ἡλίκος (LN **79.127**) (BAGD p. 345): 'how much'; 'what sized' [Lns], 'how small' [AB, HNTC; NJB], 'such a small' [**LN**; NASB], 'small' [Herm, WBC; NIV, NRSV], 'how tiny' [NAB], 'tiny' [TEV], 'tiniest' [REB, TNT], 'little' [BAGD, NIC], probably different text 'little' [KJV].

b. pres. act. indic. of ἀνάπτω (LN **14.65**) (BAGD p. 60): 'to kindle' [BAGD, HNTC, LN, Lns; KJV], 'to ignite' [AB, LN], 'to set fire to' [NJB], 'to set ablaze' [LN, WBC; NAB, TNT], 'to set alight' [NIC]; as a passive voice 'to be set aflame' [NASB], 'to be set ablaze' [Herm; NRSV, REB], 'to be set on fire' [**LN**; NIV, TEV]. This verb refers to getting the fire started [Alf, Hb, Lg(M)].

c. ἡλίκος (LN **79.127**) (BAGD p. 345): 'how much' [NIC], 'what sized' [Lns], 'how great' [Herm, HNTC; KJV, NASB, NRSV], 'how large' [BAGD, **LN**; TEV], 'how extensive' [LN], 'what a great' [NIV], 'what a vast amount of' [REB], 'vast' [TNT], 'great' [WBC], 'huge' [NAB, NJB], 'a mass of' [AB].

d. ὕλη (LN **3.3**; **3.64**) (BAGD 1. p. 836): 'forest' [BAGD, Herm, HNTC, **LN** (3.3), Lns, NTC, WBC; all versions except KJV, REB], 'timber' [REB], 'brushwood' [NIC], 'wood' [AB, BAGD, LN], 'pile of wood' [**LN** (3.64)], 'firewood' [BAGD], 'matter' [KJV]. The word refers to a forest [Hb, Herm, HNTC, ICC, Lg, Lns, My, NBC, WBC; all versions

except KJV] or standing brushwood [NIC, TNTC], or wood in general, such as firewood [AB], or to flammable materials in general [Blm; KJV].
QUESTION—How is this clause related to its context?
It forms the transition to what follows [My, Tsk, WBC], pointing out that the tongue is as dangerous as a fire [ICC, TNTC, Tsk, WBC].
QUESTION—What is the function of ἰδού 'look'?
1. It is an emphatic particle [Hb; KJV, NASB], directing attention to the following illustration [Hb, Tsk]: Look! This word separates the preceding example of good power from the following negative example [Lg].
2. It is used as a verb [NAB, NIV, NJB]: look at how much fire kindles how much forest!
QUESTION—What is the area of meaning of the two uses of ἡλίκος 'how much'?
This word refers to a quantity, either large or small [Hb, HNTC, Lg, Lns, May, My, TNTC, WBC]; the force of the statement here is increased by the author's not specifying the size of the two examples but depending on his readers' knowledge of this common situation to interpret it correctly [Hb, HNTC]; the context gives the interpretation [May]. The use of the same word with opposite meanings adds emphasis [My]. The two phrases which include this adjective are emphasized by being placed together before the verb [Hb]. The point is the havoc which a small fire can produce [Lg].

DISCOURSE UNIT: 3:6–8 [BKC]. The topic is the perversity of the tongue.

3:6 **and the tongue (is a) fire; the world**[a] **of-the unrighteousness**[b] **the tongue is-set**[c] **among**[d] **our members,**
TEXT—Some manuscripts add οὕτως 'thus' after ἀδικίας 'unrighteousness'. GNT does not mention this variant; only Blm and KJV include this word.
LEXICON—a. κόσμος (LN 59.55) (BAGD 8. p. 447): 'world' [AB, Herm, HNTC, LN, Lns, NIC, WBC; all versions except NAB], 'universe' [NAB], 'tremendous amount' [LN], 'sum total' [BAGD], 'totality' [BAGD].
b. ἀδικία (LN 88.21) (BAGD 2. p. 18): 'unrighteousness' [BAGD, LN], 'evil' [NIV], 'iniquity' [AB, Lns; KJV, NASB, NRSV], 'wickedness' [BAGD, WBC; TNT], 'malice' [NAB], 'injustice' [BAGD], 'unjust deed' [LN], 'wrong' [TEV]. This noun is also translated as an adjective: 'wicked' [HNTC; NJB, REB], 'evil' [Herm], 'sinful' [NIC]. With the definite article this noun refers to the well-known force of evil which Christians must resist [Hb].
c. pres. mid./pass. indic. of καθίστημι (LN 13.9; 37.104) (BAGD 3. p. 390): 'to designate' [LN], 'to appoint' [LN], 'to make' [BAGD, LN], 'to cause' [BAGD]. This is translated as passive: 'to be set' [WBC; NASB], 'to be placed' [AB; NRSV], 'to be constituted' [Lns]; as middle: 'to present oneself' [Herm], 'to appoint oneself' [HNTC]; as active: 'to represent' [REB], 'to stand' [NIC], 'to occupy one's place' [TEV], 'to exist' [NAB], 'to be' [KJV, NJB, TNT]; not explicit [NIV]. Some commentators take it

JAMES 3:6

as the passive voice [AB, Lns, May, WBC; NASB, NRSV], others as the middle voice, implying appointing or constituting itself [BKC, Hb, Herm, HNTC, ICC, Lg(M), My, TNTC]. It implies a development in contrast with the natural state [EGT, May]. The meaning is that the tongue dominates the members of the body [Lg].

d. ἐν with dative object (LN 83.9; 83.13): 'among' [AB, Herm, HNTC, LN, Lns, NIC, WBC; all versions except REB, TEV], 'in' [LN; REB, TEV].

QUESTION—What relationship is indicated by καί 'and'?

It joins the preceding examples to the following reference to the tongue as a fire [Hb, ICC, My, NTC].

QUESTION—What is the phrase ὁ κόσμος τῆς ἀδικίας 'the world of unrighteousness' connected with?

1. It is connected with what follows [AB, Hb, Herm, HNTC, ICC, Lg, Lns, May, Mit, NBC, NIGTC, NTC, TNTC, Tsk, WBC; NAB, NIV, NJB, NRSV, REB, TEV]: the tongue is set among our members as a world of unrighteousness. It is a predicate nominative [Hb, Herm, ICC, May, NIGTC, TNTC, Tsk, WBC], standing first in its clause for emphasis [Hb, May]. This phrase continues the description of the tongue [Lg, May].

    1.1 The tongue typifies the unrighteous world among the parts of the body [AB, ICC, May, Mit, NIGTC, TG, TNTC, Tsk], containing in itself the sins of the fallen world [TNTC], referring to the world which is dominated by unrighteousness [May, NBC, TG, TNTC].

    1.2 The tongue is prominent among the body parts as the unrighteous world [Lg].

    1.3 The tongue is *the* huge system of unrighteousness, as the definite article indicates [Hb, Lns], the embodiment of all iniquity [Lns].

2. It is connected with what precedes [Alf, Bg, BKC, Blm, My, NIC; KJV, NASB, TNT].

    2.1 It is in apposition with ἡ γλῶσσα 'the tongue' [Alf, My]: the tongue is a fire; that is, it is a world of unrighteousness.

    2.2 It is a further description of the tongue [EBC]: the tongue is a fire and it is also a world of evil. This phrase pictures all the wickedness of the world as being contained in the mind, which is expressed through the tongue [EBC].

    2.3 It tells why the tongue is called a fire [Bg]: the tongue is a fire because it is a world of unrighteousness. It is also an illustration of the last part of 3:5 [Bg].

QUESTION—How are the two nouns related in the genitive construction ὁ κόσμος τῆς ἀδικίας 'the world of unrighteousness'?

1. κόσμος 'world' is described by ἀδικίας 'unrighteousness' [Hb, Herm, HNTC, ICC, Lns, May, Mit, NBC, NIC, NIGTC, TG, TNTC, Tsk, WBC; NJB, REB]: the unrighteous world. The world is so called because it does unrighteousness [NBC], because it is controlled by evil [TG]. It is a vast system of iniquity [Hb], an organized system of evil [TG].

2. Ἀδικίας 'unrighteousness' is described by κόσμος 'world' [Blm, EBC, My; NAB, NASB]: the great amount of unrighteousness.

QUESTION—What is implied by the repetition of ἡ γλῶσσα 'the tongue'?
1. It adds emphasis [Bg, WBC] to the importance of the tongue [Hb].
2. The second instance was added because the predicate phrase was forefronted [May].

the-(one) staining[a] all the body and inflaming[b] the course[c] of-the nature[d] and being-inflamed[e] by[f] the Gehenna.[g]

LEXICON—a. pres. act. participle of σπιλόω (LN 79.58) (BAGD p. 762): 'to stain' [BAGD, Herm, LN; NRSV], 'to spot' [LN], 'to defile' [BAGD, HNTC, Lns, NIC; KJV, NAB, NASB], 'to corrupt' [WBC; NIV], 'to pollute' [REB], 'to contaminate' [AB], 'to infect' [NJB], 'to spread infection' [TNT], 'to spread evil' [TEV]. It refers to moral stains [Hb]. The present tense indicates a characteristic activity [Hb].

b. pres. act. participle of φλογίζω (LN **14.65**) (BAGD p. 862): 'to set on fire' [BAGD, Herm, LN, WBC; KJV, NASB, NIV, NRSV, TEV], 'to set fire to' [NIC; NJB], 'to set alight' [REB], 'to set light to' [HNTC], 'to set ablaze' [TNT], 'to set aflame' [Lns], 'to inflame' [AB]. The phrase καὶ φλογίζουσα τὸν τροχὸν τῆς γενέσεως 'and inflaming the course of nature' is translated 'its flames encircle our course from birth' [NAB].

c. τροχός (LN 61.5; 67.83) (BAGD p. 828): 'course' [LN, WBC; KJV, NAB, NASB, NIV, REB, TEV], 'pattern' [LN (61.5)], 'circling course' [NIC], 'cycle' [Herm, LN (67.83); NRSV], 'round' [TNT], 'wheel' [AB, BAGD, HNTC, Lns; NJB].

d. γένεσις (LN **13.71**) (BAGD 4. p. 154): 'existence' [LN, Lns; REB, TEV, TNT], 'human existence' [WBC], 'being' [AB], 'becoming' [Herm], 'origin' [BAGD], 'nature' [KJV, NRSV], 'creation' [NIC; NJB], 'birth' [NAB], 'life' [HNTC; NASB, NIV].

e. pres. pass. participle of φλογίζω (LN 14.65): 'to be set on fire' [Herm, LN, NIC, WBC; KJV, NASB, NIV, NRSV], 'to be set ablaze' [LN], 'to be set alight' [HNTC], 'to be set aflame' [Lns], 'to be inflamed' [AB]; as an active voice: 'to catch fire' [NJB]. This participle is translated as a phrase: 'its fire is kindled' [NAB], 'its own fire comes' [TNT], 'its flames are fed' [REB], 'with the fire that comes to it' [TEV]. The present tense indicates habitual action [Alf, Hb, Lg, My], not a future condemnation [Alf, Lg, My].

f. ὑπό with genitive object (LN 90.1): 'by' [AB, Herm, HNTC, LN, Lns, NIC, WBC; NAB, NASB, NIV, NRSV, REB], 'of' [KJV]; with an active voice verb: 'from' [NJB, TEV, TNT].

g. γέεννα (LN 1.21) (BAGD p. 153): 'Gehenna' [AB, BAGD, Herm, HNTC, LN, Lns, WBC], 'hell' [BAGD, LN, NIC; all versions]. This word, originally referring to the Valley of Hinnom in Jerusalem, became a symbol for the Devil [Blm, EBC, Hb, Mit, NBC, NIGTC, NTC] and his angels [Blm, Hb, Mit], or eternal punishment [EBC, EGT, Hb, HNTC, ICC, Mit, NTC, TG, TNTC, Tsk, WBC].

QUESTION—What relationship is indicated by the participle ἡ σπιλοῦσα 'the one staining'?

It is attributive (but non-restrictive), modifying ἡ γλῶσσα 'the tongue' [Alf, Bg, Blm, Hb, ICC, Lns, May, My, NBC, NIC, NIGTC, NTC, TNTC]: the tongue, which stains the whole body. It is in apposition with the preceding statement concerning the tongue [Hb]. It is a second description of the tongue [NTC].

QUESTION—What relationship is indicated by the participles φλογίζουσα…καὶ φλογιζομένη 'inflaming…and being inflamed'?

1. They are parallel to ἡ σπιλοῦσα 'the one staining', continuing the description of the tongue [Herm, My, NIC, NTC, WBC; NASB, NIV, NRSV, REB]; and καί…καί is 'and…and' [Herm, My, NIC; NASB, NIV, NRSV, REB]: it stains the whole body and sets on fire…and is set on fire.
2. They are subordinate to the first participle ἡ σπιλοῦσα 'the one staining', adding further details about the tongue [Hb, Lns; NJB], explaining why the tongue inflames the whole body [Bg], explaining the extent of the inflammation [Lns]; the καί…καί is 'both…and' [Hb, Lns]. It stains the whole body, both setting on fire…and being set on fire.

QUESTION—What is meant by τὸν τροχὸν τῆς γενέσεως 'the course of nature'?

1. It refers to the whole course of life with its varied relationships from beginning to end [Blm, EBC, Hb, HNTC, Lg, Lns, Mit, My, NIC, NIGTC, NTC, TG, TNTC, Tsk, WBC]. Our existence moves as does a wheel [Lns]; Christians considered life as moving toward a goal, not as cyclical [Mit].
2. It means existence [AB] or life [Herm].
3. It means 'the whole cycle of creation'; the reference is necessarily to something material [Alf].
4. It refers to the body and its temperament [Bg, EGT].
5. It refers to the worldly spirit of human life which is at enmity with God [May].
6. It refers to the circle formed by humanity, with each speaker setting the circle afire by the unrighteous expressions of his tongue [NBC].

QUESTION—How are the two nouns related in the genitive construction τὸν τροχὸν τῆς γενέσεως 'the course of nature'?

The commentaries do not deal specifically with this important point, but the following interpretations seem to be implied by their treatment of the phrase.

1. The genitive expresses the beginning of the course [My; NAB] which each person's birth sets in motion [NIC], presumably a genitive of source: the course from birth.
2. It means the course which a person's life follows [EBC, HNTC, Lns, NTC, TG, TNTC, Tsk], presumably a subjective genitive.

3. It refers to the whole area of human life [Mit], presumably a partitive genitive.
4. The two nouns are combined to mean 'existence' [AB], 'life' [Herm].

DISCOURSE UNIT: 3:7–8 [Hb]. The topic is how untamable the tongue is.

3:7 For every species/nature[a] both of-animals[b] and of-birds, both of-reptiles and of-sea-creatures,[c] are-being-tamed[d] and are-tamed[e] by-the species/nature[f] the human,[g]

LEXICON—a. φύσις (LN **58.24**) (BAGD 4. p. 870): 'species' [Herm, LN, WBC; NASB, NRSV], 'genus' [NIC], 'class' [LN], 'kind' [AB, HNTC, **LN**, Lns; KJV, NIV, TNT], 'form of life' [NAB], 'creature' [BAGD; TEV], 'nature' [LN], not specific [NJB, REB].

b. θηρίον (LN **4.4**) (BAGD 1.a.β. p. 361): 'animal' [**LN**; NIV], 'wild animal' [BAGD, **LN**; NJB, TEV], 'beast' [AB, BAGD, Herm, HNTC, Lns, NIC, WBC; KJV, NASB, NRSV, REB, TNT], 'quadruped' [LN], 'four-footed' [NAB]. The reference is to four-footed animals [Alf, Lg, My], to wild beasts [Hb, May, NIC, TG, WBC].

c. ἐνάλιος (LN **4.58**) (BAGD p. 261): 'sea creature' [BAGD, Herm, HNTC, LN, NIC, WBC; NRSV], 'creature of the sea' [**LN**; NASB, NIV], 'creature that swims in the sea' [REB], 'thing in the sea' [Lns; KJV], 'sea animal' [AB], 'fish' [LN; TEV, TNT], 'fish of every kind' [NJB], 'swimming' [NAB].

d. pres. pass. indic. of δαμάζω (LN **37.1**) (BAGD 1. p. 170): 'to be tamed' [AB, BAGD, Herm, HNTC, WBC; KJV, NAB, NASB, NIV, NJB, NRSV], 'to be controlled' [**LN**], 'to be brought under control' [LN], 'to be subdued' [BAGD, Lns, NIC; REB], 'to be held in check' [LN]. This is also translated in the active voice: 'to tame' [TEV, TNT]. The meaning is to subdue, which may be done without domestication [Hb, Lns, Mit, NIC], and to tame [Mit, NIC].

e. perf. pass. indic. of δαμάζω: 'to be tamed'. See d. above.

f. φύσις (LN **58.8**; **58.24**) (BAGD 2. p. 869; 4. p. 870): 'species' [Herm, LN; NRSV], 'kind' [LN], 'class' [LN], 'race' [NASB], 'nature' [BAGD, LN]. The phrase τῇ φύσει τῇ ἀνθρωπίνῃ 'the human nature' is translated 'people' [**LN**], 'man' [NIV, REB, TEV, TNT], 'mankind' [AB, BAGD, Lns, NIC; KJV, NAB], 'human(s)' [WBC; NJB], 'humankind' [BAGD, HNTC, **LN**].

g. ἀνθρώπινος (LN **9.6**) (BAGD 2. p. 67): 'human' [BAGD, Herm, LN; NASB, NRSV]. The position of this word at the end of the clause indicates emphasis [WBC].

QUESTION—What relationship is indicated by γάρ 'for'?

It indicates the grounds for giving the preceding description of the tongue [Alf, Blm, EBC, Hb, ICC, Lg, Mit, My, NBC, NIC, TNTC, WBC]. Following the concession clause in 3:7, the grounds are stated in 3:8 [Hb, Lg, Mit, My, WBC]. The untamable nature of the tongue is proof that the tongue receives its power from hell [TNTC].

QUESTION—What is the meaning of πᾶσα 'every'?
> It is a literary exaggeration and does not mean all creatures without exception [EGT, Hb, May].

QUESTION—What is meant by φύσις 'species/nature'?
1. It refers to the species, and the genitive nouns give the examples [AB, Blm, EBC, EGT, Herm, HNTC, ICC, Lns, May, Mit, NIC, NIGTC, NTC, TNTC, Tsk, WBC; all versions]: every species of animals is tamed by mankind.
2. It refers to characteristics or nature [Alf, Bg, BKC, Hb, Lg, My, NBC]. The contrast is between human nature and animal nature in general, no matter how animal nature differs in various species [My].

QUESTION—What is implied by the use of both present and perfect tenses, δαμάζεται 'is being tamed' and δεδάμασται 'is tamed'?
1. The present tense means that they are habitually tamed (that they can be tamed or subdued [AB, NIGTC, TG, Tsk; NAB, NJB, NRSV, REB, TEV, TNT]) [EBC, ICC, Lns, NBC, NIGTC], as can be seen daily [Alf, Hb]; the perfect tense adds emphasis [Lns] and implies that the taming has been accomplished [AB, Alf, EBC, Hb, ICC, Lns, My, NBC, NIGTC, TG, Tsk] (and it is still in effect), and was granted to mankind from the beginning [TNTC, Tsk, WBC]; the combination of the two verbs adds emphasis [May]. The two verbs point to the proof of the superiority of human nature over animal nature [Hb].
2. The double use of the verb is merely a rhetorical formulation [Herm].

QUESTION—What is the meaning of the dative case of the phrase τῇ φύσει τῇ ἀνθρωπίνῃ 'the human species'?
1. It expresses the agency (the means [NTC], the instrument [WBC]) of the taming [AB, Alf, Lg(M), Lns, May, My, NTC, WBC; all versions]: tamed by the human species.
2. It refers to obedience to mankind [Bg, HNTC, ICC]: tamed to obey mankind.

3:8 but the tongue no-one of-men is-able to-tame,[a]

LEXICON—a. aorist act. infin. of δαμάζω: 'to tame'. See this word at 3:7. The aorist tense indicates inability to tame the tongue as an effective achievement [Hb] or to even tame it once [Alf].

QUESTION—What relationship is implied by δέ 'but'?
> It indicates a contrast (an exception [Alf]) to the preceding statement [Alf, Hb, My, NIGTC, WBC]: almost all things can be tamed, but the tongue is an exception. The contrast is further indicated by the emphatic forefronting of τὴν γλῶσσαν 'the tongue' [NIGTC, TNTC, WBC].

QUESTION—What is implied by this statement?
1. It implies that the unredeemed person (any person [May]) cannot control his tongue; only with Christ's help can the tongue be controlled [AB, EBC, Hb, Lg, May].
2. It means that complete control of the tongue is not to be expected [ICC].

3. The statement is an hyperbole, with an implied exhortation to try to do what is stated as an impossibility [HNTC]: no one can tame the tongue, but you should try to tame it.

QUESTION—What is the genitive noun ἀνθρώπων 'men' connected with?

1. It is connected with οὐδείς 'no one' [AB, Alf, BKC, EBC, Hb, HNTC, ICC, Lg, Lns, Mit, NIC, NIGTC, NTC, TNTC, WBC; all versions]: no one of men. The reference is to one's own tongue [EBC, Lg, Lns, My, NTC]. This word is emphatic by its final position in the clause [Hb, May, WBC].
2. It is connected with γλῶσσαν 'tongue' [Blm]: the tongue of men.

(an) unstable[a] evil,[b] full[c] of-deathbearing[d] poison.[e]

TEXT—Instead of ἀκατάστατον 'unstable', some manuscripts have ἀκατάσχετον 'unruly'. GNT chooses 'unstable' with a B rating, indicating that the text is almost certain. Ἀκατάσχετον 'unruly' is read by only KJV, Blm.

LEXICON—a. ἀκατάστατος (LN 37.32) (BAGD p. 30): 'unstable' [BAGD, Lns], 'restless' [Herm, HNTC; NAB, NASB, NIV, NRSV, REB], 'disorderly' [WBC], 'irreducible to order' [NIC], 'uncontrolled' [LN], 'not controlled' [LN], 'uncontrollable' [AB; TEV, TNT], 'which cannot be controlled' [LN], 'which no one can control' [LN], different text 'unruly' [KJV]. The phrase ἀκατάστατον κακόν 'an unstable evil' is translated 'it is a pest that will not keep still' [NJB].

b. κακός (LN 88.106) (BAGD 2. p. 398): 'evil' [AB, BAGD, Herm, HNTC, LN, NIC, WBC; all versions except NJB], 'injurious' [BAGD], 'pernicious' [BAGD], 'base' [Lns].

c. μεστός (LN 59.39) (BAGD 1. p. 508): 'full' [AB, BAGD, Herm, HNTC, Lns, NIC; all versions except REB], 'very full' [LN], 'charged' [REB], 'replete' [WBC].

d. θανατηφόρος (LN 23.115) (BAGD p. 350): 'death-bearing' [Lns], 'death-bringing' [BAGD], 'deadly' [Herm, HNTC, LN, NIC; all versions], 'lethal' [AB, WBC].

e. ἰός (LN 8.74) (BAGD 1.b p. 379): 'poison' [AB, BAGD, Herm, HNTC, LN, Lns, WBC; all versions except REB], 'venom' [LN, NIC; REB].

QUESTION—What relationship is implied by these two phrases?

They give the reason why the tongue cannot be tamed [BKC, NIGTC]: it cannot be tamed because it is an unstable evil and full of deadly poison.

QUESTION—What is the phrase ἀκατάστατον κακόν 'unstable evil' connected with?

It does not directly modify γλῶσσαν 'tongue', but is an independent nominative [AB, Alf, Herm, Lns, May, Mit, My, NIC, NIGTC, WBC; all versions]: it is an unstable evil thing.

QUESTION—What is the adjective μεστή 'full' connected with?

It is feminine, agreeing with the accusative γλῶσσαν 'tongue' [Alf, NTC]; but, since μεστή 'full' is nominative [Bg, Hb, Herm, Lns, My, NTC], it implies a different clause [AB, Hb, Herm, Lns, Mit, My, NTC; all versions]: it (the tongue) is full of death-bearing poison.

QUESTION—How are these two phrases related to the preceding clause?
The first phrase is the figure of a ferocious beast [EBC, Hb, WBC]. The second is the figure of the bite of a poisonous snake [Blm, EBC, NTC, TG].

DISCOURSE UNIT: 3:9-12 [BKC, Hb, NTC]. The topic is the tongue's inconsistency [Hb], the pollution of the tongue [BKC], praising and cursing [NTC].

3:9 With[a] it we-bless[b] the Lord and Father,

TEXT—Instead of κύριον 'Lord' some manuscripts have θεόν 'God'. GNT chooses 'Lord' with an A rating, indicating that the text is certain. Only Bg, EGT, and KJV read 'God'.

LEXICON—a. ἐν with dative object (LN 90.10): 'with' [AB, Herm, HNTC, LN, NIC, WBC; NASB, NIV, NRSV], 'in connection with' [Lns], 'by' [LN]. The phrase ἐν αὐτῇ 'with it' is translated 'therewith' [KJV], 'we use it' [NAB, NJB, REB, TEV, TNT]. This preposition is instrumental in both phrases [Alf, Hb, Lg, May, My, WBC]; it means 'in connection with' [Lns].

b. pres. act. indic. of εὐλογέω (LN **33.356**) (BAGD 1, p. 322): 'to bless' [AB, Herm, HNTC, Lns, NIC, WBC; KJV, NASB, NJB, NRSV], 'to praise' [BAGD, **LN**; NAB, NIV, REB, TNT], 'to extol' [BAGD], 'to give thanks to' [TEV], 'to speak well of' [LN]. The meaning is to praise [Lg, My, TG].

QUESTION—How is this verse related to its context?
It continues the thought of 3:8 [ICC], showing how the tongue is an unstable evil thing, used in an inconsistent manner [Alf, BKC, Blm, EBC, Hb, HNTC, Mit, My, NIGTC, NTC, TNTC, Tsk]. It begins a new aspect of the argument [Hb], changing from metaphor to factual statements [NIGTC, WBC] with specific examples of the tongue's instability [WBC].

QUESTION—What is implied by the repetition of the phrase ἐν αὐτῇ 'with it'?
It adds emphasis to the double use of the tongue [Lns, May, My].

QUESTION—Who is meant by the two verb subjects 'we'?
1. It refers to mankind in general [Alf, IIb, Herm] but does not mean that James himself was guilty [Hb].
2. It refers to Christians [Mit, My, NIGTC, WBC].
2.1 It includes James [My, NIGTC]. James feels that he shares the human weaknesses of the group enough to use "we" [NIGTC].
2.2 It does not include James, but he identifies himself with his readers [Mit].
3. It refers to the Jews, who praised God but cursed the Christians [Lg]. James speaks as a representative of his guilty people [Lg].

QUESTION—What is indicated by the present tense of the two verbs εὐλογοῦμεν 'we bless' and καταρώμεθα 'we curse'?
It indicates that these are repeated actions [Hb] presently occurring [WBC].

JAMES 3:9

QUESTION—What relationship is indicated by the double reference τὸν κύριον καὶ πατέρα 'the Lord and Father'?
Both terms refer to God [AB, Alf, EGT, Hb, HNTC, ICC, Lg, Lns, May, Mit, My, NIC, TG; all versions] as indicated by the one definite article governing both nouns [Hb, Lns]. 'Lord' refers to God's power [Alf, Hb, My], or refers to him as the God of revelation [Lg], or as governor [May], and reflects James's Jewish upbringing [Mit]. 'Father' refers to God's love [Alf, EGT, Hb, My], or refers to him as Creator [HNTC, May], and reflects James's Christian insights [Mit].

and with[a] it we-curse[b] the men[c] the-(ones) made[d] in-accordance-with[e] (the) likeness[f] of-God.

LEXICON—a. ἐν with dative object: 'with'. See this word in the preceding clause.

    b. pres. mid./pass. (deponent = act.) of καταράομαι (LN 33.471) (BAGD p. 417): 'to curse' [AB, BAGD, Herm, HNTC, LN, Lns, NIC, WBC; all versions except REB], 'to invoke curses' [REB]. This word refers to personal verbal abuse [EGT, Hb, Mit], calling a curse upon someone [Hb], disputes and slanderous comments [NIC].

    c. ἄνθρωπος (LN 9.1; 9.24): 'man' [AB, HNTC, LN, NIC; KJV, NAB, NASB, NIV, TNT], 'fellow-man' [REB, TEV], 'fellow' [WBC], 'person' [LN], 'human being' [Herm, LN, Lns]; as a plural: 'people' [NJB], 'those' [NRSV]. This word is generic, referring to mankind in general [Alf, NTC].

    d. perf. act. participle of γίνομαι (LN 13.3; 13.80): 'to be made' [AB, Herm, HNTC, WBC; all versions except TEV], 'to be formed' [LN], 'to be created' [NIC; TEV], 'to come to exist' [LN], 'to be' [LN, Lns]. The perfect tense indicates that the past creation in God's image is still true [Hb, NTC].

    e. κατά with acc. object (LN 89.8) (BAGD II.5.b.α. p. 407): 'in accordance with' [BAGD, LN], 'in' [Herm, HNTC, NIC, WBC; all versions except KJV], 'after' [AB, Lns; KJV].

    f. ὁμοίωσις (LN **64.3**) (BAGD p. 568): 'likeness' [AB, BAGD, Herm, HNTC, LN, Lns, NIC, WBC; all versions except KJV, NJB], 'resemblance' [BAGD], 'similitude' [KJV], 'image' [NJB].

QUESTION—What is implied by the phrase τοὺς καθ' ὁμοίωσιν θεοῦ γεγονότας 'who are made in the likeness of God'?
It implies (by the perfect tense of the participle [Hb]) that God's image remains in mankind [Alf, EBC, Lns, Mit, My], reflected in man's personality, intellect, and emotions [EBC, Hb, Lns], although marred by sin [Alf, EBC, Lns, Mit, My, NIC]. It implies that to curse a human being amounts to cursing God [EGT, Hb, HNTC, NIGTC, NTC, Tsk].

QUESTION—How are the two nouns related in the genitive construction ὁμοίωσιν θεοῦ 'likeness of God'?
The genitive θεοῦ 'of God' is evidently an objective genitive, which is implied by the commentaries but not overtly stated: they are made like God.

3:10 Out-of[a] the same mouth there-comes-out blessing[b] and cursing.[c]
LEXICON—a. ἐκ with genitive object (LN 84.4; 90.16): 'out of' [HNTC, LN, Lns, NIC, WBC; KJV, NAB, NIV, NJB, REB, TNT], 'out from' [LN; TEV], 'from' [AB, Herm, LN; NASB, NRSV].
  b. εὐλογία (LN 33.356; **33.470**) (BAGD 3.a.α. p. 322): 'blessing' [AB, BAGD, Herm, HNTC, **LN**, Lns, NIC, WBC; KJV, NAB, NASB, NJB, NRSV], 'the act of blessing' [BAGD], 'praise' [LN (33.356); NIV, REB, TNT], 'word of thanksgiving' [TEV].
  c. κατάρα (LN **33.470**; **33.471**) (BAGD p. 417): 'cursing' [AB, Herm, LN, Lns, NIC, WBC; KJV, NASB, NIV, NRSV, TEV], 'curse' [BAGD, HNTC; NAB, NJB, REB, TNT], 'imprecation' [BAGD].
QUESTION—How is this verse related to its context?
It is a compact summary of the argument [NIGTC], further emphasizing the inconsistency of the tongue's activity [Alf, EBC, Hb, Lns, My, NIC, NIGTC], and emphasizing that it is the *same* tongue which utters both blessing and cursing [My].

Not it-is-fitting,[a] my brothers,[b] (for) these-things thus[c] to-occur.[d]
LEXICON—a. χρή (LN **71.22**) (BAGD p. 885): 'it is fitting', 'it is necessary' [BAGD], 'it ought' [BAGD], 'ought' [AB, Herm, LN, Lns; KJV, NAB, NASB, NRSV, TNT], 'should' [HNTC, **LN**, WBC; NIV, REB, TEV]. The phrase οὐ χρή 'it is not fitting' is translated 'it is wrong' [NIC] and is very emphatic [NIC]. This entire phrase is translated 'my brothers, this must be wrong' [NJB]. This word implies fitness or congruity [Hb, Tsk].
  b. ἀδελφός (LN 11.23): 'brother' [AB, Herm, HNTC, LN, Lns, NIC, WBC; all versions except NRSV, REB], '(Christian) brother' [LN], 'brother and sister' [NRSV], 'fellow believer' [LN], 'friend' [REB].
  c. οὕτως (LN 61.9): 'thus' [LN], 'so' [AB, Herm, HNTC, LN, Lns, NIC; KJV, NRSV, REB, TNT], 'this way' [NASB], 'in this way' [LN], 'the case' [WBC], not explicit [NAB, NIV, TEV].
  d. pres. mid./pass. (deponent = act.) infin. of γίνομαι (LN 13.3; 13.107) (BAGD II.1. p. 160): 'to occur' [LN], 'to happen' [LN; TEV], 'to be' [AB, BAGD, Herm, HNTC, LN, Lns, NIC, WBC; all versions except NJB, TEV].
QUESTION—What is the meaning of this clause?
It means that the good words should not be mixed up with evil comments in such a manner [Bg], even if not expressed at the same time [NBC]. It condemns such conduct [My] as incongruous [BKC] and inappropriate [Mit]. It does not mean, however, that cursing is permissible if it is not mixed with blessing [EGT, May]; rather, the cursing negates the blessing [May], and raises doubts about the reality of the worship [NBC]. It is only

the cursing that James condemns [NIGTC, WBC]. It assumes that what is in the heart is necessarily expressed through the mouth [WBC]. In the phrase ταῦτα οὕτως 'these things thus', the former word emphasizes the contents of the words and the latter emphasizes their form [My].

QUESTION—What is implied by the phrase ἀδελφοί μου 'my brothers'?

It indicates that James is speaking to believers as well as to others [EBC], and that he is speaking gently and affectionately [Hb]. Believers are able to control their tongue through the power of the Holy Spirit, but they may fail to appropriate that power [EBC].

3:11 Surely-not[a]—(does) the fountain[b] out-of[c] the same opening[d] pour-forth[e] the sweet[f] and the bitter[g]?

LEXICON—a. μήτι (LN 69.16) (BAGD p. 520): (interrogative particle indicating expectation of emphatic negative response) [BAGD, LN], 'surely not' [HNTC], 'do you suppose' [Lns], 'no' (in statement form) [TEV], not explicit [AB, Herm, NIC, WBC; all versions]. This word expects a strong negative reply [Lns, NTC]; it implies that anyone knows that the answer is "No" [Hb].
  b. πηγή (LN 1.78) (BAGD 1. p. 655): 'fountain' [AB, BAGD, NIC; KJV, NASB, REB], 'spring' [BAGD, Herm, HNTC, LN, Lns, WBC; NAB, NIV, NRSV, TNT], 'spring of water' [TEV], 'water supply' [NJB]. The definite article makes this word represent springs in general [Alf, Hb, ICC, My].
  c. ἐκ with genitive object (LN 84.4; 90.16): 'out of' [LN, Lns; NJB], 'out from' [LN], 'from' [AB, Herm, HNTC, LN, NIC, WBC; all versions except KJV, NJB], 'at' [KJV].
  d. ὀπή (LN **1.53**) (BAGD p. 574): 'opening' [BAGD, Herm, HNTC, LN; NASB, NRSV, TEV, TNT], 'hole' [BAGD, **LN**], 'outlet' [NIC; NAB, REB], 'source' [WBC], 'cleft' [Lns], 'pipe' [NJB], 'spout' [AB], 'place' [KJV], not explicit [NIV]. It refers to a split in a rock (or the ground [NTC]) from which water flows [NIGTC, Tsk].
  e. βρύω (LN **14.31**) (BAGD p. 148): 'to pour forth' [BAGD, Herm; NRSV], 'to pour out' [TEV], 'to pour' [AB], 'to gush forth' [HNTC, Lns; NAB], 'to spout forth' [NIC], 'to send forth' [KJV], 'to send out' [NASB, TNT], 'to cause to gush out' [**LN**], 'to give a flow' [NJB], 'to flow' [NIV, REB], 'to yield' [WBC]. This word implies an abundant gushing [Hb, ICC, NTC] that runs over [Lg].
  f. γλυκύς (LN **79.39**) (BAGD p. 162): 'sweet' [AB, BAGD, **LN**, Lns, NIC; KJV, TEV, TNT], 'fresh' [Herm, HNTC, LN, WBC; NAB, NASB, NIV, NJB, NRSV, REB], 'good' [LN]. It refers to water good for drinking [EBC, Hb, Lns].
  g. πικρός (LN 79.41) (BAGD 1. p. 657): 'bitter' [AB, BAGD, HNTC, LN, Lns, NIC; KJV, NASB, TEV, TNT], 'foul' [NAB], 'salt' [WBC; NIV, NJB], 'brackish' [Herm; NRSV, REB]. It refers to water unfit for drinking [EBC, Hb, Lns, Mit].

QUESTION—How is this verse related to its context?
This illustration from nature emphasizes the author's point [BKC, EBC, Hb, NTC] that the two kinds of speech referred to are incompatible [Hb, Herm, TNTC] and contrary to nature [AB, Alf, HNTC, Lg, Lns, My, NIGTC, WBC]. It is stated as a rhetorical QUESTION [NIGTC, NTC, TG, TNTC, WBC] expecting a strong negative response [BKC, Blm, Hb, NTC, TNTC, WBC] to an impossible situation [TG].

QUESTION—What do the two adjectives γλυκύ 'sweet' and πικρόν 'bitter' refer to?
They refer to water [Alf; all versions], and the point is the contrast between these two adjectives [Alf].

3:12 No[a]—is-able, my brothers, a fig-tree to-produce[b] olives or a grapevine figs?

LEXICON—a. μή (LN 69.15): (a marker indicating that a negative response to a QUESTION is expected) [LN], 'no', 'surely not' [HNTC], 'of course not' [TNT], 'do you suppose' [Lns], 'not' (in statement form) [NAB, TEV], not explicit [AB, Herm, NIC, WBC; KJV, NASB, NIV, NJB, NRSV, REB]. This word expects a negative reply, implying the impossibility of the following QUESTION [Bg, BKC, Hb].

b. aorist act. infin. of ποιέω (LN 13.9) (BAGD I.1.b.η. p. 681): 'to produce' [BAGD, HNTC, NIC, WBC; NAB, NASB, REB, TNT], 'to bear' [BAGD; NIV, TEV], 'to yield' [AB, BAGD, Herm, Lns; KJV, NJB, NRSV], 'to make' [LN].

QUESTION—How is this verse related to its context?
It further illustrates (and concludes [EBC]) the argument against contradictory speech [BKC, HNTC, Lg, Lns, Mit, My, NIGTC, WBC], showing that it is against nature [AB, Alf, Hb, HNTC, Lg, Mit, My, NIGTC]. The point is that if the mouth utters evil speech it becomes like a brackish spring and is unable to utter truly good speech [Alf, Lns, My].

Neither (is) salt[a] water (able) to-produce sweet.[b]

TEXT—Some manuscripts insert οὕτως 'thus' before οὔτε 'neither'. GNT omits this word with a B decision, indicating that the omission is almost certain. 'Thus' is added by Bg, Blm, and KJV.

LEXICON—a. ἁλυκός (LN 5.26) (BAGD p. 41): 'salt' [AB, HNTC, Lns, NIC; KJV, NASB, NRSV, REB, TNT], 'salt spring' [Herm; NIV], 'salty' [BAGD, LN], 'salty spring' [TEV], 'salt-water spring' [WBC], 'sea water' [NJB], 'brackish' [NAB]. This adjective modifies the following noun ὕδωρ 'water' [Lns]. The reference is to a salt spring [Hb, ICC, NIGTC, TG, TNTC].

b. γλυκύς: 'sweet', 'fresh' [NIC]. See this word at 3:11.

QUESTION—How is this clause related to the preceding clause?
1. For those who do not add οὕτως 'thus' at the beginning of this clause.
  1.1 It is parallel to the preceding clause, giving an additional example [Alf, BKC, Herm, Lns, May; NAB] as a climax to the illustrations [Lns]: a

grapevine cannot produce figs, nor can a salt spring produce sweet water.
1.2 It gives a conclusion to the preceding clause [My, NTC]: a grapevine cannot produce figs, and therefore a salt spring cannot produce sweet water.
2. For those who add οὕτως 'thus' at the beginning of this clause, it gives a conclusion to the preceding clause [Bg; KJV]: a grapevine cannot produce figs, and thus a salt spring cannot produce sweet water.

QUESTION—How are the words ἁλυκόν 'salt' and γλυκύ 'sweet' related to one another?

'Ἁλυκόν 'salt' describes the subject of the clause and γλυκύ 'sweet' the object [My]. These two words are placed beside each other for emphasis [My].

DISCOURSE UNIT: 3:13–4:12 [Herm; REB]. The topic is several comments against being contentious [Herm], the sin of envy [REB].

DISCOURSE UNIT: 3:13–18 [AB, BKC, EBC, GNT, Hb, HNTC, ICC, Lns, Mit, NIC, NIGTC, NTC, TG, TNTC, Tsk, WBC; NAB, NASB, NIV, NJB, TEV]. The topic is two varieties of wisdom [EBC, Lns, NTC, Tsk, WBC; NIV], true wisdom and its opposite [Mit; NJB], true wisdom [TG; NAB], true wisdom which is from above [GNT; TEV], the wisdom which is from above [HNTC; NASB], having true wisdom produces peace [TNTC], having true wisdom includes living humbly [AB], the kind of wisdom which controls the tongue [Hb], a description of a wise man's wisdom [ICC], the contrast between the tongue's controversies and the results of wisdom [NIC], an exhortation to cultivate right thoughts [BKC], pure speech having its source in true wisdom [NIGTC].

3:13 Who (is) wise[a] and understanding[b] among[c] you?

LEXICON—a. σοφός (LN 32.33) (BAGD 3. p. 760): 'wise' [AB, BAGD, Herm, HNTC, LN, Lns, WBC; all versions], 'understanding' [LN], 'prudent' [LN], 'a man of wisdom' [NIC]. This word refers to moral perception and ability to deal with practical matters [BKC, ICC, NIC], to acquired knowledge [Lg], to wisdom acquired from God [Blm, Lg(M)], to the characteristic of a teacher [EBC].

b. ἐπιστήμων (LN **32.27**) (BAGD p. 300): 'understanding' [BAGD, Herm, HNTC, **LN**, Lns, WBC; all versions except KJV, REB], 'insightful' [LN], 'perceptive' [AB], 'learned' [BAGD; REB], 'intelligent' [LN], 'endued with knowledge' [KJV], 'a man of knowledge' [NIC]. This word refers to intellectual insight [BKC], to natural wisdom needed by a teacher [Blm], to knowledge acquired by experience [Lg], to the result of special training [EBC, Lg(M)], an expert [ICC]. This and the preceding adjective are essentially synonymous [Hb, Lns, Mit, My, TG]. This word qualifies the preceding adjective [NTC].

c. ἐν with dative object (LN 83.9): 'among' [AB, Herm, HNTC, LN, Lns, NIC, WBC; KJV, NASB, NIV, NJB, NRSV, TEV], 'of' [REB], not explicit [NAB]. The phrase ἐν ὑμῖν 'among you' is translated 'in your company' [TNT].

QUESTION—What is the function of this QUESTION?

It is a rhetorical question [Herm, Mit, Tsk] putting forth the principal point of the discussion [My] and challenging the readers [Mit, TG] (the teachers only [NBC, NIC, Tsk]) to examine themselves in the area described in the following clause [Hb, HNTC, Lns, NTC, TNTC, WBC] and to examine one another to determine who are worthy to be followed as models [Lns]. The QUESTION implies that all should be wise, but not all are wise [Lns].

Let-him-show[a] from[b] the good conduct[c] the deeds[d] of-him in[e] gentleness[f] of-wisdom.[g]

LEXICON—a. aorist act. impera. of δείκνυμι (LN **28.47**) (BAGD 2. p. 172): 'to show' [AB, Herm, LN, Lns, NIC; KJV, NAB, NASB, NIV, NRSV], 'to demonstrate' [HNTC, **LN**, WBC], 'to prove' [BAGD; TEV], 'to make known' [LN], 'to give evidence' [NJB]. The phrase δειξάτω τὰ ἔργα αὐτοῦ 'let him show his deeds' is translated 'let him give practical proof of it' [REB]. The phrase δειξάτω ἐκ τῆς καλῆς ἀναστροφῆς τὰ ἔργα αὐτοῦ 'let him show from the good conduct his deeds' is translated 'let his life and conduct be an example' [TNT]. The meaning is to give proof [NTC]. The aorist tense looks at each individual act rather than the habitual conduct [Alf]; it calls for an effective demonstration [Hb].

b. ἐκ with genitive object (LN 89.77): 'from' [HNTC, LN, Lns], 'out of' [KJV], 'of' [NJB], 'by' [Herm, NIC, WBC; NASB, NIV, NRSV, REB, TEV], 'by means of' [LN], 'through' [AB]. The phrase ἐκ τῆς καλῆς ἀναστροφῆς τὰ ἔργα αὐτοῦ 'from the good conduct the deeds of him' is translated 'in practice' [NAB].

c. ἀναστροφή (LN 41.3) (BAGD p. 61): 'conduct' [AB, BAGD, LN, Lns, WBC; REB], 'behavior' [BAGD, LN; NASB], 'life' [Herm, LN; NIV, NJB, NRSV, TEV], 'way of life' [BAGD, NIC], 'mode of life' [HNTC], 'conversation' [KJV].

d. ἔργον (LN 42.11; 42.12) (BAGD 1.c.β. p. 308): 'deed' [BAGD, LN, WBC; NASB, NIV, NJB, TEV], 'work' [Herm, HNTC, Lns, NIC; KJV, NRSV], 'act' [LN], 'accomplishment' [BAGD], 'achievement' [AB], 'workmanship' [LN].

e. ἐν with dative object (LN 13.8; 89.80; 89.84): 'in' [AB, Herm, LN, NIC, WBC; NASB, NIV, NJB], 'with' [HNTC, LN; KJV, NRSV, REB, TEV], 'in connection with' [Lns], 'through' [NAB], not explicit [TNT].

f. πραΰτης (LN 88.59) (BAGD p. 699): 'gentleness' [BAGD, LN; NASB, NJB, NRSV], 'humility' [AB, BAGD, HNTC, WBC; NAB, NIV, TEV, TNT], 'courtesy' [BAGD], 'considerateness' [BAGD], 'mildness' [LN], 'meekness' [BAGD, LN, Lns, NIC; KJV], 'modesty' [REB], as an adjective 'meek' [Herm]. It is the gentleness of strength under control [EBC, Hb].

g. σοφία (LN 32.32) (BAGD 2. p. 759): 'wisdom' [BAGD, Herm, HNTC, LN, Lns, NIC, WBC; all versions except NAB], 'good sense' [NAB], as an adjective 'wise' [AB]. See this word at 1:5.

QUESTION—What relationship is indicated by ἐν 'in'?

1. It is connected with the verb δειξάτω 'let him show' and indicates the means by which he shows it [Alf, My]: let him show by gentleness of wisdom.
2. It is connected with ἔργα 'works' and specifies the kind of work [HNTC, WBC; NIV, NJB, NRSV, TEV]: let him show that his works are performed in gentleness of wisdom.
3. It is connected with all of the preceding clause [Lg]: the deeds of a good lifestyle should culminate in gentleness of wisdom.

QUESTION—How are the two nouns related in the genitive construction πραΰτητι σοφίας 'gentleness of wisdom'?

1. Σοφίας 'wisdom' describes πραΰτητι 'gentleness' [AB, BKC, EBC, ICC, Lns, My, TNTC, Tsk; NAB, NIV, NRSV, REB, TNT]: wise gentleness. It is gentleness which is to be demonstrated, not wisdom [ICC].
2. Πραΰτητι 'gentleness' describes the character of the genitive noun σοφίας 'wisdom' [Alf, Blm, Hb, Herm, Lg, May, Mit, NTC]: gentle wisdom. Meekness is a characteristic of true wisdom [Hb].
3. The two nouns are treated as parallel [TEV]: gentleness and wisdom.

3:14 But/And[a] if you-have bitter[b] jealousy[c] and selfish-ambition[d] in[e] your heart,

LEXICON—a. δέ (LN 89.124, 89.94): 'but' [AB, Herm, Lns, NIC, WBC; all versions except NAB, NRSV], 'instead' [NAB], 'for' [NRSV], not explicit [HNTC].

b. πικρός (LN 88.170) (BAGD 2. p. 657): 'bitter' [AB, BAGD, Herm, HNTC, Lns, NIC; all versions except NJB, TEV], 'harsh' [WBC], 'resentful' [LN]. This adjective is also translated as a noun: 'bitterness' [NJB]. The phrase ζῆλον πικρὸν ἔχετε καὶ ἐριθείαν 'you have bitter jealousy and selfish ambition' is translated 'you are jealous, bitter, and selfish' [TEV]. This word is emphatic by its position [EGT] and indicates a harsh attitude [Hb, Lg]; it strengthens the negative sense of ζῆλον 'zeal' [My].

c. ζῆλος (LN 88.162) (BAGD 2. p. 337): 'jealousy' [AB, BAGD, Herm, HNTC, LN, NIC; NAB, NASB, NJB, REB], 'zeal' [Lns], 'envy' [BAGD, LN, WBC; NIV, NRSV, TNT], 'envying' [KJV], 'resentment' [LN]. In a good sense, the word means 'zeal', but with the adjective πικρόν 'bitter', it is to be taken in the bad sense of jealousy and envy [BAGD]. It is a fanatical zeal for an evil cause [EBC], a bitter aggressiveness [AB]. The person regards himself as jealous for the truth and manifests a harsh zeal or rivalry [NIGTC, WBC]. It is a strong feeling of resentment and jealousy against others [LN]. The phrase 'bitter jealousy' is forefronted for emphasis [Hb].

d. ἐριθεία (LN 39.7; 88.167) (BAGD p. 309): 'selfish ambition' [BAGD, HNTC, LN, WBC; NAB, NASB, NIV, NJB, NRSV, TNT], 'selfishness' [BAGD, Lns], 'ambition' [AB], 'rivalry' [LN], 'spirit of rivalry' [REB], 'resentfulness' [LN], 'hostility' [LN], 'strife' [KJV], 'faction' [NIC], 'party spirit' [Herm]. It refers to unethical self-seeking to gain advantage [EBC, Hb, ICC, NBC, TG].

e. ἐν with dative object (LN 83.13): 'in' [AB, Herm, HNTC, LN, Lns, NIC, WBC; all versions except NJB], 'within' [LN], 'inside' [LN]. The phrase ἐν τῇ καρδίᾳ ὑμῶν 'in your heart' is translated 'at heart' [NJB].

QUESTION—What relationship is indicated by δέ 'but/and'?

1. It indicates contrast [AB, Alf, Hb, Herm, NIC, NIGTC, NTC, WBC; all versions except NRSV]. The meek person in 3:13 is contrasted with the selfish person in this verse [NIGTC, NTC, WBC]. It points to the consequences of the opposite course of that in 3:13 [Alf].

2. It indicates continuance, not contrast [ICC].

QUESTION—What is implied by the conditional clause with εἰ 'if' and the indicative mood ἔχετε 'you have'?

It implies that some do have this attitude [Alf, EBC, Hb, NTC], although the use of the conditional clause softens the statement [Hb]: if you do, as some of you do. (Note: The εἰ 'if' clause with the indicative means merely that they either do or do not presently have this attitude; only the *context* implies that they *do* have it.) However, boasting and lying would be prohibited even if they were not the result of selfish ambition and jealousy [HNTC, TNTC]. The meaning is that if these qualities are in their heart they should not express them [ICC].

QUESTION—What is the phrase ἐν τῇ καρδίᾳ ὑμῶν 'in your heart' connected with?

It is connected with both ζῆλον πικρόν 'bitter jealousy' and ἐριθείαν 'selfish ambition' [Hb]: both bitter jealousy and selfish ambition in your heart.

(do) not boast[a] and lie[b] against[c] the truth.[d]

LEXICON—a. pres. mid. (deponent = act.) impera. of κατακαυχάομαι (LN 33.370; 88.194) (BAGD 1. p. 411): 'to boast' [AB, BAGD, Herm, HNTC, Lns; NIV], 'to be boastful' [NJB, NRSV], 'to boast against' [LN (33.370)], 'to brag' [BAGD, WBC], 'to be arrogant' [NASB], 'to glory' [NIC; KJV], 'to degrade' [LN], 'to despise' [LN (88.194)], 'to look down on' [LN]. The phrase μὴ κατακαυχᾶσθε καὶ ψεύδεσθε 'do not boast and lie' is translated 'at least refrain from arrogant and false claims' [NAB], 'stop making false claims in defiance of' [REB], 'don't sin by boasting of your wisdom' [TEV], 'do not make false claims for yourselves and fly in

the face of' [TNT]. The prefixed κατα- adds the meaning of 'against' [Alf, My]. The sense is gloating in assumed superiority [Hb].
b. pres. mid. (deponent = act.) of ψεύδομαι (LN 33.253) (BAGD 1. p. 891): 'to lie' [AB, BAGD, HNTC, LN, Lns; KJV, NASB], 'to be false' [NRSV], 'to deny' [WBC], as a phrase 'with lies' [Herm], 'in your lies' [NIC]. The phrase καὶ ψεύδεσθε κατὰ τῆς ἀληθείας 'and lie against the truth' is translated 'or deny the truth' [NIV], 'or hide the truth with lies' [NJB]. The negative μή 'not' applies to this verb as well as to the preceding verb [Hb].
c. κατά with genitive object (LN 90.31) (BAGD I.2.b.β. p. 406): 'against' [AB, BAGD, HNTC, LN, Lns, NIC; KJV, NAB, NASB, TEV], 'in defiance of' [Herm], 'to' [NRSV], 'in conflict with' [LN], not explicit [WBC; REB, TNT].
d. ἀλήθεια (LN 72.2) (BAGD 2.a. p. 35): 'truth' [AB, BAGD, Herm, HNTC, LN, Lns, NIC, WBC; all versions]. With the definite article, the meaning is objective truth [Alf], the Christian truth [Hb, ICC, Lns], the truth of God's revelation [Lg], the facts of the present case [May], reality rather than mere appearance [Mit].

QUESTION—How are the two verbs κατακαυχᾶσθε 'boast' and ψεύδεσθε 'lie' related?

The present tenses imply continuation [NIC, NTC, WBC]: don't continue to boast and lie. They have been boasting [WBC]. (Note: The present imperative with μή 'not' means 'don't be doing this', and only the context can indicate whether or not they have been doing it.)

1. The two are parallel [EBC, EGT, HNTC, Lg, Lns, My, NBC, NTC; KJV, NAB, NIV, NJB] and redundant [Herm]: don't boast and don't lie.
2. The second verb is the result of the first [Hb, May, NIC, TG, TNTC, WBC; NASB, TEV]: don't lie by boasting.

QUESTION—What is the phrase κατὰ τῆς ἀληθείας 'against the truth' connected with?

1. It is connected with both verbs [Herm, HNTC, Lg, Lns, Mit, My; NAB, REB]: don't boast against the truth and lie against it.
2. It is connected with only ψεύδεσθε 'lie' [EBC, EGT, Hb, ICC, May, NBC, NIC, NTC, TG, TNTC, WBC; KJV, NASB, NIV, NJB, TEV, TNT]: don't lie against the truth.

3:15 Not is this the wisdom coming-down[a] from-above[b]

LEXICON—a. pres. mid. (deponent = act.) participle of κατέρχομαι (LN 15.107) (BAGD 2. p. 422): 'to come down' [AB, BAGD, Herm, HNTC, LN, Lns, WBC; NASB, NIV, NRSV, TEV, TNT], 'to descend' [LN, NIC; KJV], 'to come' [NAB, NJB, REB]. The present tense implies continual coming down [Lg]. It implies that it comes down from God, the source of this wisdom [LN].

b. ἄνωθεν (LN 84.13) (BAGD 1. p. 77): 'from above' [AB, BAGD, Herm, HNTC, LN, Lns, NIC; all versions except NIV, TEV], 'from heaven' [WBC; NIV, TEV].

QUESTION—What is the subject of the verb in this verse?

1. The subject of the verb is αὕτη ἡ σοφία 'this wisdom' [AB, BKC, EBC, Herm, Lg, Lns, Mit, My, NBC, NIC, NIGTC, TG, WBC; KJV, NAB, NIV, NRSV, TEV]: this wisdom is not coming down from above. The verb phrase ἔστιν κατερχομένη 'is coming down' is periphrastic [NTC, WBC].
2. The subject of the verb is αὕτη 'this' and ἡ σοφία 'the wisdom' is the predicate of ἔστιν 'is' [AB, Alf, Blm, Hb, Herm, HNTC, Lns, May; NASB, NIV, NIGTC; NJB, REB, TNT]: this is not the wisdom that comes down from above.
   2.1 The participle κατερχομένη 'coming down' is treated as indefinite attributive [Alf, Hb, Lns, May, NIC]: this wisdom is not one which comes down from above.
   2.2 The participle κατερχομένη 'coming down' is treated as definite attributive [Blm, Herm, HNTC, NIGTC; NASB, NJB, REB, TNT]: this wisdom is not *the one* which comes from above. (Note: this violates Greek grammar, since this participle has no definite article.)

but (it is) earthly,ᵃ unspiritual,ᵇ demonic.ᶜ

LEXICON—a. ἐπίγειος (LN **9.7**) (BAGD 1. p. 290): 'earthly' [AB, BAGD, Herm, HNTC, Lns; KJV, NASB, NIV, NJB, NRSV, TNT], 'of the earth' [NIC], 'on the earth' [LN], 'earthbound' [WBC; NAB, REB], 'belongs to the world' [TEV], 'human' [LN], 'characteristic of people' [**LN**], 'that people produce' [**LN**]. This word expresses strong contrast with ἄνωθεν 'from above' [Alf, EGT, My, NTC], referring to the turbulence of unregenerated human life [Hb, ICC, Lns], to earthly motives [Tsk], to what is essentially human [EGT]. It reflects the attitude of those who oppose God [WBC].

b. ψυχικός (LN 41.41) (BAGD 1. p. 894): 'unspiritual' [BAGD, HNTC, LN; NIV, NRSV, TEV, TNT], 'sensual' [AB, Lns, WBC; KJV, REB], 'psychical' [Herm], 'worldly' [LN], 'of this life' [NIC], 'natural' [LN; NASB], 'human' [NJB], 'animal' [NAB]. It refers to wisdom arising from fallen humanity [Hb, Tsk]. The meaning is decisively negative [Herm, TNTC], referring to the natural life [Lns] which both people and animals have [ICC] and in contrast with πνευματικός 'spiritual' [Mit, NIC], meaning devoid of the Holy Spirit [NIGTC, Tsk], having only human reasoning [TNTC].

c. δαιμονιώδης (LN **12.40**) (BAGD p. 169): 'demonic' [AB, BAGD, Herm, **LN**, WBC; NASB, REB, TEV, TNT], 'demoniacal' [Lns], 'demon-like' [HNTC], 'devilish' [LN; KJV, NAB, NJB, NRSV], 'of the devil' [NIC; NIV]. It refers not to the devil but to unclean spirits, demons [Hb]. It refers to the way in which a demon acts [LN].

QUESTION—What relationship is indicated by the three adjectives describing this so-called wisdom?

They form a climax, each one indicating greater alienation from God [Hb, Herm, ICC, Mit, My, NIGTC, NTC, WBC].

3:16 For[a] where (there is) jealousy[b] and selfish-ambition,[c] there (is) disorder[d] and every evil[e] thing.[f]

LEXICON—a. γάρ (LN 89.23): 'for' [AB, Herm, HNTC, LN, Lns, NIC, WBC; KJV, NASB, NIV, NRSV, REB, TNT], 'because' [LN], not explicit [NAB, NJB, TEV].

b. ζῆλος: 'jealousy'. See this word at 3:14.

c. ἐριθεία: 'selfish ambition'. See this word at 3:14.

d. ἀκαταστασία (LN 39.34; 39.36) (BAGD 2. p. 30): 'disorder' [BAGD, Herm, WBC; NASB, NIV, NRSV, REB, TEV], 'disturbance' [Lns], 'confusion' [NIC; KJV], 'chaos' [TNT], 'disharmony' [NJB], 'instability' [AB, HNTC], 'inconstancy' [NAB], 'unruliness' [BAGD], 'revolt' [LN (39.34)], 'riot' [LN (39.36)]. It refers to turmoil in the church [EBC, Hb, NBC] by the disappearance of order, a spirit opposing God's plan [Lg].

e. φαῦλος (LN 88.116) (BAGD 1. p. 854): 'evil' [BAGD, LN, NIC, WBC; KJV, NASB, NIV], 'bad' [BAGD, LN, Lns], 'base' [BAGD], 'foul' [AB], 'vile' [Herm; NAB], 'mean' [HNTC, LN], 'worthless' [BAGD]. The phrase πᾶν φαῦλον πρᾶγμα 'every evil deed' is translated 'wickedness of every kind' [NJB, NRSV], 'every kind of evil' [TEV, TNT], 'the practice of every kind of evil' [REB].

f. πρᾶγμα (LN 13.105) (BAGD 4. p. 697): 'thing' [BAGD, Lns; NASB], 'matter' [BAGD], 'affair' [BAGD], 'event' [LN], 'happening' [LN], 'action' [HNTC], 'work' [KJV], 'deed' [AB], 'practice' [Herm, WBC; NIV], 'behavior' [NAB], not explicit [NIC].

QUESTION—What relationship is indicated by γάρ 'for'?

It indicates the grounds of the comment in the preceding verse [Alf, Hb, Herm, ICC, Lg, My, NIGTC, TNTC, Tsk, WBC].

QUESTION—What is the meaning of this clause?

It indicates that this false wisdom results in all sorts of evil matters [AB, EBC, Hb, Lg, Lns, Mit, NIC, Tsk, WBC], destroying spiritual life [EBC]. Ὅπου 'where' (pointing back to 3:14 [My]) introduces the manifestations of this so-called wisdom, and ἐκεῖ 'there' introduces its results [Hb, My, NTC].

QUESTION—What is meant by πᾶν φαῦλον πρᾶγμα 'every evil thing'?

It sums up the discussion [EGT] and refers to deeds that are bad because no real benefit can ever result from them [EBC, Hb]. James does not mean that every local church will have all sorts of evil practices [NBC].

3:17 But the wisdom from-above[a] is indeed/on-the-one-hand[b] first pure,[c] then peaceable,[d] gentle,[e] obedient,[f] full[g] of mercy[h] and good[i] fruits,[j] impartial,[k] genuine.[l]

LEXICON—a. ἄνωθεν 'from above'. See this word at 3:15.

b. μέν (LN 91.6) (BAGD 2.c. p. 503): 'indeed' [LN], 'then' [LN], 'by contrast' [NAB], 'essentially' [NJB], not explicit [AB, Herm, HNTC, Lns, NIC, WBC; all versions except KJV, NAB].

c. ἁγνός (LN 88.28) (BAGD 2. p. 12): 'pure' [AB, BAGD, Herm, HNTC, LN, Lns, NIC, WBC; all versions except NAB], 'without defect' [LN], 'innocent' [NAB]. It is the basic quality (the inner quality [May, My]) of this wisdom [EBC, Hb, TNTC, WBC], and the following terms are specifics of it [EBC, Hb, Herm, ICC, NIC, NIGTC], as the introductory ἔπειτα 'then' implies [ICC]; it implies purity from defilements of any kind [Bg, Hb, ICC, My, NIC, Tsk, WBC], without moral flaw [HNTC, TNTC], pure in motives and tendency [Blm, NIC, NTC], sincerely following God's moral directives [NIGTC, WBC], pure in the sense of single-mindedness [Mit]. It is inseparable from the concept of holiness [EGT, NTC].

d. εἰρηνικός (LN 25.249) (BAGD p. 228): 'peaceable' [BAGD, Herm, HNTC, Lns, NIC; KJV, NAB, NASB, NJB, NRSV], 'peaceful' [AB, LN; TEV, TNT], 'peace-loving' [NIV, REB], 'peacemaking' [WBC], 'free from worry' [LN]. This word is the general concept, the following words are the specifics [Bg]. It is the opposite of the attitudes mentioned in the preceding verse [EBC]. It deals with relations to others [Lns], desiring peace and working to bring it about [Hb, Mit]. This word is further described by the two following adjectives [TNTC, WBC].

e. ἐπιεικής (LN 88.63) (BAGD p. 292): 'gentle' [BAGD, Herm, LN, WBC; KJV, NASB, NRSV, TEV, TNT], 'forbearing' [LN], 'gracious' [LN], 'considerate' [NIV, REB], 'humane' [NIC], 'reasonable' [AB], 'equitable' [HNTC], 'yielding' [BAGD, Lns], 'kind' [BAGD], 'kindly' [NJB], 'lenient' [NAB]. It means not insisting on the letter of one's rights [EBC, Mit, NBC, NIC, TNTC, WBC], avoiding severity in dealing with other persons [Hb, NIC].

f. εὐπειθής (LN **33.305**) (BAGD p. 324): 'obedient' [BAGD, Lns], 'compliant' [BAGD], 'submissive' [NIV], 'deferential' [WBC], 'docile' [NAB], 'reasonable' [NASB, TNT], 'open-minded' [REB], 'open to reason' [LN], 'persuadable' [HNTC], 'willing to yield' [NRSV], 'yielding to persuasion' [NIC], 'tractable' [AB, Herm], 'easy to be entreated' [KJV], 'considerate' [NJB], 'friendly' [TEV]. It implies willingness to learn from others and yield to others when no moral principle is involved [Hb, NBC, NIGTC, NTC, WBC]. It is the opposite of self-seeking and obstinacy [EBC, ICC, Lg, Mit].

g. μεστός (LN **78.45**) (BAGD 2.a. p. 508): 'full' [AB, BAGD, Herm, HNTC, LN, Lns, NIC, WBC; all versions except NAB, REB], 'rich' [NAB, REB]. The phrase μεστὴ ἐλέους 'full of mercy' is translated 'entirely merciful' [**LN**]. It implies an abundant measure [My].

h. ἔλεος (LN 88.76) (BAGD 1. p. 250): 'mercy' [AB, BAGD, Herm, HNTC, LN, Lns, NIC, WBC; KJV, NASB, NIV, NJB, NRSV, TNT], 'compassion' [BAGD; REB, TEV], 'pity' [BAGD], 'clemency' [BAGD], 'sympathy' [NAB]. It implies compassionate help for those in need [Blm, Hb, ICC, Mit, NBC, NIGTC, TNTC].

i. ἀγαθός (LN 88.1): 'good' [AB, Herm, HNTC, LN, Lns, NIC, WBC; KJV, NASB, NIV, NRSV]. The phrase καρπῶν ἀγαθῶν 'good fruits' is translated 'produces a harvest of good deeds' [TEV], 'produces a harvest of goodness' [TNT], 'kindly deeds that are its fruit' [NAB], 'deeds of kindness that are its fruit' [REB], 'shows itself by doing good' [NJB]. The goodness here is moral beneficence [Hb, Lns].

j. καρπός (LN 42.13) (BAGD 2.a. p. 405): 'fruit' [AB, Herm, HNTC, Lns, NIC, WBC; KJV, NASB, NIV, NRSV], 'deed' [LN], 'product' [BAGD], 'activity' [LN], 'result' [BAGD]. The plural here refers to many acts [Hb]. It is practical help to the needy [Mit].

k. ἀδιάκριτος (LN **88.242**) (BAGD p. 17): 'impartial' [AB, BAGD, LN, WBC; NAB, NIV, TNT], 'without partiality' [KJV], 'without a trace of partiality' [NRSV], 'nor is there any trace of partiality in it' [NJB], 'free from prejudice' [**LN**; TEV], 'not making distinctions' [HNTC], 'straightforward' [REB], 'harmonious' [Herm], 'unwavering' [BAGD; NASB], 'without vacillation' [Lns], 'undivided in mind' [NIC]. It means not making improper distinctions [NBC], for example, between the high and the humble [Bg], not acting with duplicity [Hb], showing no favoritism [Mit].

l. ἀνυπόκριτος (LN 73.8) (BAGD p. 76): 'genuine' [BAGD, LN], 'sincere' [BAGD, Herm, LN, WBC; NAB, NIV, REB, TNT], 'free from insincerity' [BAGD], 'without dissimulation' [HNTC, Lns], 'not hypocritical' [AB], 'free from hypocrisy' [TEV], 'without hypocrisy' [KJV, NASB], 'untainted with hypocrisy' [NIC], 'without a trace of hypocrisy' [NRSV], 'nor is there any trace of hypocrisy in it' [NJB]. It means free from pretense [Hb].

QUESTION—Why is this clause mentioned?

It describes heavenly wisdom [Alf, Blm, Mit, My, NIGTC, TNTC, WBC] and praises it [Alf], telling what it does for people [My, NBC, TNTC, WBC]. The conjunction δέ 'but' indicates a contrast with the preceding verse [Alf, WBC]. The qualities fall into three groups [NJB, REB, TEV, TNT]: (1) three adjectives describing social virtues [Lg], describing the attitude of the wise man [NTC], describing the manifestations of this wisdom [My], (2) a phrase introduced by μεστή 'full,' describing the wise man's actions [NTC], and (3) two adjectives similar to one another in sound [ICC, Lns, My], describing the wise man's judgment [NTC]. 'Peaceable' is more subjective, the remaining qualities are social [NIC].

QUESTION—What is the meaning of μέν 'indeed/on the one hand'?

Here it has an emphasizing sense [Bg, Hb], followed by ἔπειτα 'then', implying addition [Hb]: indeed. With πρῶτον 'first' it separates the quality ἁγνή 'pure' from the following qualities [My].

3:18 And[a] (the) fruit[b] of-righteousness[c] is-sown[d] in[e] peace[f] for/by-the-(ones) doing[g] peace.[f]

LEXICON—a. δέ (LN 89.87; 89.94): 'and' [AB, HNTC, LN, NIC; KJV, NASB, NRSV, TEV], 'and then' [LN], 'moreover' [Lns], not explicit [Herm, WBC; NAB, NIV, NJB, REB, TNT]. It adds to the preceding [Hb, Lns] and introduces the result of the preceding thought [Alf, Hb].
- b. καρπός (LN 43.15)(BAGD 2.a. p. 404): 'fruit' [AB, BAGD, Herm, HNTC, LN, Lns, NIC, WBC; KJV, NASB], 'harvest' [LN; all versions except KJV, NASB]. This word refers to the seed which results in the fruit [Herm, Lg, My].
- c. δικαιοσύνη (LN 88.13) (BAGD 2.b. p. 196): 'righteousness' [AB, BAGD, Herm, HNTC, LN, Lns, NIC, WBC; KJV, NASB, NIV, NRSV, REB, TNT], 'uprightness' [BAGD], 'doing what is right' [LN], 'doing what God requires' [LN], 'goodness' [TEV], 'justice' [NAB, NJB]. This word refers to the heavenly wisdom expressed in a holy life [Blm], the true righteousness which all Christians should manifest [Lns], ethical righteousness [My, TG].
- d. pres. pass. indic. of σπείρω (LN 43.6) (BAGD 1.b.γ. p. 761): 'to be sown' [AB, BAGD, Herm, HNTC, LN, Lns, NIC, WBC; KJV, NAB, NASB, NJB, NRSV, TNT]; as an active voice: 'to sow' [NIV], 'to plant' [TEV]. The phrase ἐν εἰρήνῃ σπείρεται 'is sown in peace' is translated 'peace is the seed-bed' [REB]. The present tense refers to customary practice [Hb]. The unnamed sower is the righteous man [Hb, ICC, My].
- e. ἐν with dative object (LN 13.8; 89.84): 'in' [Herm, HNTC, LN, Lns, NIC, WBC; KJV, NAB, NASB, NIV, NRSV, TEV], 'with' [LN], not explicit [NJB]. The phrase ἐν εἰρήνῃ 'in peace' is translated 'peaceably' [TNT], 'which is peace' [AB].
- f. εἰρήνη (LN 22.42) (BAGD 1.b. p. 227): 'peace' [BAGD, Herm, HNTC, LN, Lns, NIC, WBC; all versions except TNT], 'tranquility' [LN]. The primary reference is to peace in the community [Mit].
- g. pres. act. participle of ποιέω (LN 90.45) (BAGD I.1.b.γ. p. 681): 'to do' [LN], 'to make' [BAGD, Herm, HNTC, LN, Lns, WBC; KJV, NASB, NRSV], 'to bring about' [BAGD], 'to practice' [LN], 'to establish' [BAGD], 'to cultivate' [NIC; NAB]. The phrase τοῖς ποιοῦσιν εἰρήνην 'the ones doing peace' is translated 'the peacemakers' [NIV, NJB, REB, TEV, TNT], 'the peaceful' [AB]. The present tense indicates characteristic behavior [Hb]; they are peaceful and work to promote peace [Hb, ICC, NIC, NTC, TG].

QUESTION—How is this verse related to its context?
1. It gives the result of the peaceable spirit described in the preceding verse [Alf, Blm, EGT], an emphatic conclusion [WBC]. The link is the concept of peace [Mit]; it expands on this concept [EBC, Lns, NIGTC, TNTC, WBC] and closes the argument [NIC], leading on to the following passage [NIGTC, WBC]. It is expressed in the form of a popular proverb [NIGTC, NTC, TNTC, WBC].

2. It is an isolated saying, not connected with either the preceding or the following verses [Herm].

QUESTION—How are the two nouns related in the genitive construction καρπὸς δικαιοσύνης 'fruit of righteousness'?
1. 'Righteousness' is a genitive of apposition [Alf, Mit, My, NIC, NIGTC, TG, TNTC, Tsk, WBC; NASB, TEV]: the fruit is righteousness.
2. 'Righteousness' is a subjective genitive [AB, Hb, HNTC, ICC, Lns, NBC]: the fruit that righteousness produces. The fruit is peace [AB], it is wisdom [HNTC].

QUESTION—What is the meant by καρπὸς σπείρεται 'the fruit is sown'?
It is a prolepsis, referring to the fruit which will result from the sowing [Alf, Hb, Lg, Lns, May, Mit, My, NIC, NTC]; the seed of the fruit is sown [Herm, TG].

QUESTION—What is the phrase ἐν εἰρήνῃ 'in peace' connected with?
It is connected with the verb σπείρεται 'it is sown' [Alf, Bg, Herm, HNTC, ICC, Lns, Mit, My, NIC, NIGTC, NTC, TG, WBC; NAB, NASB, NIV, NRSV, REB, TEV, TNT]: it is sown in peace.

QUESTION—What is the meaning of the phrase ἐν εἰρήνῃ 'in peace'?
1. It indicates where the sowing is done [NIC; REB].
   1.1 It is sown in peace as its seed-bed [REB].
   1.2 It is sown in peace-loving persons [NIC].
2. It refers to the circumstances in which the seed is sown [Hb]: it is sown in peaceable circumstances. The phrase is emphatic by forefronting [Hb].
3. It indicates the manner of the sowing [Alf, NIGTC; TNT]: it is sown peaceably.
4. It describes the purpose of the sowing [TG]: it is sown for peaceful purposes.
5. It describes the righteousness [ICC]: it is peaceable.
6. 'Peace' is what is sown [AB, BKC; NJB]: the peacemakers sow peace.

QUESTION—What relationship is indicated by the dative case of the participial phrase τοῖς ποιοῦσιν εἰρήνην 'for/by those who make peace'?
1. It indicates the beneficiaries of the sowing [Bg, Herm, HNTC, May, My, NTC, WBC; NAB, NRSV, REB, TNT]: it is for those who make peace.
2. It indicates the agents of the sowing [AB, Alf, EBC, ICC, Lns, Mit, NIGTC, TG, TNTC, Tsk; NASB, NIV, NJB, TEV]: it is sown by those who make peace.
3. It includes both the beneficiaries and the agents [Hb, NIC].

DISCOURSE UNIT: 4:1–5:20 [ICC, WBC]. The topic is the contrast between worldly conduct and Christian conduct [ICC], giving testimony concerning divine providence [WBC].

DISCOURSE UNIT: 4:1–5:12 [Hb]. The topic is faith's reactions to worldly conduct.

DISCOURSE UNIT: 4:1–5:6 [ICC]. The topic is worldliness in opposition to God as life's goal.

DISCOURSE UNIT: 4:1–17 [BKC, NBC, NTC; NASB]. The topic is submission [NTC], contrite submission [BKC], peace-breaking and loving the worldly system [NBC], things to avoid [NASB].

DISCOURSE UNIT: 4:1–12 [AB, Hb, ICC, NTC; NIV, NJB]. The topic is the quarrelsomeness of the recipients of the letter [AB], disunity among believers [NJB], the pursuit of pleasure as the cause of the evils of life [ICC], the testing of faith by its reaction to selfish fighting [Hb], submission to God [NTC; NIV].

DISCOURSE UNIT: 4:1–10 [EBC, GNT, HNTC, Lns, NIC, NIGTC, TG, Tsk, WBC; NAB, TEV]. The topic is the worldly attitude [EBC], worldly desires [NAB], desires and divisions [HNTC], friendship with the world [GNT, TG; TEV], friendliness to the world means enmity to God [Lns], love for the world contrasted with love for God [NIC], conflict and compromise [Tsk], the solution to the community's malaise [WBC], a description of pure prayer [NIGTC].

DISCOURSE UNIT: 4:1–6 [BKC, Hb]. The topic is turning hate into humility [BKC], the condition which shows worldliness [Hb].

DISCOURSE UNIT: 4:1–3 [Lg, Mit, NIGTC, NTC, TNTC]. The topic is praying angrily and with desire [NIGTC], praying with wrong motives [NTC], dissensions arising from evil desires [TNTC].

4:1 From-where[a] (come) wars[b] and from-where[a] (come) fightings[c] among[d] you?

LEXICON—a. πόθεν (LN 84.6) (BAGD 2. p. 680): 'from where?' [HNTC, LN; NRSV, TEV, TNT], 'from whence?' [KJV], 'whence?' [AB, LN, Lns], 'where originate?' [NAB], 'where start?' [NJB], 'from what source?' [BAGD], 'what is the source of?' [NIC, WBC; NASB], 'what causes?' [Herm; NIV, REB]. The double use of this word adds emphasis to the QUESTION [Hb, My, NIGTC, WBC].
  b. πόλεμος (LN **39.26**) (BAGD 2. p. 685): 'war', [HNTC, Lns, NIC, WBC; KJV, NJB], 'fight' [AB; NIV, TEV], 'fighting' [REB, TNT], 'strife' [BAGD], 'conflict' [BAGD, Herm; NAB, NRSV], 'quarrel' [BAGD; NASB], 'struggle' [LN]. The reference is to continuing enmity [BKC, EGT, Hb, ICC, Lg, May, Mit, My, NBC], to wide disputes [Lns].
  c. μάχη (LN 39.23) (BAGD p. 496): 'fighting' [BAGD, Herm, Lns, NIC; KJV], 'fight' [LN], 'battle' [HNTC; NJB], 'quarrel' [AB, BAGD; NIV, REB, TEV], 'quarreling' [TNT], 'conflict' [WBC; NASB], 'strife' [BAGD], 'dispute' [BAGD; NAB, NRSV], 'struggle' [LN]. The reference is to specific outbursts [BKC, EGT, Hb, ICC, Lg, May, Mit, My, NBC], to smaller conflicts [Lns].
  d. ἐν with dative object (LN 83.9): 'among' [AB, Herm, HNTC, LN, Lns, NIC; all versions except NJB], 'between' [NJB]. The phrase ἐν ὑμῖν 'among you' is translated 'in your midst' [WBC].

QUESTION—What is the function of this question?
It is a rhetorical question [BKC, Tsk, WBC] introducing a new topic [BKC, Herm, HNTC, Mit, TNTC], admonishing [Herm] and challenging the readers to identify the source of their quarrels [Hb]. Some commentators see no link to the preceding section [HNTC]. Others think it is closely linked to the preceding section [NTC], giving the reason for the conflicts previously mentioned [My, NIGTC, TNTC].

QUESTION—What is the meaning of πόλεμοι καὶ μάχαι 'wars and fightings'?
They are real quarrels and fights [AB], partisan quarrels in the church [Hb, ICC, Lns, NIGTC, NTC], antagonistic attitudes [EBC], verbal conflicts [TNTC], both civil and religious [Blm], quarrels arising from selfish desires [Alf, Blm]. The two terms are essentially synonymous [Herm, My, TG, WBC] and add emphasis [NIC]. The plurals refer to repeated or continuing conflicts [Hb, NTC].

QUESTION—To whom does the phrase ἐν ὑμῖν 'among you' refer?
It refers to conflicts within the group [AB, Alf, EBC, Hb, Lns, NTC]. It means among the members of the group [AB, EBC, Hb, ICC, Lns, NTC, WBC; all versions]: among you.

(Is it) not from-this,[a] from your pleasures[b] the-(ones) warring[c] in[d] your members?[e]

LEXICON—a. ἐντεῦθεν (LN 92.34) (BAGD 2. p. 268): 'from this' [AB, BAGD, LN], 'hence' [Lns; KJV], 'in this' [NIC], 'there' [HNTC], 'the source' [NASB], not explicit [Herm, WBC; all versions except KJV, NASB]. This word carries on the thought of the preceding πόθεν 'from where?' [May, NIC, WBC]; it opens the way to the answer [WBC] and emphasizes the source which is being mentioned [EGT, Hb, May, My, NIC].

b. ἡδονή (LN **25.27**) (BAGD 1. p. 344): 'pleasure' [HNTC, Lns, WBC; NASB], 'desire for pleasure' [BAGD, LN; TEV], 'desire' [LN; NIV, NJB], 'selfish desire' [TNT], 'craving' [NRSV], 'inner craving' [NAB], 'appetite' [REB], 'passion' [Herm, LN], 'lust' [AB, BAGD, NIC; KJV]. This word refers to desires for personal satisfaction [Mit, TG], desires carried out in sensual indulgence [Lg, Tsk], desires for earthly riches [My]. It always has a bad implication [Hb, TG, TNTC, Tsk, WBC]. The focus is on the object of the desire [HNTC].

c. pres. mid. (deponent = act.) participle of στρατεύω (LN 55.4) (BAGD 2. p. 770): 'to war' [HNTC; KJV, REB], 'to make war' [NIC; NAB], 'to wage war' [WBC; NASB], 'to be at war' [Herm; NRSV], 'to battle' [LN; NIV], 'to fight' [LN; NJB, TEV, TNT], 'to be in conflict' [AB], 'to campaign' [Lns]. This participle describes the activity of the ἡδονῶν 'pleasures'; the present tense refers to continuing action [Hb].

d. ἐν with dative object (LN 83.13): 'in' [AB, Herm, HNTC, LN, Lns, NIC; KJV, NASB, REB], 'inside' [NJB], 'within' [NAB, NIV, NRSV, TEV, TNT], 'among' [WBC].

JAMES 4:1

e. μέλος (LN 8.9; 63.17) (BAGD 1. p. 501): 'member' [BAGD, Herm, HNTC, LN, Lns, NIC, WBC; KJV, NAB, NASB], 'limb' [BAGD], 'body' [AB; REB], 'body part' [LN]. The phrase τοῖς μέλεσιν ὑμῶν 'your members' is translated 'you' [NIV, NRSV, TEV, TNT], 'your own selves' [NJB].

QUESTION—What is the function of this question?
1. It is a separate question [NIC, Tsk; all versions (expressed as a statement TEV)], a rhetorical question [NTC, Tsk, WBC], indicating the answer to the preceding question [Alf, BKC, EBC, Mit, TG, WBC; TEV], expecting an affirmative answer [EBC, Hb, NTC, TG, WBC] and identifying the source of the quarreling [Hb, Tsk].
2. It is part of the preceding question [Lg, My].

QUESTION—What is meant by μέλεσιν 'member' and who are the participants in the conflict?
1. The members are the parts of the human body [AB, Alf, BKC, EBC, Hb, HNTC, Lg, NIC, NIGTC, NTC, TNTC, Tsk]. The 'pleasures' are sinful pleasures [TNTC], such as rancor, malice, and tendencies towards violence [AB], hedonism [BKC, EBC], and lust [Alf, Lg]. The term 'members' is used collectively for the personality, which is the abode of the passions which fight against righteousness [NIC]. They wage battle in people's hearts [BKC]. These desires fight within a person's body against his conscience [NIGTC] and soul [TNTC, Tsk]. Lusts battle in order to be satisfied [EBC]. Lusts are compared to soldiers on a military campaign and their aim is to satisfy their cravings [Hb]. The lusts are encamped within a person [Alf].
2. The members are the members of the church, each a part of Christ's body [ICC, WBC]. The fighting is among different individuals and is related to social or political issues [WBC]. The pleasures of one person war against those of another [ICC].

QUESTION—Who is the warring directed against?
1. It is against other members of the community [AB, Alf, Hb, ICC, Lns, NTC, TG, Tsk, WBC]; some persons, because of selfish desires [Alf] are attempting to exalt themselves and put down others [Alf].
2. It is against anything that hinders the fulfillment of the desires [EBC, My; TNT].
3. It is against the person's conscience [NIGTC], his soul [TNTC, Tsk], himself [HNTC; NIV].
4. It is against righteousness [NIC].

QUESTION—What is the meaning of the phrase ἐν τοῖς μέλεσιν ὑμῶν 'in your members'?
1. It means that the attitudes arise in the individuals [Alf, BKC, Lns, May, NIC, NIGTC, NTC; TNT]. It is in the body of an individual Christian [NIGTC].
2. It means that the warfare is carried on in the human personality [AB, EBC, Hb, HNTC, TNTC, Tsk; NIV, NJB, NRSV, REB, TEV].

3. It means conflict among church members [ICC, WBC].

4:2 You-desire[a] and (do) not have,[b]

LEXICON—a. pres. act. indic. of ἐπιθυμέω (LN 25.12; 25.20) (BAGD p. 293): 'to desire' [AB, BAGD, Herm, HNTC; NAB], 'to desire very much' [LN (25.12)], 'to have desires' [WBC], 'to want' [NIV, NJB, NRSV, REB, TEV, TNT], 'to long for' [BAGD, LN], 'to lust' [LN (25.20), Lns, NIC; KJV, NASB]. The desire is evil [Hb, My], for worldly possessions [Alf, My, TG] and honors [Alf]. The present tense of this verb and the following one indicate repeated actions [Hb, Lns].

b. pres. act. indic. of ἔχω (LN 57.1): 'to have' [Herm, HNTC, LN, Lns; KJV, NASB, NRSV, REB, TEV, TNT], 'to possess' [LN], 'to obtain' [NAB], 'to acquire' [AB], 'to get' [WBC; NIV], 'to have satisfaction' [NIC]. The phrase οὐκ ἔχετε 'you do not have' is translated 'you lack' [NJB].

QUESTION—How is this verse related to its context?

1. It further explains the charge made in the preceding verse [Alf, ICC, My] and expresses its result [Hb]. It is a warning of what will happen if they engage in wrong desires [ICC, Tsk], but is stated as indicatives for didactic effect [HNTC, Tsk]: if you do these things, this will result. The reference is to Christians in general, not to a particular Christian community [ICC, Tsk].
2. The sense is concessive [Lns]: although you desire, you do not have.

you-murder[a] and are-jealous[b] and (are) not able to-obtain,[c]

TEXT—Instead of φονεύετε 'you murder', φθονεῖτε 'you envy', a conjectural emendation with no manuscript support, is read by Herm, NIC, and possibly May. GNT does not mention this conjecture.

LEXICON—a. pres. act. indic. of φονεύω (LN 20.82) (BAGD p. 864): 'to murder' [BAGD, HNTC, LN, Lns; REB, TNT], 'to commit murder' [LN; NASB, NRSV], 'to resort to murder' [NAB], 'to kill' [AB, BAGD, WBC; KJV, NIV, NJB], 'to be ready to kill' [TEV]; different text 'to be jealous' [Herm], 'to covet' [NIC]. This is the result of the frustrated desire just mentioned [Alf, Hb].

b. pres. act. indic. of ζηλόω (LN 25.21; 88.163) (BAGD 2. p. 338): 'to be jealous' [HNTC, LN (88.163)], 'to be filled with jealousy' [BAGD], 'to envy' [NIC; NAB], 'to be envious' [Herm, LN; NASB, REB], 'to be filled with envy' [BAGD], 'to desire to have' [KJV], 'to covet' [LN (25.21); NIV, NRSV], 'to desire strongly' [TEV], 'to be determined to get' [TNT], 'to have an ambition' [NJB], 'to be a fanatic' [AB], 'to use zeal' [Lns]. This verb is also translated as a phrase: 'out of jealousy' [WBC].

c. aorist act. infin. of ἐπιτυγχάνω (LN 57.60) (BAGD p. 304): 'to obtain' [AB, BAGD, Herm, HNTC, LN, Lns; KJV, NASB, NRSV], 'to attain' [BAGD, LN; REB], 'to acquire' [LN; NAB], 'to have' [NIV], 'to get'

[TEV, TNT], 'to get one's desire' [NIC], 'to get what one wants' [WBC], 'to reach' [BAGD], 'to satisfy' [NJB].

QUESTION—How are the two verbs related in the phrase φονεύετε καὶ ζηλοῦτε 'you murder and you are jealous'?
1. The two verbs are to be taken together [AB, Bg, Lns, My, NBC, NIGTC, WBC; KJV, NIV (but reading a different text [Herm, NIC])]: you murder and are jealous. That the stronger verb precedes the weaker is not significant; they simply present the negative and positive aspects of the conduct [Lg]; the second verb is more comprehensive [Lns] and gives the inner motive for the killing [Bg, NBC, WBC].
2. The two verbs are to be separated [Hb, HNTC, ICC, Mit, TNTC, Tsk; all versions except KJV, NIV]: you kill; you covet and cannot obtain. This avoids an unacceptable anticlimax with the following ζηλοῦτε 'you are jealous' [ICC]; φονεύετε 'you murder' expresses the result of the preceding phrase [HNTC, May, Tsk; all versions except KJV, NIV].

QUESTION—What is meant by φονεύετε 'you murder'?
1. It is to be taken figuratively [Blm, EBC, Hb, Lns, My]. It is to be understood in an ethical sense as also are 'fight' and 'make war' [Lns].
2. It is to be taken literally [ICC, TNTC, WBC]. It is possible that some of them were in the Zealot movement which fought against the Roman rule [WBC].

you-fight[a] and make-war;[b]

LEXICON—a. pres. mid. (deponent = act.) of μάχομαι (LN 39.23) (BAGD 2. p. 496): 'to fight' [AB, BAGD, Herm, LN, Lns, NIC; KJV, NASB], 'to battle' [HNTC], 'to quarrel' [BAGD; NAB, NIV, REB, TEV, TNT], 'to dispute' [BAGD], 'to engage in disputes' [NRSV], 'to clash severely' [LN], 'to contend' [WBC]. The phrase μάχεσθε καὶ πολεμεῖτε 'you fight and make war' is translated 'you fight to get your way by force' [NJB]. The sense is metaphorical [Hb].
b. pres. act. indic. of πολεμέω (LN **39.26**) (BAGD 2. p. 685): 'to join in war' [WBC], 'to war' [LN, Lns, NIC; KJV], 'to make war' [HNTC], 'to fight' [**LN**; NAB, NIV, REB, TEV, TNT], 'to quarrel' [NASB], 'to engage in conflicts' [NRSV], 'to strive' [AB, Herm]. The sense is metaphorical [Hb].

QUESTION—What is this phrase connected with?
1. It forms the final answer to πόθεν 'from where?' in the preceding verse [Alf].
2. It indicates the result of coveting and not being able to obtain [Hb, HNTC, May; all versions except KJV, NIV]: you are not able to attain, so you fight.
3. It includes both of the above [My].
4. It forms the third unit of the condemnation [Lg].

you-have[a] not on-account-of[b] your not asking.[c]

LEXICON—a. pres. act. indic. of ἔχω: 'to have'. See this word above.

b. διά with accusative object (LN 89.26; 90.44): 'on account of' [LN], 'because of' [LN], 'because' [AB, Herm, HNTC, NIC, WBC; all versions], 'by reason of' [LN], 'for the reason that' [Lns]. This preposition expresses cause [NTC].
c. pres. mid. infin. of αἰτέω (LN 33.163): 'to ask' [Herm, HNTC, NIC, WBC; all versions except NJB, REB], 'to ask for' [LN], 'to ask for oneself' [Lns], 'to pray' [AB; NJB, REB]. The middle voice implies asking in their own interests [Hb] wrongly [NTC]; it focuses more specifically on prayer [NIC]. The subject of this infinitive is ὑμᾶς 'you' [NTC]. The meaning is to pray to God [AB, Alf, Bg, BKC, EBC, HNTC, Lg, NIC, NTC, TG, Tsk, WBC; NJB, REB, TEV, TNT]. What they do not ask for is what would really satisfy them, that is, peace and happiness [Blm, Mit], wisdom [WBC].

QUESTION—How is this related to the preceding verse?

It does not mean that their lusts were not satisfied because they failed to ask God to fulfill their evil desires; rather, it reveals the source of their conflicts to be in hearts turned away from God [BKC]. Perhaps they felt that what they wanted was unworthy of requesting God for them [Hb]. They needed to desire those things that God would want to give them [ICC, Tsk].

4:3 You-ask[a] and (do) not receive[b] because you-ask wrongly,[c]

LEXICON—a. pres. act. indic. of αἰτέω: 'to ask'. See this word at 4:2.
b. pres. act. indic. of λαμβάνω (LN 57.55): 'to receive' [AB, Herm, HNTC, LN, Lns, NIC, WBC; all versions except REB, TNT], 'to acquire' [LN], 'to obtain' [LN]. The phrase οὐ λαμβάνετε 'you do not receive' is translated 'your requests are not granted' [REB], 'you are not answered' [TNT].
c. κακῶς (LN 72.22) (BAGD 2. p. 398): 'wrongly' [AB, HNTC, LN; NAB, NJB, NRSV], 'with wrong motives' [BAGD; NASB, NIV], 'with the wrong motive' [Herm], 'from wrong motives' [REB], 'in the wrong spirit' [WBC], 'badly' [BAGD], 'incorrectly' [LN], 'amiss' [KJV], 'in a base way' [Lns]. The phrase διότι κακῶς αἰτεῖσθε 'because you ask wrongly' is translated 'because your motives are bad' [TEV], 'because your motives are wrong' [TNT], 'because of your corrupt asking' [NIC].

QUESTION—What is the meaning of the clause αἰτεῖτε καὶ οὐ λαμβάνετε 'you ask and do not receive'?

1. The meaning is that they do ask [KJV, NAB, NASB, NRSV], but with wrong motives [My]: you ask but do not receive.
2. The implied meaning is conditional [REB, TNT], concessional [HNTC], temporal [NIV, NJB, TEV]: if/even if/when you do ask, you do not receive.

QUESTION—What is implied by the change from middle to active to middle voice of αἰτέω 'to ask' in this and the preceding verse?
1. There is no difference in meaning [Alf, EGT, ICC, NIC, TNTC], although the middle voice here refers more specifically to prayer than does the active voice [NIC].
2. The middle voice has middle meaning [BKC, Hb, Lns, May, My]; the active voice focuses on asking in contrast to receiving [My].
   2.1 It implies asking in one's own interest [BKC, Hb, Lns, My]: you ask for yourself.
   2.2 It implies earnestness [May]: you ask earnestly.

in-order-that[a] you-might-spend[b] (it) on[c] your pleasures.[d]
LEXICON—a. ἵνα (LN 89.59): 'in order that' [Lns, NIC], 'in order to' [AB, Herm, HNTC, LN; NRSV, REB], 'for the purpose of' [LN], 'so that' [LN; NASB], 'with a view to' [NAB], 'that' [KJV, NIV]. The phrase αἰτεῖσθε ἵνα δαπανήσητε 'you ask in order that you may spend' is translated 'you ask for things to use' [TEV]. This entire clause is translated 'you only want to indulge your selfish desires' [TNT], 'wanting to indulge your passions' [NJB], 'to indulge your sinful pleasures' [WBC].
b. aorist act. subj. of δαπανάω (LN **57.149**) (BAGD 1. p. 171): 'to spend' [BAGD, Herm, HNTC, NIC; NASB, NIV, NRSV], 'to spend completely' [LN], 'to consume' [KJV], 'to waste' [**LN**, Lns], 'to squander' [NAB, REB], 'to indulge' [WBC; NJB, TNT], 'to dissipate' [AB]. The aorist tense indicates that their complete intention was the indulging of their pleasures [Hb]. The implied object of this verb is the things they asked for [AB, Herm, Lns, My, NIC; KJV, NAB, NASB, NIV, NRSV, REB].
c. ἐν with dative object (LN 83.13): 'in' [AB, LN, Lns], 'on' [Herm, HNTC, NIC; NAB, NASB, NIV, NRSV, REB], 'upon' [KJV], 'for' [TEV].
d. ἡδονή (LN 25.111) (BAGD 1. p. 344): 'pleasure' [BAGD, HNTC, LN, Lns, WBC; NAB, NASB, NIV, NRSV, REB, TEV], 'that which is pleasurable' [LN], 'enjoyment' [BAGD], 'desire' [TNT], 'passion' [Herm; NJB], 'lust' [AB, NIC; KJV]. The reference is to worldly goods [AB, EBC, TG] for luxurious living [AB]. See this word at 4:1.

QUESTION—What relationship is indicated by ἵνα 'in order that'?
It indicates the purpose of the asking [BKC, EBC, Hb, ICC, Lns, My] and also explains why they were asking wrongly [ICC, Lns, May, My]: you ask wrongly, viz. in order to indulge your pleasures.

QUESTION—What relationship is indicated by the phrase ἐν 'in'?
It refers to the state of the persons [Alf], to the sphere in which they intended to use what they received [Hb, ICC]. This phrase is emphatic by forefronting [Hb].

DISCOURSE UNIT: 4:4–17 [Lg]. The topic is the sixth admonition.

DISCOURSE UNIT: 4:4–10 [TNTC]. The topic is an exhortation to repent.

JAMES 4:4

DISCOURSE UNIT: 4:4–6 [Mit, NIGTC, NTC]. The topic is a condemnation of compromising [NIGTC], friendship with the world [NTC].

4:4 Adulteresses,ᵃ not do-you-knowᵇ that the friendshipᶜ of-the worldᵈ is enmityᵉ of-the God?

TEXT—Instead of μοιχαλίδες 'adulteresses', some manuscripts read μοιχοὶ καὶ μοιχαλίδες 'adulterers and adulteresses'. GNT has the shorter reading with an A decision, indicating that the text is certain. The longer reading is accepted by Bg, Blm, and KJV.

LEXICON—a. μοιχαλίς (LN **31.101**) (BAGD 2.b p. 526): 'adulteress' [BAGD, Herm, HNTC, Lns, NIC; KJV, NASB], 'adulterer' [AB; NJB, NRSV], 'unfaithful creature' [REB]; as a plural: 'you adulterous people' [NIV], 'you unfaithful people' [**LN**, WBC], 'unfaithful people' [TEV], 'O you unfaithful ones' [NAB]. This noun is also translated as an adjective: 'adulterous' [BAGD, LN], 'unfaithful' [LN]; as a phrase: 'you are not to be trusted' [TNT].

   b. perf. (with pres. meaning) act. indic. of οἶδα (LN 28.1, 32.4): 'to know' [AB, Herm, HNTC, LN, Lns, NIC, WBC; KJV, NASB, NIV, NRSV, REB, TEV], 'to understand' [LN; TNT], 'to comprehend' [LN], 'to realize' [NJB], 'to be aware' [NAB].

   c. φιλία (LN **25.33**) (BAGD p. 859): 'friendship' [AB, BAGD, Herm, HNTC, Lns, NIC, WBC; KJV, NASB, NIV, NRSV], 'affection' [LN], 'love' [BAGD; NAB, NJB, REB]. The phrase ἡ φιλία τοῦ κόσμου 'the friendship of the world' is translated 'to be the world's friend' [TEV], 'if you love the world' [TNT]. This word refers to affection and kind feelings [Hb].

   d. κόσμος (LN 41.38) (BAGD 7. p. 446): 'world' [AB, BAGD, Herm, HNTC, LN, Lns, NIC, WBC; all versions]. 'world system' [LN]. The reference is to the affairs of mankind in general apart from and hostile to God [Alf, Hb, HNTC, Lg, Lns, Mit, NTC], the corrupt part of the world [Blm] controlled by Satan [EBC].

   e. ἔχθρα (LN **39.10**) (BAGD p. 331): 'enmity' [AB, BAGD, Herm, HNTC, Lns, NIC; KJV, NAB, NRSV, REB], 'hostility' [NASB], 'hatred' [WBC; NIV, NJB]. The phrase ἔχθρα τοῦ θεοῦ ἐστιν 'is enmity of God' is translated 'to be God's enemy' [TEV], 'you are God's enemies' [TNT], 'is being at enmity with God' [LN]. It is hostility, the opposite of friendship [Hb]. The enmity is on man's part, not God's [ICC].

QUESTION—Why is the feminine form μοιχαλίδες 'adulteresses' used?

   1. It is used figuratively. The feminine form reflects the relationship of all believers, both men and women, to God as their spiritual Lord and husband [Alf, EBC, Hb, Herm, HNTC, ICC, Lns, May, Mit, NBC, NIC, NIGTC, NTC, TG, TNTC, Tsk, WBC] and to Christ as his bride [EBC, Hb, HNTC, ICC, Lg, Lns, May, NBC, NIC, NIGTC, NTC, Tsk]. James may have used the feminine form thinking of Hosea's unfaithful wife [Tsk]. This strong word is used intentionally to awaken the readers [EBC].

The plural form refers to the individuals who were guilty [Hb, HNTC, ICC, May, NIGTC]; it relates to churches, not individuals [My], to Judaism in general [Lg]. The reference is to God's people loving the world [Lns], their desire for material things, which was spiritual idolatry [AB, Hb, NIC], spiritual adultery [Blm, Lns, NBC, TNTC, Tsk]; it is near to apostasy [WBC].
 2. It is used literally. This focuses especially on women [EGT].
QUESTION—What is this QUESTION connected with?
 1. It is connected with the preceding thought [HNTC]. Although prayer implies a good relationship with God, it can be used for self-gratification and thus expresses a relationship with the world [HNTC].
 2. It is connected only with what follows [Herm, NIGTC]. This is an abrupt transition to a new unit [NIGTC].
QUESTION—What is implied by οὐκ 'not' which introduces this QUESTION?
 It indicates that an affirmative answer is expected [Hb, NBC, TG, WBC], and implies that the readers were knowledgeable in this matter [Hb, ICC, Lns, TG] and that their consciences will agree [Hb].
QUESTION—How are the two nouns related in the genitive construction ἡ φιλία τοῦ κόσμου 'the friendship of the world'?
 Κόσμου 'world' is an objective genitive [AB, Blm, EBC, Hb, Herm, ICC, Lns, NIC, Tsk; NASB, NIV, NJB, NRSV, TNT]: loving the world.
QUESTION—How are the two nouns related in the genitive construction ἔχθρα τοῦ θεοῦ 'enmity of God'?
 Θεοῦ 'God' is an objective genitive [AB, Hb, Herm, Lns, NIC; NASB, NIV, NJB, NRSV]: he shows enmity toward God.

Who ever therefore^a chooses^b to-be a-friend^c of-the world makes-himself^d an-enemy^e of-God.

LEXICON—a. οὖν (LN 89.50) (BAGD 5. p. 593): 'therefore' [Herm, LN; KJV, NASB, NRSV], 'consequently' [LN], 'so' [HNTC, LN], 'then' [LN, Lns], 'so then' [LN], 'accordingly' [LN], not explicit [AB, NIC, WBC; NAB, NIV, NJB, REB, TEV, TNT].
 b. aorist pass. (deponent = act.) subj. of βούλομαι (LN 25.3; 30.56) (BAGD 1. p. 146): 'to choose' [NIC; NAB, NIV, NJB, REB, TNT], 'to be determined' [WBC], 'to will' [LN (30.56); KJV], 'to intend' [LN, Lns], 'to purpose' [LN], 'to want' [BAGD, HNTC, LN (25.3); TEV], 'to desire' [BAGD, LN], 'to wish' [AB, BAGD, Herm; NASB, NRSV]. The reference is to the set of the mind, but with no emphasis on the verb [Alf]; it refers to a deliberate completed choice [EBC, Hb, Lns, Tsk, WBC]. The aorist tense refers to the time of the decision [Hb].
 c. φίλος (LN 34.11) (BAGD 2.a.α. p. 861): 'friend' [AB, BAGD, Herm, HNTC, LN, Lns, NIC, WBC; all versions except TNT]. The phrase φίλος εἶναι τοῦ κόσμου 'to be a friend of the world' is translated 'to love the world' [TNT].

d. pres. mid. indic. of καθίστημι (LN 13.9; 37.104) (BAGD 3. p. 390): 'to make oneself' [BAGD, LN (13.9); NASB, REB, TEV], 'to cause oneself to be' [BAGD, LN], 'to establish oneself' [Lns], 'to set oneself' [WBC], 'to designate oneself' [LN (37.104)], 'to appoint oneself' [HNTC], 'to commit oneself to being' [TNT], 'to prove oneself to be' [Herm]. This is also translated in the active voice: 'to be' [KJV], 'to become' [NIC; NIV, NRSV], 'to turn out to be' [AB]; in the passive voice: 'to be marked out' [NAB], 'to be constituted' [NJB]. The sense is to become (to take one's stand [Hb, ICC]) by the very fact of choosing friendship with the world [Alf, EBC, Hb]. The verb is middle voice [Bg, Lns], meaning to act upon oneself [Bg], to take one's stand [Lns], to act by one's own choice [Hb]. The present tense indicates a continuing condition [Hb, ICC]; it refers to any case at any time [Lns].

e. ἐχθρός (LN 39.11) (BAGD 2.b.β. p. 331): 'enemy' [AB, BAGD, Herm, HNTC, LN, Lns, NIC; all versions]; as a phrase 'at enmity' [WBC], 'being an enemy' [LN].

QUESTION—What relationship is indicated by οὖν 'therefore'?

It indicates the result of the preceding clause [Alf, Hb, My, TG]. The preceding observation is now given as a general principle [Hb], showing how loving the world amounts to enmity against God [NIC].

QUESTION—How are the two nouns related in the genitive construction φίλος τοῦ κόσμου 'friend of the world'?

Κόσμου is an objective genitive [Lns; TNT]: loving the world.

QUESTION—How are the two nouns related in the genitive construction ἐχθρὸς τοῦ θεοῦ 'enemy of God'?

Θεοῦ 'God' is an objective genitive [Lns, Tsk]: the person has enmity against God; God, however, continues to love him [Tsk]. This phrase is emphatic by forefronting [Hb].

4:5 Or[a] do-you-think[b] that in-vain[c] the Scripture says,

LEXICON—a. ἤ (LN 89.139): 'or' [Herm, HNTC, LN, Lns, NIC, WBC; NASB, NIV, NRSV, REB], not explicit [AB; KJV, NAB, NJB, TEV, TNT]. It introduces an alternative [Hb, May, NBC], a QUESTION giving an alternative proof [ICC], to convince the readers if they will not accept the preceding conclusion [Alf, EBC, May, NBC].

b. pres. act. indic. of δοκέω (LN 31.29) (BAGD 1.d. p. 202): 'to think' [AB, BAGD, HNTC, LN, Lns; KJV, NASB, NIV, TEV, TNT], 'to suppose' [BAGD, Herm, LN, NIC; NAB, NRSV, REB], 'to imagine' [LN, WBC], 'to consider' [BAGD], 'to believe' [BAGD, LN]. The phrase δοκεῖτε ὅτι κενῶς ἡ γραφὴ λέγει 'do you think that vainly the Scripture says' is translated 'can you not see the point of the saying in scripture' [NJB].

c. κενῶς (LN 89.64) (BAGD p. 428): 'in vain' [AB, BAGD, Herm, LN; KJV], 'in an empty manner' [BAGD], 'in an empty way' [Lns], 'idly' [BAGD], 'for no purpose' [LN], 'to no purpose' [BAGD; NAB, NASB], 'to no effect' [HNTC], 'for nothing' [NRSV, TNT], 'without reason'

[NIV]. The phrase κενῶς λέγει 'in vain says' is translated 'has no point when it says' [REB]. The phrase κενῶς ἡ γραφὴ λέγει 'the scripture in vain says' is translated 'there is no truth in the scripture that says' [TEV], 'there is no ground in what Scripture says' [WBC], 'it is an idle saying in the scriptures' [NIC]. To be 'in vain' means that it has no bearing on guilt or salvation [Bg], or on our conduct [Hb]. This word is emphatic by forefronting as the point of the author's concern [Hb].

QUESTION—How is this verse related to its context?

It adds scriptural authority for the preceding statement that friendship with the world is incompatible with friendship with God [Hb, NIGTC, TNTC, Tsk]. He finishes his analysis with a rebuke [WBC]. It gives further evidence for the point the author has been making [Alf, Tsk] and by implication expects a negative answer [EBC, Lns, TG].

QUESTION—What is the structure of this verse?

1. It is one question [AB, Herm, NIC, Tsk, WBC; all versions (expressed as a statement [TEV])]: Do you think…in us?
2. It is a (rhetorical [TG]) question followed by a statement [Hb, Lns]: Do you think…? The Spirit/spirit…in us.
3. It consists of two questions [Blm, HNTC]: Do you think…to no effect? Does the Spirit/spirit…in us?

QUESTION—What is the source of the quotation given in this verse?

1. It is a quotation from an unknown source [AB, Herm, NIC, NIGTC, NTC]. The author doubtless expected his readers to be familiar with this quotation [NIGTC].
2. The reference is to the general sense of Scripture on this subject [Blm, Hb, HNTC, Lg(M), May, Mit, Tsk, WBC].
3. It refers to specific passages. It refers to Psalms 37:1 and 73:3 [Lg], It is a general reference to passages such as Ex. 20:5 [EBC, ICC, TNTC] and 34:14 [EBC, TNTC]. It possibly refers to the sense of Deut. 32:10–11 [Alf]. It refers to Gal. 5.17 and 1 Pet. 2:1, 2, 5 [Bg]; to various Pauline passages, thus demonstrating the late date of this epistle [EGT]. The scripture the author has in mind is not the second half of this verse but rather the quotation from Prov. 3:34, which he quotes in 4:6 [BKC, My].

"To[a] jealousy[b] yearns[c] the spirit/Spirit[d] which he-caused-to-live[e] in[f] us"?

TEXT—Instead of κατῴκισεν 'he caused to live', some manuscripts read κατῴκησεν 'he/it lived'. GNT reads 'he caused to live' with a B rating, indicating that the text is almost certain. 'He/it lived' is read by only Bg, Blm, Lg, NIC, KJV.

LEXICON—a. πρός with accusative object (LN 78.51) (BAGD III.6. p. 711): 'to' [KJV], 'toward' [NAB], 'to the point of' [LN]. The phrase πρὸς φθόνον 'to envy' is translated 'jealously' [BAGD, Herm, Lns; NASB, NRSV, TNT], 'with jealousy' [AB], 'enviously' [HNTC]. The phrase πρὸς φθόνον ἐπιποθεῖ 'yearns to envy' is translated 'envies intensely' [NIV], 'is filled with envious longings' [REB], 'is prone to envious lust'

[NIC], 'is filled with fierce desires' [TEV], 'the longing is a jealous longing' [NJB], 'opposes envy' [WBC].
- b. φθόνος (LN 88.160) (BAGD p. 857): 'jealousy' [BAGD, LN; NAB], 'envy' [BAGD, LN; KJV]. It can refer to legitimate passionate jealousy [AB, Alf, EBC, EGT, Hb, Herm, ICC, Lg(M), Lns, May, Mit, My, NBC, NIGTC, TNTC], or it can have a bad connotation [NTC] of envy resulting from friendship with the world [Bg, Lg] and spiteful envy [NIC].
- c. pres. act. indic. of ἐπιποθέω (LN **25.18**) (BAGD p. 297): 'to yearn' [BAGD, Herm, Lns; NRSV, TNT], 'to long' [HNTC, **LN**], 'to long for' [BAGD], 'to desire' [BAGD; NASB], 'to be filled with desire' [**LN**], 'to lust' [KJV], 'to claim' [AB], 'to tend' [NAB]. It means claiming a right over [AB], to long for [EBC]; it refers to envious longing [HNTC].
- d. πνεῦμα (LN 12.18; 26.9) (BAGD 5.d.α. p. 677): 'spirit' [AB, Herm, HNTC, LN (26.9), NIC; all versions except NASB], 'Spirit' [BAGD, LN (12.18), Lns, WBC; NASB], 'spiritual nature' [LN].
- e. aorist act. indic. of κατοικίζω (LN **85.82**) (BAGD p. 424): 'to cause to live' [BAGD; NIV], 'to cause to dwell' [**LN**], 'to make to dwell' [Herm, HNTC, Lns, WBC; NASB, NRSV, TNT], 'to send to dwell' [NJB], 'to put' [**LN**], 'to place' [TEV], 'to implant' [NAB, REB], 'to settle' [AB]. The implied subject is God [Hb, HNTC]; the aorist tense points to the time when the indwelling occurred [Hb].
- f. ἐν with dative object (LN 83.13): 'in' [AB, HNTC, LN, Lns, NIC, WBC; all versions], 'within' [Herm].

QUESTION—What is the meaning of the second half of this verse?
1. Τὸ πνεῦμα is the human spirit [AB, EBC, Herm, HNTC, ICC, Mit, My, NBC, NIC, NIGTC, NTC, Tsk; KJV, NAB, NRSV, REB, TEV, TNT].
   1.1 The human spirit is the subject of the verb [HNTC, NIC, NTC; KJV, NAB, NIV, REB, TEV].
   1.1.1 It means that our human spirit tends toward envious lust [NIC, NTC; KJV, NAB, NIV], envious longings [REB], fierce desires [TEV]: our human spirit tends toward envious desires.
   1.1.2 In question form, it implies that scripture indicates that man's longing is directed to God, not controlled by envy [HNTC]: Is man's spirit directed by envy? No, according to Scripture it is directed to God.
   1.2 The human spirit is the predicate of the verb [AB, Alf, EBC, Herm, ICC, Mit, My, NBC, NIGTC, TNTC, Tsk; NRSV, TNT]. It means that God created the human spirit [AB, ICC, NIGTC] and longs for it [Herm, Mit, My, NBC, NIGTC, Tsk; NRSV, TNT], passionately demands exclusive control over it [AB], jealously seeks the loyalty of the human spirit [ICC, TNTC], through the Holy Spirit [Alf] he jealously longs for his people to love him [Alf, EBC]: God yearns jealously over the spirit he has caused to dwell in us.
2. Τὸ πνεῦμα is the Holy Spirit [Alf, Bg, Blm, EGT, Hb, Lg, Lns, May, WBC; NASB].

2.1 The Holy Spirit is the subject of the verb [Alf, Blm, EGT, Hb, Lg, Lns, May, WBC].
2.1.1 It means that the Holy Spirit jealously yearns for our love and devotion [Alf, EGT, Hb, Lg(M), Lns, May]: the Holy Spirit whom God caused to dwell in us yearns jealously over us.
2.1.2 It means that the Holy Spirit in us expresses a longing against the human envy which causes fightings [Lg, WBC]: the Holy Spirit whom God caused to dwell in us opposes human envy.
2.1.3 In question form, it implicitly denies that the Holy Spirit expresses envious desires [Blm]: Does the Holy Spirit in us envy lustfully? No.
2.2 The Holy Spirit is the predicate of the verb [NASB]: God jealously desires the Spirit which he has made to dwell in us.

4:6 But he gives more grace.^a
LEXICON—χάρις (LN 25.89; 57.103; 88.66) (BAGD 3.b. p. 878): 'grace' [AB, BAGD, Herm, HNTC, LN (88.66), Lns, NIC, WBC; all versions except NAB], 'favor' [LN (25.89)], 'good will' [LN], 'kindness' [LN], 'gift' [LN (57.103); NAB]. It refers to God's gracious gift of help to fulfill his requirements [ICC, Mit].
QUESTION—What is this clause related to?
1. It is a new sentence [AB, Blm, EBC, Herm, ICC, NIC, TG, WBC; all versions] anticipating the quotation which follows [My, NBC]: But he gives more grace.
2. It continues the question begun in 4:5 [GNT]: ...in us, but he gives more grace.
QUESTION—What relationship is indicted by δέ 'but'?
1. It is continuative, introducing a further thought related to the preceding [Hb, HNTC, Lns]: in addition, he gives more grace.
2. It introduces a contrast, indicating that there is hope for one who seeks worldly pleasures [NTC]: but he gives more grace.
QUESTION—What is the subject of the verb δίδωσιν 'he gives'?
God is the subject [AB, Alf, Bg, EBC, Hb, Herm, HNTC, ICC, Lns, My, NIC, NIGTC, NTC, WBC; all versions]: God gives more grace.
QUESTION—What is compared in the phrase μείζονα χάριν '*greater* grace'?
1. It means that his standards are high, but he gives more grace than is needed to meet the standards [EBC, ICC, NBC, WBC], and grace greater than what was given at birth [NBC].
2. It means that the person who gives himself completely to God will receive a greater supply of grace than if he did not so give himself [May].
3. It means that God gives more grace to enable us to resist envious desires [Blm], to resist the world [Hb], grace greater than the strength of man's evil spirit [NIC].
4. It means that if someone seeks worldly pleasure God does not reject him but gives him the opportunity to be forgiven [NIGTC].

5. It means that God's grace is of more concern to him than his jealous concern for obedience [Mit].
6. It means that the farther one departs from envy, the more grace God bestows [Bg].
7. Μείζονα 'greater' is used in the sense of superabundance rather than a comparison [EGT]: a superabundance of divine grace.

Therefore[a] it-says, "The God opposes[b] proud[c] (persons), but to-humble[d] (persons) he-gives grace."

LEXICON—a. διό (LN 89.47): 'therefore' [AB, Herm, LN; NASB, NRSV], 'for this reason' [LN], 'that is why' [WBC; NIV], 'which is why' [HNTC], 'for the sake of which' [NAB], 'as' [NJB, TEV], 'and so' [NIC], 'thus' [REB], 'for', [TNT], 'wherefore' [KJV], not explicit [Lns]. This word introduces the scriptural evidence for what the author has just said [Hb, My].

b. pres. mid. indic. of ἀντιτάσσω (LN 39.1) (BAGD p. 76): 'to oppose' [Herm, LN, WBC; NASB, NIV, NJB, NRSV, REB, TNT], 'to resist' [AB, BAGD, HNTC, Lns; KJV, NAB, TEV], 'to set oneself against' [NIC]. The middle voice indicates that God sets himself against the proud [Hb, May].

c. ὑπερήφανος (LN **88.214**) (BAGD p. 841): 'proud' [BAGD, Herm, HNTC, WBC; all versions except REB], 'haughty' [BAGD, **LN**, Lns, NIC], 'arrogant' [AB, BAGD, LN; REB]. The absence of the definite article emphasizes the character of these persons rather than their identity [Hb].

d. ταπεινός (LN 88.52) (BAGD 2.b. p. 804): 'humble' [AB, BAGD, Herm, HNTC, LN, NIC, WBC; all versions except NAB], 'lowly' [BAGD, Lns; NAB]. The absence of the definite article points to the character of these persons, which is emphasized by the forefronted word order [Hb].

QUESTION—What is the subject of the verb λέγει 'he says'?
1. God is the subject [May; KJV]: God says.
2. The Holy Spirit is the subject [Alf, Lg(M)]: the Holy Spirit says. It is the Holy Spirit who speaks in Scripture [Alf, Lg(M)].
3. Scripture is the subject [Bg, Lg, My; NIV, NJB, REB, TEV, TNT]: Scripture says.
4. The subject is impersonal [AB, Herm, HNTC, NIC, WBC; NAB, NASB, NRSV]: it is written.

QUESTION—Why is the O.T. quotation mentioned?
The second part of the quotation is the relevant part [EBC, Herm, HNTC, ICC, Lns, Mit, TNTC]. Both parts are emphasized [Alf, NIGTC, NTC, Tsk, WBC].
1. It gives the scriptural assurance that God gives grace [HNTC, Lns] sufficient to resist the world and to be loyal to him [EBC, ICC, TNTC], grace for forgiveness to the penitent [Mit, NIGTC].

2. It shows that those who seek for worldly honors are God's enemies but the humble receive his favors [Alf].

DISCOURSE UNIT: 4:7–12 [BKC, Hb]. The topic is an exhortation to turn judgment into justice [BKC], an exhortation to worldly-minded persons [Hb].

DISCOURSE UNIT: 4:7–10 [Mit, NIGTC, NTC]. The topic is a call to repentance [NIGTC], coming near to God [NTC].

4:7 Submit-yourselves[a] therefore to-God,
LEXICON—a. aorist pass. impera. of ὑποτάσσω (LN 36.18) (BAGD 1.b.β. p. 848): with middle meaning 'to submit oneself' [AB, Herm, Lns, WBC; KJV, NIV, NRSV, TEV], 'to subject oneself' [BAGD]; with passive meaning 'to be subjected' [BAGD]; with active meaning 'to submit' [HNTC, LN; NAB, NASB, REB, TNT], 'to obey' [BAGD, LN], 'to give in' [NJB], 'to enlist under' [NIC]. The passive voice is used with middle meaning [Hb, ICC, Lg, Lns, NIC, NTC]. Submission is the surrender of one's will and this leads to obedience [EBC].
QUESTION—What relationship is indicated by οὖν 'therefore'?
It indicates exhortation based on what has just been said [AB, EBC, Hb, My, NBC]. This and the following clause give the practical exhortations [ICC], the basic requirement of submitting to God, which is expanded in 4:8–10 [Hb, NIGTC, TNTC]. Since God grants grace to the humble, the readers should be humble and submit to God [EBC, NIGTC, TNTC].
QUESTION—To whom are the following exhortations addressed?
They are addressed to the proud [My] and also to all [Alf, Lg, NTC].
All Christians are subject to these moral dangers [ICC].
QUESTION—What relationship is indicated by the aorist imperatives in this and the following verses?
They call for decisive action [EBC, Hb, Lns], urgent action [WBC], action once for all [NTC].

but resist[a] the devil and he-will-flee[b] from[c] you.
TEXT—Some manuscripts omit δέ 'but'. GNT does not deal with this variant. 'But' is read by EGT, Hb, HNTC, Lg, Lns, and WBC; it is omitted by Alf, Blm, KJV, and probably only for stylistic reasons and not from their Greek text by AB, Herm, NIC, NTC, and all versions except KJV.
LEXICON—a. aorist act. impera. of ἀνθίστημι (LN 39.18) (BAGD 1. p. 67): 'to resist' [AB, BAGD, Herm, HNTC, LN, WBC; all versions except REB, TNT], 'to withstand' [BAGD, Lns], 'to stand up to' [REB, TNT], 'to set oneself against' [BAGD], 'to fight' [NIC].
b. fut. mid. (deponent = act.) indic. of φεύγω (LN 15.61) (BAGD 1. p. 855): 'to flee' [AB, BAGD, Herm, HNTC, LN, Lns, NIC; KJV, NASB, NIV, NRSV], 'to take flight' [NAB], 'to run away' [LN; NJB, TEV, TNT], 'to turn and run' [REB], 'to run' [WBC]. The future tense expresses God's promise [Alf, Hb].

c. ἀπό with genitive object (LN 89.122): 'from' [AB, Herm, HNTC, LN, Lns, NIC, WBC; all versions except NAB, REB], not explicit [NAB, REB].

QUESTION—How is this clause related to the preceding clause?
> Two actions are commanded, each of which calls on the initiative of the reader [EGT]. This command to resist the devil is the reverse of the command to surrender to God's will [Mit]. Submission to God is only possible when one resists the devil [Hb, My]. They do God's will by opposing God's enemy [NBC, NIGTC]. Resisting the devil is the first step in submitting to God [WBC].

QUESTION—How do people resist the devil?
> They do not succumb to the temptation to worldliness sent by the devil [ICC]. By doing good or by total commitment to God, they refuse to submit to the devil [NIGTC].

QUESTION—What relationship is indicated by καί 'and'?
> It introduces the result of actively resisting the devil [Hb, HNTC, May, Mit, My, NTC, TNTC, Tsk, WBC]: if you resist the devil, he will flee from you.

4:8 Draw-near[a] to-God and he-will-draw-near[b] to-you.

LEXICON—a. aorist act. impera. of ἐγγίζω (LN 15.75) (BAGD 1. p. 213): 'to draw near' [AB, Herm, HNTC, LN, Lns, NIC; NASB, NRSV], 'to draw nigh' [KJV], 'to draw close' [NAB, REB], 'to come near' [BAGD, LN, WBC; NIV, NJB, TEV, TNT], 'to go near' [NJB], 'to come close' [REB], 'to approach' [BAGD, LN]. This verb implies a return to communion with God [Hb]; it affirms the Christian's privilege of free access to God through Christ [Mit]. The aorist tense refers to decisive action [Hb, Lns]. The imperative mood exhorts a response to God's call for them to return to him [Hb, NBC].

b. fut. act. indic. of ἐγγίζω: 'to draw near'. See this word above. The imperative mood plus the future indicative amounts to a conditional clause [NIGTC]: if you draw near to God, he will draw near to you.

QUESTION—How is this clause related to the preceding?
> It continues the author's exhortations [WBC] based on his concern for his readers' salvation [AB]. Their worldliness has drawn them away from God [Hb]. It expresses the positive action of drawing near to God in contrast to the negative action of the preceding verse [BKC, My, NIGTC, Tsk, WBC]: resist the devil, but, on the other hand, draw near to God.

QUESTION—What is meant by drawing near to God?
> It implies that their worldliness has distanced them from God [Hb]. This does not refer to initial conversion, but to repentance on the part of Christians [Alf, HNTC, Mit, NTC, TNTC, WBC]. They must renounce the sins referred to in 4:1–4 [WBC]. What they are to do is spelled out in 4:8b–9 [NTC, TNTC]. They are to enter communion with God as acceptable worshippers [Hb]. They are to draw strength and comfort from the sense of God's nearness [Mit].

Cleanse[a] hands, sinners, and purify[b] hearts,[c] double-minded[d] (persons).

LEXICON—a. aorist act. impera. of καθαρίζω (LN 53.28; 79.49) (BAGD 2.b.α. p. 387): 'to cleanse' [AB, BAGD, Herm, LN, Lns; KJV, NAB, NASB, NRSV], 'to clean' [HNTC, LN, NIC; NJB], 'to make clean' [LN; REB], 'to purify' [BAGD, LN, WBC], 'to wash' [NIV, TEV, TNT]. The aorist imperative implies personal duty [Hb].

    b. aorist act. impera. of ἁγνίζω (LN **88.30**) (BAGD 1.b. p. 11): 'to purify' [AB, BAGD, Herm, HNTC, LN, Lns; KJV, NAB, NASB, NIV, NRSV, TEV], 'to cleanse' [TNT], 'to purge' [NIC], 'to clear' [NJB], 'to see that (something) is pure' [REB], 'to consecrate' [WBC].

    c. καρδία (LN 26.3) (BAGD 1.b.δ. p. 404): 'heart' [AB, BAGD, Herm, HNTC, LN, Lns, NIC, WBC; all versions except NJB], 'mind' [LN; NJB], 'inner self' [LN].

    d. δίψυχος (LN **31.38**) (BAGD p. 201): 'double-minded' [AB, BAGD, Herm, HNTC, LN, Lns, NIC, WBC; KJV, NASB, NIV, NRSV, TNT], 'doubter' [**LN**], 'waverer' [NJB], 'backslider' [NAB], 'hypocrite' [TEV], 'doubting' [BAGD], 'hesitating' [BAGD], '(you) whose motives are mixed' [REB]. It connotes instability and fickleness [NTC]. They attempted to be committed to both God and the world [EBC, Hb, HNTC, Mit, NIGTC, TG, TNTC, WBC].

QUESTION—What is the relationship between this part of the verse and the first part?

    1. This part states a requirement for fulfilling the first part [BKC, Lns, My]: in order to draw near to God you must cleanse your hands and heart.

    2. Figuratively cleansing the hands is the means for resisting the devil; purifying the heart is the means for drawing near to God [Blm].

QUESTION—What is the relationship between the two exhortations addressed to ἁμαρτωλοί 'sinners' and to δίψυχοι 'double-minded persons'?

The ἁμαρτωλοί 'sinners' are those who disobey God's laws [NIGTC, NTC]; even though addressed as sinners, they are professing Christians [Hb, Mit, NIC, Tsk, WBC] who need to repent [TNTC, Tsk, WBC]. The δίψυχοι 'double-minded ones' are those who try to combine loyalty to God and desire for the world [AB, Alf, Bg, EBC, Hb, NIGTC, NTC, TG, TNTC, Tsk, WBC]. The absence of the definite article or possessive pronoun adds vividness to these two very blunt terms [TNTC].

    1. They are addressed to the same persons [Alf, Bg, HNTC, ICC, Mit, My, NIC, TNTC, WBC]: you sinners (who are also) double-minded.

    2. They are addressed to two distinct groups [NIGTC]: you sinners and also you double-minded ones.

QUESTION—What is the meaning of the exhortation to cleanse their hands?

It is an exhortation to make their outward conduct morally pure [EBC, Hb, ICC, Lns, Mit, My, NBC, NIC, NIGTC, TG, TNTC, WBC], to repent [Lg, TNTC]. The reference to their hands is symbolic of their deeds [Hb, Lns]. The hands are the external organs which put actions into effect [Alf, Lg, My] and are polluted by sinful actions [Alf]. To cleanse means to repent [Lg, Mit], to stop doing evil and to do good [My].

QUESTION—Why are the readers exhorted to purify their hearts?

It means that their inner thoughts and motives must be pure [EBC, Hb, Lns, Mit, My, NBC, NIC, NIGTC, TG, TNTC, WBC]. The heart represents the whole inner life [Hb] which must be totally committed to God [NIGTC].

4:9 Lament[a] and mourn[b] and weep.[c]

LEXICON—a. aorist act. impera. of ταλαιπωρέω (LN **25. 136**) (BAGD 1.b. p. 803): 'to lament' [BAGD, LN; NAB, NRSV], 'to be sorrowful' [**LN**; REB, TEV], 'to grieve' [NIV], 'to be miserable' [AB, WBC; NASB], 'to be wretched' [BAGD, Herm, Lns], 'to make oneself wretched' [HNTC], 'to repent' [NIC], 'to be afflicted' [KJV]. This entire clause is translated 'appreciate your wretchedness, and weep for it in misery' [NJB], 'now is the time for sorrow, mourning, and lamentation' [TNT]. The meaning is wretchedness in their minds from a recognition of their sinfulness [Alf, Hb, NIGTC] so that they will turn away from the world [Bg] and repent [EBC]. The aorist tense refers to the action of becoming wretched [Hb]. It may mean voluntarily abstaining from comforts and luxuries [May]. Others think it means no such voluntary asceticism [Mit, NIC, NIGTC, Tsk, WBC].

b. aorist act. impera. of πενθέω (LN 25.142) (BAGD 1. p. 642): 'to mourn' [AB, BAGD, Herm, HNTC, Lns, NIC, WBC; KJV, NAB, NASB, NIV, NRSV, REB], 'to be sad' [BAGD, LN], 'to grieve' [BAGD, LN], 'to cry' [TEV], 'to weep' [LN; NJB]. This verb refers to the inward state of those who weep [Mit]. 'Mourn and weep' are often used together with the word 'mourn' referring to the outward demeanor of those who grieve [Hb].

c. aorist act. impera. of κλαίω (LN **25.138**) (BAGD 1. p. 433): 'to weep' [BAGD, Herm, HNTC, **LN**, NIC; KJV, NAB, NASB, NRSV, REB, TEV], 'to cry' [BAGD], 'to wail' [AB, LN, WBC; NIV], 'to sob' [Lns], 'to lament' [LN]. This verb refers to the outward evidence of repentance [Hb, Mit], tears flowing because of sin and shame [Hb], a summons to godly sorrow [May].

QUESTION—What is the meaning of this verse?

It indicates the proper attitude for recognition of the need for cleansing [BKC, My, NBC, NIC, NIGTC, NTC], an urgent demand for repentance [Hb, HNTC], emphasizing sorrow over sins [Herm, Mit, My] in a tone of judgment [Herm]. All four (the first three [Hb, Lns]) verbs in this verse summon the readers to repentance [EBC, Hb, ICC, Lns]; the first three are essentially synonymous [TG]. The aorist imperatives refer to beginning this repentance [NIGTC; NAB]. The second and third verbs are the emotional expressions of the first [Hb, NIGTC].

Your laughter into[a] mourning[b] let-it-be-transformed[c] and the joy into[a] gloom.[d]

LEXICON—a. εἰς with accusative object (LN 13.62) (BAGD 4.b. p. 229): 'into' [AB, Lns, WBC; NAB, NASB, NRSV, REB, TEV, TNT], 'to' [Herm, HNTC, LN, NIC; KJV, NIV, NJB].
  b. πένθος (LN **25.142**) (BAGD p. 642): 'mourning' [AB, BAGD, Herm, HNTC, Lns, NIC, WBC; all versions except NJB, TEV], 'sorrow' [LN], 'sadness' [BAGD], 'grief' [BAGD, **LN**; NJB], 'crying' [TEV].
  c. aorist pass. impera. of μετατρέπω (LN **13.64**) (BAGD p. 513): 'to be transformed' [LN], 'to be turned' [AB, BAGD, Herm, HNTC, **LN**, Lns; KJV, NAB, NASB, NJB, NRSV, TNT], 'to be changed' [LN]. The passive voice is also translated as active: 'to change' [NIV, TEV], 'to turn' [NIC, WBC; REB]. The third person passive refers to a power outside themselves, and the imperative mood urges them to let that power do its work in them [Hb].
  d. κατήφεια (LN **25.296**) (BAGD p. 423): 'gloom' [AB, **LN**; NASB, NIV, NJB, REB, TEV, TNT], 'gloominess' [BAGD], 'dejection' [HNTC, Lns, WBC; NRSV], 'sorrow' [Herm; NAB], 'depression' [LN], 'heaviness' [KJV], 'dismay' [NIC]. The meaning is dejection caused by a sorrowful heart [Hb].

QUESTION—What is the meaning of this clause?
It expresses the change that will result from the three preceding imperative verbs [Lns]. It means that they should turn their worldly laughter and joy into mourning and repentance in realization of their sinfulness [Hb, Herm, Lns, Mit, NTC, TG], in order to avoid God's judgment later [TNTC]. The first part of the clause refers to the outward evidence [Lg, My], the temporary sorrow [Blm]; the second part refers to the inner state [Lg, My], the attitude of the heart [Blm].

4:10 Humble-yourselves[a] before[b] (the) Lord and he-will-exalt[c] you.
LEXICON—a. aorist pass. impera. of ταπεινόω (LN 87.62; 88.56) (BAGD 2.b. p. 804), 'to humble oneself' [AB, BAGD, Herm, LN, Lns, NIC, WBC; all versions except NAB], 'to make oneself humble' [BAGD], 'to bring oneself down low' [LN], 'to be humbled' [NAB], 'to be humble' [HNTC]. The passive voice has middle meaning [Hb, ICC, Lns, NIC, TG, TNTC]. This verb sums up the exhortations of 4:7–9 [ICC, Lns]. It means awareness of God's supreme majesty [Mit] and our unworthiness to be accepted by him [Mit, Tsk], acknowledgment of his authority over us [Mit], of our need of God [TNTC, WBC], and our willingness to submit our will to his [Mit, TNTC]. It is the state of total dependence on God [WBC].
  b. ἐνώπιον (LN 83.33; 90.20) (BAGD 5.b. p. 271): 'before' [AB, BAGD, Herm, HNTC, LN, NIC; NIV, NJB, NRSV, REB, TEV, TNT], 'in the sight of' [LN, Lns; KJV, NAB], 'in the presence of' [WBC; NASB], 'in

front of' [LN]. It means to be in the view of [Hb], in awareness of the presence of [My].
  c. fut. act. indic. of ὑψόω (LN 87.20) (BAGD 2. p. 851): 'to exalt' [AB, BAGD, Herm, HNTC, LN, Lns, NIC; NASB, NRSV, REB], 'to lift up' [BAGD; KJV, NIV, NJB, TEV], 'to raise up' [WBC; TNT], 'to raise on high' [NAB].

QUESTION—How is this verse related to its context?
It is the conclusion of the exhortation [Alf, My, NIGTC, TNTC, WBC], summing it up [My, TNTC], giving the true path to exaltation [Alf, BKC, Hb], the only path to true joy [WBC]. It picks up the thought from 4:6 [Mit, Tsk], from 4:8 [WBC]. The humbling here refers to repentance only [Lns], although the principle is a general truth [EBC].

QUESTION—Who does κυρίου 'Lord' refer to?
  1. It is God the Father [Alf, ICC, My, NIC, TG].
  2. It is Jesus Christ [Hb, Lns].
  3. It includes both God the Father and Jesus Christ [Lg]. The living God of revelation is to be recognized in Christ [Lg].

QUESTION—With reference to the clause καὶ ὑψώσει ὑμᾶς 'and he will exalt you', when doe the exaltation take place?
  1. The exaltation is in this life [Lns].
  2. It is both in this life (morally and spiritually [ICC]) (as a concealed glory [Alf, My]) and hereafter (as a manifested glory [Alf, My]) [Alf, Hb, ICC, Lg, My, Tsk].
  3. It is only hereafter [Mit, WBC].

DISCOURSE UNIT: 4:11–17 [NIC, WBC]. The topic is some cautionary advice [NIC], some godless attitudes [WBC].

DISCOURSE UNIT: 4:11–12 [EBC, GNT, HNTC, Lns, Mit, NIC, NIGTC, NTC, TG, TNTC, Tsk; NAB, TEV]. The topic is faultfinding [EBC], backbiting and judging [Tsk], speaking against a fellow-believer [Lns, NIC], judging a Christian brother [GNT, NTC, TG; NAB], forbidding critical speech [TNTC], pure speech which does not condemn others [NIGTC], comments about passing judgment on others [HNTC; TEV].

4:11 (Do) not speak-againstᵃ one-another, brothers.
LEXICON—a. pres. act. impera. of καταλαλέω (LN 33.387) (BAGD p. 412): 'to speak against' [BAGD, HNTC; NASB], 'to speak evil of' [BAGD, LN; KJV, TNT], 'to speak evil against' [NRSV], 'to speak ill of' [NIC; NAB, REB], 'to speak disdainfully of' [WBC], 'to talk against' [Lns], 'to slander' [BAGD, Herm, LN; NIV, NJB], 'to defame' [AB, BAGD], 'to criticize' [TEV]. The reference is to unfavorable judgment of someone's character and motives [Alf], speaking against someone in his absence [ICC, Tsk], slander [Lg, NIGTC, TNTC] and opposition [Lg], derogatory comments intended to influence others against the person [Hb, Mit], anything said harshly or unkindly [EBC, HNTC, ICC], any kind of

harmful speech [TNTC], denouncing persons who were alleged not to be keeping the Torah [EGT].

QUESTION—What is this verse connected with?

1. It is connected with the spirit of the preceding discussion [Alf, Herm, Lg, Lns, My, NTC, WBC] from 4:7, with 4:7–10 relating to God and 4:11–12 relating to man [Hb], and closely connected with the following verse [NTC]. He now addresses those who speak against the worldly-minded believers whom he has just condemned [My].

2. Verses 11–12 form a new section, self-contained [HNTC].

QUESTION—What relationship is indicated by μή 'not' with the present imperative μὴ καταλαλεῖτε ἀλλήλων 'don't be speaking against one another'?

It is a command to cease speaking against one another, which they were doing [EBC, Hb, ICC, NBC, NTC, TNTC]: stop speaking against one another. (Note: this must be implied from the context; the construction can mean either to cease doing something or not to be doing it in the future.) The present tense condemns a habit [Hb, NIC, NTC].

QUESTION—What is implied by ἀδελφοί 'brothers'?

It is an affectionate address [NBC]. This and the two following mentions of 'brother' indicate a change of attitude and a new appeal [NIC].

The-(one) speaking-against[a] (a) brother or judging[b] his brother speaks-against law and judges law;

TEXT—Instead of ἤ 'or', some manuscripts read καί 'and'. GNT does not deal with this variant. Only May and KJV clearly read καί 'and'.

LEXICON—a. pres. act. participle of καταλαλέω: 'to speak against'. See this word above.

b. pres. act. participle of κρίνω (LN 56.30) (BAGD 6.b. p. 452): 'to judge' [AB, Herm, Lns, WBC; KJV, NAB, NASB, NIV, NRSV, TEV], 'to pass judgment on' [HNTC, NIC; REB, TNT], 'to pass an unfavorable judgment upon' [BAGD], 'to judge as guilty' [LN], 'to condemn' [BAGD, LN; NJB], 'to criticize' [BAGD], 'to find fault with' [BAGD]. The judging here amounts to condemning [TG].

QUESTION—What is meant by νόμος 'law'?

It means the second great commandment [ICC], the law of Christian love [Hb, Lg, My], the royal law [Hb, May] to which he has referred previously, and without the article it emphasizes its quality [Hb]; it is moral obligation and law in general [Blm, Lns]; it refers to Lev. 19:18, "Love your neighbor as yourself" [EBC, Herm, HNTC, Mit] as fulfilled by Jesus [Mit]; it is the Torah [EGT]. It is the teaching of Jesus in general [TNTC],

QUESTION—What is the significance of the present tense of the participles καταλαλῶν 'speaking against' and κρίνων 'judging'?

The present participles indicate habitual or characteristic action [Hb, Lg]: the one who habitually speaks against or judges his brother.

QUESTION—What is the significance of ἀδελφοῦ 'brother' without the article and the phrase τὸν ἀδελφὸν αὐτοῦ 'the brother of him' with the article and the possessive pronoun?

The first noun emphasizes the idea of the brother as a fellow Christian [Hb, My], while the second phrase emphasizes their unity in brotherhood [Hb, Lns, May, My, NIC] and thus emphasizes the shamefulness of the sin [My, NIC]: he who speaks against one who is a fellow Christian or judges the one who is his brother.

QUESTION—What relationship is indicated by ἤ 'or'?

1. It joins the two participial phrases, indicating that the second refers to the same activity as the first from a different aspect [Hb, Lns, NIGTC, Tsk]: who speaks against or, to say it differently, judges. This interpretation is supported by the fact that the two participles are governed by the same article [Hb, Lns].
2. It shows that they are distinct ideas, although closely related [My].

QUESTION—What is implied by the phrases καταλαλεῖ νόμου 'speaks against the law' and κρίνει νόμον 'judges the law'?

1. It implies setting oneself above the law [Alf, EBC, Lg, NIC, NIGTC, NTC, TG, WBC] and judging another person's observance of it [Alf, Lg], deciding on the validity of the law [EBC, Hb, Lg, Lns, Mit, My, Tsk] and rejecting it [EBC, Hb, Lg, Lns, Mit, My, TNTC]. It means violating (setting aside [NTC]) the law of love [Hb, HNTC, May, Mit, NIGTC, NTC, TG, WBC] and implicitly making oneself superior to it [ICC, Mit], thus implying that it is invalid or unnecessary [HNTC, May, Mit], and exempting oneself from obeying it [Hb, NBC], usurping God's office as judge [Hb, Mit, NIC, NIGTC, NTC, TG, Tsk, WBC]. Failure to do the law implies a denial of the law's authority [TNTC].
2. Here it refers to misinterpreting the Torah and criticizing others who did not follow the misinterpretation [EGT].

but/now[a] if you-are-judging law, not are-you (a) doer[b] of-law but (a) judge.[c]

LEXICON—a. δέ (LN 89.87; 89.124): 'but' [Herm, NIC; KJV, NASB, NJB, NRSV, REB], 'however' [NAB], 'and' [AB, HNTC, WBC], not explicit [NIV, TEV, TNT].

b. ποιητής (LN 42.20) (BAGD 2. p. 683): 'doer' [AB, BAGD, Herm, HNTC, LN, Lns; KJV, NASB, NRSV], 'one who practices' [TNT], 'observer' [NAB], 'servant' [NIC], 'one who obeys' [TEV]. This noun is also translated as a verb: 'to keep' [NIV, REB], 'to observe' [WBC]. The phrase οὐκ εἶ ποιητὴς νόμου 'you are not a doer of law' is translated 'you have ceased to be subjected to it' [NJB].

c. κριτής (LN 56.28) (BAGD 1.b. p. 453): 'judge' [AB, BAGD, Herm, HNTC, LN, Lns, NIC; KJV, NAB, NASB, NJB, NRSV], 'one who judges' [TEV, TNT]. This noun is also translated as a verb: 'to judge' [WBC], 'to sit in judgment' [NIV, REB]. He is a judge because in judging a person's action he judges whether it is a violation of the law [Alf].

QUESTION—What relationship is indicated by δέ 'but/now'?
1. It indicates contrast [Herm, NIC; KJV, NAB, NASB, NJB, NRSV, TEV]: but.
2. It indicates transition, calling attention to what follows [AB, Hb, HNTC, My, WBC]: now if you are judging the law.

QUESTION—What relationship is indicated by the conditional clause in the indicative mood εἰ κρίνεις 'if you are judging'?

It refers to actual conduct [Alf, Hb]; the shift from the second person plural to the singular places the emphasis on each individual [Hb]: if you individually are judging. (Note: only the context implies that they were in fact judging; the construction could be used if they were or were not guilty; cf. Jn. 15:20.) It means that to judge the law usurps God's prerogative as judge [Mit].

4:12 One[a] is (the) lawgiver[b] and judge, the-(one) being-able to-save[c] and to-destroy;[d]

TEXT—Some manuscripts omit the definite article ὁ 'the' before νομοθέτης 'lawgiver'. GNT includes 'the' with a C rating, indicating difficulty in deciding which variant to place in the text. The presence of the article should require the translation 'one is the lawgiver', but various translations and commentaries do not appear to make this distinction and it cannot be determined which reading they accept.

TEXT—Some manuscripts omit καὶ κριτής 'and judge'. GNT does not mention this variant. Only Bg, Blm, and KJV omit this phrase.

LEXICON—a. εἷς (LN 60.10) (BAGD 2.b. p. 231): 'one' [AB, Herm, HNTC, LN, Lns, NIC, WBC; all versions except TEV], 'one alone' [BAGD]. The clause 'one is the lawgiver and judge' is translated 'God is the only lawgiver and judge' [TEV]. It emphasizes the uniqueness of the one who is referred to [Hb, Herm, ICC]. It also points out that the same person is both lawgiver and judge [Lg, Lns], since one definite article governs both nouns [Lns].

b. νομοθέτης (LN 33.340) (BAGD p. 542): 'lawgiver' [AB, BAGD, Herm, HNTC, LN, Lns, WBC; all versions], 'dispenser of law' [NIC].

c. aorist act. infin. of σῴζω (LN 21.27) (BAGD 2.a.α. p. 798): 'to save' [AB, BAGD, Herm, HNTC, LN, Lns, WBC; all versions], 'to preserve from eternal death' [BAGD]. The phrase ὁ δυνάμενος σῶσαι καὶ ἀπολέσαι 'the one being able to save and to destroy' is translated 'he who has power of life and death' [NIC].

d. aorist act. infin. of ἀπόλλυμι (LN 20.31) (BAGD 1.a.α. p 95): 'to destroy' [AB, BAGD, Herm, LN, Lns, WBC; all versions].

QUESTION—What is the meaning of the phrase εἷς ἐστιν ὁ νομοθέτης καὶ κριτής 'one is the lawgiver and judge'?
1. 'The lawgiver and judge' is the predicate [AB, Hb, HNTC, ICC, Lns, My, WBC]: one is the lawgiver and judge.

2. 'One the lawgiver and judge' is the subject (KJV omits 'and judge') [EBC, Herm, NBC, Tsk; all versions except possibly TEV]: there is one lawgiver and judge.

QUESTION—What is the phrase ὁ δυνάμενος σῶσαι καὶ ἀπολέσαι 'the one being able to save and to destroy' connected with?

It explains the subject εἷς 'one' [Alf, Hb, ICC, Lg, My]: this 'one' is able to save and to destroy. The aorist infinitives imply the finality of God's decisions [Hb, NTC]. The definite article with the participle ὁ δυνάμενος 'the one being able' indicates that the person described here is identical with the subject εἷς 'one' [Lns]. The saving and destroying refer primarily to the final judgment [Mit, TG].

but you, who are-you the-(one) judging the neighbor?[a]

TEXT—Instead of πλησίον 'neighbor', some manuscripts read ἕτερον 'other (person)'. GNT does not deal with this variant; only Bg and KJV read 'other'.

LEXICON—a. πλησίον (LN 11.89) (BAGD 1.b. p. 672): 'neighbor' [AB, BAGD, Herm, HNTC, LN, Lns, WBC; all versions except TEV; different text KJV], 'someone else' [TEV], 'fellow' [NIC]. It emphasizes the close relationship [Hb].

QUESTION—What is implied by the emphatic σύ 'you'?

It sarcastically implies the feebleness of man in contrast with the power of God [Alf, Blm, EBC, Hb, Herm, May, Mit, My, NIC, Tsk, WBC], the presumptuousness of a man in judging his neighbor [HNTC, Mit, Tsk]: but you—who are you?

QUESTION—What relationship is indicated by ὁ κρίνων 'the one judging'?

It modifies the emphatic σύ 'you' [Hb, Lns], and the present tense implies characteristic activity [Hb].

DISCOURSE UNIT: 4:13–5:11 [TNTC]. The topic is what is implied by a Christian world-view.

DISCOURSE UNIT: 4:13–5:6 [Herm, NIGTC; NJB, REB]. The topic is some sayings directed against worldly-minded wealthy and business people [Herm], a warning for wealthy and self-confident persons [NJB], the danger of riches [REB], testing through riches [NIGTC].

DISCOURSE UNIT: 4:13–17 [AB, BKC, EBC, GNT, Hb, HNTC, ICC, Lns, Mit, NIC, NIGTC, NTC, TG, TNTC, Tsk; NAB, NIV, TEV]. The topic is business ethics [AB], an exhortation to change boasting into belief [BKC], making one's business plans without consideration of God's will [Lns], being submissive to God's will [NTC], presuming on God's goodness [TG], presumptuous self-confidence [Tsk], against being presumptuous about tomorrow [GNT, NIC; NAB, NIV], warning against boasting [TEV], boastful self-sufficiency [EBC], an example of arrogance condemned [HNTC, TNTC], the test of riches [NIGTC], faith tested by its response to presumptuous planning [Hb].

DISCOURSE UNIT: 4:13–15 [NTC]. The topic is an example of being submissive to God's will.

DISCOURSE UNIT: 4:13–14 [Hb]. The topic is a rebuke to self-sufficiency.

4:13 Come[a] now, the-(ones) saying, "Today or tomorrow we-will-go into[b] this-or-that[c] the city and we-will-stay[d] there (a) year and we-will-do-business[e] and we-will-gain[f]"

TEXT—Instead of ἤ 'or', some manuscripts read καί 'and'. GNT does not deal with this variant; only Alf, Blm, and Lg read 'and'.

TEXT—Instead of the future indicative 'we will . . .' of the four verbs in the quotation, some manuscripts read the aorist subjunctive 'let us . . .' by reading -ω- in the verb ending instead of -ο-. GNT does not deal with this variant; only Bg and Blm clearly read the subjunctive.

TEXT—Instead of ἐνιαυτόν '(a) year', some manuscripts add ἕνα 'one' and read 'one year'. GNT does not deal with this variant; only Alf, Bg, Lg, and My read 'one year'.

LEXICON—a. pres. act. impera. (used as an interjection) of ἄγω (LN **91.13**) (BAGD p. 8): 'come' [AB, BAGD, Herm, HNTC, Lns, NIC; NAB, NASB, NRSV], 'come then' [BAGD], 'go to' [KJV], 'listen' [LN; NIV, TEV], 'pay attention' [**LN**], 'well' [NJB], 'a word' [REB], not explicit [TNT]. The phrase ἄγε νῦν 'come now' is translated 'attend to this' [WBC]. It is a summons [My, TG] and implies disapproval [EGT, Hb], insistence [ICC], and the added νῦν 'now' adds to the urgency [Hb, ICC, Lns, My] and implies a connection with the preceding thoughts [My].

b. εἰς with accusative object (LN 84.22): 'into' [Herm, LN; KJV], 'to' [AB, HNTC, Lns, NIC, WBC; all versions except KJV]. It implies going to and going into upon arrival [My].

c. ὅδε (LN **92.33**) (BAGD 3. p. 553): 'this or that' [BAGD, HNTC, **LN**, WBC; NIV, NJB, TNT], 'such and such' [AB, BAGD, Herm, LN; NAB, NASB, NRSV, REB], 'such' [KJV], 'this' [Lns], 'a certain' [TEV], 'some particular' [NIC].

d. fut. act. indic. of ποιέω (LN 90.45; 42.41) (BAGD I.1.e.δ. p. 682): 'to stay' [BAGD, NIC; TEV, TNT], 'to spend' [AB, BAGD, Herm, HNTC, Lns, WBC; NAB, NASB, NIV, NJB, NRSV, REB], 'to continue' [KJV], 'to do' [LN], 'to work' [LN]. It indicates activity, not mere presence [Hb].

e. fut. mid. (deponent = act.) of ἐμπορεύομαι (LN **57.196**) (BAGD 1. p. 256): 'to do business' [Lns, WBC; NRSV, TNT], 'to carry on business' [BAGD, Herm; NIV], 'to engage in business' [LN; NASB], 'to go into business' [**LN**; TEV], 'to trade' [AB, HNTC, LN, NIC; NAB, NJB, REB], 'to buy and sell' [KJV].

f. fut. act. indic. of κερδαίνω (LN **57.189**) (BAGD 1.a. p. 429): 'to gain' [BAGD, LN], 'to get gain' [Lns; KJV], 'to earn' [LN], 'to profit' [HNTC], 'to make a profit' [AB, BAGD, Herm, **LN**, NIC; NASB], 'to come off with a profit' [NAB], 'to make money' [WBC; NIV, NRSV,

REB, TNT], 'to make some money' [NJB], 'to make a lot of money' [TEV]. This verb expresses the final goal of the plans [My].

QUESTION—What is this section connected with?
1. It is independent [Herm].
2. It is another example of an arrogant spirit [HNTC, Mit], an example of neglecting God in one's plans [ICC, Lns, Mit, NTC].

QUESTION—To whom is this exhortation addressed?
1. It is addressed to Jewish merchants [Alf, BKC, Blm, My, Tsk, WBC]. Although the section from 4:13–5:6 is addressed to rich and ungodly Jews outside the church, it applies to Christians insofar as they identify with those merchants [Alf, My].
2. It is addressed to Christian businessmen [EBC, NIGTC, NTC, TNTC], especially Jewish Christians [Hb], but possibly non-Christians as well [TNTC].
3. It is addressed to all people who make their future business plans without taking God into consideration [Herm, Mit, NBC, NIC], both non-Christians and Christians [NIC].

QUESTION—What is the function of the phrase ἄγε νῦν 'come now'?
It is brusque [BKC, TNTC] and intended to draw the readers' attention to what follows [Bg, BKC, Blm, EBC, Mit, Tsk]. It indicates that the matter is serious [EBC] and urgent [Hb]. It indicates that a different group is now being addressed [Mit].

QUESTION—What relationship is indicated by the present tense participial phrase οἱ λέγοντες 'the ones saying'?
The participial phrase is the vocative case of direct address identifying the addressees [Hb, Lns], and the present tense indicates that this was a common occurrence [EBC, Hb, Lg]: you who commonly say. The 'saying' was in their minds [ICC]; it was actual speech [Lg, WBC].

QUESTION—Why is the quotation given here?
It is an example of a boastful declaration by businessmen who make their plans without consulting God [BKC, Blm, EBC, Hb, NIC, NTC, TNTC, Tsk].

QUESTION—What is implied by the phrase ἤ/καὶ αὔριον 'or/and tomorrow'?
1. If ἤ 'or' is read, it implies an alternative [Alf, Hb, Lns, NIC, TG] expressed by the same person or by another person [Bg], implying that plans are definite [Lns, Tsk], or are still indefinite [TG]: today or perhaps tomorrow.
2. If καί 'and' is read.
2.1 It means that the journey will require two days [Alf, Hb, My]: today and tomorrow we will journey. It indicates confidence for both days [My].
2.2 It adds to the false sense of security [Lg]: today, and tomorrow as well.

QUESTION—What is implied by the forms of the four verbs in this quotation?
The future indicative forms indicate the false certainty of the speakers' assumption [Alf, Hb, Lg, Lns, My, NBC, NIC, NIGTC, NTC]: we will definitely do this.

QUESTION—What is meant by the phrase τήνδε τὴν πόλιν 'this or that city'?
1. It indicates indefiniteness [AB, Hb, Herm, NIGTC, NTC, TG, WBC; all versions except KJV, TEV]: this or that city.
2. The reference is to the particular city in the speaker's mind [Alf, Bg, EBC, ICC, Lg(M), Lns, May, My, NIC] or which he mentions [Tsk]: the city I'm thinking about.
3. It means that first one city and then another is intended [Lg]: one city and later another city.

4:14 —(you) who (do) not know[a] the (thing) of-the tomorrow of-what-sort[b] (is) your life;

TEXT—Instead of τὸ τῆς αὔριον 'the thing of tomorrow', some manuscripts read τὰ τῆς αὔριον 'the things of tomorrow', and others read τῆς αὔριον 'of tomorrow'. GNT reads 'the thing of tomorrow' with a B rating, indicating that the text is almost certain. 'The thing of tomorrow' is read by Alf, Bg, Blm, Hb, ICC, Lns, May, NIC, WBC; 'the things of tomorrow' is read by Lg; 'of tomorrow' is read by EGT.

TEXT—Some manuscripts add γάρ 'for' after ποία 'what sort'. GNT omits γάρ 'for' with a B rating, indicating that the text is almost certain. 'For' is omitted by AB, BKC, EGT, Hb, HNTC, ICC, Lns, NBC, NIGTC, Tsk, WBC, and all versions except KJV; it is included by Alf, Bg, Blm, Herm, Lg, My, NIC, and KJV.

LEXICON—a. pres. mid. (deponent = act.) indic. of ἐπίσταμαι (LN 28.3; 32.3) (BAGD 2. p. 300): 'to know' [AB, BAGD, Herm, HNTC, LN Lns, NIC, WBC; all versions except NAB, REB], 'to understand' [LN], 'to be aware of' [LN], 'to have an idea' [NAB, REB]. This word implies accurate knowledge [Hb].
b. ποῖος (LN 58.30) (BAGD 1.a.β. p. 684): 'of what sort' [Lns], 'what sort of' [BAGD, LN], 'what kind of' [LN; NAB], 'what' [AB, Herm, WBC; NASB, TEV, TNT], 'what?' [HNTC, NIC; KJV, NIV, NRSV, REB], not explicit [NJB]. It is qualitative, referring to the nature of life [Tsk]; it implies depreciation here, meaning how fleeting life is [Alf, Blm, Hb, My].

QUESTION—How is this verse related to its context?
It is parenthetical [Alf, Blm, Hb, Lg, My] so that 4:15 picks up from 4:13 [Alf, Bg, Blm, EBC, Hb, Herm, HNTC, ICC, Lg, Lns, My, NIC, TNTC, Tsk].

QUESTION—What is the meaning of the various forms of the phrase τὸ τῆς/τὰ τῆς/τῆς αὔριον 'the thing of/the things of/of tomorrow'?
Whichever form of the text is read, it means that life itself tomorrow is uncertain [Blm, EBC, ICC, Lg, Lns, My, NIC]. They do not know the actual situation on the morrow [Hb].

QUESTION—What is the structure of this part of this verse?
1. If γάρ 'for' is not added following ποία 'of what sort'.

1.1 It consists of one statement [AB; NAB, NASB, NJB, NRSV, TEV, TNT]: you who do not know about tomorrow what your life will be.
1.2 It consists of a statement followed by a question [EGT, Hb, HNTC, NBC, Tsk; NIV, REB]: you who do not know about tomorrow; of what sort is your life?
2. If γάρ 'for' is added following ποῖα 'of what sort', it is a statement followed by a question [Alf, Blm, Lg, My; KJV]: you do not know about tomorrow; for what is your life? 'For' introduces the justification for saying that they do not know about tomorrow [Alf, My].

QUESTION—What is the meaning of οἵτινες 'who'?

1. It is qualitative, characterizing the persons referred to [Alf, Hb, ICC, Lg, Lns, My, TNTC, Tsk, WBC]: you who belong to this class of persons.
2. It is concessive [Blm, Lg(M), May, NIC, NTC; KJV]: although you do not know.

for^a you-are (a) mist^b the-(one) appearing^c for^d a-little,^e then even disappearing^f—

TEXT—Some manuscripts omit γάρ 'for' following ἀτμίς 'mist'. GNT includes this word with a C rating, indicating difficulty in deciding which variant to place in the text. 'For' is included by AB, Alf, Bg, Blm, EGT, Hb, Herm, ICC, Lg(M), Lns, May, NBC, WBC, and NRSV; it is omitted by HNTC, and all versions except NRSV, although some translations may omit it for stylistic reasons only.

TEXT—Instead of ἐστε 'you are', some manuscripts read ἔσται 'it will be', and other manuscripts read ἐστιν 'it is'. GNT reads ἐστε 'you are' and discusses it with the preceding variant, but the C decision cannot apply to ἐστε. 'You are' is read by AB, Alf, EGT, Hb, Herm, HNTC, ICC, Lg, Lns, May, My, NIC, WBC, and all versions except KJV; 'it will be' is read by Bg; 'it is' is read by Blm, and KJV.

LEXICON—a. γάρ (LN 89.23) (BAGD 1.f. p. 152): 'for' [AB, Herm, LN; NRSV], 'because' [LN, WBC], 'pray' [BAGD].

b. ἀτμίς (LN **1.36**) (BAGD p. 120): 'mist' [BAGD, HNTC, WBC; NIV, NJB, NRSV, REB], 'vapor' [AB, BAGD, **LN**, Lns, NIC; KJV, NAB, NASB], 'steam' [LN], 'smoke' [Herm], 'a puff of smoke' [TEV, TNT].

c. pres. pass. (deponent = act.) participle of φαίνομαι (LN 24.18) (BAGD 2.b. p. 851): 'to appear' [AB, BAGD, Herm, HNTC, LN, Lns, WBC; all versions except REB], 'to become visible' [BAGD, LN], 'to show' [NIC]; as a passive: 'to be seen' [REB]. The present tense indicates repeated action [Hb].

d. πρός with accusative object (LN 67.106) (BAGD III.2.b. p. 710): 'for' [AB, BAGD, Herm, HNTC, Lns, NIC, WBC; all versions except NAB]. The phrase πρὸς ὀλίγον is translated 'for a little while' [LN], 'briefly' [AB].

e. ὀλίγος (LN 59.13) (BAGD 3.b. p. 564). 'little' [LN, NIC], 'little while' [AB, HNTC, Lns; NASB, NIV, NJB, NRSV, REB, TNT], 'little time'

[Herm; KJV], 'short time' [BAGD], 'short while' [WBC], 'moment' [TEV].
   f. pres. pass. (deponent = act.) participle of ἀφανίζω (LN 13.98; **24.27**) (BAGD p. 124): 'to disappear' [AB, BAGD, Herm, HNTC, LN, WBC; NJB, REB, TEV], 'to vanish' [**LN**, NIC; NAB, NIV, NRSV, TNT], 'to vanish away' [Lns; KJV, NASB].

QUESTION—How is this clause related to the preceding part of the verse?
1. If γάρ 'for' is included following ἀτμίς 'mist'.
   1.1 It expresses the justification for the preceding depreciative comment about their life [Alf, Blm, Hb, ICC, May, My, NBC]: it is appropriate to say that, for you are only a mist. Not merely their life but they themselves (ἐστε 'you are') are a smoke [My].
   1.2 It describes the nature of the life and the persons [Lns]: indeed, your life and you are a vapor.
2. If γάρ 'for' is omitted.
   2.1 It is a further statement [NAB, NASB, NJB, TEV, TNT]: you do not know about tomorrow; you are a vapor.
   2.2 If ἐστιν 'it is' is read instead of ἐστε 'you are', it is the answer to the preceding question [KJV]: what is your life? It is a vapor.

QUESTION—What relationship is indicated by the participial phrase 'which appears...and then disappears'?
It describes the mist/smoke [My].

QUESTION—What is meant by ἔπειτα 'then'?
It implies that the disappearance is certain to follow [Hb].

QUESTION—What is meant by καί 'even'?
It implies manner [Alf, Lg, Lns, May, My]: disappearing even as it appeared.

DISCOURSE UNIT: 4:15 [Hb]. The topic is an indication of the correct attitude.

4:15 Instead-of[a] your saying, "If the Lord should-will,[b] both we-will-live[c] and we-will-do this or that."

TEXT—Instead of the future indicative ζήσομεν 'we will live', some manuscripts read the aorist subjunctive ζήσωμεν 'we should live'. GNT does not deal with this variant. Only AB (apparently), Bg, and Blm read the aorist subjunctive form.

LEXICON—a. ἀντί with genitive object (LN **89.133**) (BAGD 3. p. 74): 'instead of' [BAGD, Herm, Lns; NAB, NJB], 'instead' [AB, HNTC, LN; NASB, NIV, NRSV], 'for that' [KJV]. The phrase ἀντὶ τοῦ λέγειν ὑμᾶς 'instead of your saying' is translated 'say rather' [WBC], 'what you ought to say is' [REB, TNT], 'what you should say is this' [TEV], 'what you should say instead is' [NIC].
   b. aorist act. subj. of θέλω (LN 25.1; 30.58) (BAGD 2. p. 355): 'to will' [AB, BAGD, Herm, HNTC, Lns, NIC; KJV, NAB, NASB, TNT], 'to be willing' [TEV], 'to be (someone's) will' [WBC; NIV, NJB, REB], 'to

desire' [LN (25.1)], 'to want' [BAGD, LN], 'to wish' [BAGD, LN; NRSV], 'to purpose' [LN (30.58)].

c. fut. act. indic. of ζάω (LN 23.88) (BAGD 1.a.δ. p. 336): 'to live' [AB, Herm, HNTC, LN, Lns, NIC, WBC; all versions except NJB, TNT], 'to live on' [BAGD], 'to remain alive' [BAGD], 'to be still alive' [NJB, TNT]. Even living is dependent on God's will [HNTC, Lg, WBC].

QUESTION—How is this verse related to its context?

1. It states the desired alternative to the attitude expressed in 4:13 [AB, Alf, Bg, BKC, Blm, Hb, Herm, HNTC, ICC, Lg, Lns, Mit, My, NIC, NIGTC, NTC, TG, TNTC; all versions except NAB]: you make your own plans instead of saying, "If it is the Lord's will." Verse 14 is a parenthesis [Alf, Hb, Lg].

2. It states the desired alternative to 4:16 [NAB]: instead of saying "If the Lord wills," you make boastful claims.

QUESTION—What is the meaning of the articular infinitive phrase ἀντὶ τοῦ λέγειν ὑμᾶς 'instead of your saying'?

1. This dependent infinitive phrase is treated as an independent clause [AB, Bg, HNTC, Mit; all versions except NAB] implying an imperative meaning [Bg]: instead, you ought to say.

2. It is a subordinate phrase [Alf, Blm, EBC, Hb, Herm, ICC, NIGTC; NAB]: instead of saying, "If the Lord wills."

QUESTION—What is included in the conditional clause introduced by ἐάν 'if'?

1. It includes only the first of the verbs [Alf, Bg, BKC, Hb, Herm, HNTC, ICC, Lg, Lns, Mit, NBC, NIGTC, Tsk; all versions]: if the Lord should will, we will live and do this or that.

2. For some who read the subjunctive ζήσωμεν 'we should live', it includes the second verb as well [AB, Blm]: if the Lord should will and we should live, we will do this or that.

QUESTION—What relationship is indicated by the conditional clause ἐάν 'if' with the subjunctive mood?

It leaves open the question of what God's will may be in any specific situation but expresses the Christian's proper desire to do God's will [Hb]: if God desires it, we will live and do this or that. It implies the believer's responsibility to plan, but to do so in cooperation with God [Hb, Mit, NIGTC].

QUESTION—To whom does ὁ κύριος 'the Lord' refer?

It refers to God [Alf, BKC, EGT, Hb, Herm, HNTC, ICC, Lg, Lns, Mit, NBC, NIC, NIGTC, TNTC, Tsk, WBC]. There is no thought of separating the persons of the godhead [Hb].

QUESTION—What is the meaning of καί...καί 'both/and...and'?

1. It means 'both...and' [Alf, Bg, EGT, Hb, Herm, HNTC, ICC, My, NIGTC, NTC, WBC; NASB] in the clause giving the consequence of the preceding conditional clause [BKC, Lg, Lns, May, Mit, My, NBC, TNTC, Tsk], specifying both verbs [Herm, Lg, May, My, Tsk; NASB]: we will both live and do this or that.

2. The second καί 'and' introduces the purpose of ζήσομεν 'we will live' [NAB, NJB, REB]: we will live to do this or that.
3. For some who read the subjunctive ζήσωμεν 'we should live', the first καί 'and' connects ζήσωμεν 'we should live' with the preceding verb [AB, Blm]: if the Lord should will and we should live, we will do this or that. (This incorrectly omits καί 'and' before ποιήσομεν 'we will do' [Bg].)

DISCOURSE UNIT: 4:16–17 [Hb, NTC]. The topic is the evil of their present attitude [Hb], good and evil [NTC].

4:16 But now you are-boasting^a in^b your pretensions;^c

LEXICON—a. pres. mid. (deponent = act.) of καυχάομαι (LN 33.368) (BAGD 1. p. 425): 'to boast' [AB, BAGD, Herm, HNTC, LN, Lns, WBC; NASB, NIV, NRSV, REB, TEV, TNT], 'to vaunt oneself' [NIC], 'to glory' [BAGD], 'to pride oneself' [BAGD], 'to rejoice' [KJV]. This entire clause is translated 'all you can do is make arrogant and pretentious claims' [NAB], 'but as it is, how boastful and loud-mouthed you are' [NJB]. This word refers to unwarranted certainty in one's plans [WBC] and self-congratulation based on disregard for God [Mit]. Their language in 4:13 is a proud boast [Hb].

b. ἐν with dative object (LN 13.8; 83.13; 89.5; 89.80; 89.119): 'in' [Herm, HNTC, LN, Lns, NIC; KJV, NASB, NRSV], 'with' [LN], 'with regard to' [LN], 'about' [AB, LN, WBC]. The phrase ἐν ταῖς ἀλαζονείαις 'in your pretensions' is translated 'and brag' [NIV, REB], 'you are proud' [TEV], 'you are too sure of yourselves' [TNT]. This preposition indicates the state [Alf], the grounds of the boasting [EBC].

c. ἀλαζονεία (LN **88.219**) (BAGD p. 34): 'arrogance' [BAGD, Herm, HNTC; NASB, NRSV], 'false arrogance' [LN], 'pretension' [BAGD, Lns, WBC], 'pretentious pride' [**LN**], 'boastful haughtiness' [LN], 'boasting' [KJV], 'bragging' [NIC], 'presumptuous plan' [AB]. This word expresses the source of the boasting [Alf, My]; it refers to unfounded confidence in one's knowledge concerning future conditions [Alf, Bg, EBC, EGT, Hb, Lns, May, My] as expressed in 4:13 [Herm, NBC], empty pretensions [Hb]. The plural indicates repeated occasions [Hb, TNTC], different manifestations in various circumstances [My].

QUESTION—What relationship is indicated by δέ 'now'?
It indicates a contrast with the proper spirit just mentioned [Alf, Hb, My, NBC, NIC, NIGTC, Tsk, WBC; NAB]. It reiterates the condemnation of the wrong attitude mentioned in 4:13 [BKC], and identifies the sin involved [WBC]. To ignore God in one's plans implies arrogantly claiming to be in command of the future [EBC].

QUESTION—What is meant by νῦν 'now'?
It is temporal [Alf, Blm, EGT, Hb, ICC, May, My, NBC, NIC, TG, WBC; NASB, NIV, NJB, NRSV]: as matters now actually stand. The situation occurs too often [Blm].

all such boasting[a] is evil.[b]

LEXICON—a. καύχησις (LN **33.368**) (BAGD 1. p. 426): 'boasting' [AB, BAGD, Herm, HNTC, LN, Lns, WBC; all versions except KJV], 'vaunting' [NIC], 'rejoicing' [KJV]. This word refers to the action of boasting rather than the content of boasting [NIC].

b. πονηρός (LN 88.110) (BAGD 1.b.β. p. 691): 'evil' [AB, BAGD, Herm, HNTC, LN, WBC; KJV, NASB, NIV, NRSV, TNT], 'wicked' [BAGD, LN, NIC], 'bad' [BAGD], 'wrong' [NJB, REB, TEV], 'reprehensible' [NAB].

QUESTION—What is the meaning of τοιαύτη 'such'?

It is qualitative, meaning that this type of boasting is evil [Alf, EGT, Hb, HNTC, May, My, NIGTC, NTC, Tsk; NJB]: this kind of boasting is evil. There is a proper boasting [Hb, HNTC, May, My, NIGTC, NTC, Tsk].

4:17 **Therefore to-(one)-knowing[a] to-do good[b] and not doing (it), it-is sin[c] to-him.**

LEXICON—a. perf. (with pres. meaning) act. participle of οἶδα (LN 28.1) (BAGD 3. p. 556): 'to know' [BAGD, LN, Lns, WBC; all versions except TNT], 'to know how' [AB, HNTC, NIC; TNT], 'to be able' [Herm]. The emphasis is on this word [Lg]. The reference is to the knowledge which the readers have previously had [My].

b. καλός (LN 88.4) (BAGD 2.b. p. 400): 'good' [Herm, HNTC, LN, Lns; KJV], 'the good' [NIV, TEV], 'morally good' [BAGD], 'praiseworthy' [LN], 'right' [NIC; TNT], 'the right thing' [WBC; NAB, NASB, NJB, NRSV, REB], 'rightly' [AB]. Without the definite article the reference is to something good [NTC].

c. ἁμαρτία (LN 88.289): 'sin' [AB, Herm, HNTC, LN, Lns, NIC; KJV, NASB]. The phrase ἁμαρτία αὐτῷ ἐστιν 'it is sin to him' is translated 'he sins' [WBC; NAB, NIV], 'he commits a sin' [NJB], 'he commits sin' [NRSV], 'we are guilty of sin' [TEV], 'he is a sinner' [REB, TNT]. This word is emphatic by forefronting [Hb].

QUESTION—What relationship does this clause have with its context?

1. It furnishes the conclusion to the preceding remarks [Alf, Bg, BKC, Blm, EBC, EGT, Hb, ICC, Lns, May, My, NIC, NIGTC, NTC, TNTC, Tsk, WBC] about boasting [EBC, Hb], about acting rightly [AB], to all of the advice thus far given [BKC, May], concerning the brevity of life [Alf], to counter a possible retort by readers that they already know what he has told them [Blm]. It is a proverb [Tsk] of unknown origin [ICC, NIGTC, NTC, TNTC, WBC], reminding the readers that he has now told them what is right, and if they fail to do it they are sinning [EBC, ICC, TNTC, Tsk].

2. It is an additional thought that because of the uncertainty concerning tomorrow and O.T. warnings on this subject, omissions will now be considered to be sins [HNTC].

3. It is a completely independent statement concerning sins of omission [Herm, Mit].

QUESTION—What relationship is indicated by the two participles without definite articles, εἰδότι 'knowing' and μὴ ποιοῦντι 'not doing'?

The absence of the article makes the participles refer to anyone who knows what he should do and fails to do it [Hb, Lns]. The sense of the tenses of these participles indicates a characteristic of knowing and not doing [Hb, Lg].

QUESTION—What relationship is indicated by the phrase καλὸν ποιεῖν 'to do good'?

1. This infinitive phrase is the object of εἰδότι [AB, Alf, EGT, Hb, HNTC, My; KJV, TNT].
   1.1 With εἰδότι meaning 'knowing' [Alf, Hb, My; KJV]: knowing to do good/knowing that he should do good.
   1.2 With εἰδότι meaning 'knowing how' [AB, EGT, HNTC; TNT]: knowing how to do good.
2. Καλόν 'good' is the object of εἰδότι 'knowing' and governs ποιεῖν 'to do' [NAB, NASB, NIV, NJB, NRSV, REB]; knowing (what is) the right thing to do.

QUESTION—What is the meaning of καλὸν ποιεῖν 'to do good'?
1. It refers to good behavior, not good works [AB].
2. It refers to doing acts of goodness [HNTC].

QUESTION—What is the meaning of μὴ ποιοῦντι 'not doing (it)'?
1. It means omitting doing something which one ought to do [Bg, EGT, Mit, NTC, TNTC, WBC], which may be as sinful as doing wrong [EGT, Mit, NTC, TNTC, Tsk, WBC].
2. It refers to doing evil in spite of knowing to do good, not merely failing to do good [Alf, Lg(M), My]; failure to do good, as making one's plans without considering God's will [NIGTC], is necessarily doing evil [My, NIC, NIGTC].

QUESTION—What is the meaning of μὴ ποιοῦντι 'not doing (it)'?
1. It means omitting doing something which one ought to do [Bg, EGT, Mit, NTC, TNTC, WBC], which may be as sinful as doing wrong [EGT, Mit, NTC, TNTC, Tsk, WBC].
2. It refers to doing evil in spite of knowing to do good, not merely failing to do good [Alf, Lg(M), My]; failure to do good, as making one's plans without considering God's will [NIGTC], is necessarily doing evil [My, NIC, NIGTC].

DISCOURSE UNIT: 5:1–20 [BKC, NTC]. The topic is sharing with concern [BKC], patience [NTC].

DISCOURSE UNIT: 5:1–18 [NIC]. The topic is the conclusion.

DISCOURSE UNIT: 5:1-11 [Hb, HNTC]. The topic is the testing of faith by its response to unjust treatment [Hb], the approach of the end of the age [HNTC].

DISCOURSE UNIT: 5:1-6 [AB, BKC, EBC, GNT, Hb, ICC, Lg, Lns, Mit, NBC, NIC, NIGTC, NTC, TG, TNTC, Tsk, WBC; NAB, NASB, NIV, TEV]. The topic is condemnation of persons who misuse their riches [TNTC; NASB], judgment on unrighteous wealthy persons [AB, EBC, Hb, ICC, Lns, NIC, WBC], a warning to wealthy persons [TG; NAB, TEV], a warning to those who oppress others [GNT; NIV], retribution for the rich [Tsk], accusations against wealthy persons [NBC], impatience with the wealthy [NTC], testing by the rich [NIGTC], condemnation of Judaists [Lg], sharing one's possessions [BKC].

5:1 Come[a] now (you) the rich-ones, weep[b] wailing[c] over[d] your miseries[e] the-(ones) coming-upon[f] (you).

LEXICON—a. pres. act. impera. (used as an interjection) of ἄγω: 'come'. See this word at 4:13.

  b. aorist act. impera. of κλαίω (LN 25.138) (BAGD 1. p. 433): 'to weep' [BAGD, Herm, HNTC, LN, NIC, WBC; all versions except NJB], 'to cry' [BAGD], 'to wail' [LN], 'to lament' [AB, LN; NJB], 'to sob' [Lns]. The aorist imperative implies urgency [Alf, Hb]. It is the weeping of despair [Lns].

  c. pres. act. participle of ὀλολύζω (LN **25.140**) (BAGD p. 564): 'to wail' [AB, Herm, HNTC; NAB, NIV, NRSV, REB, TEV, TNT], 'to howl' [Lns, NIC, WBC; KJV, NASB], 'to cry aloud' [BAGD, **LN**], 'to cry out' [BAGD], 'to make a loud cry' [LN], 'to weep' [NJB]. This participle describes the manner of the weeping [Alf, NTC], weeping accompanied by cries of pain [NTC]. It is stronger than κλαύσατε 'weep' [Alf, My], referring to utter woe [Lns]. The present tense indicates habitual action [Alf], or repeated action when Christ returns [Hb].

  d. ἐπί with dative object (LN 89.27; 90.23) (BAGD II.1.b.γ. p. 287): 'over' [AB, NIC; NAB, REB, TEV], 'for' [KJV, NASB, NJB, NRSV, TNT], 'because of' [HNTC, LN; NIV], 'in view of' [WBC], 'about' [LN], 'at' [Herm], 'on the basis of' [LN], 'concerning' [LN], 'with respect to' [LN], 'with reference to' [LN], 'upon' [BAGD], 'in' [Lns].

  e. ταλαιπωρία (LN 22.11) (BAGD p. 803): 'misery' [BAGD, Herm, HNTC, NIC, WBC; all versions except REB], 'miserable fate' [REB], 'wretchedness' [BAGD, LN], 'wretched condition' [Lns], 'distress' [BAGD], 'trouble' [BAGD], 'calamity' [AB].

  f. pres. mid. (deponent = act.) participle of ἐπέρχομαι (LN 13.119) (BAGD 1.b.β. p. 285): 'to come upon' [AB, BAGD, Herm, LN; KJV, NASB, NIV, TEV, TNT], 'to happen to' [LN], 'to overtake' [LN; REB], 'to impend' [NAB], 'to come to' [NJB, NRSV], 'to come one's way' [WBC], 'to come' [HNTC, Lns, NIC]. The meaning is that the miseries are already coming upon them [Tsk], they are already approaching and about to strike [Hb].

QUESTION—To whom is this paragraph addressed?
This is apostrophe [EBC, NBC, NIC, NTC, Tsk], where the rich are addressed as though they were recipients of the letter. James wants to show his Christian readers the folly of depending on riches or envying those who are wealthy [Tsk]. Whether the rich would hear this rebuke was questionable, but the poor and oppressed Christians would derive comfort from knowing that God knew of their hardships. It is written to encourage Christians to endure the oppression of rich unbelievers [Bg, ICC, NIC], to wait for their reward from God [NIC], and to encourage them not to be envious of the wealthy [Hb, ICC, Mit].

QUESTION—Who are οἱ πλούσιοι 'you rich people'?
This phrase is vocative [AB, Lns, NIC, NTC, TNTC, WBC; all versions], and the definite article indicates reference to this class of people [Lns, NIC, NTC].
1. They are unbelievers [Bg, EBC, Hb, Lg, Mit, My, NIGTC, NTC, TNTC], rich non-Christian (Jewish [Hb, Lg, TNTC]) landowners who oppress the poor [Hb, NIGTC, TNTC], or primarily unbelievers but perhaps this applies to all who fit the description [AB, Herm, HNTC, ICC, May].
2. They are worldly-minded Christians [Blm, NIC], but including non-Christians as well [NIC], any Christians who may be tempted by riches [Tsk].

QUESTION—Why is this warning mentioned?
It is a warning of the woes which will come upon οἱ πλούσιοι 'the rich' [all commentaries] at the final judgment [ICC, Mit], at the return of Christ [Alf, Hb], preceding Christ's return [My], at the fall of Jerusalem [Bg, Lg].
1. This is not a call to repentance for the persons condemned [BKC, EBC, Hb, Herm, HNTC, My, NBC, NIC, NIGTC, NTC, TNTC, Tsk, WBC].
2. The implied goal is repentance for the persons condemned [Alf, Lg].

5:2 Your riches are-rotted[a] and your garments[b] have-become moth-eaten,[c]

LEXICON—a. perf. act. indic. of σήπω (LN **23.205**) (BAGD p. 749): 'to rot' [AB, Herm, LN, Lns, NIC; NAB, NASB, NIV, NJB, NRSV], 'to rot away' [**LN**; REB, TEV], 'to become rotten' [WBC; TNT], 'to be rotten' [HNTC], 'to decay' [LN], 'to be corrupted' [KJV]. This verb is general, not limited to actual rotting [Lns, My, NBC, TNTC], and the two following verbs give its specifics [Lns]. The sense is metaphorical, meaning to waste away [Herm].

b. ἱμάτιον (LN 6.162) (BAGD 1. p. 376): 'garment' [AB, BAGD, Herm, HNTC; KJV, NASB], 'clothes' [NIC, WBC; NIV, NJB, NRSV, TEV, TNT], 'fine clothes' [REB], 'clothing' [BAGD, LN], 'apparel' [LN], 'fine wardrobe' [NAB]. Garments were a recognized form of wealth [Hb, ICC, May, TG, Tsk].

c. σητόβρωτος (LN 20.20) (BAGD p. 749): 'moth-eaten' [AB, BAGD, Herm, HNTC, **LN**, Lns, NIC, WBC; all versions except NIV, TEV], 'eaten by moths' [TEV], 'ruined by moths' [LN]. The phrase τὰ ἱμάτια ὑμῶν σητόβρωτα γέγονεν 'your garments have become moth-eaten' is translated 'moths have eaten your clothes' [NIV].

QUESTION—What is implied by the perfect tense of the two verbs in this verse?

1. They are used prophetically, as if the misfortune had already occurred [AB, Alf, EGT, Herm, May, Mit, My, NIC, NIGTC, TG, WBC].
   1.1 The reference is to physical loss [AB, Alf, EGT, Herm, May, WBC].
   1.2 The reference is to the worthlessness of physical wealth at the final judgment [Mit].
2. They relate to existing conditions [EBC, Hb, HNTC, ICC, Lg, Lns, NBC, TNTC, Tsk].
   2.1 It means that their wealth has already rotted and their clothing has already become moth-eaten [EBC, Lns, NBC, Tsk]. They have stored up so much that it is rotting [EBC, NBC]. These people prefer to let their possessions deteriorate rather than share them with other people [Tsk].
   2.2 It means that their material riches are worthless in securing spiritual benefits or hope [Hb, HNTC, ICC, TNTC]. The reality will be revealed at the day of judgment [Hb].
   2.3 It means that the spiritual wealth of external Jewish righteousness is worthless [Lg].

QUESTION—What is meant by ὁ πλοῦτος ὑμῶν 'your riches'?

1. It refers to all kinds of wealth [Herm, Lg, LN, May, NIGTC, TNTC], further specified in what follows [Alf, EBC, HNTC, Lns, My, NIC]: your wealth of various kinds. They are things that make a person rich [LN].
2. It refers to perishable grain [Hb, May, Mit, NTC, Tsk]: your riches consisting of grain. This is in keeping with the natural meaning of 'is rotten' and with the literal destruction of clothing [Hb].

5:3 Your gold and (your) silver are-rusted[a]

LEXICON—a. perf. pass. indic. of κατιόω (LN 2.61) (BAGD p. 424): 'to be rusted' [Herm, HNTC, Lns; NASB, NRSV], 'to become rusty' [BAGD, LN], 'to be covered with rust' [TEV, TNT], 'to become tarnished' [BAGD, LN, WBC], 'to corrode' [AB; NAB, NJB], 'to be corroded' [LN, NIC; NIV, REB], 'to be cankered' [KJV]. The prefixed preposition κατα- is intensive, indicating entirety [Alf, EGT, Hb, ICC, Lns, May, My].

QUESTION—What is implied by the use of the verb κατίωται 'they are rusted' with regard to gold and silver?

1. The reference is physical [AB, Alf, BKC, Blm, EBC, EGT, Herm, May, My, NBC, WBC].
   1.1 It is merely an imprecise general term, implying the destruction of their gold and silver [AB, Alf, Herm, My].
   1.2 It means that the gold has lost its luster and the silver has become tarnished [BKC, EBC, NBC, WBC].
   1.3 It refers to the deterioration of the alloys combined with the gold and silver [Blm].

1.4 It refers to filth accumulating on these metals [EGT].
1.5 The rusting of gold and silver is a supernatural act in a supernatural disaster [NIC]. James knows that gold does not rust [NIC].
2. The reference has a spiritual application [Hb, HNTC, ICC, Lg, Lns, Mit, NIGTC, NTC].
   2.1 It is an intentional hyperbole, implying that at the judgment day their wealth would be as worthless as rusted iron [Hb, HNTC, ICC, Lns, Mit] and a symbol of their impending ruin [ICC]; they are temporal and useless [NIGTC]. These persons have let their riches decay rather than share them with the poor [Hb, NIGTC].
   2.2 It means that to hoard wealth, simply to possess it, is useless; it refers also to the ultimate worthlessness of material goods [NTC].
   2.3 It is a figurative reference to the corruption of the glory of Israel by the corruption of its rich men in legalism [Lg].

and the rust[a] of-them shall-be for[b] (a) testimony[c] for-you

LEXICON—a. ἰός (LN 2.60) (BAGD 2. p. 379): 'rust' [BAGD, Herm, HNTC, Lns; KJV, NASB, NRSV, TEV, TNT], 'tarnish' [LN], 'corrosion' [AB, NIC, WBC; NAB, NIV, NJB, REB]. It is the substance that results from oxidation of metals [LN].

b. εἰς with accusative object (LN 89.57) (BAGD 4.d. p. 229): 'for' [BAGD, Lns, NIC], 'for the purpose of' [LN], 'as' [BAGD]. The phrase εἰς μαρτύριον ὑμῖν ἔσται 'will be for a testimony for you' is translated 'will be a testimony against you' [HNTC; NAB], 'will be a witness against you' [AB; KJV, NASB, NJB, TEV], 'will be evidence against you' [WBC; NRSV, REB, TNT], 'will testify against you' [Herm; NIV].

c. μαρτύριον (LN 33.262) (BAGD 1.a. p. 494): 'testimony' [BAGD, HNTC, LN, Lns; NAB], 'witness' [AB, LN; KJV, NASB, NJB, TEV], 'evidence' [NIC, WBC; NRSV, REB, TNT], 'proof' [BAGD].

QUESTION—To what does αὐτῷ 'of them' refer?
It refers to the gold and silver [My]: the rust of your gold and silver.

QUESTION—What is meant by the phrase μαρτύριον ὑμῖν 'testimony for you'?
1. The rust will be used as evidence against them. [Bg, BKC, HNTC, NBC, NIC, NTC, WBC; NRSV, REB, TNT]. It will be proof that, instead of helping the poor, they allowed their wealth to sit idle [NTC] because of their economic carelessness and social callousness [NBC]
2. The rust will testify against them [EBC, EGT, Hb, Herm, NIGTC, TNTC, Tsk; NIV]. It will bear witness that the rich neglected their duty to give alms [Herm]; they hoarded their wealth because of greed and selfishness [EBC, Hb].
3. The rust will be proof to them [Alf, ICC, Lns, May, Mit, My]. It will be a sign to the rich of the perishability of wealth and of the certain ruin awaiting those who have no other hope [ICC]. The ruin of their gold and

silver will indicate their own coming ruin [Alf]. It will give proof of the perishableness of all earthly things [May, Mit].

and it-will-eat[a] your flesh[b] as[c] fire.
LEXICON—a. fut. mid. (deponent = act.) indic. of ἐσθίω (LN 20.44) (BAGD 2. p. 313): 'to eat' [HNTC, Lns; KJV, NIV, NJB, NRSV], 'to eat up' [TEV], 'to consume' [BAGD, LN; NASB, REB], 'to devour' [AB, BAGD, Herm, NIC, WBC; NAB, TNT], 'to destroy' [LN].
  b. σάρξ (LN 8.63) (BAGD 1. p. 743): 'flesh' [AB, BAGD, Herm, HNTC, LN, Lns, NIC, WBC; all versions except NJB], 'body' [NJB]. This word refers to the person [NIGTC], to a person's physical existence and possessions [NTC].
  c. ὡς (LN 64.12): 'as' [AB, LN, Lns], 'as it were' [KJV], 'like' [Herm, HNTC, LN, NIC, WBC; all versions except KJV].
QUESTION—What is implied by the use of the plural σάρκας 'flesh'?
  1. The plural refers to the flesh of the body in contrast with the singular for the body as a whole [EGT, May, My]. It refers to the animated bodies of these persons [Lns], focusing attention on their primary concern for their physical comforts [Hb, Lns, My].
  2. The plural is used in the same sense as the singular [ICC].
  3. It refers to the externals of religious, civil, and individual life [Lg].
QUESTION—What is the phrase ὡς πῦρ 'as a fire' connected with?
  1. It is connected with what precedes it [Alf, Blm, EBC, EGT, Hb, Herm, HNTC, Lg, Lns, May, Mit, My, NIC, NIGTC, NTC, TG, TNTC, Tsk, WBC; all versions except NJB]: it will eat your flesh like fire. It is the riches that will eat the flesh; they will be wrath for these persons [NIC]. It means that their bodies will be destroyed as any material is destroyed by fire [Alf, EBC, Herm, HNTC, Lns, NIGTC, NTC, TG]. It implies swift and complete destruction [Bg], terrible misery and woe [Blm, Hb], by God's judgment [HNTC, My, NTC, TNTC]. Their greed will destroy them [BKC]. The failure of their wealth will bring ruin on them [Mit, Tsk] since they have nothing else to depend on [Mit]. It means that their selfishness will destroy the finer qualities of their souls in swift destruction as fire destroys [May]. Another view is that their legalism will eat through their ceremonies and destroy their very lives [Lg].
  2. It is connected with what follows as a comment on the preceding clause [AB; NJB]: it is like a fire you have stored up for the last days. They have stored up the fire of the underworld, to be destroyed by it when the end comes [AB]. It means that their covetous behavior has stored up a fire of destruction for themselves for the last days [AB].
  3. It is connected with what follows as a grounds for the preceding clause [ICC]: it will eat your flesh, since you have stored up fire which shall be in the last days. It is the fire of Gehenna that he refers to [ICC].

JAMES 5:3

You-have-stored-up[a] in/for[b] (the) last days.
LEXICON—a. aorist act. indic. of θησαυρίζω (LN 13.135) (BAGD 1. p. 361): 'to store up' [BAGD; NAB, NJB], 'to store up treasure' [BAGD, Herm, HNTC; NASB], 'to lay up treasure' [Lns, NIC; NRSV], 'to heap treasure together' [KJV], 'to pile up riches' [TEV, TNT], 'to pile up wealth' [REB], 'to amass wealth' [WBC], 'to hoard wealth' [NIV], 'to gather' [AB].
  b. ἐν with dative object (LN 83.13): 'in' [Herm, LN, Lns, NIC; NASB, NIV, REB, TEV], 'for' [AB, LN, WBC; KJV, NJB, NRSV], 'during' [HNTC, LN], 'in the course of' [LN], 'within' [LN], 'against' [NAB]. The phrase ἐν ἐσχάταις ἡμέραις 'in the last days' is translated 'while the world is coming to an end' [TNT].
QUESTION—What is meant by ἐν 'in/for'?
  1. They have stored up treasures in or during these last days [Alf, EBC, Hb, Herm, HNTC, Lg, Mit, My, NBC, NIC, NIGTC, NTC, TNTC, Tsk; NASB, NIV, REB, TEV, TNT]. These are the last days before the Lord comes [Alf, Hb, My]. The 'last days' are the whole time between the first and second coming of Christ [EBC, Lns, NIGTC, NTC, Tsk]. This is stated ironically; the rich even at the end of this present age continue to gather material wealth, but what actual treasure it really is will soon be revealed [HNTC, Lg, NIGTC]. The rich are blind or else unconcerned [NBC]. God's coming judgment should have been a strong stimulus to share their treasures rather than hoard them [TNTC].
  2. They had stored up treasure to use in the last days [Bg, BKC, Blm, WBC; KJV, NRSV].
  3. They have stored up fire and will be destroyed by it when the last day comes [AB, ICC; NJB]. The last days refer to God's judgment [ICC].
  4. It is really judgment that they have stored up for the last day [NAB].

5:4 Behold, the pay of-the workers the-(ones) having-mowed[a] your fields, the-(one) defrauded[b] by/from[c] you calls-out,[d]
TEXT—Instead of ἀπεστερημένος 'defrauded', some manuscripts read ἀφυστερημένος 'held back'. GNT selects 'defrauded' with an A rating, indicating that the text is certain. BAGD gives 'held back' as an alternative translation of ἀπεστερημένος, so it may not be possible to determine which word is being translated by those who read 'held back' or something similar. However, ἀπεστερημένος 'defrauded' is clearly read by Alf, Blm, Lns, My, NTC, TG, KJV, NRSV; ἀφυστερημένος 'held back' is read by EGT, Hb, HNTC, ICC, May, NIC, WBC.
LEXICON—a. aorist act. participle of ἀμάω (LN **43.13**) (BAGD p. 44): 'to mow' [AB, BAGD, Herm, LN, Lns, NIC; NASB, NIV, NJB, NRSV, REB], 'to reap' [WBC], 'to reap down' [KJV], 'to harvest' [HNTC; NAB], 'to gather one's harvests' [TNT]. This entire clause is translated 'You have not paid any wages to the men who work in your fields. Listen

to their complaints!' [TEV]. The reference is to reaping [TG]. The aorist tense indicates that the work has been completed [Hb, Lns, NTC].
   b. perf. pass. participle of ἀποστερέω (LN 57.248) (BAGD p. 99): 'to be defrauded' [LN], 'to be stolen' [BAGD], 'to be kept back by fraud' [Lns; KJV], 'to be held back' [BAGD], 'to be withheld' [AB, Herm; NASB]; as an active voice: 'to withhold' [NIC; NAB], 'to keep back' [NJB], 'to keep back by fraud' [NRSV], 'to fail to pay' [NIV]. The phrase ὁ μισθὸς ὁ ἀπεστερημένος 'the pay defrauded' is translated 'the wages have never been paid' [TNT], 'the wages you never paid' [REB]. The perfect tense implies that the injustice remains [Hb, Lns].
   c. ἀπό with genitive object (LN 90.7): 'by' [AB, Herm, HNTC, LN, Lns, WBC; NASB], 'of' [KJV], not explicit [NIC; NAB, NIV, NJB, NRSV, REB, TNT]. This word indicates the source of the action [Hb, May]; it indicates the agent of a passive verb [Lns].
   d. pres. act. indic. of κράζω (LN 33.83) (BAGD 2.b.β. p. 448): 'to call out' [BAGD, HNTC], 'to call' [BAGD], 'to cry out' [AB, Herm, Lns; NASB, NIV, NJB, NRSV], 'to cry' [BAGD; KJV], 'to cry aloud' [NIC; NAB, REB], 'to shout' [LN], 'to shout aloud' [WBC], 'to shout out loud' [TNT], 'to scream' [LN]. The present tense implies continual crying out [Hb, Lns] at present, not at the final judgment [NBC].
QUESTION—Why is this verse mentioned?
   1. It describes another (a specific [HNTC, ICC, Lg, WBC]) injustice of the wealthy, the failure (of some farmers [NIC, WBC]) to pay their workmen [EBC, HNTC, ICC, Lns, Mit, My, TNTC, Tsk, WBC]. It amplifies the preceding comment [Herm]. It is a general accusation, not directed to known persons [HNTC].
   2. It is a figurative reference; the 'wealthy' are Israel, who are rejecting the 'harvest' of blessing, which is the testimony of the 'workers', who are the Christian witnesses [Lg].
QUESTION—What is the phrase ἀφ' ὑμῶν 'by/from you' connected with?
   1. It is connected with the preceding participle [AB, Hb, Herm, HNTC, Lns, May, NIC, NTC, Tsk, WBC; all versions]: defrauded/withheld by you.
   2. It is connected with κράζει 'calls out' [Alf, Lg, My]: the withheld pay cries out from you—that is, from your coffers.

and the cries[a] of-the-(ones) having-reaped[b] have-entered[c] into[d] the ears of-(the)-Lord Sabaoth.[e]
LEXICON—a. βοή (LN **33.82**) (BAGD p. 144): 'cry' [AB, BAGD, Herm, HNTC, LN, WBC; all versions except NASB, REB], 'outcry' [NIC; NASB, REB], 'shout' [BAGD, LN, Lns].
   b. aorist act. participle of θερίζω (LN 43.14) (BAGD 1. p. 359): 'to reap' [LN, Lns; KJV], 'to harvest' [Herm, LN], 'to do the harvesting' [NASB], 'to gather in one's crops' [TEV]. This is also translated as a noun: 'harvester' [AB, BAGD, WBC; NAB, NIV, NRSV, TNT], 'reaper' [HNTC, NIC; NJB, REB]. This articular participle indicates a group of

workers [Hb], and the aorist tense indicates that they have completed their work [Hb, Lns].
c. perf. act. indic. of εἰσέρχομαι (LN 15.93) (BAGD 2.b. p. 233): 'to enter' [HNTC, LN, Lns; KJV], 'to come into' [LN], 'to come in' [BAGD], 'to come' [AB], 'to go into' [LN], 'to go in' [BAGD], 'to go up' [Herm], 'to reach' [NIC, WBC; all versions except KJV]. This word is emphatic by word order [Hb]. The perfect tense indicates that the cries have remained in God's ears [Lns]; he has heard them and has begun his judgment [WBC].
d. εἰς with accusative object (LN 84.22): 'into' [LN, Lns; KJV], 'to' [AB, Herm], not explicit [HNTC, NIC, WBC; all versions except KJV].
e. Σαβαώθ (LN 12.8) (BAGD p. 738): 'Sabaoth' [BAGD; NJB], 'of Sabaoth' [HNTC, Lns; KJV, NASB], 'of Hosts' [AB, BAGD, Herm, NIC; NAB, NRSV, REB, TNT], 'of the armies' [BAGD], 'Almighty' [LN, WBC; NIV, TEV]. This word is used intentionally as a biblical term [HNTC]. It implies God's great power and majesty [ICC, Lns, May, Mit, NIC, NIGTC, Tsk, WBC]. It refers to God's heavenly armies [AB, My, NIC, NTC, TNTC, Tsk] and earthly [NTC, TNTC, Tsk], to the hosts of angels [May] or the stars [May, Mit].

QUESTION—What is implied by this clause?
It implies that God not only hears, but that he will answer [AB, Bg, BKC, Blm, EBC, Lns, NBC, NIC, NIGTC, TNTC, Tsk].

QUESTION—How many groups of workers are referred to in this verse?
There is only one group; the mowers and the harvesters are the same workers [Alf, Bg, Hb, Herm, HNTC, Lns, May, NBC, NTC, Tsk].

5:5 You-have-lived-in-luxury[a] on[b] the earth and you-have-lived-in-self-indulgence,[c]

LEXICON—a. aorist act. indic. of τρυφάω (LN **88.253**) (BAGD p. 828): 'to live in luxury' [Herm, HNTC, NIC, WBC; NIV, NRSV, TNT], 'to live a life of luxury' [LN], 'to lead a life of luxury' [BAGD], 'to live luxuriously' [NASB], 'to live in high style' [Lns], 'to live in pleasure' [KJV], 'to live lavishly' [AB], 'to lead a life of self-indulgence' [BAGD], 'to live with intemperance' [**LN**], 'to revel' [BAGD, LN], 'to carouse' [BAGD, LN]. The phrase ἐτρυφήσατε καὶ ἐσπαταλήσατε 'you have lived in luxury on the earth and you have lived in self indulgence' is translated 'you lived in wanton luxury' [NAB, REB], 'you have had a life of comfort and luxury' [NJB], 'your life has been full of luxury and pleasure' [TEV]. This word refers to soft luxury and self-indulgence [EBC, Hb, ICC, Lg, Lns, Mit, My, Tsk]. The aorist tense summarizes the condition [ICC].
b. ἐπί with genitive object (LN 83.46): 'on' [Herm, HNTC, LN, Lns, NIC; all versions], 'upon' [AB, LN]. The phrase ἐπὶ τῆς γῆς 'on the earth' is translated 'off the land' [WBC].

c. aorist act. indic. of σπαταλάω (LN **88.252**) (BAGD p. 761): 'to live in self-indulgence' [HNTC, WBC; NIV, TNT], 'to live indulgently' [LN], 'to live with indulgence' [**LN**], 'to live in indulgence' [BAGD], 'to live luxuriously' [BAGD], 'to luxuriate' [Lns], 'to live sumptuously' [AB], 'to live voluptuously' [BAGD], 'to live in pleasure' [Herm; NRSV], 'to live in wantonness' [NIC], 'to lead a life of wanton pleasure' [NASB], 'to be wanton' [KJV]. This word refers to wasteful self-indulgence [EBC, Hb, Lns, Mit, My, Tsk], riotousness [ICC, Lg], immorality [ICC, Lg, NIC], and vice [NIC].

QUESTION—Why is this verse mentioned?

It lists another charge against the wealthy, that is,. they have lived in luxury [EBC, Hb, Herm, Mit, My, NIC, TNTC, Tsk, WBC], in self-indulgence [EBC, Hb], have gathered riches and lived riotously [Herm].

QUESTION—What is implied by the phrase ἐπὶ τῆς γῆς 'upon the earth'?

It implies that their concerns were centered on this world [Hb, ICC, Lns, May, Mit, My, NIGTC]. It implies a contrast between their lavish living in this life with their future fate [EGT, Hb, NIC, NIGTC, TNTC], a contrast with the coming day of slaughter [Tsk]. It implies that their lifestyle will come to an end [HNTC]. It means that they were living "off the land" in continual prosperity, that their earthly riches would come to an end, and that punishment and misery were awaiting them [WBC].

QUESTION—What is implied by the aorist tense of all three verbs in this verse?

1. They look at these persons' lifestyle as a whole [NTC], from the point of view of the judgment day [Hb].
2. They view the present conduct as constantly occurring [My].

you-have-nourished[a] your hearts[b] in[c] (a) day[d] of-slaughter.[e]

TEXT—Some manuscripts add ὡς 'as' before ἐν 'in'. GNT does not deal with this variant. Only Bg, Blm, KJV read 'as in a day of slaughter'.

LEXICON—a. aorist act. indic. of τρέφω (LN 23.6; 35.45) (BAGD 1. p. 825): 'to nourish' [BAGD; KJV], 'to fatten' [AB, BAGD, Herm, Lns, NIC; NAB, NASB, NIV, NRSV, TNT], 'to fatten up' [HNTC], 'to make fat' [TEV], 'to gorge' [WBC; REB], 'to feed' [BAGD], 'to provide with food' [BAGD], 'to provide food for' [LN (23.6)], 'to take care of' [LN (35.45)]. The phrase ἐθρέψατε τὰς καρδίας ὑμῶν 'you have nourished your hearts' is translated 'you went on eating to your heart's content' [NJB]. The meaning is to fatten and satiate [Hb, HNTC], to fatten for butchering [Lns], to indulge [WBC]. Their luxurious living has fattened them for slaughter [BKC, Hb] like fattened animals [Hb].

b. καρδία (LN 26.3) (BAGD 1.a. p. 403): 'heart' [AB, BAGD, Herm, HNTC, LN, Lns, NIC; KJV, NASB, NJB, NRSV], 'inner self' [LN]. The phrase τὰς καρδίας ὑμῶν 'your hearts' is translated 'yourselves' [WBC; NAB, NIV, REB, TEV, TNT]. The heart is the self [NTC], the inner life

[Hb, ICC, Lg] where the satisfaction of fattening their bodies is felt [Alf, Hb, My]; the passions and desires [NIGTC, WBC].
- c. ἐν with dative object (LN 67.33; 67.136): 'in' [HNTC, WBC; KJV, NASB, NIV, NJB, NRSV], 'on' [Herm; REB], 'during' [LN], 'at the time of' [LN], 'in connection with' [Lns], 'for' [AB, NIC; NAB, TEV], not explicit [TNT].
- d. ἡμέρα (LN **56.33**; 67.142) (BAGD 3.b.β. p. 347): 'day' [AB, BAGD, Herm, HNTC, **LN**, Lns, WBC; all versions except NJB], 'time' [LN (67.142); NJB], 'period' [LN]. The phrase ἡμέρα σφαγῆς 'day of slaughter' is translated 'slaughtering-day' [NIC].
- e. σφαγή (LN 20.72; **56.33**) (BAGD p. 796): 'slaughter' [AB, BAGD, Herm, HNTC, LN, Lns, WBC; all versions], 'condemnation' [**LN**].

QUESTION—What is implied by the phrase ἐν ἡμέρᾳ σφαγῆς 'in a day of slaughter'?

'Day of slaughter' means a time when slaughter will occur [Bg, BKC, Blm, Hb, HNTC, My, NIGTC; REB].
1. It means that they have indulged themselves without being aware of an impending judgment, just as cattle fatten themselves without being aware of their impending slaughter [EBC, EGT, Herm, HNTC, ICC, Lg, Lns, May, NIGTC, NTC, TG, TNTC, Tsk, WBC].
2. It means that they have been indulging themselves like victorious warriors do at a victory feast for which cattle have been slaughtered [Bg, NIC].

QUESTION—What relationship is indicated by the preposition ἐν in the phrase 'in a day of slaughter'?
1. It means *in* a day of slaughter/judgment [EBC, EGT, Herm, HNTC, Lg, My, NBC, NIGTC, NTC, TNTC, WBC; all versions except NAB, TEV].
2. It means in connection with a day of slaughter [Hb, Lns].
3. It means in preparation for the day of slaughter [AB, ICC, TG; NAB, TEV]. Their lifestyle has made their hearts heavy for the day of slaughter [AB].

5:6 You-have-condemned,[a] you-have-murdered[b] the righteous[c] (person); not does-he-resist[d] you.

LEXICON—a. aorist act. indic. of καταδικάζω (LN 56.31) (BAGD p. 410): 'to condemn' [AB, BAGD, Herm, HNTC, LN, Lns, NIC, WBC; all versions]. The aorist tense refers to actions done at various times [Blm, Hb, Lns].
- b. aorist act. indic. of φονεύω (LN 20.82) (BAGD p. 864): 'to murder' [BAGD, Herm, HNTC, LN, Lns, NIC; NIV, NRSV, REB, TEV], 'to put to death' [NASB], 'to kill' [AB, BAGD, WBC; KJV, NAB, NJB, TNT]. The aorist tense refers to actions done at various times [Blm, Hb, Lns].
- c. δίκαιος (LN 88.12): 'righteous' [AB, Herm, HNTC, LN, Lns; NASB, NRSV], 'just' [LN, NIC, WBC; KJV, NAB], 'upright' [NJB], 'innocent' [NIV, REB, TEV, TNT]. The righteousness of the righteous person provokes the enmity of the unrighteous wealthy person [Alf, Bg, Hb, Mit].

d. pres. mid. indic. of ἀντιτάσσω (LN 39.1) (BAGD p. 76): 'to resist' [AB, BAGD, HNTC, NIC, WBC; KJV, NAB, NASB, NRSV, TEV, TNT], 'to offer resistance' [BAGD, Herm; NJB, REB], 'to withstand' [Lns], 'to oppose' [BAGD, LN; NIV]. The meaning is to withstand, implying inability to overcome the oppressors [Lns]. The present tense refers to the present continuing attitude of meekness by these righteous persons [Alf, My]; it presents the situation graphically [Lns, May].

QUESTION—What relationship does this verse have with its context?

It describes another charge [Hb, HNTC, Mit, NIGTC, TNTC], an even worse kind of persecution by the wicked wealthy persons [Blm, EBC, Herm, My, NTC, Tsk, WBC].

QUESTION—What is implied by the phrase κατεδικάσατε τὸν δίκαιον 'you have condemned the righteous person'?

1. It means that wealthy persons have secured condemnation of innocent persons in courts [AB, BKC, EBC, Hb, ICC, Lns, Mit, My, NIGTC, NTC, WBC].
2. It refers specifically to Christ—people have condemned and killed Christ, the Just One [Lg].

QUESTION—What is meant by the phrase ἐφονεύσατε τὸν δίκαιον 'you have murdered the righteous person'?

It means that they have secured the death of righteous persons by judicial sentence [AB, BKC, EBC, Hb, ICC, Lns, My, NIGTC, NTC, WBC]. It could also refer to incidental taking of life by taking away the means of making a living [ICC, Mit, NTC, TNTC].

QUESTION—What is implied by the singular phrase τὸν δίκαιον 'the righteous one'?

1. The singular is collective [Alf, Bg, BKC, Blm, EBC, Hb, Herm, HNTC, Lns, May, Mit, My, NBC, NIC, NIGTC, NTC, TG, TNTC, Tsk, WBC]: righteous persons in general. It refers also to Christ [Bg] and prophetically to the death of James the Just, the author of this epistle [Bg, May], and others such as Stephen and James son of Zebedee, the class of persons known as the righteous; these are examples, not specific references [EBC].
2. It refers specifically to Christ [Lg]: Christ, the Righteous One.

QUESTION—What is implied by the phrase οὐκ ἀντιτάσσεται ὑμῖν 'he does not resist you'?

1. It is a statement [AB, Alf, Bg, Blm, EBC, EGT, Hb, Herm, HNTC, My, NIC, TNTC, Tsk, WBC; all versions]: he does not resist you.
   1.1 It implies that the righteous persons do not resist their persecutors [Blm, EBC, EGT, Hb, HNTC, My, NIC, TNTC, Tsk] and doubtless could not [Blm, EBC, EGT, Herm, NIC, TNTC, WBC], but endure in patience [My]; or that they were following Christ's teaching against resisting the evil person [Hb] and accepting their suffering [HNTC], and also that their hopes were on the future [EGT] and the coming vengeance by God

[My]. The condemnation of the rich is increased by the helplessness of their victims [NIC].
  1.2 It means that Christ does not stop these persons as they head toward death [Lg]; it is ironical [Lg(M)]: he does not stand in your way.
 2. It is a question [ICC, NIGTC]: does he not resist you? Yes, he does. Even though dead, the just one does resist the rich by calling for justice before God's throne [NIGTC]. This is the witness of the poor at God's coming judgment day [ICC].

DISCOURSE UNIT: 5:7–20 [EBC, Herm, ICC, Lg, NIGTC; GNT, NASB, NJB, REB, TEV]. The topic is sayings on various subjects [EBC, Herm], an exhortation [NASB], counsels for the Christian life-style [ICC], the final topic and conclusion [Lg], the closing statement [NIGTC], patience and prayer [GNT, REB, TEV], the Lord's return [NJB].

DISCOURSE UNIT: 5:7–12 [BKC; NAB, NIV]. The topic is patience [NAB], sharing in patience [BKC], patience in suffering [NIV].

DISCOURSE UNIT: 5:7–11 [AB, EBC, Hb, ICC, Lns, Mit, NBC, NIC, NIGTC, NTC, TG, TNTC, Tsk, WBC]. The topic is waiting patiently for Christ's return [AB, Lns, NBC, NIC, Tsk], an exhortation concerning patience [EBC, NTC, TG, TNTC, WBC], exhortations to suffering Christians [Hb], the reward of being constant and forbearing [ICC], endurance during testing [NIGTC].

5:7 **Be-patient[a] therefore, brothers, until the coming[b] of-the Lord.**
LEXICON—a. aorist act. impera. of μακροθυμέω (LN 25.168) (BAGD 1. p. 488): 'to be patient' [AB, Herm, HNTC, LN, Lns, WBC; all versions], 'to remain patient' [LN], 'to wait patiently' [LN], 'to have patience' [BAGD], 'to hold out in patience' [NIC]. It implies being content to wait for deliverance [EGT, HNTC, Lg, NIC, NIGTC, TG, TNTC, Tsk, WBC], patiently enduring wrongs [Lns, Mit, My, TG], not trying to get even for the wrongs done to them [EBC, Hb, Tsk]. The aorist tense indicates a constant attitude [Hb].
  b. παρουσία (LN 15.86) (BAGD 2.b.α. p. 630): 'coming' [AB, BAGD, Herm, HNTC, LN, NIC, WBC; KJV, NAB, NASB, NIV, NJB, NRSV], 'advent' [BAGD], 'Parousia' [Lns]. The phrase ἕως τῆς παρουσίας τοῦ κυρίου 'until the coming of the Lord' is translated 'until the Lord comes' [REB, TEV, TNT]. It is a specific event [Hb]. The term implies Christ's presence as a result of his coming [Hb].
QUESTION—What relationship is indicated by οὖν 'therefore'?
  It indicates exhortation based on the preceding verses [EBC, EGT, Hb, HNTC, My, NBC, NIGTC]. The preceding condemnation of the wealthy is the basis for the present appeal to the readers [EGT, Hb, HNTC]; patience is warranted because the judgment on the rich (at the return of Christ [NBC]) is near [My, NBC, NIGTC, TNTC].

QUESTION—What is implied by ἀδελφοί 'brothers'?

It is a friendly term [BKC, NTC, TNTC] indicating that he is now turning to the faithful believers [EBC, Lg, Mit, TNTC]; it is in contrast with the previously mentioned οἱ πλούσιοι 'the rich' [Alf, My].

QUESTION—What is the meaning of τῆς παρουσίας τοῦ κυρίου 'the coming of the Lord'?

It means the return of Christ [AB, Alf, Bg, Blm, EBC, Hb, HNTC, ICC, Lg, Lns, May, Mit, My, NIC, NIGTC, TG, TNTC, Tsk, WBC]: until Christ returns.

Behold, the farmer waits-for the precious[a] fruit[b] of-the earth,

LEXICON—a. τίμιος (LN 65.2) (BAGD 1.b. p. 818): 'precious' [AB, BAGD, Herm, HNTC, LN, Lns, NIC; all versions except NIV], 'valuable' [LN; NIV], 'choice' [WBC].

b. καρπός (LN 43.15) (BAGD 1.a. p. 404): 'fruit' [AB, BAGD, Herm, HNTC, LN, Lns, NIC; KJV, NJB, TNT], 'harvest' [LN], 'crop' [LN, WBC; NIV, NRSV, REB, TEV], 'produce' [NASB], 'yield' [NAB], 'grain' [LN].

QUESTION—Why is the illustration concerning the farmer mentioned?

It is intended to encourage the Christians to await patiently the coming victory [AB, Blm, Hb, My], and to encourage the church leaders to await patiently the maturing of the implanted word in the believers [AB]; the farmer is mentioned as an illustration of patience [BKC, EBC, Hb, ICC, TG, TNTC, Tsk, WBC].

QUESTION—What is implied by the phrase τίμιον καρπόν 'precious fruit'?

It is precious because it refers to the grain from which bread, the most necessary food, is made [Blm], because it is produced by hard work [Hb] and because it is necessary for physical life [Hb, Tsk, WBC]. Its preciousness justifies the patience [May, My].

being-patient[a] over[b] it until it-receives early-rain[c] and late.[d]

TEXT—Some manuscripts insert ὑετόν 'rain' before πρόϊμον 'early (rain)'. GNT omits this word with a B rating, indicating that the text is almost certain. However, 'rain' is understood with or without this word, so the translation will be the same regardless of which reading is accepted. Ὑετόν is specifically omitted by Alf, Blm, EGT, Hb, Herm, ICC, Lg, May, Mit, NIGTC, TNTC.

LEXICON—a. pres. act. participle of μακροθυμέω: 'to be patient'. See this word above. The present participle implies a constant attitude [Hb].

b. ἐπί with dative object (LN 90.23) (BAGD II.1.b.γ. p. 287): 'over' [NIC], 'for' [AB, WBC; KJV], 'for the sake of' [Lns], 'concerning' [LN], 'about' [LN; NASB], 'to' [NAB], 'with' [Herm, HNTC; NRSV], 'with responsibility for' [LN], 'with respect to' [LN], not explicit [NIV, NJB, REB, TEV, TNT]. The meaning is to watch over [Alf] with focused interest [Hb, Lg(M)], to be patient with it [Herm].

JAMES 5:7

c. πρόϊμος (LN 14.14) (BAGD p. 706): 'early rain' [AB, BAGD, Herm, HNTC, **LN**, Lns; KJV, NASB, NRSV, REB, TNT], 'early rainfall' [WBC], 'autumn rain' [LN; NIV, NJB, TEV], 'winter rain' [NIC; NAB]. This is the rain which comes after sowing [Bg, EBC, May, Tsk], before sowing [HNTC, Lg, Mit, NTC], at sowing time [Lns,], in late autumn [TNTC], in September or October [LN], in October and November [EBC, Hb, HNTC, ICC, Lg(M), Mit, NTC, TG, WBC].

d. ὄψιμος (LN **14.13**) (BAGD p. 601): 'late' [BAGD], 'late rain' [AB, Herm, HNTC, **LN**, Lns; NASB, NRSV, REB, TNT], 'late rainfall' [WBC], 'latter rain' [KJV], 'spring rain' [LN, NIC; NAB, NIV, NJB, TEV]. This is the rain which comes prior to harvest time [Bg, EBC, HNTC, Lg, May, Mit, NTC, Tsk], in the spring [Lns, TNTC], in April and May [EBC, Hb, HNTC, ICC, LN, Mit, NTC, TG], in March and April [Lg(M), NIGTC, WBC].

QUESTION—What is the subject of λάβῃ 'it receives'?

1. The subject is the earth [EGT, Hb, Mit]: until the earth receives the early and late rains.
2. The subject is καρπός 'fruit' [ICC, Lg, Lns, May, My, NIGTC]: until the fruit receives the early and late rains.

5:8 Be-patient[a] you also, establish[b] your hearts,[c] because the coming[d] of-the Lord has-approached.[e]

LEXICON—a. aorist act. impera. of μακροθυμέω: 'to be patient'. See this word at 5:7.

b. aorist act. impera. of στηρίζω (LN 74.19) (BAGD 2. p. 768): 'to establish' [BAGD, Herm], 'to stablish' [KJV], 'to strengthen' [AB, BAGD, HNTC, LN; NASB, NRSV], 'to steady' [NAB], 'to make firm' [Lns], 'to make more firm' [LN], 'to confirm' [WBC], 'to fortify' [NIC]. The phrase στηρίξατε τὰς καρδίας ὑμῶν 'establish your hearts' is translated 'do not lose heart' [NJB], 'you must be stout-hearted' [REB], 'you must be courageous' [TNT] 'stand firm' [NIV], 'keep your hopes high' [TEV]. The aorist tense implies a decisive act [Hb].

c. καρδία (LN 26.3) (BAGD 1.b.ε. p. 404): 'heart' [AB, BAGD, Herm, HNTC, LN, Lns, NIC; KJV, NAB, NASB, NRSV], 'inner self' [LN], 'mind' [LN], 'life' [WBC].

d. παρουσία: 'coming'. See this word at 5:7.

e. perf. act. indic. of ἐγγίζω (LN 67.21) (BAGD 5.b. p. 213): 'to approach' [BAGD, LN], 'to be near', [AB, HNTC, NIC; NIV, NRSV, REB, TEV], 'to come near' [BAGD, LN, Lns], 'to draw nigh' [KJV], 'to be at hand' [Herm, WBC; NAB, NASB], 'to be soon' [NJB], 'to take place soon' [TNT]. The perfect tense indicates that Christ's return is near but has not actually occurred [Hb, NBC, NIC, NTC].

QUESTION—What relationship does this verse have with its context?
It gives the application of the reference to the farmer's patience [Herm, NBC, NTC]. It is the completion of the exhortation [My]. It is the conclusion to be drawn from the example in 5:7 [NIGTC].

QUESTION—What is implied by καὶ ὑμεῖς 'you also'?
It means the readers as well as the farmer mentioned in 5:7 [Alf, BKC, EBC, Hb, Lg, My, NBC, NIC]: you also as well as the farmer. This phrase indicates emphasis [NTC].

QUESTION—What is the meaning of the phrase στηρίξατε τὰς καρδίας ὑμῶν 'establish your hearts'?
It means to be courageous [AB, ICC, TG] and purposeful [ICC], to be strong in their inner being [EBC, Hb], firm in their faith [NIGTC, TNTC], not giving away to doubt [NIGTC]. It indicates how they are to be patient [My, NIGTC].

QUESTION—What relationship is indicated by ὅτι 'because'?
It gives the grounds for the preceding exhortation [Hb, NIC]: become strong, because the Lord will soon return.

5:9 Grumble[a] not, brothers, against[b] one-another, in-order-that[c] you not be-judged;[d]

LEXICON—a. pres. act. impera. of στενάζω (LN **33.384**) (BAGD p. 766): 'to grumble' [AB, Herm, NIC; NAB, NIV, NRSV], 'to complain' [HNTC, LN, WBC; NASB, TEV], 'to make complaints' [NJB, TNT], 'to groan' [Lns], 'to groan against' [BAGD], 'to complain of' [BAGD], 'to grudge' [KJV]. The phrase μὴ στενάζετε κατ' ἀλλήλων 'do not grumble against one another' is translated 'do not blame your troubles on one another' [REB]. This verb refers to inner feelings [EBC, EGT, Hb, May] of faultfinding [Hb]. Μή 'not' with the present imperative commands them to stop grumbling [EBC, Hb, NTC] (Note: however, it can equally command not to be doing something which is not yet being done).
  b. κατά with genitive object (LN 90.31) (BAGD I.2.b. p. 406): 'against' [BAGD, Herm, LN, Lns, NIC; all versions except REB], 'at' [AB], 'about' [HNTC], 'of' [WBC].
  c. ἵνα (LN 89.59): 'in order that' [Lns], 'in order to' [LN], 'for the purpose of' [LN], 'so that' [AB, LN; NRSV, TEV], 'that' [NASB], 'so as' [NJB]. The phrase ἵνα μή 'in order that not' is translated 'lest' [Herm, HNTC, NIC; KJV, NAB]. The phrase ἵνα μὴ κριθῆτε 'in order that you may not be judged' is translated 'or you will be judged' [NIV], 'or you will fall under judgment' [REB], 'then you yourselves will not be judged' [TNT], 'that leads to condemnation' [WBC]. This word introduces the grounds for the command [Hb, ICC, Mit, NIGTC].
  d. aorist pass. subj. of κρίνω (LN 56.30) (BAGD 4.b.α. p. 452): 'to be judged' [AB, Herm, Lns; NASB, NIV, NRSV, TNT], 'to be brought to judgment' [NJB], 'to be condemned' [BAGD, LN, NIC; KJV, NAB]. The phrase μὴ κριθῆτε 'you may not be judged' is translated 'God will not

judge you' [TEV]. The judging will bring condemnation [Alf, Hb, NIC, Tsk]; the aorist tense indicates that the judgment will be final [Hb, Lg(M), NIC].

QUESTION—Why is this verse mentioned?
1. It is to urge mutual forbearance [Alf, HNTC, Mit, My, NIGTC, NTC, TG, WBC], as indicated by ἀλλήλων 'one another' [Hb]. They are not to blame one another for the distresses they are suffering [ICC, Lns, My]; they are not to allow pressures to make them censorious against one another [Mit]. The term ἀδελφοί 'brothers' shows that the exhortation is based on brotherly concern [Hb, NBC, NTC]. This verse is isolated from the preceding verse [Herm].
2. It tells what is meant by μακροθυμήσατε 'be patient' in 5:8 [Lns, NIGTC].

QUESTION—To whom does ἀλλήλων 'one another' refer?
1. It refers to the Christians [AB, EBC, Hb, HNTC, Mit, My, NBC, NTC, TG, TNTC, Tsk, WBC]: you Christians must not complain against one another.
2. It refers to all of the quarrels among the Jews [Lg].

behold, the judge stands[a] before[b] the doors.
LEXICON—a. perf. act. indic. of ἵστημι (LN 17.1): 'to stand' [AB, Herm, HNTC, LN, Lns, NIC, WBC; all versions except NJB, TEV], 'to wait' [NJB]. This entire clause is translated 'the Judge is near, ready to appear' [TEV].
b. πρό with genitive object (LN **67.58**; 83.33) (BAGD 1. p. 701): 'before' [BAGD, Lns; KJV], 'in front of' [BAGD, LN], 'at' [AB, BAGD, Herm, HNTC, LN, NIC, WBC; all versions except KJV, TEV]. The phrase ἕστηκεν πρὸ τῶν θυρῶν 'stands before the doors' is translated 'is coming soon' [**LN**]

QUESTION—Why is this clause mentioned?
It means that they must not complain against one another [AB, BKC, Blm, Lg, Mit, NIGTC, NTC, TNTC, Tsk].
1. Because the Judge is coming soon [AB, BKC, Blm, Lg(M)].
2. Because if they do they will be judged [Mit, NIGTC, NTC, TNTC, Tsk].

QUESTION—Who is the judge?
1. He is Christ [Alf, Bg, BKC, Hb, Lg, My, NTC, TNTC] at his return [Hb, Lg, My, NIGTC].
2. He is God [HNTC, ICC, NIC, WBC; TEV].

QUESTION—What is implied by the phrase πρὸ τῶν θυρῶν 'before the doors'?
It means that his coming is imminent [NIGTC, TG, TNTC, Tsk, WBC]. This is an idiom meaning that the event to follow is regarded as having almost begun [LN (67.58)].

5:10 (As an) example[a] of-suffering[b] and of-patience,[c] brothers, take[d] the prophets who spoke in[e] the name of-(the)-Lord.

LEXICON—a. ὑπόδειγμα (LN 58.59) (BAGD 1. p. 844): 'example' [AB, BAGD, Herm, HNTC, LN, Lns, WBC; all versions except NAB, REB], 'model' [BAGD, LN, NIC; NAB], 'pattern' [BAGD; REB]. This word is emphatic by word order [Hb, NTC].

    b. κακοπάθεια (LN 24.89) (BAGD p. 397): 'suffering' [NASB, NIV, NRSV, TEV, TNT], 'long-suffering' [AB], 'affliction' [Herm], 'suffering affliction' [KJV], 'suffering of what is bad' [Lns], 'suffering hardship' [LN; NAB], 'hardship' [HNTC], 'ill-treatment' [REB], 'endurance in affliction' [NIC], 'putting up with persecution' [NJB], 'adversity' [WBC], 'perseverance' [BAGD]. The meaning is endurance [EGT], enduring evils [Bg], affliction [Lg, My], vigorous efforts to endure misfortune [Hb].

    c. μακροθυμία (LN 25.167) (BAGD 1. p. 488): 'patience' [AB, BAGD, Herm, HNTC, Lns, WBC; all versions except NJB, TEV], 'patient endurance' [TEV], 'persevering patience' [NIC], 'endurance' [BAGD], 'steadfastness' [BAGD]. The phrase τῆς κακοπαθίας καὶ τῆς μακροθυμίας 'the suffering and the patience' is translated 'patience in the face of suffering' [LN], 'patiently putting up with persecution' [NJB].

    d. aorist act. impera. of λαμβάνω (LN 31.50) (BAGD 1.a. p. 464): 'to take' [AB, BAGD, Herm, HNTC, Lns, NIC; all versions except TNT], 'to accept' [LN], 'to receive' [LN], 'to come to believe' [LN], 'to think of' [TNT], 'to consider' [WBC]. The meaning is to hold before their mind [Hb]; the aorist tense implies a definite act [Hb].

    e. ἐν with genitive object (LN 90.30): 'in' [AB, Herm, HNTC, Lns, NIC, WBC; all versions]. The meaning is 'on behalf of' [AB].

QUESTION—Why is this verse mentioned?

    It is a further encouragement to be patient in afflictions [Alf, Blm, EBC, Hb, Mit, My, NTC].

QUESTION—How are the two nouns related in the phrase τῆς κακοπαθίας καὶ τῆς μακροθυμίας 'the suffering and the patience'?

1. It refers to two distinct ideas [Alf, EBC, Hb, Lns, My, NTC; KJV, NAB, NASB, NRSV]: they suffered and they were patient. The definite articles indicate definite experiences and imply that they were like the readers' experiences [Hb, Lns].
2. It refers to one idea: they were patient under suffering [BKC, HNTC, ICC, Mit, WBC; NIV, REB, TEV], or they patiently suffered [TNTC; NJB]. The phrase is a hendiadys [HNTC, ICC, NIGTC, WBC].

QUESTION—How are the two accusative nouns ὑπόδειγμα 'example' and προφήτας 'prophets' related?

    'Prophets' is the predicate of λάβετε 'take' and 'example' is in apposition with it (implied by the translation or discussion but not overtly stated) [AB, Alf, Hb, Herm, Lg, Lns, NBC, NIC, TNTC, Tsk, WBC; all versions]: take the prophets as an example. The reference is to the OT prophets [Hb].

QUESTION—What relationship is indicated by the relative clause 'who spoke in the name of the Lord'?

It refers to the prophets as a whole (implied by the translation or discussion but not overtly stated) [AB, Bg, EBC, Hb, HNTC, ICC, Lg, Lns, Mit, My, NBC, NIGTC, NTC, TG, Tsk]: take the prophets in general; they spoke in the name of the Lord.

QUESTION—What relationship is indicated by the phrase ἐν τῷ ὀνόματι κυρίου 'in the name of the Lord'?

It means that they understood that what they spoke had God's authority [HNTC, Tsk]; they spoke as representatives of God [May, Tsk]; they received the message from the Lord and spoke it [Lns, Mit, TG]. They were speaking in behalf of the Lord Jesus [AB].

QUESTION—Who is the 'Lord'?
1. It is God [Alf, Hb, HNTC, Mit, NIGTC, TG, WBC].
2. It is Jesus [AB].

5:11 Behold,ᵃ we-consider-blessedᵇ the-(ones) having-endured;ᶜ

LEXICON—a. ἰδού (LN 91.13) (BAGD 1.c. p. 371): 'behold' [Herm; KJV, NASB], 'lo' [Lns], 'look' [LN], 'see' [NIC], 'listen' [LN], 'pay attention' [LN], 'indeed' [AB; NRSV], 'remember' [BAGD, HNTC; NJB], 'consider' [BAGD], 'as you know' [WBC; NIV], not explicit [NAB, REB, TEV, TNT]. This word calls particular attention to the example of Job [Hb, NIGTC, WBC].

b. pres. act. indic. of μακαρίζω (LN **25.120**) (BAGD p. 486): 'to consider blessed' [BAGD, Herm; NIV], 'to regard as blessed' [AB], 'to reckon as blessed' [WBC], 'to call blessed' [BAGD, HNTC, Lns; NAB, NRSV], 'to count blessed' [NASB], 'to say to be the blessed ones' [NJB], 'to call fortunate' [BAGD], 'to consider fortunate' [BAGD], 'to regard as fortunate' [**LN**], 'to call happy' [BAGD; TEV], 'to consider happy' [BAGD; TNT], 'to regard as happy' [LN]. 'to count happy' [NIC; KJV, REB]. By saying 'we', the author joins with his readers in the evaluation [Hb, Lg, TG], and the present tense indicates a common practice [Hb, ICC, Lg].

c. aorist act. participle of ὑπομένω (LN 25.175) (BAGD 2. p. 845): 'to endure' [AB, BAGD, HNTC, LN, NIC; KJV, NAB, NASB, TEV], 'to show endurance' [NRSV], 'to persevere' [NIV], 'to persevere bravely' [Lns], 'to have perseverance' [NJB], 'to bear up' [LN]. 'to demonstrate endurance' [LN], 'to be steadfast' [Herm], 'to stand fast' [WBC], 'to stand firm' [REB], 'to stand one's ground' [BAGD], 'to hold out' [BAGD], 'to remain' [BAGD], 'to remain firm to the end' [TNT]. It means steadiness under stress [Mit], remaining brave under trials [Hb]. The articular participle in the aorist tense indicates the general class of persons [Hb, ICC, NTC]; the aorist tense indicates a reference to persons in the past [Hb, My, NIC, WBC], but not limited to prophets [My], referring to the blessedness which comes in God's presence after death [WBC]; it is timeless, not limited to the past [NIGTC, NTC].

QUESTION—How is this clause related to what precedes?

1. It is another example of patience given by the author [Alf, BKC, EBC, Herm, Mit, NTC], giving a new reason for the preceding exhortation [My], and summarizing the general reference to the prophets [Hb, TNTC, WBC]: we Christians consider those who endure to be blessed. Having previously discussed μακροθυμία, patience under abuse, he now turns to ὑπομονή, perseverance in distressful situations [Lns].

2. It is a quotation attributed to the prophets just mentioned [AB]: the prophets said, "We consider those who endure to be blessed."

the perseverance[a] of-Job you-have-heard and the end[b] of-(the)-Lord you-have-seen,[c]

LEXICON—ὑπομονή (LN 25.174) (BAGD 1. p. 846): 'perseverance' [AB, BAGD; NIV, NJB], 'brave perseverance' [Lns], 'endurance' [BAGD, HNTC, LN; NASB, NRSV], 'steadfastness' [BAGD, Herm, WBC; NAB], 'fortitude' [BAGD], 'patience' [BAGD, NIC; KJV, TEV]. The phrase τὴν ὑπομονὴν Ἰώβ 'the patience of Job' is translated 'how Job stood firm' [REB], 'how Job remained firm' [TNT]. This word is emphatic by word order [NIGTC].

b. τέλος (LN 89.40) (BAGD 1.a., 1.c., p. 811): 'end' [BAGD, HNTC, LN; KJV], 'result' [LN], 'outcome' [BAGD, Herm, LN; NASB], 'consummation' [NIC], 'goal' [BAGD, Lns], 'purpose' [WBC; NJB, NRSV], 'termination' [BAGD], 'cessation' [BAGD]. The phrase τὸ τέλος κυρίου 'the end of the Lord' is translated 'the Lord's final dealing' [AB], 'what the Lord did in the end' [NAB], 'what the Lord did for him in the end' [TNT], 'how the Lord treated him in the end' [REB], 'how the Lord provided for him in the end' [TEV], 'what the Lord finally brought about' [NIV].

c. aorist act. indic. of βλέπω or ὁράω (LN 24.7; 27.5) (BAGD 1.a. p. 220): 'to see' [BAGD, Herm, HNTC, LN, NIC, WBC; all versions except NJB, TEV], 'to perceive' [BAGD], 'to become aware of' [LN], 'to understand' [NJB], 'to learn about' [LN], 'to find out about' [LN], 'to know' [Lns; TEV], not explicit [AB].

QUESTION—How are the two nouns related in the genitive construction τὴν ὑπομονὴν Ἰώβ 'the patience of Job'?

It means that Job exercised patience [TG], stood firm [REB, TNT] (a subjective genitive): the perseverance which Job demonstrated. Job remained loyal to God under tremendous testing [Hb].

QUESTION—How are the two nouns related in the genitive construction τὸ τέλος κυρίου 'the end of the Lord'?

1. It is a subjective genitive [Lns, May, My], a genitive of agency [Hb], telling what the Lord did for Job [Alf, Bg, BKC, Blm, EBC, Hb, Herm, HNTC, ICC, Lns, May, NBC, NIC, NIGTC, NTC, TG, TNTC, Tsk;

NAB, NIV, REB, TEV, TNT], the outcome of Job's sufferings [My]: the result which the Lord brought about for Job. It refers to the reward that resulted from Job's suffering [NIC].
2. It states God's purpose for Job [EGT, Hb, WBC; NJB, NRSV]: the purpose God had in mind for Job. It is the end designed by the Lord, the reward he gave Job [WBC]. The goal God had in mind in allowing Job to suffer has been revealed; it was to refute Satan's slander and to vindicate and strengthen Job's faith [Hb].
3. It refers to the death of Jesus [Lg]: the death of the Lord Jesus.

that/because[a] very-compassionate[b] is the Lord and merciful.[c]
LEXICON—a. ὅτι (LN 89.33; 90.21): 'that' [LN; KJV, NASB, NJB], 'the fact that' [LN], 'how that' [Lns], 'how' [NRSV], 'because' [AB, LN, WBC], 'since' [LN], 'for' [Herm, HNTC, LN, NIC; REB, TEV], not explicit [NAB, NIV, TNT].
   b. πολύσπλαγχνος (LN **25.52**) (BAGD p. 689): 'very compassionate' [LN, WBC], 'compassionate' [AB, Herm; NAB, NRSV], 'full of compassion' [HNTC; NASB, NIV], 'full of pity' [TNT], 'kind' [NJB], 'very pitiful' [Lns, NIC; KJV], 'merciful' [REB], 'full of mercy' [TEV].
   c. οἰκτίρμων (LN 88.81) (BAGD p. 561): 'merciful' [AB, Herm, HNTC, LN, WBC; NAB, NASB, NRSV], 'compassionate' [LN, Lns, NIC; NJB, REB], 'full of compassion' [TEV, TNT], 'full of mercy' [NIV], 'of tender mercy' [KJV].
QUESTION—What relationship is indicated by ὅτι 'that/because'?
1. Ὅτι means 'that' and introduces what they have seen [Bg, Hb, Lns, May, My, NIC; KJV, NASB, NJB]: you have seen . . . that God is compasssionate and merciful. This clause further explains the preceding reference to Job [May, My].
2. Ὅτι means 'because' [AB, Alf, Herm, HNTC, TG, WBC; REB, TEV].
2.1 It indicates the reason for thinking of how God treated Job [Alf,]: you should think about this, because you will find that God is compassionate and merciful.
2.2 It indicates the reason for God's dealing with Job [TG, WBC]: God dealt well with Job, because God is compassionate and merciful.
2.3 It indicates the reason for looking at the result of Christ's sufferings [Lg]: you should think about this, because it is a result of God's mercy.

DISCOURSE UNIT: 5:12–20 [AB, HNTC, Lns, TNTC]. The topic is instructions concerning discipline [AB], religious conversation in the present life [HNTC], final exhortations [Lns, TNTC].

DISCOURSE UNIT: 5:12–18 [ICC, WBC]. The topic is how to express strong emotions in a religious manner, and the effectiveness of prayer [ICC], issues concerning the group, including taking oaths and reactions to problems and sins [WBC].

DISCOURSE UNIT: 5:12–13 [AB]. The topic is an exhortation not to swear but to sing and pray [AB].

DISCOURSE UNIT: 5:12 [EBC, Hb, Lns, Mit, NBC, NIC, NIGTC, TG, TNTC, Tsk]. The topic is an exhortation concerning oaths [EBC, Lns, TNTC], swearing forbidden [NBC, NIC, NIGTC, Tsk], faith evaluated by how it responds to selfish oaths [Hb], a comment on making promises [TG].

5:12 But above^a all, my brothers, swear^b not, neither (by) the heaven nor the earth nor any other oath;^c

> LEXICON—a. πρό with genitive object (LN **65.54**) (BAGD 3. p. 702): 'above' [AB, BAGD, Herm, LN, NIC, WBC; all versions], 'more important than' [**LN**], 'of greatest importance' [LN], 'most importantly' [HNTC], 'before' [Lns]. The phrase πρὸ πάντων 'above all' is translated 'especially' [BAGD].
>
> b. pres. act. impera. of ὀμνύω (LN 33.463) (BAGD p. 566): 'to swear' [AB, BAGD, Herm, LN, Lns; KJV, NASB, NIV, NJB, NRSV], 'to swear an oath' [NIC, WBC; NAB], 'to make an oath' [LN], 'to use an oath' [HNTC; REB, TEV, TNT]. The present imperative with μή 'not' is a command to stop swearing [Hb, Lns, NIGTC, NTC, WBC] (Note: this form is also used to command not to *be doing* something which is not now being done). It refers to strengthening one's statements by an oath [WBC], by an appeal to the name of God [TG, TNTC, WBC] or a substitute for his name [TG, TNTC].
>
> c. ὅρκος (LN 33.463) (BAGD p. 581): 'oath' [AB, BAGD, Herm, HNTC, LN, Lns, NIC; KJV, NAB, NASB, NJB, NRSV], not explicit [WBC; NIV, REB, TEV, TNT].

QUESTION— What is this verse connected with?

> 1. It is connected with the preceding comments, as indicated by the introductory phrase πρὸ πάντων 'above all' [AB, Hb, May, NIC], by the opening phrase of 5:13 [Alf, Bg], by the theme of judgment in 5:9 [NBC], by the common theme of discipline of the tongue [NIC, WBC]. It is the conclusion based on the preceding exhortations [BKC] concerning three types of worldliness [Hb]. The introductory δέ is to be rendered as 'now' or 'and', since no contrast is indicated [Hb, Lns].
> 2. It is merely another of several exhortations concerning the readers' conduct [My, NTC]. There is a general connection in concern about the tongue and the danger of judgment, but no specific connection to what precedes; a new section begins here [HNTC, NIGTC] as is indicated by both δέ 'but' and ἀδελφοί μου 'my brothers' [NIGTC].
> 3. This verse has no connection with what precedes [EGT, Herm, Mit] nor with what follows [Herm, Mit].

QUESTION—Why is this verse mentioned?

> It prohibits careless swearing as a means of assuring the truth of a statement [My, NIGTC, WBC], which James regards as especially to be avoided [My]; it prohibits the careless addition of oaths to one's conversation [NIC]. It

prohibits using supposedly non-binding oaths to strengthen one's statements, since these actually appeal to God's name [NTC]. It is intended to emphasize the need for patience [AB]; their suffering just referred to might result in impatience which could tempt them to swear oaths [Alf, Blm].

QUESTION—What relationship is indicated by the phrase πρὸ πάντων 'above all'?

1. This phrase refers to importance here [Hb, ICC, NIC, TG]: especially. The comparison is only with previously-mentioned sins of speech [NIC, Tsk, WBC]. It is important because this evil was so prevalent [Hb].
2. It is an emphatic introductory phrase, calling attention to what is to follow [HNTC, Mit, NIGTC, TNTC, WBC] and indicating that the author is near the close of his letter [WBC]. It does not mean that 5:12 is more important [NIGTC].
3. It is temporal [Lns]: before you do anything else.

QUESTION—What relationship is indicated by the three accusative nouns οὐρανόν 'heaven', γῆ 'earth', and ὅρκον 'oath'?

They are substitutes for using the name of God [TG, Tsk].

1. They are accusatives of the thing by which the oath is sworn [Alf, Hb, HNTC, ICC, Lg, My, NIGTC, WBC; all versions except NAB, NJB]: do not be swearing by heaven nor by earth nor by anything else. The author is counseling against introducing such oaths into ordinary affairs where a simple "yes" or "no" should be used [Alf, Hb]. They express more specifically the meaning of μὴ ὀμνύετε 'don't swear' [My].
2. The first two are accusatives of the thing by which the oath is sworn; the third means not to swear any other oath [Lns; NAB, NJB]: don't be swearing by heaven nor by earth, and don't swear any other oath.

but of-you the "Yes" let-it-be yes and the "No" (let it be) no, in-order-that[a] not you-may-fall[b] under[c] judgment.[d]

LEXICON—a. ἵνα (LN 89.59): 'in order that', 'in order to' [LN], 'for the purpose of' [LN], 'so that' [AB, Herm, LN; NASB, NRSV], 'in this way' [NAB], 'then' [TNT], 'and then' [TEV]. The phrase ἵνα μή 'in order that not' is translated 'lest' [HNTC, Lns, NIC; KJV], 'otherwise' [WBC; NJB], 'for fear' [REB]. It introduces the reason for not swearing [My].

b. aorist act. subj. of πίπτω (LN **90.71**) (BAGD 2.a.γ. p. 660): 'to fall' [BAGD, Herm, HNTC, Lns, NIC; KJV, NASB, NRSV], 'to come' [AB, WBC; TEV, TNT]. The phrase ὑπὸ κρίσιν πέσητε 'you may fall under judgment' is translated 'to experience condemnation' [LN]. The aorist tense indicates a single act [NTC].

c. ὑπό with accusative object (LN 37.7; **56.32**): 'under' [AB, Herm, HNTC, LN, Lns, NIC; NASB, NRSV, TEV, TNT], 'into' [KJV], 'to' [WBC]. The phrase ὑπὸ κρίσιν πέσητε 'you may fall under judgment' is translated 'you may be condemned' [**LN**], 'you will incur condemnation' [NAB].

d. κρίσις (LN **56.30**) (BAGD 1.a.β. p. 452): 'judgment' [AB, BAGD, HNTC, Lns, WBC; NASB, TEV, TNT], 'condemnation' [Herm, LN,

NIC; KJV, NAB, NRSV]. The clause ἵνα μὴ ὑπὸ κρίσιν πέσητε 'in order that you may not fall under judgment' is translated 'or you will be condemned' [LN; NIV], 'otherwise you make yourselves liable to judgment' [NJB], 'for fear you draw down judgment on yourselves' [REB]. The judgment will be condemnation [Hb, Lg, Mit, My] at the final judgment [NIC, NIGTC]. The danger of judgment would be because the appeal to God's name in the oath would place the speaker under greater obligation to fulfill his promise [WBC].

QUESTION—What relationship is indicated by the phrase 'let your "Yes" be yes and your "No" be no'?

It gives the proper alternative to adding oaths to one's statements [My, TG, TNTC; all versions]: just say "Yes" or "No," without adding oaths. It means that their declarations should be definite [AB], should need no oaths to verify them [Alf, BKC, EBC, Herm, HNTC, ICC, Lg, May, Mit, My, NIC, NTC, Tsk]; if they hedge, they will be judged [AB]. Their speech should be so honest that no oaths would be needed [EBC, Hb, Herm, Lns, Mit, NIC, NTC]. The present imperative verb ἤτω 'let it be' implies that this should be habitual [Hb].

DISCOURSE UNIT: 5:13–20 [BKC, Hb, NBC; NAB, NIV]. The topic is sharing in prayer [BKC], applying spiritual principles [NBC], anointing and prayer [NAB], the prayer of faith [NIV], closing remarks [Hb].

DISCOURSE UNIT: 5:13–18 [Hb, Lns, Mit, NIC, NIGTC, NTC, TG, TNTC, Tsk]. The topic is faith tested by resorting to prayer [Hb], comments about prayer [EBC, TG], prayer and healing [TNTC], praying in all circumstances [Tsk], comments about prayer in times of trouble and times of illness [Lns], situations where the church needs to act [NIC], mutual help through prayer [NIGTC], being persistent in prayer [NTC].

DISCOURSE UNIT: 5:13 [BKC, Hb, NTC]. The topic is being sensitive to needs [BKC], turning to prayer in emotional responses [Hb], praying and praising [NTC].

5:13 Is-suffering-misfortune[a] anyone among[b] you? He-should-pray.[c]

LEXICON—a. pres. act. indic. of κακοπαθέω (LN 24.89) (BAGD 1. p. 397): 'to suffer misfortune' [BAGD], 'to suffer hardship' [LN; NAB], 'to suffer distress' [LN], 'to suffer pain' [LN], 'to suffer ill' [Lns], 'to suffer' [AB, Herm; NASB, NRSV], 'to be afflicted' [KJV], 'to be in affliction' [NIC], 'to be in trouble' [NIV, NJB, REB, TEV, TNT], 'to be in difficulty' [HNTC], 'to face adversity' [WBC]. This verb refers to misfortune [Hb, My, WBC], to be unfortunate, or to suffer [My] difficulties [TG], trouble [Mit] of every sort [NIC, TNTC], all sorts of calamities [ICC]. It emphasizes the inner feelings resulting from misfortune [NIGTC].

    b. ἐν with dative object (LN 83.9): 'among' [Herm, HNTC, LN, Lns; KJV, NAB, NASB, NRSV, REB, TEV], 'of' [AB, NIC, WBC; NIV, NJB, TNT]

JAMES 5:13

c. pres. mid. (deponent = act.) impera. of προσεύχομαι (LN 33.178) (BAGD p. 713): 'to pray' [AB, BAGD, Herm, HNTC, LN, Lns, NIC, WBC; all versions]. The prayer is to be for help from God [TG]. The present tense indicates habitual practice whenever such situations arise [Hb].

QUESTION—What is the form of this verse and the first part of the following verse?
1. It consists of three questions and hortatory answers [Alf, BKC, Hb, HNTC, May, NBC, NIC, NIGTC, NTC, Tsk, WBC; all versions except NAB, NJB]: Is anyone...? He should.... The singular verbs point to individual response [Hb]. A conditional sense is implied by the questions [NIGTC, Tsk].
2. It is translated as three conditions and consequences [AB, My]: If anyone...he should...
3. It consists of two conditions and consequences in 5:13 and a question and hortatory answer in 5:14 [NAB]: If anyone...he should....Is anyone...? He should...
4. It is translated as three indefinite statements [NJB]: Anyone who...should...
5. It is translated (punctuated [GNT]) as three pairs of statements [Herm; GNT]: Someone is..., he should...

Is-happy[a] anyone? He-should-sing-psalms.[b]
LEXICON—a. pres. act. indic. of εὐθυμέω (LN 25.146) (BAGD p. 320): 'to be happy' [AB; NIV, TEV], 'to feel happy' [NIC], 'to be cheerful' [BAGD, Herm; NASB, NRSV], 'to feel cheerful' [HNTC; TNT], 'to be in good spirits' [Lns, WBC; NAB, NJB], 'to be in good heart' [REB], 'to be merry' [KJV], 'to be encouraged' [LN]. The reference is to inner cheerfulness [WBC]. It means to be joyful or of good courage even if the situation is difficult [NIGTC].
b. pres. act. impera. of ψάλλω (LN 33.111) (BAGD p. 891): 'to sing psalms' [Herm, LN; KJV, NJB], 'to sing praises' [BAGD, HNTC, LN, Lns, NIC; NASB, REB, TEV], 'to sing hymns' [AB], 'to sing a hymn of praise' [NAB], 'to sing songs of praise' [NIV, NRSV], 'to sing a song' [WBC], 'to sing' [LN; TNT]. The verb includes any kind of sacred song [Hb]. It means to sing and praise God [NIGTC]. The reference is to songs of thanksgiving to God [NIC, TG] and is a form of prayer [TNTC].

DISCOURSE UNIT: 5:14–18 [AB, BKC]. The topic is healing sick persons [AB], praying for needs [BKC].

DISCOURSE UNIT: 5:14–16a [Hb]. The topic is prayer for a believer's needs.

5:14 Is-sick/weak[a] someone among[b] you?
LEXICON—a. pres. act. indic. of ἀσθενέω (LN 23.144; 74.26) (BAGD 1.a. p. 115): 'to be sick' [AB, BAGD, Herm, HNTC, LN (23.144), Lns; KJV,

NAB, NASB, NIV, NRSV, TEV], 'to be ill' [LN, NIC; NJB, REB, TNT], 'to be weak' [LN (74.26), WBC].
  b. ἐν with dative object: 'among'. See this word at 5:13.
QUESTION—What is the meaning of ἀσθενεῖ 'one is sick/weak'?
  1. It refers to physical illness [AB, Alf, Bg, EBC, EGT, Hb, Herm, HNTC, ICC, Lns, May, Mit, My, NIGTC, NTC, TNTC, Tsk, WBC], which is severe [Blm, NIGTC, Tsk]: Is someone sick? The sickness may include a spiritual element [Hb].
  2. It refers to spiritual weakness [BKC, Lg]: Is someone spiritually weak? Although the word is used for physical illness in the Gospels, it is used in Acts (20:35) and the Epistles (Rom. 4:19; 14:1—2, 21; 1 Cor. 8:9–12) to refer to a weak faith or a weak conscience. Here it refers to people who have grown weary in the midst of suffering and are morally or spiritually weak [BKC].

He-should-summon[a] the elders[b] of-the church[c] and they-should-pray[d] over[e] him,
  LEXICON—a. aorist mid. impera. of προσκαλέω (LN 33.312) (BAGD 1.a. p. 715): 'to summon' [BAGD, WBC], 'to send for' [NIC; NJB, REB, TEV], 'to ask for' [NAB], 'to call for' [Herm; KJV, NASB, NRSV], 'to call on' [BAGD], 'to call to (oneself)' [Lns], 'to call' [AB, HNTC, LN; NIV, TNT]. The middle voice implies that the sick person himself should summon the elders [Hb, NBC, NTC]; it expresses the reference to the patient [Lg(M), WBC], but the actual summoning is by himself [Lg(M), NTC] or by other persons [Lg(M), My, NIGTC, NTC]. The aorist tense implies a definite act of summoning [Hb, NTC], urgency [WBC].
  b. πρεσβύτερος (LN 53.77) (BAGD 2.b.α. p. 700): 'elder' [AB, BAGD, Herm, HNTC, LN, Lns, NIC, WBC; all versions except NAB], 'presbyter' [BAGD; NAB]. It refers to church leaders [AB, Alf, BKC, Blm, Hb, Herm, HNTC, ICC, Lns, May, Mit, My, NBC, NIC, NIGTC, NTC, TG, TNTC, WBC], especially the pastors [Bg, EBC]. They act for the congregation [Alf, Bg, My].
  c. ἐκκλησία (LN 11.32): 'church' [Herm, HNTC, LN, Lns, NIC; all versions], 'congregation' [AB, LN, WBC]. The reference is to the believer's local congregation [Alf, Hb, Herm, HNTC, Lg(M), Lns, May, Mit, My, NBC, NIGTC, NTC, WBC].
  d. aorist pass. (deponent = act.) impera. of προσεύχομαι: 'to pray'. See this word at 5:13. This is the principal act of the elders in this situation [EBC, Hb, Lg, Lns, My, NIGTC, NTC] and is intended to bring about the healing [HNTC, My, Tsk]. The aorist tense suggests urgency [WBC].
  e. ἐπί with accusative object (LN 90.40) (BAGD III.1.a.ζ. p. 288): 'over' [BAGD, Herm, HNTC, Lns, NIC, WBC; all versions except TEV], 'for' [AB, LN; TEV]. Motion, figuratively or literally, is involved [Alf, NIGTC, TNTC], implying standing at his bedside [TG], extending their

hands over the patient [Hb, May, Mit, NIGTC], or prayer directed toward him [NIGTC]; it implies praying for his salvation [Lg].

having-anointed[a] him with-oil[b] in[c] the name of-the Lord.
LEXICON—a. aorist act. participle of ἀλείφω (LN 47.14) (BAGD 1. p. 35): 'to anoint' [AB, BAGD, Herm, HNTC, LN, NIC, WBC; all versions except TEV], 'to oil' [Lns], 'to rub on' [TEV]. This action is secondary to praying [EBC, Hb, Lns, My, NIGTC, NTC].
  b. ἔλαιον (LN 6.202) (BAGD 1. p. 247): 'oil' [AB, Herm, HNTC, LN, Lns, NIC, WBC; all versions except TEV], 'olive oil' [BAGD, LN; TEV].
  c. ἐν with dative object (LN 90.23): 'in' [AB, Herm, HNTC, LN, Lns, NIC, WBC; all versions].
QUESTION—What relationship is indicated by the aorist participle ἀλείψαντες 'having anointed'?
  1. It is temporal [Alf, Hb, Lns]: after they have anointed.
  2. It is an accompanying action to praying [AB, Alf, HNTC, ICC, My, NIC, NIGTC, TNTC; NIV, NJB, REB]: praying and anointing. The aorist tense refers to the anointing as a completed act [NIC] as part of the act of prayer [NIGTC].
QUESTION—What was the function of the anointing?
  1. It means ceremonial anointing [Alf, Blm, Hb, Herm, NIGTC, TG, TNTC] as a symbolic rather than sacramental action [TNTC, WBC], for miraculous healing [Bg, Blm, Herm], as an accompaniment of the divine healing [TG, Tsk].
  2. It means medicinal application of oil [EBC].
  3. It means both of the above [HNTC, ICC].
  4. It means merely rubbing oil on the body [BKC, Lns] for bestowing honor or refreshment [BKC].
QUESTION—What is the meaning of the phrase ἐν τῷ ὀνόματι τοῦ κυρίου 'in the name of the Lord'?
  1. It means in dependence on the Lord's help [Blm, Hb, NIGTC], by divine authority [TNTC], under the command [HNTC, Mit] and by the power of Jesus [HNTC, Lg, Mit], and invoking the name of Jesus [NIGTC]. It means 'on behalf of the Lord' [AB].
  2. It means 'while invoking the name of the Lord' [Herm, My].
QUESTION—What is the phrase 'in the name of the Lord' connected with?
  1. This phrase modifies ἀλείψαντες 'having anointed' [Alf, Hb, ICC, Lg, My]: having anointed him in the name of the Lord. However, the prayer was also in the name of the Lord [Hb].
  2. It modifies both προσευξάσθωσαν 'let them pray' and ἀλείψαντες 'having anointed' [Bg, Blm, Mit]: let them pray in the name of the Lord, having anointed him in the name of the Lord.
QUESTION—Who is τοῦ κυρίου 'the Lord'?
  1. It is Jesus [AB, Alf, Bg, Hb, Herm, HNTC, Lg, My, WBC].
  2. It is God [Blm].

5:15 And the prayerᵃ of-the faithᵇ will-saveᶜ the-(one) being-ill/being-discouragedᵈ and the Lord will-raiseᵉ him;

> LEXICON—a. εὐχή (LN **33.178**) (BAGD 1. p. 329): 'prayer' [AB, BAGD, Herm, HNTC, LN, Lns, NIC; all versions except TNT], 'request' [WBC]. The phrase καὶ ἡ εὐχὴ τῆς πίστεως 'and the prayer of faith' is translated 'if those who pray also have faith' [TNT]. The definite article with this noun indicates the specific prayer offered by the elders [Hb]. This word refers to a fervent petition [TNTC, WBC].
> b. πίστις (LN 31.85) (BAGD 2.a. p. 663): 'faith' [AB, BAGD, Herm, HNTC, LN, Lns, NIC, WBC; all versions]. The reference is to the faith exercised by the elders [Hb, Lns, NIC, NIGTC, TNTC, Tsk, WBC] and also by the patient [Lns, NIC, Tsk].
> c. fut. act. indic. of σῴζω (LN 21.27; 23.136) (BAGD 1.c. p. 798): 'to save' [AB, BAGD, HNTC, LN (21.27), NIC; KJV, NJB, NRSV], 'to make well' [LN (23.136), WBC; NIV], 'to get well' [TNT], 'to heal' [Herm, LN; REB, TEV], 'to restore' [NASB], 'to reclaim' [NAB], 'to rescue' [Lns].
> d. pres. act. participle of κάμνω (LN **23.142**; 25.291) (BAGD 2. p. 402): 'to be sick' [LN (23.142)], 'to be ill' [BAGD], 'to become discouraged, to be disheartened' [LN (25.291)]. The participial phrase τὸν κάμνοντα 'the one being ill' is translated 'the sick man' [BAGD, HNTC, **LN**; REB, TNT], 'the sick person' [AB, Herm; NIV, NJB, TEV], 'the sick one' [WBC], 'the sick' [NIC; KJV, NRSV], 'the one who is sick' [NASB], 'the one who is ill' [NAB], 'the patient' [Lns].
> e. fut. act. indic. of ἐγείρω (LN 13.65; **23.140**) (BAGD 1.a.β. p. 214): 'to raise up' [HNTC, Lns, NIC, WBC; KJV, NASB, NIV, NRSV], 'to raise up again' [NJB], 'to raise from one's bed' [TNT], 'to make (one) rise' [AB], 'to restore' [LN], 'to restore to health' [BAGD, Herm, **LN**; NAB, REB, TEV], 'to heal' [LN].

QUESTION—Why is this verse mentioned?

> It expresses the result of the prayer in 5:14 [Hb, My, NIGTC]

QUESTION—How are the nouns related in the genitive construction ἡ εὐχὴ τῆς πίστεως 'the prayer of faith' ?

> The prayer is offered in faith [Alf, BKC, EBC, My, NTC; NASB, NIV, REB], it is uttered in faith [NAB], it is made in faith [LN (33.178); TEV], it is based on faith [Hb, May, WBC], it is made by those who have faith [TNT]. The ones who pray believe that God will answer the prayer [TG]. They have confidence that it is the Lord's will to heal the person [Hb]. They have confidence that God is able to answer the prayer if it is his will and they have confidence that God's will is perfect [TNTC]. Some think that it is a special prayer granted by God in certain instances [Blm, Hb, Lg], while others think it is no different from other kinds of prayer since all prayers are to be made in faith [Tsk].

QUESTION—What is meant by τὸν κάμνοντα 'the one being ill/discouraged' and what is meant by that person being saved and raised?
1. It describes the person who is physically ill [Alf, EBC, Hb, Herm, ICC, Lns, May, Mit, My, NIC, NIGTC, NTC, TG, TNTC, Tsk, WBC]. The word focuses on the weariness caused by severe illness [Hb]. The word σώσει 'will save' refers to physical healing [Alf, EBC, Hb, Herm, ICC, Lns, May, My, NIC, NIGTC, TG, TNTC, Tsk, WBC; all versions]. It is restoration to total well-being, both physical health and relationship to God [Mit]. The person is raised up from his sick bed [Alf, EBC, EGT, Hb, ICC, My, NIC, NIGTC, TG, TNTC, Tsk]. It is a way of saying that he is restored to health [Herm].
2. It describes the person who is spiritually sick [Lg]. The saving is a spiritual healing of the wounds and infection caused by Judaistic confusion [Lg].
3. It describes the person who is spiritually weary and discouraged [BKC]. He is saved in the sense that the Lord will restore him from discouragement and spiritual defeat [BKC].

QUESTION—Who is ὁ κύριος 'the Lord'?
It is Jesus [Alf, EGT, Hb, Lg, My].

and-if he-may-have done[a] sins,[b] it-will-be-forgiven[c] to-him.
LEXICON—a. perf. act. participle of ποιέω (LN 90.45) (BAGD I.1.c.γ. p. 682): 'to do' [BAGD, LN], 'to commit' [AB, BAGD, Herm, HNTC, Lns, NIC, WBC; all versions except NIV], 'to be guilty of' [BAGD]. The phrase ἁμαρτίας ᾖ πεποιηκώς 'he may have done sins' is translated 'he has sinned' [NIV]. The perfect tense refers to a state resulting from having sinned [Alf, Hb, My, NBC, WBC], the resulting burden of the sins [Lg].
b. ἁμαρτία (LN 88.289) (BAGD 1. p. 43): 'sin' [AB, BAGD, Herm, HNTC, LN, Lns, NIC, WBC; all versions except NIV]. This word is emphatic by forefronting, and the plural refers to repeated sins [Hb, Lns], sins which caused the illness [Blm, ICC].
c. fut. pass. indic. of ἀφίημι (LN 40.8) (BAGD 2. p. 126): 'to be forgiven' [AB, Herm, HNTC, LN, NIC, WBC; all versions except NAB], 'to be pardoned' [BAGD, LN], 'to be remitted' [BAGD, Lns]. The phrase ἀφεθήσεται αὐτῷ 'it will be forgiven to him' is translated 'forgiveness will be his' [NAB]. The singular verb implies 'his sinning' as its subject [Alf, Bg, Lg, My]; it is an impersonal construction meaning that forgiveness will be given [Hb, ICC, Lns, May], lumping the sins together [Hb]. The healing of the illness is included [My].

QUESTION—What is implied by this comment?
It implies that the sick person must confess his sins in order to be healed [AB].

QUESTION—What is the conditional clause κἂν ἁμαρτίας ᾖ πεποιηκώς 'and if he may have done sins' connected with?

It is connected with the clause which follows [AB, Alf, Bg, BKC, Blm, EBC, EGT, Hb, Herm, HNTC, ICC, Lg, Lns, Mit, My, NIC, NIGTC, NTC, TG, TNTC, Tsk, WBC; all versions]: if he has sinned, he will receive forgiveness.

QUESTION—What relationship is indicated by κἂν 'and if'?

1. Κἂν 'and if' [Bg, EGT, Hb, Herm, ICC, May, NIGTC, TG, TNTC, Tsk] indicates that the illness may or may not have been caused by sin [Bg, Hb, Herm, May, Mit, NIC, NIGTC, TG, TNTC, Tsk, WBC]: and if his sin is the cause of this illness.
2. Κἂν 'and if' is translated 'even if' [Alf, My]: even if he may have sinned. It suggests that the illness was caused by the sin he is to confess [Alf, My], that the sins made the illness more severe [Lg].

5:16 Confess[a] therefore to-one-another the sins[b] and pray[c] for[d] one-another in-order-that/that[e] you-may-be-healed.[f]

TEXT—Some manuscripts omit οὖν 'therefore'. GNT does not mention this variant. 'Therefore' is omitted by Blm, KJV, TNT, but TNT may omit it for stylistic reasons only.

TEXT—Instead of τὰς ἁμαρτίας 'the sins', some manuscripts read τὰ παραπτώματα 'the trespasses'. GNT does not mention this variant; only Alf, Blm, KJV clearly read 'trespasses' (KJV 'faults').

LEXICON—a. pres. mid. impera. of ἐξομολογέω (LN 33.275) (BAGD 2.a p. 277): 'to confess' [AB, BAGD, Herm, HNTC, LN, Lns, NIC, WBC; all versions except NAB], 'to admit' [BAGD, LN], 'to declare' [NAB]. The prefixed preposition ἐκ- is intensive, implying open and full confession in acknowledging personal guilt [Hb]. Confession is to be made to the person wronged [NIC, NTC]; it is the necessary prerequisite to praying for one another [My]. The confession relates primarily to sinful involvement in Judaistic practices, but also to other sins [Lg].

b. ἁμαρτία: 'sin'. See this word at 5:15.

c. pres. mid. (deponent = act.) of εὔχομαι (LN 33.178) (BAGD 1. p. 329): 'to pray' [AB, Herm, HNTC, LN, Lns, NIC, WBC; all versions].

d. ὑπέρ with genitive object (LN 90.36): 'for' [AB, Herm, HNTC, LN, Lns, NIC, WBC; all versions], 'on behalf of' [LN].

e. ὅπως (LN 89.59) (BAGD 2.b. p. 577): 'in order that' [LN, NIC], 'so that' [AB, LN, WBC; NASB, NIV, NRSV, TEV], 'that' [BAGD, Herm, HNTC, Lns; KJV, NAB, REB, TNT]. The phrase ὅπως ἰαθῆτε 'in order that you may be healed' is translated 'to be cured' [NJB].

f. aorist pass. subj. of ἰάομαι (LN 23.136) (BAGD 2. p. 368): 'to be healed' [AB, BAGD, Herm, HNTC, LN, Lns, NIC, WBC; KJV, NASB, NIV, NRSV, REB, TEV], 'to be cured' [NJB, TNT], 'to be restored' [BAGD], 'to find healing' [NAB]. The reference is to physical healing [AB, Alf, Bg, EBC, Hb, Herm, ICC, Lns, May, Mit, NIC, NIGTC, WBC] but may include spiritual healing as well [Hb, HNTC, Mit], primarily spiritual but may include physical healing [Lg, Tsk], healing from sin [BAGD, HNTC], healing of the soul [BKC].

QUESTION—What relationship is indicated by οὖν 'therefore'?

It indicates the inference to be drawn from the preceding exhortation [Alf, BKC, EBC, Hb, Lg, May, My, NBC, NIGTC, NTC, TNTC, Tsk, WBC]: since prayer for the sick or weak is effective, prayer should be practiced by all. 'You' denotes readers generally [AB, Lg, Mit, NIGTC, Tsk] and implies that, in some sense, all need healing [Hb, NBC]. The statement is potential, whenever the specific need arises [Hb].

QUESTION—What relationships are implied by the structure of the two clauses exhorting to confess and to pray?

The present tense of the verbs imply a general practice [Hb, Lns, NTC, WBC] and the two coordinate second person verbs suggest group action [Hb]. The two references to 'one another' imply activity by the believers in general, not merely the ministers [Alf, EBC, Hb, Lns, Mit, My, NIC, NIGTC, NTC, TG, Tsk, WBC]. The definite article with ἁμαρτίας 'sins' implies that specific sins are to be confessed, not general sinfulness [Hb]. Confession of their wrongdoings against other Christians are meant [Alf, EBC, Hb, NIC, NTC, Tsk], and against God [Alf, May, My, NTC]. It concerns whatever sins burden their consciences and for which they feel a need for intercession [Hb]. This is not indiscriminate confession in public, but is appropriate to small groups of fellow believers [Hb, NTC]. The confession is to be made to the injured person by the one who injured him [Blm, EBC, NTC]. The confession is to be made by the sick person [Bg, ICC, TG];.The prayer is made for the sick person [ICC]; it is to be a prayer of forgiveness made by the injured person for the person who injured him [Bg, Blm]; it is to be by the offender and the offended following confession [NTC]. The prayer for one another must follow the confession; otherwise the confession may prove harmful [Hb]. This exhortation refers only to cases of critical illness, where confession and reconciliation might aid recovery [Blm].

QUESTION—What relationship is indicated by the clause ὅπως ἰαθῆτε 'that/in order that you may be healed'?

1. It expresses the purpose of the preceding [AB, EBC, Hb, HNTC, Mit, My, NIC, NIGTC, TG, WBC; NASB, NIV, NRSV, TEV]: in order that you may be healed.

   1.1 It gives the purpose of both preceding clauses [AB, EBC, HB, HNTC, Mit, TG]: the purpose of confessing . . . and praying . . . is healing.

   1.2 It gives the purpose of praying only [WBC]: the purpose of praying for one another is healing.

2. It expresses the content of the prayer [NJB]; pray to be healed.

DISCOURSE UNIT: 5:16b–18. The topic is the power of the petition by a godly man.

5:16b Much is-powerful[a] (the) supplication[b] of-a-righteous[c] (man) in-(its)-working.[d]

  LEXICON—a. pres. act. indic. of ἰσχύω (LN 74.9) (BAGD 2.a. p. 383): 'to be powerful' [BAGD, HNTC, NIC, WBC; NAB, NIV, NRSV, REB, TNT], 'to have power' [BAGD, Herm], 'to be strong' [BAGD], 'to have the strength' [LN], 'to be able' [BAGD, LN], 'to be able to do' [BAGD], 'to be very capable of' [LN], 'to be effective' [AB], 'to avail' [Lns; KJV]. This verb is translated 'can accomplish' [NASB]. The phrase πολὺ ἰσχύει 'much is powerful' is translated 'works very powerfully' [NJB]. The phrase πολὺ ἰσχύει...ἐνεργουμένη 'much is powerful...in its working' is translated 'has a powerful effect' [TEV]. This word with the adjective πολύ 'much' is emphatic by forefronting [Hb, My].

  b. δέησις (LN 33.171) (BAGD p. 172): 'prayer' [AB, BAGD, Herm, HNTC, LN, NIC, WBC; all versions except NAB], 'plea' [LN], 'petition' [Lns; NAB], 'request' [LN], 'entreaty' [BAGD]. It is petitionary prayer [Hb, ICC, Lns, Mit]; it is not different in meaning from the two other words for prayer used in these verses [TNTC, WBC]. The absence of the article means that the petition is not defined [Hb].

  c. δίκαιος (LN 88.12) (BAGD 1.b. p. 195): 'righteous' [AB, BAGD, Herm, HNTC, LN, Lns, NIC, WBC; KJV, NASB, NIV, NRSV], 'just' [BAGD, LN], 'upright' [BAGD; NJB], 'good' [REB, TEV, TNT], 'holy' [NAB]. This word is related to holiness here [AB]; it is the person whose faith is shown by his deeds [Alf, Hb], one who has confessed his sins and been forgiven [EBC, Hb, Lns, NTC, Tsk], one who by faith fulfills the royal law [May, My], one who does what is morally right [Mit]; it includes all who sincerely trust in God [Herm, HNTC, Lg, NIGTC, TNTC] and seek to do God's will [TNTC]. The singular noun is generic, referring to anyone of this class [Hb].

  d. pres. mid. participle of ἐνεργέω (LN 42.3) (BAGD 1.b. p. 265): 'to work' [BAGD, LN], 'to be at work' [BAGD, LN], 'to function' [LN], 'to operate' [BAGD], 'to be effective' [BAGD]; as an adjective 'effective' [NASB, NIV, NRSV, REB], 'effectual' [KJV], 'energetic' [Herm], 'active' [HNTC], 'fervent' [NAB], 'vigorous' [AB], 'heartfelt' [NJB]. This participle is translated 'in its effectiveness' [WBC], 'in its operation' [NIC], 'when putting forth its energy' [Lns], 'because God is at work in it' [TNT]. It is emphatic by its position at the end of the clause [Lns, May]. The sense is middle voice [WBC], meaning its effect is powerful [NTC]; it is passive, 'energized by the Holy Spirit' [May]. It adds very little to the meaning of the clause [ICC, Mit].

QUESTION—Why is this clause mentioned?

  It gives the grounds of assurance for (an illustration of [HNTC], an encouragement to fulfill [Lg], a strengthening of [My]) the preceding exhortation concerning prayer [Blm, EBC, Hh, TNTC, WDC]: pray for one another, because prayer accomplishes much.

QUESTION—What relationship is indicated by the present participle ἐνεργουμένη 'working'?
1. It indicates the field or its effect [Alf, Hb, My, NIC, TNTC]: it is powerful in its working. That it is 'working' is assumed [Alf, My].
2. It is temporal [ICC, My, NBC]: it is powerful when it is working. Even a righteous man is not always praying [NBC], but when he does pray, it has great effect [ICC].
3. It refers to earnestness and perseverance [Lns]: when it is earnestly working.
4. It is the equivalent of an adjective [Herm]: it is an energetic prayer.

5:17 Elijah was a-man of-like-feelings^a to-us,

LEXICON—a. ὁμοιοπαθής (LN 25.32) (BAGD p. 566): 'of like feelings', 'of like sensations' [Lns], '(with the) same kinds of feelings' [LN], '(with the) same kinds of desires' [LN], 'subject to like passions' [KJV], 'with the same nature' [BAGD], 'with a nature like' [WBC; NASB], 'with experiences similar' [AB], 'of the same limitations' [NIC], 'as frail as' [NJB], 'like' [Herm; NAB, NRSV], 'just like' [HNTC; NIV, REB, TNT], 'the same kind (of person) as' [TEV]. The word stresses Elijah's humanity, with the same experiences and feelings as ordinary persons [Hb, Mit, My, NTC, TG, Tsk]; it refers to feelings [Alf]; it refers to occasions of suffering [AB, ICC, Lns, WBC] and limitations [WBC]; it refers to both feelings and sufferings [Bg]; it implies that he could suffer and be tempted [Lg].

QUESTION—How is this verse related to its context?
This verse and the following one present an example of effectual prayer [Alf, BKC, EBC, Hb, Herm, HNTC, Lns, My, NIC, NIGTC, TNTC, Tsk, WBC] and a confirmation of the power of prayer [ICC, Lns]. The illustration is a tacit concession-contraexpectation, implying that although Elijah was an ordinary human being, nevertheless, when he prayed, it ceased to rain and then rained again [Herm, May]. It presents Elijah as a righteous man who is an ordinary human being; his example is therefore relevant for ordinary Christians [AB, Alf, Hb, Herm, HNTC, ICC, May, Mit, NIC, NIGTC, NTC, TNTC, WBC].

and with-prayer he-prayed the not to-rain,

QUESTION—What is the meaning of the phrase προσευχῇ προσηύξατο 'with prayer he prayed'?
It means that he prayed earnestly [Bg, BKC, EBC, TG, TNTC, Tsk, WBC]. It is an intensification of the idea of prayer [Herm, HNTC, Lg, Lns, May, My, NIC, NTC]. The addition of προσευχῇ 'with prayer' emphasizes the idea of prayer [ICC]. He made it a matter of special prayer [Alf].

QUESTION—What relationship is indicated by the articular infinitive phrase τοῦ μὴ βρέξαι 'the not to rain'?
The aorist tense of the infinitive implies a single action [NTC], that is, that there should be no more rain [Hb].

1. It is an indirect command [NTC], an object clause, expressing the content of the prayer [ICC, Lns, NTC; all versions]: he prayed, asking that it not rain.
2. It combines the purpose and the content of the prayer [Alf, Hb, My]: he prayed in order that, and asking that, it might not rain.
3. It expresses the purpose of the prayer [Lg(M)]: he prayed, in order that it might not rain.

and it-rained not upon[a] the earth[b] (for) three years and six months.

LEXICON—a. ἐπί with genitive object (LN 83.46): 'upon' [AB, Herm, LN], 'on' [HNTC, LN, Lns, NIC, WBC; all versions except NJB, REB]; the phrase οὐκ ἔβρεξεν ἐπὶ τῆς γῆς 'it did not rain upon the earth' is translated 'the land had no rain' [REB], 'no rain fell' [NJB].

b. γῆ (LN 1.39; 1.60; 2.14): 'earth' [AB, Herm, HNTC, LN, Lns, NIC; KJV, NASB, NRSV], 'land' [LN, WBC; NAB, NIV, REB, TEV], 'ground' [LN; TNT], 'soil' [LN], not explicit [NJB]. It refers to the idolatrous kingdom of Israel [Hb, TG]; it refers to the earth [My].

QUESTION—What relationship is indicated by καί 'and'?

It introduces the result of Elijah's prayer [Hb, My]: and as a result it did not rain.

QUESTION—What relationship is indicated by the accusative phrase ἐνιαυτοὺς τρεῖς καὶ μῆνας ἕξ 'three years and six months'?

It is an accusative of extent of time, but none of the commentaries mention this point: it did not rain for the extent of time of three years and six months.

5:18 And again he-prayed, and the heaven[a] gave[b] rain and the earth[c] produced[d] its fruit.[e]

LEXICON—a. οὐρανός (LN 1.5) (BAGD 1.b. p. 594): 'heaven' [AB, BAGD, Herm, HNTC, Lns; KJV, NRSV], 'heavens' [WBC; NIV, TNT], 'sky' [LN, NIC; NAB, NASB, NJB, TEV]. The phrase ὁ οὐρανὸς ὑετὸν ἔδωκεν 'the heaven gave rain' is translated 'the rain poured down' [REB].

b. aorist act. indic. of δίδωμι (LN **13.128**) (BAGD 1.b.γ. p. 193): 'to give' [AB, Herm, HNTC, LN, Lns, NIC, WBC; KJV, NIV, NJB, NRSV, TNT], 'to produce' [**LN**], 'to yield' [BAGD], 'to burst forth' [NAB], 'to pour' [NASB], 'to pour down' [REB], 'to pour out' [TEV].

c. γῆ: 'earth'. See this word at 5:17.

d. aorist act. indic. of βλαστάνω (LN **23.199**) (BAGD 1. p. 142): 'to produce' [AB, BAGD, HNTC, LN, NIC, WBC; NAB, NASB, NIV, TEV, TNT]. 'to bring forth' [Herm; KJV], 'to bear' [REB], 'to yield' [NRSV], 'to give' [NJB], 'to sprout up' [Lns].

e. καρπός (LN **23.199**; 43.15) (BAGD 1.a. p. 404): 'fruit' [AB, Herm, HNTC, **LN**, Lns, NIC; KJV, NASB], 'harvest' [LN; NRSV], 'crop' [BAGD, LN; NAB, NIV, NJB, REB, TEV, TNT], 'harvest crop' [WBC].

QUESTION—What relationship is indicated by the second and third occurrences of καί 'and'?
   They introduce the results of the prayer [Hb, My, NTC]: he prayed, and as a result the heavens gave rain and the earth produced its harvest.
QUESTION—What is meant by ὁ οὐρανὸς ὑετὸν ἔδωκεν 'the heaven gave rain'?
   1. 'Heaven' refers to the sky [LN, Mit, NIC; NAB, NASB, NJB, TEV, TNT]: the sky poured forth rain. It means that rain fell from the clouds in the sky [Mit].
   2. 'Heaven' is used as a substitute for the name 'God' [Hb, NIC, Tsk]: God in heaven gave rain.

DISCOURSE UNIT: 5:19–20 [AB, BKC, EBC, Hb, ICC, Lns, Mit, NIC, NIGTC, NTC, TG, TNTC, Tsk, WBC]. The topic is the salvation of apostates [AB], a comment concerning wanderers [EBC], the privilege of serving those who wander [ICC], rescuing the backslider [NTC, Tsk], the great reward for saving souls [NIC], the importance of needs [BKC], church discipline [TG], a concluding word of encouragement [NIGTC], a closing summons to action [TNTC], closing words and a brotherly admonition [WBC], the conclusion [Hb].

5:19 My brothers, if someone among[a] you wanders[b] from[c] the truth[d] and someone turns-back[e] him,
   TEXT—Some manuscripts omit μου 'my'. GNT does not mention this variant; only Blm, KJV omit this word.
   LEXICON—a. ἐν with dative object (LN 83.9): 'among' [Herm, HNTC, LN, Lns, NIC; NAB, NASB, NRSV], 'of' [AB, WBC; KJV, NIV, NJB, REB, TEV, TNT]
   b. aorist pass./pass. (deponent = act.) subj. of πλανάω/πλανάομαι (LN **31.67**) (BAGD 2.c.β. p. 665): 'to wander' [Herm, LN; NIV, NRSV], 'to wander away' [BAGD; TEV], 'to stray' [HNTC, **LN**, NIC, WBC; NAB, NASB, REB, TNT], 'to stray away' [NJB], 'to go astray' [AB, LN], 'to stray from the truth' [LN], 'to err' [Lns; KJV]. A few take it to be passive: 'be seduced' [Alf]; it means to be led aside through sin [Bg].
   c. ἀπό with genitive object (LN 89.122): 'from' [AB, Herm, HNTC, LN, Lns, NIC, WBC; all versions].
   d. ἀλήθεια (LN 72.2) (BAGD 2.b. p. 36): 'truth' [AB, BAGD, Herm, HNTC, LN, Lns, NIC, WBC; all versions]. It refers to the gospel [AB, Alf, EBC, Lns, NTC, TG], to all that the gospel involves [TNTC], to the truth of salvation [Lns], to the whole of Christian knowledge and precepts [ICC]. It is primarily moral, referring to God's revealed will [Mit].
   e. aorist act. subj. of ἐπιστρέφω (LN 16.13) (BAGD 1.a. p. 301): 'to turn back' [HNTC, Lns, WBC; NASB], 'to turn around' [LN], 'to turn toward' [LN], 'to turn' [BAGD], 'to bring back' [Herm, NIC; NAB, NIV, NJB, REB, TEV, TNT], 'to convert' [AB; KJV]; as a passive voice 'to be brought back' [NRSV].

QUESTION—What is this and the following verse connected with?

It refers to persons who have been involved in the various evils dealt with through the epistle [Hb, NIC, WBC]. The reference to sin and pardon in 5:15–16 prompted a return to this theme in the conclusion of the letter [WBC]. It is closely connected with the preceding exhortations concerning confession and prayer for one another [Lns, My], concerning prayer in all occasions [Tsk]. It continues the theme of patience [NTC]. It returns to the subject of 5:16 [May, Mit].

QUESTION—What is implied by the phrase ἀδελφοί μου 'my brothers'?

It introduces the conclusion of the epistle [Bg, WBC]. It signifies an abrupt change of subject [ICC]. It indicates that believers are being addressed [EBC]. It implies love [Hb, Lns, Mit, Tsk] and sympathetic concern [Hb, Tsk]. It is emphatic by forefronting [NTC].

QUESTION—What is implied by this conditional clause?

1. It is a condition of expectancy which the author presumes will occur [Lns]. It implies that it is possible for a Christian to wander away from the gospel [Tsk]. The reference is to members of the church (a believing Christian [Mit, NIC]) and not to unevangelized persons [Hb, Mit, WBC], as the phrase ἐν ὑμῖν 'among you' makes clear [Hb].

2. It refers only to persons who have heard the gospel but have turned away instead of accepting it [NBC], whose profession of faith has not been real, because a Christian can never lose his salvation [EBC].

QUESTION—What is the meaning of the phrase πλανηθῇ ἀπὸ τῆς ἀληθείας 'wander from the truth'?

It means to turn away from salvation into sin and spiritual death [Lns], apostasy [NIGTC, WBC], rejection of God's will [NIGTC, WBC], not demonstrating faith in practice [WBC], to be involved in doctrinal errors or failure in conduct [Blm, ICC, Tsk], to have sinned by turning away from righteous living [Herm], moral failure [HNTC, NIGTC]. It does not refer to single sins but to alienation from basic Christian principles [Lg, My], turning away to Judaism and related errors [Lg, Lns].

QUESTION—What is implied by the second τις 'someone'?

It implies that this duty extends to all the believers [May, Mit, NIC, NTC, TG, TNTC, Tsk, WBC], to each one individually who might be at hand [Mit].

5:20 let-him-know[a] that the-(one) having-turned-back[b] a-sinner from[c] (the) error[d] of-his way[e] will-save[f] his soul[g] from[h] death

TEXT—Instead of γινωσκέτω 'let him know' (third person imperative), some manuscripts read γινώσκετε 'you know' (indicative) or 'know' (second person imperative). GNT reads 'let him know' with a B rating, indicating that the text is almost certain. 'Let him know' is read by Bg, Blm, Hb, Herm, HNTC, ICC, Lg, Lns, Mit, My, NIC, NIGTC, NTC, TG, TNTC, Tsk, WBC, KJV, NASB, and NJB; 'you know' (indicative) is read by May; 'know (second person imperative)' is read by Alf and Lg(M); the second person imperative is read by AB; NAB, NIV, NRSV, REB, TEV, and TNT also, but it is not certain which text some of these follow.

TEXT—Instead of ψυχὴν αὐτοῦ ἐκ θανάτου 'his soul from death', some manuscripts read ψυχὴν ἐκ θανάτου αὐτοῦ 'a soul from death itself', and others read ψυχὴν ἐκ θανάτου 'a soul from death'. GNT reads 'his soul from death' with a C rating, indicating difficulty in deciding which variant to place in the text. 'His soul from death' is read by AB, Bg, HNTC, ICC, NIGTC, NTC, WBC, and all versions except KJV and REB; 'a soul from death' is read by Alf, Blm, Hb, Herm, Lns, May, Mit, NIC, Tsk, KJV, and REB.

LEXICON—a. pres. act. impera. of γινώσκω (LN 28.1; 32.16): 'to know' [Herm, HNTC, LN; KJV, NASB, NRSV], 'to come to understand' [LN], 'to comprehend' [LN], 'to realize' [Lns, NIC], 'to be sure' [NIV, NJB, REB, TNT], 'to be assured' [WBC], 'to consider' [AB], 'to remember' [NAB, TEV].

b. aorist act. participle of ἐπιστρέφω: 'to turn back'. See this word at 5:19.

c. ἐκ with genitive object (LN 84.4) (BAGD 1.a. p. 234): 'from' [AB, BAGD, Herm, HNTC, LN, Lns, NIC, WBC; all versions], 'away from' [BAGD], 'out from' [LN], 'out of' [BAGD, LN]. This means to turn from error to the way of truth [ICC].

d. πλανή (LN 31.8; 31.10) (BAGD p. 666): 'error' [AB, BAGD, Herm, HNTC, LN, Lns, NIC, WBC; KJV, NASB, NIV, TNT], 'delusion' [BAGD], 'deception' [BAGD, LN], 'misleading belief' [LN], 'deceptive belief' [LN], 'mistaken view' [LN], not explicit [NAB]. The phrase πλάνης ὁδοῦ αὐτοῦ 'the error of his way' is translated 'his erring ways' [NJB, REB], 'his wrong way' [TEV], 'wandering' [NRSV]. This word describes ὁδός 'way' [My].

e. ὁδός (LN 41.16) (BAGD 2.b. p. 554): 'way' [AB, Herm, HNTC, Lns, NIC, WBC; all versions except NRSV], 'way of life' [BAGD, LN].

f. fut. act. indic. of σῴζω (LN 21.18; 21.27) (BAGD 2.a.β. p. 798): 'to save' [AB, BAGD, Herm, HNTC, LN, Lns, NIC; all versions except REB], 'to deliver' [LN], 'to rescue' [LN, WBC; REB]. Only God can save, but man can be his agent [Mit, NTC].

g. ψυχή (LN 9.20) (BAGD 1.c. p. 893): 'soul' [AB, BAGD, Herm, HNTC, Lns, NIC; all versions except NIV], 'person' [LN]. The phrase ψυχὴν αὐτοῦ 'his soul' is translated 'him' [WBC; NIV]. The reference is to the whole person [NIGTC], the eternal part of the person [WBC], the person's inner life [Hb].

h. ἐκ with genitive object (LN 84.4) (BAGD 1.c. p. 234): 'from' [AB, BAGD, Herm, HNTC, LN, Lns, NIC, WBC; all versions], 'out from' [LN], 'out of' [LN].

and will-cover[a] a-multitude[b] of-sins.

LEXICON—a. fut. act. indic. of καλύπτω (LN 79.114) (BAGD 2.a. p. 401): 'to cover' [AB, BAGD, Herm, HNTC, LN, WBC; NASB, NRSV], 'to cover

over' [LN; NIV, NJB], 'to hide' [Lns; KJV], 'to cancel' [NAB, REB], 'to wipe out' [NIC], 'to bring about forgiveness' [TEV], 'to cause to be forgiven' [TNT]. The meaning is forgiveness of sins [Hb, HNTC, ICC, Lns, Mit, My, NIC, NIGTC, NTC, TG, TNTC, Tsk, WBC]. It means to cause the sin to be forgiven by God [Hb, HNTC, Mit, My, NIC, NIGTC, TNTC, WBC].

b. πλῆθος (LN **59.9**) (BAGD 2.a. p. 668): 'multitude' [AB, BAGD, Herm, HNTC, **LN**, Lns; KJV, NAB, NASB, NIV, NRSV, REB], 'host' [BAGD, NIC], 'large number' [LN]. The phrase πλῆθος ἁμαρτιῶν 'a multitude of sins' is translated 'many sins' [WBC; TEV, TNT], 'many a sin' [NJB]. It implies the great extent of the forgiveness [WBC].

QUESTION—Why is this verse mentioned?

It gives the two results of restoring a sinner [Hb].

QUESTION—Who is the implied subject of γινωσκέτω 'let him know'?

1. It is the person who restores the sinner [Alf, Hb, Herm, Lg, Mit, My, TG, Tsk, WBC].
2. It is both the one who restores and the one who is restored [Bg].

QUESTION—To whom does ψυχὴν αὐτοῦ 'his soul' refer?

It refers to the soul of the restored sinner [AB, Bg, Hb, Herm, HNTC, ICC, Lns, Mit, My, NIC, NIGTC, NTC, TG, TNTC, Tsk, WBC; NRSV, TEV, TNT].

QUESTION—What is the meaning of θανάτου 'death'?

It is the eternal death of the soul [Bg, EBC, Hb, Herm, Lg, Lns, My, NIC, NIGTC, NTC, TG, TNTC, WBC]. It is both separation from God in this life and eternal death [Mit]. It is the penalty of sin [NIC]. Some commentators assume that the sinner was not a genuine believer before he is converted from his sin [EBC, NBC]. The congregation must have had unconverted people who called themselves Christians [NBC]. Others think that this is concerned with erring Christians who need to be restored to the church and God [EBC, Herm, HNTC, ICC, Mit, NIC].

QUESTION—Whose sins will be covered?

1. It is the sins of the erring person [AB, Alf, Bg, BKC, Blm, EBC, Hb, Lg, Lns, My, NIC, NIGTC, NTC, TG, TNTC, Tsk, WBC]. The salvation of these persons prevents future sins [AB].
2. It is the sins of the restorer [Herm, HNTC, ICC, Mit, NIC]. Good deeds and sin are recorded opposite one another and the restorer thus cancels out many of his own sins [Herm].

www.ingramcontent.com/pod-product-compliance
Lightning Source LLC
Chambersburg PA
CBHW052042300426
44117CB00012B/1942